Virginia Woolf

A WRITER'S LIFE

Virginia Woolf

A
WRITER'S
LIFE

LYNDALL GORDON

OXFORD UNIVERSITY PRESS

Oxford University Press, Walton Street, Oxford OX2 6DP

London New York Toronto
Delhi Bombay Calcutta Madras Karachi
Kuala Lumpur Singapore Hong Kong Tokyo
Nairobi Dar es Salaam Cape Town
Melbourne Auckland
and associated companies in
Beirut Berlin Ibadan Mexico City Nicosia

Oxford is a trade mark of Oxford University Press

First published 1984
Reprinted 1984

British Library Cataloguing in Publication Data
Gordon, Lyndall
Virginia Woolf.
1. Woolf, Virginia—Biography 2. Authors,
English—20th century—Biography
I. Title
823'.912   PR6045.072Z/
ISBN 0-19-811723-X

Library of Congress Cataloging in Publication Data
Gordon, Lyndall.
Virginia Woolf, a writer's life.
Bibliography: p.
Includes index.
1. Woolf, Virginia, 1882-1941—Biography.
2. Novelists, English—20th century—Biography.
I. Title.
PR6045.072Z653 1984   823'.912 [B]   84-3903
ISBN 0-19-811723-X

Printed in Great Britain
at the University Press, Oxford
by David Stanford
Printer to the University

For Siamon

Acknowledgements

THIS book is dedicated to my husband, Siamon Gordon, whose quick good sense and editorial flair shaped it at every stage. I benefited too from talks with many students, with Greta Verdin on 'moments of being' and with Frances Partridge on Virginia Woolf's pacifism. Lola Szladits, Curator of the Berg Collection, supplied the title; Gila Bercovitch, insight and early encouragement; and Jenny Joseph, detailed comments on the completed typescript.

The notes do not adequately acknowledge my dependence on Anne Olivier Bell's impeccable edition of *The Diary of Virginia Woolf* and on Quentin Bell whose biography of his aunt must remain the authoritative account. A new life would be superfluous if, with undue modesty, he had not declined to assess her writing. This is a complementary effort to link the writing with the life. It could not have been done without the splendid resources of the Berg Collection in New York and the help of other librarians, particularly Michael Halls, Modern Archivist at King's College, Cambridge and John Burt at the University of Sussex.

Quentin Bell has allowed quotations from the unpublished papers of Virginia Woolf, and Trekkie Parsons from Leonard Woolf's papers; Virginia Woolf's literary estate, the Hogarth Press, and Harcourt Brace Jovanovich have allowed quotations from published works.

I should finally like to thank Hugo Brunner for cycling through wind and rain with helpful material, Nigel Nicolson for an original photograph, Terence Pepper for tracing two other photographs, Pam Woodward for meticulous typing and, too, the Fellows of Jesus College, Oxford, for the hospitality of their Common Room and a grant for final expenses.

Contents

Plates

The cover shows a portrait of Virginia Woolf painted by her sister, Vanessa Bell, c.1911–12.

VICTORIAN MODELS

We are born with the dead:
See, they return, and bring us with them.

Four Quartets

1. *Life Has a Base*

VIRGINIA WOOLF said that 'if life has a base' it is a memory. Her life as a writer was based on two persistent memories: the north Cornwall shore and her parents. Early one morning, lying in the nursery of her family's summer home at St Ives, she heard 'the waves breaking, one, two, one, two, . . . behind a yellow blind'. Lying half asleep, half awake in her warm bed, she heard that rhythm and saw a moment's light as the wind blew the blind out and knew 'the purest ecstasy I can conceive'. Years later, she wanted the waves' rhythm to sound all through her greatest books, *To the Lighthouse* and *The Waves*. The rising and breaking came to represent the maximum possibilities of existence and its finality.

Virginia Woolf was born Adeline Virginia Stephen* in 1882, the third child of unconventional Victorians, Julia and Leslie Stephen, of whom she found it hard to say which was the more remarkable. The memory of the waves must have been early. The memory of her parents was of another kind, a memory not of the senses but of the analytic intelligence. They came into focus for Virginia at the age of eight or ten. Her father was an eccentric mountaineer and distinguished editor whose abrasive intellectual honesty both appalled and enlivened his children. Her mother had a consuming vocation for the troubled and sick, whom she nursed with practical wisdom and exquisite sympathy.

There is a dim photograph of Julia Stephen reading with her four younger children in about 1894. Virginia's furtive face is too long for symmetry, her bones thin and delicate, and her observant eyes are rounded at their lower edge like pears. The photograph breathes the perfect stillness of the children's absorption. More than thirty years later Virginia Woolf recorded a similar scene in *To the Light-house*. As the mother, Mrs Ramsay, reads aloud, she sees a son's eyes darken, sees a daughter drawn by an imaginative word, and concludes that 'they were happier now than they would ever be again'.

---

* It is difficult to know what to call a writer whose name was changed by marriage and who shares surnames with men who were well known in their own right. It is therefore often convenient to use her Christian name but all references to her as author will use the name on her books.

Julia Stephen was the most arresting figure in a Victorian past which her daughter tried to reconstruct and preserve. Julia's death in 1895 was closely followed in 1897 by that of Stella, her daughter by an earlier marriage, and then by the deaths of Leslie Stephen in 1904 and a son, Thoby, in 1906. That decade of deaths sealed off Virginia's youth and divided it sharply from the rest of her life. 'So many horrors', she said, 'were pressed to our eyes.' The dead haunted her imagination: '. . . The ghosts', she wrote in her diary at the age of fifty, 'change so oddly in my mind; like people who live, & are changed by what one hears of them.'

As a writer, Virginia Woolf took hold of the past, of ghostly voices speaking with increasing clarity, perhaps more real for her than were the people who lived by her side. When the voices of the dead urged her to impossible things they drove her mad but, controlled, they became the material of fiction. With each death, her sense of the past grew. Her novels were responses to these disappearances. '. . . The past is beautiful', she said, 'because one never realises an emotion at the time. It expands later, & thus we don't have complete emotions about the present, only about the past.' Filled out in memory, the dead could take a final form; the living were unformed, like herself still in the making, though this did not deter her from shaping them, too, in her imagination. She transformed people whom she loved—parents, brother, sister, friends, husband—into figures fixed in attitudes that could outlive their time.

This biography will follow her creative response to such memories. At her strongest she did not wish to dwell on death itself but to paint durable portraits. These portraits were not photo-graphic: she would distort her subject to fit private memory to some historical or universal pattern. The selfless Mrs Ramsay, based on Virginia's memory of her mother, is transformed as the quintessential Victorian and the very pattern of motherhood as she reads to her child. In this way, Virginia Woolf brought back the dead and perpetuated them on paper as Lily Briscoe, the artist in *To the Lighthouse*, perpetuates the Victorian family on canvas.

The insistent modernity of the early 1920s was the image Virginia Woolf imprinted on the public until, in the 1960s, this image shifted to another partial truth: the feminist Virginia Woolf who underpins the struggle for women's rights. Now that it is possible to see these images in the perspective of the complete works, published and unpublished, it is clear that her phase as high priestess of the modern novel was quite short and that her feminist polemic was an attempt to rewrite rather than discard the Victorian model of womanhood. She looked backward for her models and her career may be, in part, defined by the play of memory, by an acute sense of the past, especially by ties with the nineteenth century. It may be defined, in part too, by a craving for anonymity which became more explicit towards the end of her career. This was a move away from the self-conscious superiority of modern writers towards the lives of the obscure, particularly the lives of women, in whom she sought a counter-history to that of power, of kings with golden teapots on their heads.

Art mattered, and the fate of women, but aesthetic experiment and polemic were subsidiary to the tug of the unknown. 'I have some restless searcher in me', she wrote in her diary. It is this search above all that compelled her work, not causes. Yeats saw that there is for everyone 'some one scene, some one adventure . . . that is the image of his secret life'. Virginia Woolf's recurring image was a voyage of discovery or the fin of a submerged form lurking in the waves. 'Why is there not a discovery in life?' she went on. 'Something one can lay hands on & say "This is it?"' . . . I have a great & astonishing sense of something there. . . .' Every afternoon, when she took long walks, London itself beckoned as the 'unexplored land'. She did not float on a self-indulgent stream of consciousness; she was a curious explorer in the wake of the Elizabethan voyagers or say, Darwin, seeking to know what she called 'the infinite oddity of the human position'.

Virginia Woolf shaped and defended the modern novel and left nearly 4,000 letters and thirty volumes of a diary. No writer's life can be so fully documented. Yet, the woman writing remains elusive—and must always remain so, for there is no end to understanding a life. As a leading figure of an advanced, artistic set in Bloomsbury and as a writer of letters, she flaunted different colours, according to her company. 'How queer', she acknowledged, 'to have so many selves.' But the writer of fiction was kept out of sight. She told a friend: 'I must be private, secret, as anonymous and submerged as possible in order to write.'

Virginia Woolf's visible life in Bloomsbury, her famous wild flights of fancy and withdrawals into sickness, and the associated legends of an invalid lady, a frigid body, a precious aesthete withdrawn from the world, have been endlessly repeated. Here are the invisible events that shaped her work: the memories of childhood, the odd education, the volcanic matter of her madness, the unusual marriage. To put the more fertile memories together is to find overwhelming evidence of a writer's life that ran parallel with but distinct from the well-known facts of her public life. When she came, herself, to analyse the writer's life in a draft of *The Waves*, she remarked 'a certain inevitable disparity' between the public and private self '—between the outer & and inner'. The outer facts are here, but only as a prop for the unfolding creative side.

This, then, is a writer's life. In the official biography, Quentin Bell, with exemplary candour, gives an exact record of what it was like to know Virginia Woolf as a member of a family and a figure in Bloomsbury. This life will draw more on her works and use different sources: the unfinished memoirs, the drafts of novels, and some less-known or unpublished pieces like the early 'Memoirs of a Novelist' which lays the course of her career and her last, unfinished book, *Anon*.

'Every secret of a writer's soul', Virginia Woolf said, 'every experience of his life, every quality of his mind is written large in his works.' This is a deliberate extravagance but, in her case, nothing is so true as her fiction to her most cherished experience. 'I wonder', she asked herself, 'whether I . . . deal . . . in autobiography & call it fiction?' Fiction exaggerates, of course, and selects so that to read back from the work to the life is a delicate task, but certain of her novels, taken together with diaries and memoirs, do record the defining moments on which her life turned. These I shall try to follow to see a Virginia Woolf not as she appeared to others but as she appeared to herself. She believed that there are only a few essential hours of life. In the lives of most people they would have to be imagined: 'the moment from which all that we know them by proceeds.' She herself, attentive always to the 'blind' moment, set it down. It was, she found, determined by a 'shock-receiving capacity'. The shocks, silent, invisible, are the scaffold of a life and yet, she added, often left out. To follow the 'shocks' as they emerge in a sequence of their own, I shall bring in books out of the order in which they were published.

Only writing, Virginia Woolf said, could compose 'the synthesis of my being'. She wrote every day for about thirty-five years. Most of her writing—including notebooks, drafts, unpublished sketches, early diaries, even reading plans—has survived, but much of this is not synthesized with the established works so as to define exactly the nature of her endeavour. She eludes our usual categories, and for this reason the mass media, in particular, have tended to cling to convenient labels of madwoman and snob which bypass the work. My aim is not to bring in every work but to bring out the essence of her career. To see its coherence, I shall follow Virginia Woolf's view of lives latent in her novels. There she suggests repeatedly that the high-points of existence are not the traditional markers of birth, marriage, and death but hidden away among the ordinary events of an ordinary day. The diary of 1921 looks back to an ordinary summer day in August 1890, to the sound of the sea and the children in the garden, and concludes that all her life was 'built on that, permeated by that: how much so I could never explain'.

I see Virginia Woolf's life in three phases. The first is the childhood scenes—the places, people, and Victorian conventions— which became a subject for some of her novels. 'Books', she said, 'are the . . . fruit stuck here and there on a tree which has its roots deep down in the earth of our earliest life, of our first experiences.' In particular, the first part of this biography will look at Julia and Leslie Stephen, then at the way their daughter remembered them in *To the Lighthouse*. Although there are many references in diary and letters to Leslie Stephen as the source for the temperamental Victorian father, Mr Ramsay, it is risky to equate a living person with a figure in a novel. Leslie Stephen's own memoirs and unpublished letters give a different, more lovable view of him than his daughter's fiction which has become, if anything, too influential. In *To the Lighthouse* the Ramsay parents appear first close-up in their own time. Then, after a passage of years, they are seen from the perspective of an artist, looking back at Victorians after the first world war. Lily Briscoe, composing their portrait, enacts the obsessive drama of Virginia Woolf, the transforming of personal memory into impersonal art.

The play of actual and composed character, of actual and composed event, will continue in the second part of the life. There follows a phase of twenty years when Virginia suffered from her losses, schooled herself to be a writer, and thought up the theories that were to shape her novels. This is the underground phase of development when she began to see herself as an explorer of the deep, as sunken sea-monster or gallant voyager. An account of her long apprenticeship, mental solitude, recurring illness, and self-education will offset her story of a young woman's precarious journey to enlightenment in *The Voyage Out*.

The third phase is a long one of action and achievement. Virginia Woolf's mature efforts to compose her life, with her abandonment of respectable Kensington, her search for new freedom in Blooms-bury, her unconventional union with Leonard Woolf, and renewed stages of effort and experiment, will offset her formal diagram of the lifespan in *The Waves*.

This book will rock back and forth between the life and the work, coming to rest always on the work. For Virginia Woolf, life and work were complementary. There were, of course, other influences from literature and history, but her life was her main source. She turned early tragedies, discoveries, and moments of bliss into art which, at the same time, casts its perspective on her life.

Yeats spoke of the development of a writer through his art as 'the birth of a new species of man'. The same could be said of Virginia Woolf as a new species of woman. She was, she once told a friend, 'trained to silence'. For all the verbal freedom and wit with which she later presided over the intellectual London of her day, she reserved a side of herself for her novels alone. The death of the strange, searching Rachel in *The Voyage Out* and the suicide of the mad, past-ridden Septimus in *Mrs. Dalloway* are fictional versions of the self that was potentially creative, potentially distorted, and always threatened with extinction. Her reserve made publication an agony.

The memory 'base', the 'moments of being', the woman's silence: these clues will be the guides to a unique career. But Virginia Woolf was also shaped by the platitudes and manners of the preceding age. Her biographic theory is incomplete without what she called 'invisible presences'.

Kensington in the 1880s and 1890s, the prevailing ideal of womanhood, the covert sexuality of well-bred men, the educational privileges reserved for brothers: these conditions of Victorian society all shaped Virginia in her very struggle against them.

The greatest struggle was to be with the image of staunch Victorian womanhood which was to dog her longer perhaps than other women of her generation. In her fifties she was annoyed to find herself and her sister acting, with unconscious automatism, as angels of mercy when Duncan Grant languished over nothing more serious than a cold. In a speech to professional women in 1931 she said: 'You who come of a younger and happier generation may not have heard of the Angel of the house. She was intensely sympathetic. She was immensely charming. She was utterly unselfish. . . . Almost every respectable Victorian house had its angel. And when I came to write . . . the shadow of her wings fell upon the page; I heard the rustling of her skirts in the room. Now this creature . . . never had any real existence. She had—what is more difficult to deal with—an ideal existence, a fictitious existence. She was a dream, a phantom. . . .' This angel whispered to the young girl writing her first reviews that to succeed it was necessary to conciliate. 'I turned upon that Angel and caught her by the throat. I did my best to kill her. . . . If I had not killed her, she would have killed me—as a writer.'

Another struggle was to be against the shuttered life of the Victorian girl, not only against physical enclosures and restraints, but against induced ignorance and the habitual silencing of feelings. The Stephen home in Kensington, 22 Hyde Park Gate, was towards the end of a cul-de-sac; it was quiet and sedate. All they heard was the distant clatter of wheels where the street approached Kensington Gardens, and the horses stamping in the mews. All they looked out on was old Mrs Redgrave in her Bath chair with the glass pane let down so that she looked like a museum case on wheels.

This shuttered life was associated, of course, with the ingrained respectability that was to make Virginia's and her sister Vanessa's revolt so insistent and, at the same time, so reticent. One night, when Virginia was about fifteen, she heard an old man raving obscenely. Next morning she was told that it had been a cat. Her lifelong dislike of her half-brothers was to be for her a reasonable response to their suppressed sexuality. When she was about six her grown-up half-brother, Gerald Duckworth, lifted her on to a table and explored her private parts. The child was bewildered by the covertness which demanded her complicity and which, she instinctively knew, was too shaming to mention. 'I still shiver with shame at the memory', she confessed to a friend in 1941.

In her 'Sketch of the Past' Virginia Woolf recalled how she and her sister were trained to 'sit passive and watch the Victorian males go through their intellectual hoops'. *To the Lighthouse* regards imperial administrators and university fellowships with comic detachment. Such positions were the approved goals of her upper-middle-class family. Quentin Bell explained that the men of their family always worked for a living but never with their hands. They did not belong to a leisure class or hereditary ruling class nor were they engaged in any sort of commerce. They were professionals. Their sons were educated carefully because success would depend on their efforts. For the last century the family had regularly produced, on the mother's side, officials of the East India Company and, on the Stephen side, lawyers, judges, and heads of schools and colleges. Virginia observed with an irritation not unmixed with envy the series of hurdles which were reserved for the boys in her family and at which they seemed invariably to excel. 'All our male relations were adepts at the game', she wrote. 'They knew the rules and attached immense importance to them. Father laid enormous stress upon schoolmasters' reports, upon scholarships, triposes and fellowships. The Fishers [their cousins], the male Fishers, took every prize, honour, degree.'

The arguments in the way of women's education were 'tough as roots but intangible as sea mist'. Men who enjoyed the utmost rigours of education wished to preserve the tender home bloom of maidenly innocence, sweetness, chastity, which might suffer if women were allowed to read Latin and Greek. One Victorian mother agreed to send her daughter to Girton College only on condition that she should return 'as if nothing had happened'.

Writing was the most accessible of the arts yet not entirely approved. As Virginia noted, Fanny Burney's first manuscripts were burnt and later she sewed in the mornings to forestall her stepmother's blame for writing in the afternoons. 'Literature cannot be the business of a woman's life', Robert Southey wrote to Charlotte Brontë. She reassured him that, as a governess, her daily duties did not allow 'a moment's time for one dream of the imagination'. She went on: 'In the evenings, I confess, I do think, but I never trouble any one else with my thoughts. I carefully avoid any appearance of preoccupation and eccentricity, which might lead those I live amongst to suspect the nature of my pursuits. . . . I have endeavoured not only attentively to observe all the duties a women ought to fulfil, but to feel deeply interested in them.

I don't always succeed, for sometimes when I'm teaching or sewing I would rather be reading or writing; but I try to deny myself. . . .'

However much Virginia criticized the Victorians for their attitudes, she was nostalgic for their manners. She compared the Victorians to her own generation in the scene in *Night and Day* (1919) where Katharine and her mother, Mrs Hilbery, turn the pages of the family album. Mrs Hilbery was modelled on Thackeray's daughter, Anny Ritchie, whose sister was Leslie Stephen's first wife. To Mrs Hilbery, looking at people she had personally known, the Victorians seem 'like ships, like majestic ships, holding on their way, not shoving or pushing, not fretted by little things, as we are, but taking their way, like ships with white sails'. In *The Years*, Peggy, a disillusioned doctor in the 1930s, admires only her elderly Victorian aunt, the force she put into words 'as if she still believed with passion—she, old Eleanor—in the things that man had destroyed. A wonderful generation, she thought, as they drove off. Believers. . . .'

As a young woman Virginia listened to old Lady Strachey reading plays aloud. With only one eye, she could go on for two and a half hours, acting every part. It was the Victorian lady—'many-sided, vigorous, adventurous, advanced'—who intrigued Virginia, the high-handed way in which she baffled age and disaster; the exuberance and energy with which she pursued the noble and poetic. To Virginia the social manner of the Victorian lady had a beauty founded upon restraint, sympathy, unselfishness—all civilized qualities.

Her own mother's performance of Victorian womanhood had been flawless: all men worshipped her and she was, truly, a selfless woman. Beneath the beauty and the playfulness, there was the tireless nurse; beneath the emotional generosity, she was stern in judgement. Her very walk declared her decisiveness and backbone. She would hold her black umbrella erect and move with an 'indescribable air of expectation', her head tilted a little upwards, so that the eye looked straight at you. To her husband she was the embodiment of Wordsworth's ideal, a woman nobly planned to warn, to comfort, and command. Virginia remembered how, each evening, her mother would write letters of advice, warning, and sympathy, 'her wise brow and deep eyes presiding, . . . so profoundly experienced that one could hardly call them sad'. Her effort was so exactly directed that there was scarcely any waste. For this reason alone her mark on others was 'ineffaceable, as though branded'.

Virginia Woolf's celebrated modernity was, in a sense, spurious, an effort to move away from the past to create a contemporary form. But the nineteenth century holds sway in her polite, sidelong manner, in her reticence, in the longing for education and liberty, in the attention to the obscure (like Wordsworth and Hardy) and, above all, in her emphasis on moments of sublimity which links her to the Romantic poets.

The childhood summers at St Ives were marked in memory as the irrecoverable paradise. The waves, the walks, the seaside garden awoke the 'sense sublime'. Cornwall gave Virginia, as the Lakes Wordsworth, a sense of emotional reality in nature that no experience in later life could surpass.

In the spring of 1882, just after Virginia's birth, Leslie Stephen, on one of his habitual tramps in Cornwall, came across 'one of the loveliest walks imaginable'. He saw a gradually sloping moor of gorse broken by masses of primroses and bluebells, and the St Ives bay and its sandhills in the distance. Delicious breezes crossed the open moor. The air, he reported, was as soft as silk, with 'a fresh sweet taste like new milk'.

On an impulse he inspected Talland House which was offered for rental. It had been built in the 1840s or 1850s by the Great Western Railway, though the railway was only extended to St Ives in the early 1880s. At that time the large, square house was still outside the town, on a hill. There was no furniture in the upstairs rooms nor did the cold-water tap work, but there was a perfect view across the bay to Godrevy lighthouse. Leslie Stephen spent the night in the house and lay in bed, he told his wife, with the blinds open in order to 'see the Children sport upon the shore'. An easy path led to the sandy cove below, down which, he wrote, 'the babies will be able to go quite comfortably'.

So from mid-July to mid-September the Stephen family moved each year to what was then an unspoilt St Ives, still much as it had been in the sixteenth century: a scramble of houses crusting the steep slope like a bunch of rough shellfish, oysters or mussels, all crowded together. The whitewashed, granite houses had thick walls to withstand the sea and gales. It was a rugged, windy, narrow-streeted fishing town—a natural world remote from the narrow, stuffy London house which shut in the other ten months of the year.

When Virginia recalled Talland House, she tended to think of children in the garden. The acre or two of garden, running down the slope to the sea, was in fact a dozen gardens with terraces divided by hedges of escallonia. Each corner and lawn was named: the coffee garden; the cricket ground; the kitchen garden; the pond. There were slopes down which children could slide, intricate thickets of gooseberries and currants, a fountain, remote beds of potatoes and peas, and all kinds of summer fruit: strawberries, grapes, peaches. 'Altogether', wrote Leslie Stephen in 1884, 'a pocket paradise. . . .'

Every day the children had a great dish of Cornish cream sprinkled with brown sugar. Every Sunday they would walk with their father to Trencrom. From that hill, they could see both coasts of Cornwall, on the one side St Michael's Mount, on the other St Ives Bay. Little paths led between the heather to the top. 'Our legs were pricked and scratched as we climbed; and the gorse was yellow, sweet smelling, nutty.'

It was the odd memory, not the formal event, that was to be the 'base' of *To the Lighthouse*. A trip to Godrevy lighthouse in September 1892 stuck in Virginia's mind, also her younger brother's great disappointment at not being allowed to go, which was reported in the children's newspaper, 'The Hyde Park Gate News'. The novel retains Virginia's memory of Julia Stephen sitting on the porch on hot afternoons, watching the children at cricket. She also remembered how untidy and shabby Talland House was, and how overrun with guests: in a beehive chair the opium addict, Mr Wolstenholme, who was to be the source for the detached poet, Mr Carmichael, in *To the Lighthouse*; and Kitty Lushington, the source for the conventional Minta Doyle, who—obedient to Mrs Stephen's wish—became engaged to another guest under the jackmanii, a spot the children promptly called 'the Love Corner'. Also local folk: Alice Curnow who tramped up the drive leaning away from a great covered basket of washing and Jinny Berriman who cleaned the house—they too found a place in the child's tenacious memory and live on in her novel.

The Talland House idyll lasted ten years. In the summer of 1893 an 'infernal hotel' was rising in front of the house and the family foresaw the commercialization of St Ives. 'There never was a place so haunted', Leslie Stephen wrote to his wife. 'It is almost painful to me to look at the cricket ground and think of all the people who have sat there. . . .' One more summer, and then they gave up the house. Eleven years later, after both parents were dead, the brothers and sisters returned to see numerous solid white mansions where, in 1894, there had been only heather, and a broad public road where there had been only a footpath on the side of the moor.

To go back to St Ives in 1905 was, for Virginia, a pilgrimage (the word appears frequently in her Cornwall diary). Written in a consciously elegiac style, her diary on 11 August notes the prevailing hope as the four took their places in the Great Western train. There, in this little corner of England, 'we should find our past preserved, as though through all this time it had been guarded & treasured for us to come back to one day. . . . Ah, how strange it was, then, to watch the familiar shapes of land & sea unroll themselves once more . . . & to see once more the silent but palpable forms which for more than ten years we had seen only in dreams, or in the visions of waking hours.' There, again, were the cliffs tumbling in a cascade of brown rocks into the sea; there was the curve of the bay which 'seemed to enclose a great sweep of liquid mist'; and there the promontory of the island with its cluster of lights.

A branch line brought them to the sea at dusk. Walking up from the station, they fancied that they were merely coming home after a long day's outing. When they reached Talland House, they would thrust it open to find themselves among familiar sights. They passed up the carriage drive, mounted the rough steps, and peered through a chink in the escallonia hedge: 'There was the house . . . there were the stone urns, against the bank of tall flowers; all, so far as we could see was as though we had but left it in the morning. But yet, as we knew well, we could go no further; if we advanced the spell was broken. The lights were not our lights; the voices were the voices of strangers.'

They lingered in the grip of this fancy that they might yet approach their drawing-room window—it was to frame the first part of *To the Lighthouse*—but, of course, were forced to keep their distance. 'We hung there like ghosts in the shade of the hedge, & at the sound of footsteps we turned away.'

Virginia Woolf re-enacted this visitation many years later. In

May 1936, when she nearly broke down over *The Years*, she crept again into the garden of Talland House and, in the dusk, a woman of fifty-four peered through the ground-floor window to recapture the long lost Victorian summer.

It was decided at an early age that Virginia was to be a writer. Writing absorbed her, she said, 'ever since I was a little creature, scribbling a story in the manner of Hawthorne on the green plush sofa in the drawing room at St. Ives while the grown-ups dined'. She had the good fortune to be born into that small but powerful class which made much of intellectual gifts. 'Yesterday I discussed George II with Ginia', Leslie Stephen wrote to his wife from St Ives in July 1893. 'She takes in a great deal & will really be an author in time. . . .' At the age of five she told her father a story every night. Later, after Thoby went away to school, there was a communal serial in the night nursery—as in the Brontë home—a romance about the unsuspecting Dilke family next door which was made to discover gold under the nursery floor.

'Clémenté, dear child', Vanessa would encourage Virginia in the affected drawl of Mrs Dilke. Then Virginia, as Clémenté, would pick up the plot and the serial went on, while the fire flickered, until her voice ceased and one by one they dropped off to sleep.

At St Ives there was a different serial, a 'garden story about Beccage and Hollywinks; spirits of evil who lived on the rubbish heap; and disappeared through a hole in the escallonia hedge'— Virginia related these details to her mother and the American ambassador (her godfather), Mr Lowell. A few years later Virginia submitted to *Tit-Bits* a 'wildly romantic' story about a young woman on a ship—we know no more than that, but here is the scene of her first complete novel, *The Voyage Out*.

Virginia was a much-praised child. From the time she could write a letter at the age of five in a 'most lovely hand', her parents responded with pride, delighting in her talk and in her high-spirited jokes and tales in the 'Hyde Park Gate News' which she produced, at intervals, between February 1891 and April 1895. One item is an eloquent tribute to Leslie Stephen's election as President of the London Library (following Gladstone and Carlyle):

Mrs. Ritchie the daughter of Thackeray who came to luncheon the next day expressed her delight by jumping from her chair and clapping her hands in a childish manner but none the less sincerely. The greater part of Mrs. Stephen's joy lies in the fact that Mr. Gladstone is only vice-president. . . . We think that the London Library has made a very good choice in putting Mr. Stephen before Mr. Gladstone as although Mr. Gladstone may be a first-rate politician he cannot beat Mr. Stephen in writing.

There is also an uproarious serial about a henpecked but aspiring cockney, his bungling efforts at farming, and a comic power struggle between him and his wife.

At the same time as Virginia's wit was encouraged, she was bathed in protective love. This love is most striking in Leslie Stephen's letters. 'Kiss my darling little bright eyes', he ends one letter to Julia. In 1883, when Virginia was nearly two, he wrote that 'she sat on my knee to look at Bewick' (the book on birds) and every so often would put her cheek against his, demanding 'kiss'. Delighted by her boldness, a few months later he reports that, when he told her he must go to his library, she 'squeezed her little self tightly up against me & then gazed up with her bright eyes through her shock of hair & said "don't go, Papa!" She looked full of mischief all the time. I never saw such a little rogue.' Whatever Leslie Stephen became during Virginia's adolescence, certainly in her childhood there was no sign of the Victorian tyrant of common report. Slogging over his biographical dictionary in 1886, he called up Virginia's face for comfort: 'I see her eyes flash & her sweet little teeth gleam.' Her mother once caught her twisting a lock of hair as she read, in imitation of her father. On her ninth birthday, in 1891, he observed that 'she is certainly very like me'.

Virginia's imagination was shaped first by a natural scene, the Cornwall shore, then by a social scene, Victorian London, and then, as she grew older, she began to perceive the originality of her father and mother. The searching inquisitiveness that led to their portrait in *To the Lighthouse* first showed itself in a bold question launched at her elder sister when, still in the nursery, they were jumping about naked before their bath: 'She suddenly asked me which I liked best, my father or mother', Vanessa recalled. Vanessa's answer was unhesitating: 'Mother.' But Virginia went on to explain why she, on the whole, preferred their father. 'I don't think', said Vanessa, 'her preference was quite as sure and simple as mine. She had considered both critically and had more or less analysed her feelings for them which I, at any rate consciously, had never attempted.'

2. *The Most Lovable of Men**

THROUGHOUT her life Virginia was to retain a fascination for the character of 'that old wretch my father'. She was, she believed, more like him than like her mother, which made her more critical, 'but he was an adorable man, and somehow, tremendous'. She often condemned him: in her adolescence he seemed a tyrant. Later, as she grew older, she could see what had made Leslie Stephen so attractive to his contemporaries and friends. She would dip into his letters and memoirs and find there a mirror image of herself: 'a fastidious delicate mind, educated & transparent'. But the ambivalence was never resolved. Near the end of her life she could still see her father from two angles at once: 'As a child condemning; as a woman of 58 understanding—I should say tolerating. Both views true?'

The indissoluble link that made Virginia closer to her father than his other children was his profession as man of letters. All her benign memories are of the scholarly gentleman in the library, on the top floor of the tall house in Hyde Park Gate, neatly blotting an article and beginning another. He hoped to make his mark as a philosopher but it is as a critic and biographer that he is remembered, primarily for the *Dictionary of National Biography* and his *History of English Thought in the Eighteenth Century*.

Leslie Stephen's hold on his younger daughter's imagination was the result, partly, of the education he gave her, but long before she became his pupil there was the simpler bond of feeling, something in this case deeper than the routine bond of child to parent. It was a spontaneous attraction to certain qualities in Leslie Stephen that appear not so much in his famous works as in private letters and memoirs.

He wrote two entirely different memoirs. The second, *Some Early Impressions*, written in 1903 near the end of his life, was designed for publication and recorded strictly external events: his Cambridge experiences in the 1850s where until the age of thirty he was a determinedly manly and athletic don; his conquest of Alpine

---

* This phrase was used to describe LS by his American friend, James Russell Lowell.

peaks during vacations; his avowal of agnosticism and the consequent loss of his tutorship in 1863; then his years as a powerful editor and journalist in London. But all the private events of his life went into the confidential *Mausoleum Book*, written eight years earlier and not intended for publication.

'I hope', he told his children, 'that I am helping you a little by trying to fix some of the memories which will, I trust, be a lifelong possession to you all.'

His 'Letter to Julia's Children' (as he called it) pictures himself as a *gauche*, dry old don, hardly fit for marriage, a poor skeleton with long, thin arms and legs. It amazed him that he should have enjoyed the love of two exceptional women, Harriet Marion Thackeray, whom he married in 1867, and, after her death eight years later, Julia Duckworth. Leslie Stephen exaggerated his defects but, in truth, he had no great physical advantages. He had goat-like blue eyes and a curious flatness on the top of his head, accentuated by a tatty, flaring red beard into which he would mutter uncomfortable truths. This was hardly improved by a snorting, brusque manner which Julia called his 'terribleness'. His children accepted his self-caricature at face value—indeed he approximated the image as he grew old, which was when they formed their lasting impressions—but his letters to contemporaries suggest his immense lovableness. Lovableness is hard to define but I think it came from the articulate and unselfconscious ease with which this often silent and irritable man could express tenderness.

In his brief portrait of Minny Thackeray, Leslie Stephen had to confront the character of the muted woman, a problem which his daughter would take up in *The Voyage Out* and other novels. Thinking back twenty years after Minny's death on her baby-fox face, he saw the need to get behind the bland surface of the mid-Victorian girl who set down conventional sentiments in her letters. Minny's innocence, her unaffectedness, her pure-mindedness did not make her a child-wife, but she had the fearlessness and straightforwardness of a child. Her purity was the very antithesis of small-minded prudery. Minny Thackeray impressed her husband from the beginning with her fearless transparency. There seems to have been no feeling she cared to conceal, no affection she thought necessary to veil. In their last months they 'seemed to know each other's wishes and feelings at a glance and to share them'.

In his youth Leslie Stephen had a mature relationship with

a woman; in middle age a romance. His veneration for his second wife was less discerning. He made of her a goddess and was pampered in return. He became, as he grew older, more infantile and dependent, 'lopsided' and 'unreal' without her.

When Julia Duckworth's aunt, the great Victorian photographer, Julia Margaret Cameron, left England for Ceylon, the niece asked her to 'pray God that I may die soon. That is what I most want.' In her youth Julia had had a shock from which she never wholly recovered. Brought up among Pre-Raphaelite artists, she had rejected proposals from Holman Hunt and Thomas Woolner and chosen, instead, to marry a handsome, conventional man whom she idolized. Herbert Duckworth had died after only four years, just before the birth of their third child. Virginia heard that this reserved woman used to lie upon his grave. Then, when her friend, Minny, died, she came to comfort Leslie Stephen. He saw that her own blow had given her 'a deeper and keener sympathy with all who are desolate and afflicted'. He recognized, too, that her past-ridden melancholy was not only a response to shock but constitutional. A family strain, it went deeper than his own rampant moodiness.

Leslie Stephen's letters to Julia at this time show an unselfish tact and delicacy of feeling. His first proposal, on 2 February 1877, has the delightful transparency that Virginia recognized:

Dearest Julia,

I am forced to say something to you which concerns me much—and you very little. It was revealed to me a little while ago that I love you—as a man loves the woman he would marry. . . . Now a sure instinct tells me that you have no such feeling for me. *I have not the slightest illusion about this.* I feel certain too that you will never have such a feeling for me. Nay, I am convinced that even if you loved me, I could hardly make you happy as my wife. . . . Whatever happens I shall love you (in one sense) as long as I live. . . . As I write I feel half mad & half wicked, but I do *not* feel unfaithfully to my distant memories.

Leslie Stephen did not hide his more obvious defects: his 'fidgets' over money; his willingness to shuffle off his duties on to others; his rudeness; and the fact that nothing cheered him so much as a thoroughly good grumble. 'I am a sort of harmless misanthrope', he wrote. 'When you have got to know me a little you may stroke me. . . .'

Julia's hesitation had to do not with the man himself or her own

inclinations but with two practical problems. During the independent years of widowhood she had developed a vocation for
nursing. She told Stephen that she could never give it up.

'I may be called away to nurse people for weeks or have invalids
in my house for weeks', she explained, 'and be so tied as to be unable
to see you as often or as much as I want.'

This, then, was no idle charity. Julia's book on the management
of sick rooms, published in 1883, is the work of a professional. By
concentrating on one goal, the patient's well-being, physical and
mental, she shed the distractions of passing fads and panaceas so
that one may discern, in her practical rules, the pure principles of
nursing. There is exquisite attention to detail: to lift a patient's
head softly in one's palm; to be silent during bathing which is one of
the patient's very few pleasures; to listen to what a patient is saying
even if it seems wrong. Many years later, Leonard and Virginia
Woolf reprinted the book at the Hogarth Press. I doubt that it is
used in the training of nurses, but it should be. Written with feeling
and humour, it is a pleasure to read.

Leslie Stephen assured her that she would be free to work as she
saw fit: 'Go away for weeks, if you must & nurse sick people, or do
anything else. I will not complain any more. . . .' He kept his word.
During Julia's frequent absences he took charge of the household
and children. In April 1881 he wrote: 'People think me very wrong
to let you go. But, my own, I feel that it is right.' Wherever Julia
Stephen went, even to St Ives, she was called to sick-beds. Virginia
recalled the sternness of her mother's face as she would walk from
the rooms of the poor past the children's cricket ground.

Although Julia and Leslie Stephen never flouted convention, as
their daughters were to do, their writings show that their thoughts
and impulses were too forthright, too honest and clear-headed to be
wholly conventional. Before their marriage, in April 1877, he
exploded in frustration at the conventions that kept them from
visiting as often as they wished. He had to talk to her, he said
truculently, 'through a convent grating'. If Julia would not yet
consent to link herself to him in deed, would she agree to a pro
forma marriage? Julia refused because she believed a woman should
not marry unless she could accept a man with 'proper passion'.

As in the matter of vocation, so in the matter of passion, Julia
brought up a difficult issue. In August 1877, following a brief visit
from Leslie Stephen, she wrote two urgent letters to Coniston, in

the Lake District, where he was on holiday. She was not fit for marriage, she confessed, because of her 'deadness'. She had long been in a state of paralysed passivity and did not think she could ever recover.

It would be easy to misunderstand these letters as an ominous confession of frigidity but Leslie Stephen was not alarmed. His reply assured Julia that her response should be in no way forced and that she should come to him, if she decided to do so, in her own time. At length, Julia agreed, very soberly, to undertake a new life. They were married on 26 March 1878. The Coniston correspondence was probably the basis for that exemplary 'equality' to which Virginia Stephen testified in her 'Reminiscences' and for which she strove in her own marriage.

Leslie Stephen and Virginia described this marriage according to the differing points of view of husband and child, but on two facts their accounts agree. 'Let me say it confidently,' the husband records in the *Mausoleum Book*, 'my darling did come to life again.' And at the end of the first part of *To the Lighthouse* the daughter shows the vitality of her parents' love as they read together. At the same time, both husband and daughter agree that the years of widowhood had left Julia rather stern, rather melancholy. 'O my dear,' Leslie Stephen wrote reproachfully in 1885, 'what would I not give to see you a little cheerful.'

Beautiful in her grey, sober dignity, Julia Stephen was to die long before her time at the age of forty-nine. Her children decided that she had been worn out by their father's relentless emotional demands. But she died of rheumatic fever, a condition which could possibly be traced back to 1879 when she had nursed a severe case of the fever a few months after she herself had had a difficult childbirth. It is also clear from Leslie Stephen's last worried letter to her in April 1895 that she had gone off, probably to nurse, despite recurring bouts of influenza, and as usual he had let her do as she wanted. When her death was followed two years later by that of her daughter, Stella, the younger children found a scapegoat in their father, branding him as an ogre who devoured women.

The *Mausoleum Book* and correspondence show Julia Stephen's lot to have been less dreadful than it seemed to her children. Her husband's humane intelligence gave to their letters a rare quickness in intercepting signals. He believed it manly to be tender. And the strength of the woman is always visible. 'I would not, if I could, endure you to act against your judgement', Leslie Stephen wrote at an early stage. It is perhaps the unconventionality of Stephen's regard for women that gave his daughter an essential licence and, at the same time, made his blind spots seem particularly exasperating.

Much about the Stephen parents falls outside the scope of the father's memoir and, to see a complete picture, it should be balanced against the daughter's evidence. Leslie Stephen himself confessed to Julia that he would tune up his glooms ('the horrors') to exact her deliciously sensitive ministrations. To Leslie Stephen this was a minor flaw, to his children a major one. His self-dramatizations infuriated them.

Virginia Woolf's fictionalized portrait of her father as Mr Ramsay shows a baffling mutability, a lightning switch from the most lovable of men to 'famished wolfhound' and back again. There is humanity on a grand scale—he cannot sleep for thinking about fishermen and their wages—yet when he finds an earwig in his milk he sends a plate whizzing through the window. His manners can be bleak and cutting, yet he might show a sensitive courtesy that goes beyond mere politeness. He can wield truth as a weapon, grinning sarcastically as he proves to his son, James, that the weather will prevent a longed-for trip to the lighthouse. Yet his respect for facts is also a mark of the intellectual courage that he passes on to his children:

What he said was true. It was always true. He was incapable of untruth; never tampered with a fact; never altered a disagreeable word to suit the pleasure or convenience of any mortal being, least of all his own children, who . . . should be aware from childhood that life is difficult; facts uncompromising. . . .

Virginia learnt to do justice to the small fact that might, in the end, outweigh other facts. As a novelist she would gather all the often contradictory facts so as to see her characters with the judiciousness of her Stephen ancestors who, since the end of the eighteenth century, had distinguished themselves in every generation in the field of law. Her examination of Mr Ramsay in *To the Lighthouse* is like a witness-box account of the pros and cons of his nature. She puts forward one witness, then another, prosecution, defence, poised again and again in combat.

In a section cut from the manuscript of *To the Lighthouse*, the adolescent daughter, Cam, conducts an imaginary trial of her father. The trial was too personal for publication yet its complex of truths carries more conviction than the superficial ridicule of the wolfhound. At the age of six, James, her younger brother, has longed to sail to the lighthouse but his wish has been foiled by Mr Ramsay's brusque proof that bad weather will prevent the expedition. In this way, the father continues to needle his children, in particular his son, with his aggressive assertions of fact. In his teens, James charges the father with being a sarcastic brute and, to this, Cam poses 'an answer' with her picture of a quiet, grey-clothed gentleman, reading judiciously or writing his articles. In the light of the library 'neither satire & harshness existed, nor temper, nor annoyance, nor his extraordinary vanity, nor his peremptoriness, nor his tyranny (she verified each of these qualities by looking at him)'.

Cam also excuses her father on the grounds of age: 'It was inconceivable how old he was; how much he had left behind which they knew nothing of.' In the 1890s the Stephen children were growing up in the home of a man old enough to be their grandfather. (He was fifty years old when Virginia was born.) They saw an eminent mid-Victorian with a great forehead and nose, a long grey beard, and heavy eyebrows, wisps of which lowered over the eyes. In colossal hiker's boots he would hop along before or behind the family party, swinging his stick, and humming 'like a stridulous grasshopper'.

Cam finally admits that her father 'escaped' from the trial. 'You might try to lay hands on him, but then like a bird, he spread his wings, he floated off to settle out of our reach somewhere far away on some desolate stump.' Her 'sullen rage' at his outlawry suddenly switches again as she recalls how, once, he had picked a yellow flower and her mother, taking it, had stuck it in her dress. '*She* let him go too. . . . It was the same even then. He had his little perch out at sea, she thought smiling, as she did when sometimes she imagined herself like her mother.'

Leslie Stephen was broad-minded about his wife's nursing but it simply never occurred to him that a woman needed a holiday. While he took many walking trips in England and an annual climbing holiday in the Alps, it seems the only time that Julia got away was to sick-beds. Only once, when she was looking particularly worn as her husband set off for the Alps, did he propose a hotel holiday. But, when she ventured suggestions, he decided they were all too expensive and they ended up with relations in Brighton. He would go off to 'tramp' leaving her with eight children, including Laura, the disturbed child of his marriage to Minny. 'I like to think of you with the ragamice', he wrote blithely from the coast of Cornwall in 1884. 'They must be delightful.'

Of the four Stephen children, Virginia stood out from the first as the boldest, the most passionate, and the most drawn to their father. After the mother's death, when they felt like trees pressed down by the remorseless 'gale' of their father's sighs, she could not condemn him like the others. During their unhappiest years from 1895 to 1904, Thoby, the elder son, was away at school and college while Vanessa and Adrian, furiously attached to the memory of their mother, hardened into rebels. It was Virginia who felt painfully divided. In the draft of *To the Lighthouse* she described 'the entire complete misery' of the adolescent Cam as witness to the clashes between father and younger brother during lessons: '& they once dashed about the room & she could only draw aside into the window, & look at the peaceful lawn.' Cam re-enacts Virginia's conflict: drawn by Mr Ramsay's intent manner of reading, by his sensitive hands, his direct and simple language, and the unconscious dignity of his age, Cam yet has to stand by the children's compact to resist him.

It seems clear that, in the last decade of Leslie Stephen's life and perhaps before, there was a distressing deterioration which showed itself only among intimates at home. To his contemporaries he remained the most lovable of men: he continued to write the most touching letters and to charm the Alpine Club with the wit of his after-dinner speeches. Leonard Woolf, meeting him at Cambridge in 1901, saw 'one of those bearded and beautiful Victorian old gentlemen of exquisite gentility and physical and mental distinction on whose face the sorrows of all the world had traced the indelible lines of suffering nobility'. But at home there were fits of ill temper over the pettiest set-backs. Even in Julia's lifetime the bedroom door would slam in the morning. In his daughter's view, his moodiness was reinforced by the saintly indulgence of a Victorian wife.

At seventeen, Virginia wrote her first, rather affectionate caricature of her father. In the Warboys diary of 1899, she accounted for his more bizarre conduct in terms of a genetic endowment in which she, to her evident amusement, must share. The Stephens, with their long bodies, moved awkwardly, as though they resented conventionalities at every step. They could sit speechless, well knowing that it was grey and drizzling and their guests depressed and bored. This imperturbability, so admirably suited to climbing expeditions, was not, however, 'calculated to smooth a tea party'.

The prime reason for Leslie Stephen's overbearing exactions of sympathy was his sense of failure. His accents of self-abasement, still tinged by the old winning candour, can be heard in these lamentations to Julia in 1893:

I *do* wish that I had been more self-confident. . . . I have given up one thing after another & tried different lines & become a jack of all trades & only done well enough to show that I might have done better. . . . You, poor thing, get nearly all my grumblings: for I don't think that I grumble to other people & I certainly don't grumble much to myself.

He would compare himself to a sort of futile Casaubon, Halford Vaughan, the husband of Julia's unhappy eldest sister. Adeline Vaughan, he perceived, had sacrificed her life to a pretentious scholar, entirely wrapped up in vain speculations, whose sense of failure made him unbending and crotchety.

Virginia was born at a turning-point in her father's career. 1882 was the year of the failure of *The Science of Ethics* in which Leslie Stephen had tried to prove that the 'good' had survival value for society, though not necessarily for the individual. It was with this book that he had hoped to establish himself as a speculative philosopher and it had been his disappointment at its reception which had led him, in 1882, to accept the publisher, George Smith's suggestion that he compile the biographical dictionary that was, ironically, to make his name. His first volume appeared in 1885, his last in 1900, and, though Leslie Stephen retired in 1891, he continued to contribute. All through Virginia's childhood, then, her father was grinding out immense numbers of biographies. Virginia's older brother, Thoby Stephen, aged five, produced a box which he called his 'contradictionary box'. Asked the reason for its name, he said it was full of rubbish. Leslie Stephen discerned gleams of satire. It is customary to praise the 'leanness' and 'terseness' of his dictionary style but the writing, though still salty, lacks his earlier exhilaration. In his later years he retreated from the wit and vivacity of his Alpine essays to serve 'Dryasdust', the scholar. In the entry on Carlyle there is a wry burst of sympathy for the philosopher as he begins work on Cromwell in 1840. Carlyle, Stephen wrote, was 'now making acquaintance with "Dryasdust" for the first time. He had never been enslaved to a biographical dictionary; and the dreary work of investigating dull records provoked loud lamentations and sometimes despair.' In the same melodramatic manner, Leslie Stephen called the office of the *DNB* (at 15 Waterloo Place) 'my place of torture'.

In later letters to Julia, he pictures himself as a spectre or a hibernating creature, blanking out on human relations during her absences. In *To the Lighthouse* the failed philosopher demands that his wife should fertilize him. She must fill all the rooms of his house with life in which (in the draft) 'he could steep his barrenness' and Mrs Ramsay, improvising with flashing knitting-needles and her boy between her knees, 'gallantly created the whole world'. The boy, sensing his father's unnatural demand, feels words flow out of her like bounding, leaping, but perfectly controlled waves. She buoys up her husband by proclaiming all the praises she has heard and citing all the American universities that implore his presence. And only then does he feel that he is 'no forlorn spectator tangling his feet in cobwebs'. There is undoubtedly some distortion in this indignant draft portrait of Leslie Stephen. The truth appears clearly in one of his letters to Julia in 1887 which acknowledges the fault but testifies to the generosity of feeling that made this marriage so special: '. . . you know, I hope, that though you cannot give me a fresh set of nerves, all my tantarums [*sic*] and irritabilities, & oaths & lamentations are (comparative) trifles; & that I have always a huge sense of satisfaction underneath.' At the same time, one must concede an element of justice in Virginia's indignation. In the *Mausoleum Book*, Leslie Stephen confessed that he used to exaggerate his self-pity 'in order to extort from [his wife] some of her delicious compliments. They were delicious, for even if they implied error of judgement, they implied the warmest love.' What was, for him, no more than a heartening drama was, in effect, an imposition on the integrity of his wife and, later, his adolescent children. '(The strain of having told lies)', Virginia scribbled in the margin of her *Lighthouse* manuscript.

Leslie Stephen's deterioration reached its peak immediately after

Julia's death when what Virginia described as an 'Oriental' grief blinded him to his children's right to their own feelings and finally cut him off from their sympathies. Some of the vigour that in youth had gone into climbing mountains remained to him but was now directed into energetic lamentations. His daughter saw in him 'much of the stuff of a Hebrew prophet', filling the world with terrible outbursts of woe. Virginia, aged thirteen, stretched out her arms to this man as he came stumbling from Julia's deathbed but he brushed impatiently past. This scene, imprinted for life on her memory, is emblematic of the emotional impasse which was to persist in their relations from 1895 until Leslie Stephen's death in 1904.

3. A Family Portrait

THERE is a photograph of Virginia at the age of nine or ten, chin in hand, intent on Leslie and Julia Stephen as they sit quietly reading on the sofa at St Ives. There, grave-faced in dark Victorian clothes, sit the living subjects who, as Mr and Mrs Ramsay, were to be recomposed and preserved in the artifice of fiction. How did they appear to a mature imagination? It will be curious to see, in detail at this point, what final shape the parents came to take in Virginia Woolf's great novel of her childhood, *To the Lighthouse*.

In May 1925, thirty-three years after that photograph was taken, as she paced around Tavistock Square, the outline of a record rose spontaneously to her mind: the father, mother, and child in the garden; the mother's death; then the bereaved family's expedition to the lighthouse. 'But could one tell the truth? . . . About one's parents?', she heard a friend ask a month later. Already she was committed to a curious biographic experiment. She would not define her parents' lives by a conventional progression but picture them on two definitive days, about ten years apart. Treating external facts as mere punctuation (Mrs Ramsay does die, most disconcertingly, in brackets), she would strike boldly for what she considered the centre of their lives, the states of mind that uphold action. The novel comes to be about the actual painting of a portrait of the Ramsays, as a modern artist, Lily Briscoe, gives distinctive shape to her distant memories of this family. The first part of the novel shows the Ramsays close-up, their daily relations to their children, to guests, and to themselves. Here is the shapeless, raw material of family life from which, eventually, the artist must draw her 'vision'. 'This is not made up,' Virginia Woolf told herself triumphantly as she sank back into her childhood, 'it is the literal fact.' She was writing *To the Lighthouse* twenty times faster than usual, proof it seemed to her 'that what fruit hangs in my soul is to be reached there'.

At first she saw a book dominated by the Old Man: 'a single & intense character of father', she wrote in her diary on 30 July. A first impulse was to battle with an egotist whose continued life, she said later, would have extinguished her own. Yet as soon as she launched the 'attack' on 6 August, she found herself writing about her mother.

Julia Stephen was partly unknown, extended over the large surface of her exacting family, extended even further by her nursing efforts into the alleys of London. Leslie Stephen was easier to do: she had known him longer and, despite the superficial contradictions of his nature, he stood clear. But the mother was a mystery, and perhaps this is precisely what drew her on. She sensed something screened by Julia's arresting beauty which might be crucial to her own latent gifts as a writer. It was as difficult to capture the real woman, Virginia concluded many years later, as to paint a Cézanne. Since she was writing fictional biography, not biography proper, she could blend her memory of actual scenes with scenes she imagined. The son's disappointment at not being allowed to go to the lighthouse, the mother reading aloud, her visit to a sick-bed, and the superfine quickness with which she divined others' needs: these details a child could remember. Imagination filled in the gaps: what did the father and mother say when they were alone? What made their marriage, for all their differences, so extraordinarily right? As the portrait progressed she feared it was too made-up and was much relieved when her sister confirmed the portrait's accuracy when the book was published in May 1927. 'I'm in a terrible state of pleasure that you should think Mrs Ramsay so like mother', Virginia wrote to Vanessa. 'At the same time, it is a psychological mystery why she should be: how a child could know about her; except that she has always haunted me. . . .'

The main problem was how to approach a person of great distinction who had left no telling work or saying. Where there is distinction there is, usually, a characteristic note to a life, but with this Victorian woman the characteristic note is so muted that it never quite sounds. To do her mother justice, Virginia Woolf had to pass by the family memory of a beauty with whom every man fell in love and search for the source of Julia's strange authority that was derived from no formal power or status. She must focus on a shadowy area of possibility which would never have come to light if among the seven children there had not been one who wished to discover it.

To expose Mrs Ramsay's distinction, her compassion and insight, the artist must pare away the clutter of dusty habits in which it was enclosed: her Victorian sentiment and her silly worship of power:

> Indeed, she had the whole of the other sex under her protection; for reasons she could not explain, for their chivalry and valour, for the fact that they negotiated treaties, ruled India, controlled finance; finally for an attitude to herself which no woman could fail to feel or to find agreeable, something trustful, childlike, reverential . . .

In the opening scene, as Mrs Ramsay rears her son, James, she projects all her imaginative energy on the six-year-old boy and dreams of him as an imperial administrator while her bypassed daughters sport with 'infidel ideas', question the Bank of England, the Indian Empire, and all the trappings of power, the ringed fingers and deference.

Mrs Ramsay's portrait penetrates beyond childhood memory when, imagined from a critical perspective, she is seen to pander also to an air of importance. Mr Ramsay has a devotee, Charles Tansley, who is likened to 'red, energetic ants' set on one track. His thesis, 'the influence of something upon somebody', is the kind of scholarship that buries masterpieces under what Pound calls 'bare-boned factlets'. Yet because Tansley takes himself so seriously he will delude society into granting him the kind of official standing that is his dearest wish. Virginia Woolf ridicules his fantasy—he sees himself exalted in Mrs Ramsay's eyes, gowned, hooded, walking in procession—by linking it with a poster which catches Mrs Ramsay's attention at that moment, advertising circus tricks: 'fresh legs, hoops, horses, glistening reds and blues . . . a hundred horsemen, twenty performing seals . . .'.

Virginia Woolf's rebuke of Mrs Ramsay, implied in this imaginary scene, is gradually located more firmly in the interior voice of Lily Briscoe who is, all the time, giving shape to Mrs Ramsay on canvas and trying to 'place' her relation to others. Mrs Ramsay pities Tansley. Lily fears him: in him she identifies the artist's enemy. For Tansley's ineffectiveness makes him scorn women whose inferior position provides a convenient foil to vanity. Mrs Ramsay tries to humanize him by tactful little attentions which lift his morale. She invites him to walk with her to the town; on the way she manages to imply the subjection of all wives to their husbands' work. And he does respond with a clumsy burst of sentiment as he sees her:

Stepping through fields of flowers and taking to her breast buds that had broken and lambs that had fallen; with stars in her eyes and the wind in her hair—He took her bag.

Yet although Mrs Ramsay wrings from him a temporary veneration and one superfluous gesture, Tansley's egotism is too meagrely fixed to show her further consideration. Later in the day, when Mr Ramsay puts an end to his wife's hopes of sailing to the lighthouse, Tansley is quick to leap into line behind his patron: '"There'll be no landing at the Lighthouse tomorrow", said Charles Tansley, clapping his hands together as he stood at the window with her husband.'

Mrs Ramsay's indulgence of men is offset by severity to women. There is something irresistible, Lily notes, in the masterfulness with which Mrs Ramsay says 'Marry, marry'. In the dark of night she comes to Lily's bedroom to force the ideal of marriage on a young woman whose independence and stature she has not fathomed. 'An unmarried woman has missed the best of life', she states and Lily, in turn, 'would urge her own exemption from the universal law . . . she liked to be alone; she liked to be herself; . . . and so have to meet a serious stare from eyes of unparalleled depth, and confront Mrs Ramsay's simple certainty . . . that her dear Lily, her little Brisk, was a fool.'

Filled with Victorian certainties as to the high destiny of women in marriage, she inflates a young pair, Paul Rayley and Minta Doyle, with the grandeur of feelings they cannot sustain. Minta is the kind of nice girl who is fatally submissive to Mrs Ramsay. Minta is malleable because she cultivates the flaws of womanishness: too idle a rein on impulse, too easy enthusiasms. She explodes in sobs over a lost brooch. She is weeping, naturally, 'for some other loss' in having just then consented to marry. Her consolation prize is Paul's baby-blue eyes and domestic security. Paul's reward is Mrs Ramsay's approval.

With the help of picnics and house parties, Julia Stephen too had led her victims to the altar, dispatching difficulties with the high hand of some commanding empress. One of her protégées, the romantic Madge Symonds, who had written a book and travelled with her father, the writer, John Addington Symonds, was married to one of Julia's dullest relations, a schoolmaster called William Vaughan. The motherless Kitty Lushington, while under Julia's protection at St Ives, was engaged to Leo Maxse in September

1890. The Maxse marriage, like that of the Rayleys, was not a success. Kitty was heir to all that was conventional in Julia Stephen which her own daughters rejected, not without acute temptation. Kitty was 'a lady of the most delicate charm, of the most ethereal grace' who became a hostess to important men. Virginia Woolf allowed Kitty's charm a fair play in the shape of Mrs Dalloway, but finally laid this ghost with the portrait of Minta Doyle as charming victim of masterful Mrs Ramsay.

Ten years later, when Mrs Ramsay is dead and Lily Briscoe looks back at her as a Victorian, she sums up Mrs Ramsay's mistakes. Out of some sacrificial need of her own she had trained her husband in obtuseness: never to give, always to take. Her extravagances of wifely sympathy seem now, to Lily's cool modern gaze, quite archaic. Lily's tone is fastidious; a pedantic word, 'evidently', confronts Mrs Ramsay's emotions; and there is a deliberate use of the past tense. When Mr Ramsay demands sympathy from Lily, as the nearest woman available, she realizes that she cannot enact the Victorian response:

Surely she could imitate from recollection the glow, the rhapsody, the self-surrender she had seen on so many women's faces . . . when . . . they blazed up . . . into a rapture of sympathy, of delight in the reward they had, which, though the reason of it escaped her, evidently conferred on them the most supreme bliss of which human nature was capable.

The problem of Julia Stephen's portrait was not the haziness of memory, but an insistent, unforgettable image, like that of Helen passing before the old men of Troy. Her beauty, her womanliness was a flawless composite, always presented and enacted before the ravished eyes of the ten-year-old child in the drawing-room at St Ives. In Virginia Woolf's plan she saw 'a stone figure; a statue set on a height always to look the depths of night in the face'. It was her self-imposed task to look beyond the stone figure if she hoped to find the true source of her mother's distinction. The image the child had remembered was outwardly like the Angel of the House, and so, easy to criticize as a distortion of womanhood. But the portrait which Lily paints has nothing of this. She sees quite another Mrs Ramsay, almost obscured by the monument, who is yet a portent of what women may be.

Lily paints Mrs Ramsay as a purple triangle. From the first moment that Lily sets up her easel so as to see Mrs Ramsay at the window, reading to James, there is to be no attempt at a likeness but an abstract idea of shadow and silence. Lily sees, at the outset, 'a wedge-shape of darkness' just as Virginia Woolf, in her first notes for the book, imagines the antithesis to the man reciting 'The Charge of the Light Brigade'; someone retreating from the postures of action into the secret authority of her mind.

'Oh the torture of never being left alone!', Julia once said. This was the starting-point for the approach to the unknown face of Mrs Ramsay. Her daughter had merely to imagine a Victorian matron, with a large household of eight children and three guests, who would never normally be alone, suddenly left alone. As she switches off her sense of duty, the beam of the lighthouse strikes her. The magical third stroke of the lighthouse—'her stroke', Mrs Ramsay calls it—confirms Lily's intuition that this woman hides a face so deeply in shadow that it is normally 'invisible'. The artist behind her easel, the biographer behind her novel reproduce the action of the lighthouse: together they light up a woman's uncharted nature. Neither the artist nor the subject herself can say what exactly this may be.

At this moment Mrs Ramsay is infused with the beam's power to search the mind, 'purifying out of existence . . . any lie'. Her power depends on 'losing personality'. She realizes that 'our apparitions, the things you know us by, are simply childish'.

Anthropologists have noticed their poor record with female subjects who, despite apparent volubility, relay almost no information beyond what is immediately observable, their marriages and duties. Edwin and Shirley Ardener suggest that women have become a 'muted' group through centuries of adapting their perceptions to fit a language encoded by men.* Mrs Ramsay dislikes the jarring way that her husband confronts James with the disappointing fact that he cannot sail to the lighthouse. When her remonstrance provokes swearing, she quickly assumes 'there was nothing to be said'. But in the privacy of Lily's mind this silence is loaded with a challenge to Mr Ramsay's voice which has been indulged too long and booms too loud, like a brass beak.

'"I have the feelings of a woman but I have only the language

* Women are, of course, only one of many muted groups in society which must establish links between their own experience and the dominant model of events.

of men"', Virginia Woolf quoted in a 1920 review.* 'To try the
accepted forms, to discard the unfit, to create others which are more
fitting, is a task that must be accomplished. . . .' This task must be
seen in the context of her upper-middle-class training in ladylike
silence. To lift her voice as a writer could not have been easy; to
frame a statement of feeling for which no words exist demanded an
almost mad audacity. She often spoke of voices that inspired or
maddened her. Lily Briscoe finds that 'to follow her thought was
like following a voice which speaks too quickly to be taken down by
one's pencil, and the voice was her own voice saying without
prompting undeniable, everlasting, contradictory things . . .'.

As James Joyce saw the need to forge the uncreated conscience of
his subject Irish race so Virginia Woolf set out to generate the
uncreated model of her sex. Both saw a stronghold guarded by
language and that it is with language that it must be opposed. The
Irish orator in *Ulysses* gives an exemplum of the Jews as a tribe of
nomad herdsmen subject to Egypt. Only by refusing to hear the
admonitions of the dominant civilization was it possible for Moses
to come down from Sinai with a new code *'graven in the language of
the outlaw'*.

Virginia Woolf's model of her sex originated with her mother,
but her mother purified not only of the dramatic plot of her outward
life and not only of the passing conventions of Victorian womanhood, but purified of the artifice of language itself. She sees a woman
whose tables of the law are locked in their pre-verbal state. When
Lily is alone with Mrs Ramsay in the dark bedroom, 'she imagined
how in the chambers of the mind and heart of the woman . . . were
stood, like treasures in the tombs of kings, tablets bearing sacred
inscriptions, which if one could spell them out would teach one
everything, but they would never be . . . made public'. The
biographer and artist in Lily combine to ask: 'What art was there,
known to love or cunning, by which one pressed through into those
secret chambers? . . . For it was not knowledge but unity that she
desired, . . . nothing that could be written in any language known
to men, but intimacy itself, which is knowledge, she had thought,
leaning her head on Mrs. Ramsay's knee.' Mrs Ramsay is adept at
what E. M. Forster calls the secret understanding of the heart. At

---

* VW slightly misquotes Bathsheba in *Far From the Madding Crowd*. Bathsheba explains:
'It is difficult for a woman to define her feelings in language which is chiefly made by men to
express theirs.'

dinner her eyes go round the table unveiling the thoughts and feelings of her guests without effort, 'like a light stealing under water so that its ripples and the reeds in it and the minnows balancing themselves, and the sudden silent trout are all lit up hanging, trembling'. Her eyebeam lights up a hidden self, wrapped in an artifice of manners. It is an exercise of that gift to see through all lies which the beam of the lighthouse had briefly exposed.

Virginia Woolf isolated two gifts in her mother which were to form the basis of her own art. First, Julia Stephen could stamp people with their characters at once. Her bold biographic sallies in the Hyde Park Gate drawing-room on Sunday afternoons probably provided a more valuable example for Virginia than the factual items of the *DNB*.

Second, Julia passed on to her daughter the Victorian agnostic's sense of futility balanced by solicitude. With the shock of her first husband's death, Julia had become 'the most positive of disbelievers'. Her resignation to fate made her cherish, with attentive piety, minute dramas in the lives about her 'as though she heard perpetually the ticking of a vast clock'. In the draft of *To the Lighthouse* the Rayley engagement is no sooner settled than Mrs Ramsay sees it consumed by the past, as though the stream of time eddied round it at first, then rushed it into the main current: 'oh yes whenever anything happened, it was one's first thought—always death.' This omnipresent sense of termination was to find its way into all her daughter's novels, particularly *The Waves*. As Julia listened to the ticking of the clock so her daughter heard the waves beat the measure of life. Her only recourse against time passing was to squeeze the moment before it washed away in the current streaming at her back. All her most civilized characters have this power to transfix the past. Without it, their historical sense would be unendurable.

At first we see the parents close-up at the peak of their life. The first part of *To the Lighthouse* ends with Mrs Ramsay reading Shakespeare's sonnets, those testimonies to a beauty that calls for undying works of art. The author means to ensure, through Lily's painting and, by implication, through the novel itself, that the summer day of her mother's unquestionable loveliness would never fade. 'So long as men can breathe, or eyes can see,' Shakespeare wrote, 'So long lives this, and this gives life to thee.' Lily is far too modest to believe that her painting will not be relegated to attics, but all that rightly concerns her is that one moment in time, one summer afternoon at the end of the Victorian age, should be recorded.

Mrs Ramsay is immersed in the sonnet, 'From you have I been absent in the spring'. Here, the beloved seems the essence of all beauty so that, in the beloved's absence, nature's approximation— 'the deep vermilion in the rose'—is a poor substitute. The sonnet could speak for the novelist herself, for a sense of loss so great that all forms of present loveliness are but pale imitations of a perfection she had glimpsed as a child:

> Yet seem'd it winter still, and, you away,
> As with your shadow I with these did play.

This scene of the parents reading is the scene of the photograph, only little Virginia is not there. The parents are left alone and the mature novelist sums up their private relationship from an imaginative distance, like Virginia Woolf peering in at the window of Talland House, to see the beloved ghosts enact their long past drama.

The sexual feeling in this scene is suggested rather than enacted. The strength of the Ramsay marriage seems to have been based on Mr Ramsay's willingness, like Leslie Stephen's, to respond imaginatively to the silence of his wife. Mrs Ramsay cannot articulate the nature of her love, 'yet he knew'—these are the closing words.

The mutual feeling of the Ramsays is the natural outcome of a remarkable infusion of humanity which comes from their mutual draughts of great literature. Mr Ramsay, reading Scott, thinks how imbalanced, by comparison, is the sexual interest in Balzac; he slaps his thighs in delight at Scott's feeling and humour. Observing that he is absorbed by the novel and 'controlling his emotion', Mrs Ramsay allows herself to be lulled by the sonnets into a sleepy thrall. In the grip of Shakespeare's verbal wooing, stretched on the intricate mesh of those masterly definitions of love, she craves language. She wishes that Mr Ramsay would say 'anything'.

Gradually, the Ramsays draw together, 'involuntarily, coming side by side, quite close'. There is virtually no action or speech, only the measured growth of a delicate and pregnant rapport that can contain all nuances of character.

In her 'Reminiscences' Virginia said that the fifteen years of her mother's second marriage had been a late fulfilment. Marriage for her parents—and eventually for herself—held the possibility of the most fascinating of possible relationships between men and women. The Ramsays are adepts at 'seeing' each other: 'But she knew . . . he was watching. . . . He was roused.' . . . 'She turned, holding her stocking, and looked at him.' The shrewd child in the drawing-room had seen enough to imagine this. Beautiful, even to a child's eye, were their glances of unutterable delight in each other, she recalled. Their consonance was reached by 'rich, rapid scales of discord, and incongruity'. Later, when Leslie Stephen looked at the photograph of them, with Virginia in the background, he affirmed their 'deep strong current of calm inward happiness'.

With Julia's death this panoply of love, which had enfolded the Stephen family, completely vanished. Relationships at once became artificial and strained. Leslie Stephen became melodramatic and unreal; the children retreated into distrustful silence. There now began for Virginia a long struggle between the tug of the past and her need to begin anew, to compose an independent identity as writer. What happens to Lily Briscoe in the post-war section of *To the Lighthouse*, when she comes into her own as a modern artist, is a fictional account of Virginia Woolf's own self-discovery as writer, and comes into this story at a later stage.

In the mean time, there lay ahead twenty years of illness when Virginia was in the grip of the past. She lived in an era in which the past seemed to 'speak' to the present in the form of ghosts, as her mother once spoke to her at breakfast in 1915. 'Unquenchable seems to me such a presence', Henry James had written to the Stephen family after Julia's death. In such a case, the ghost sense is not some bizarre incursion but a matter of the degree to which the past is alive.

The origin of this ghost sense is suggested in a manuscript description of the Victorian mother. After dinner, Mrs Ramsay stands upon the stair, willing herself into her children's memory. It satisfies her to know that, by entering so closely into her children's emotions, she would, in a sense, overcome death. 'They would come back to this night then. And it pleased her to think how all their lives long in their memories she would be woven . . . so that her own death would matter rather less.'

It was disastrously easy to bring Julia back. Virginia had only to read her love letters or to open her old wardrobe or to overhear someone in the family with a similar laugh, ending on three notes of pure happiness, wrung out one by one. I say 'disastrous' because the excitement of this contact brought, as an inevitable sequel, the renewed pain of abandonment. In the *Lighthouse* manuscript Lily's very body felt stark and hollow with longing: 'Ghost, air, nothingness.'

Virginia's reaction to her mother's death took three forms. There were times when she was crippled by a helpless longing. She had a recurring dream in which her mother would raise to her forehead a wreath of white flowers and step, with her usual quickness, across the fields until she vanished. Then, after the deaths of Stella and Thoby, she would move off in a company of the dead, a company which Virginia tried three times to join.

In London or in the country, her eyes half-closed, she would seek in the living world some likeness to the dream. She would look down a railway carriage or at the curve of the road, and then some object would get in the way. So, in her work, reality and dream check each other. Lily cannot complete her portrait from memory; in an agony of frustration she calls on the ghost of Mrs Ramsay:

'Mrs. Ramsay! Mrs. Ramsay!' she cried, feeling the old horror come back—to want and want and not to have. Could she inflict that still?

And then the ghost steals back: 'Mrs. Ramsay—it was part of her perfect goodness to Lily—sat there quite simply, in her chair, flicked her needles to and fro, knitted her reddish-brown stocking, cast her shadow on the step.' For the space of the painting, Lily commands her presence.

Virginia's healthiest response to her mother's death was creative: the completion of Lily's portrait. Virginia Woolf saw biography as a portrait, not a compendium of facts. Her subject had to be composed like a work of art. Memories and facts were essential but, in the end, were only a guide to questions. Memory gave her the beam but only imagination could direct it. She asked two difficult questions which she answered with two great imaginative scenes. First, what was her mother to *herself*? It was an inspired stroke to let the beam of the lighthouse catch her, in a rare moment, alone. Second, what was the private scene of her parents' marriage? Working from their remembered glance, she dramatized a mounting rapport so complete that it wiped out all domestic friction.

When the portrait was published, Vanessa was amazed that such authenticity could be achieved by imagination more than by fact. She wrote:

> Villa Corsica [Cassis, France]
> 11 May [1927]

My Billy,

. . . It seemed to me that in the first part of the book you have given a portrait of mother which is more like her to me than anything I could ever have conceived of as possible. It is almost painful to have her so raised from the dead. You have made one feel the extraordinary beauty of her character, which must be the most difficult thing in the world to do. It was like meeting her again with oneself grown up and on equal terms and it seems to me the most astonishing feat of creation to have been able to see her in such a way. You have given father too I think as clearly but perhaps, I may be wrong, that isn't quite so difficult. There is more to catch hold of. Still it seems to me to be the only thing about him which ever gave a true idea. So you see as far as portrait painting goes you seem to me to be a supreme artist and it is so shattering to find oneself face to face with those two again that I can hardly consider anything else. . . .

> Your VB

Virginia had yet one other response to her mother's death that was, for her, the most simple and yet the most difficult to understand. Neither sick nor creative, it was a simple acceptance of her continued presence. 'Nothing is stronger than the position of the dead among the living', she once wrote matter-of-factly. In the manuscript of *To the Lighthouse* the modern artist thinks of the insistent presence of the Victorian mentor: not the woman of flesh and blood, but the other, hidden one who would steal back and mould one's thoughts. A decade after her death and 'still she prevailed—Faintly, almost imperceptibly she made herself felt. She had put off the robe of the flesh & taken on another.' In this way Julia Stephen continued to haunt her daughter. A decade after her death Virginia reported that 'on more occasions than I can number, in bed at night, or in the street, or as I come into the room, there she is; beautiful, emphatic, with her familiar phrase and her laugh; closer than any of the living'.

APPRENTICESHIP

Self-emancipation even in the West Indian provinces of the fancy and imagination, — what Wilberforce is there to bring that about?

Walden

4. *Twenty Dark Years*

DARK years in Virginia Stephen's life, from 1895 to 1915, began with her mother's death. The lowest point came in the last months of 1897 following the loss of her eldest sister, Stella. There was, at the age of fifteen, so much against her: the deaths of her two protectors; the emotional withdrawal of her father; and above all the mental illness that now set in, that always threatened to surface, and that often succeeded in these first, most vulnerable twenty years in bouts of varying severity, the last of which coincided with the publication of her first novel in 1915.

How did Virginia Stephen come to be a writer against such odds? The next two chapters tell of adversity; the following two of her emancipation: how she began to draw on her peculiar resources, especially her wayward education; how she turned the paternal model to effect and how she came to surpass her father; how she began to make imaginative use of the limited experience open to her and to dare to stand by odd views of society from her position as an inadequately protected and sick young woman.

Hers was an exceptionally long apprenticeship, partly the result of set-backs, but in a great part self-imposed. How did she come by her private standard, so uncompromisingly high, for what is to be published? There was in her, as in the most original of her contemporaries, T. S. Eliot, restraint. Both submitted themselves to years of silent practice; both hoarded writings without attempting publication. Patience is not a literary virtue much spoken of nowadays but they had it, a sign not of humility but of vigilant self-respect.

The third part of this book will trace Virginia Woolf's public achievements, but this second part traces what is, in a way, more interesting: a writer's formative phase. Her solitary experiments, particularly an unpublished piece, 'Memoirs of a Novelist' (written in 1909), were a reservoir of theories which eventually found expression in the novels of her maturity. All her pivotal ideas were born during this long period of adversity.

In *To the Lighthouse* the years that intervene between the Victorian scene and modern womanhood are pictured as a blank passage of time. In reality, these years were filled with influential figures and dramatic event, but Virginia's memories were so painful that they broke off two attempts at a memoir and produced, in her autobiographic novel, a dashing hiatus when time literally speeds up, the seasons swing round, as the faceless years fly into oblivion.

The 1897 diary and a reminiscent fragment for her 'Sketch of the Past' (1940) offer a few details of her troubled state. The fragment suggests that privately she, like Eliot, saw herself emerging from a chrysalis but, where Eliot imagined a process of self-perfection, bursting out ingenuous and pure, she stressed less the transformation, rather the vulnerability of the shell-less creature, when with 'sticky tremulous legs & antennae it pushes out of the chrysalis & emerges: waits beside the broken shell for a moment; damp: its wings still creased; its eyes dazzled; incapable of flight'. This is how she saw herself at fifteen when she took the sudden blow of Stella's death. 'Even now', she wrote ten years later, 'it seems incredible.'

Virginia's life might have shut down then and there. She might have remained mentally crippled. She might, alternatively, have striven to be 'normal', an insipid, well bred girl. Since she took neither course, a turning-point is here, in 1897.

After Stella's death the three men in the household began to prey on the two younger sisters in different ways. From the time of Julia's death, Leslie Stephen was ravenous for sympathy ('like a lion seeking whom he could devour'). Between 1895 and 1897 Stella had taken the brunt of this and fed him reassurance and praise. After Stella's death he 'showed himself strangely brisk' as he eyed the next eldest daughter, Vanessa. It was Vanessa's cool unresponsiveness, according to Virginia, which now provoked unprecedented shows of 'violence' from their father. On Wednesdays, she remembered, if weekly accounts went over £11 'down came his fist on the account books. There was a roar. His vein filled. His face flushed. Then he shouted "I am ruined." Then he beat his breast. . . . Vanessa stood by his side absolutely dumb. . . . Never have I felt such rage and such frustration. For not a word of my feeling could be expressed.'

The second man was Stella's bereaved husband, Jack Hills, who played on their emotions. Virginia recalled a scene with Jack in a garden house where they were on holiday, at Painswick, near

Stroud, a month after Stella's death: 'He grips my hand in his. He groans. "It tears one asunder" he groaned. He was in agony. He gripped my hand to make his agony endurable; as if he were in physical torture. "But you can't understand" he broke off. "Yes, I can", I murmured. Subconsciously I knew that he meant that his sexual desires tore him asunder, together with his anguish at her loss. Both were torturing him. And the [leafless] tree, outside in the dark garden, was to me the emblem, the symbol, of the skeleton agony to which her death had reduced him; and us; everything.' In Jack's case the girls were willing victims, though now and again Virginia rebelled. He exacted minute analysis of his grief but gave little recognition in return except to draw Vanessa temporarily into a futile intimacy.

Finally, there were George's embraces which went beyond the bounds of decency but which he masqueraded, even to himself, as overmastering brotherly affections. This is the most sinister kind of predator, the kind who masquerades as protector. His apparent solicitude led them, intermittently, to trust him. In any case, convention forbade any mention of it, for to complain of George would reflect on the purity of their own minds.

All this emotional violence Mrs Stephen and Stella had held at bay. When they died 'some restraint seemed to burst'. In *To the Lighthouse* Lily perceives that it was 'a house full of unrelated passions' which had once cohered around the older women but were now unleashed. George, who had been a childhood hero, who had taken them for bus rides and had given them tea at City Inns and had taught them how to play cricket with a straight bat, was now 'a sea of racing emotions'. The two young girls, little more than adolescents, could exert no control. They could only withdraw. And so they 'walked alone' whenever they could.

They used to escape to Kensington Gardens, then comparatively wild, where they had read *Tit-Bits*, lying in the long grass, slowly eating a penny chocolate. The sisters now found privacy in a glass-enclosed room, overlooking the back garden. Vanessa would paint while Virginia read aloud from Thackeray and George Eliot. It was then, said Virginia, that 'Nessa and I formed together a very close conspiracy. In that world of many men, coming and going, we formed our private nucleus.'

In her 'Sketch of the Past' Virginia stressed the unbecoming side to death: its legacy of bitterness, bad-temper, ill-adjustment. The immediate effect of Julia's death was to conjure an atmosphere of unreal gloom in which a genuine pang of grief would have been almost welcome. 'We had but a dull sense of the gloom which could not honestly be referred to the dead; unfortunately it did not quicken our feeling for the living; but hideous as it was, obscured both living and dead . . .'. Slowly, Virginia was alerted to the implications of her mother's death by the emotions which seeped through the morbid silence of shut bedrooms, the black clothes, the writing paper so heavily bordered in black that there was scarcely space to write. Her father, closeted with a determined stream of avid mourners or with the long-suffering Stella, would give vent to explosive cries which the children could hear as doors opened and shut. They sat at meals staring dumbly at their father as he protested again and again his wish to die. They were too young and miserable to regard his histrionics with charity, let alone with humour. As he passed his children's room, stumbling upstairs to his study, they heard him say to himself: 'I wish I were dead, I wish I were dead—I wish my whiskers would grow.'

Their estrangement had another cause. The children regarded death with a modern reticence. It was unmentionable. Leslie Stephen, on the other hand, responded with the emotional licence of an earlier generation which had made the death scene the centre of its dramas. The children felt that their father was morbid, yet his volubility seems more natural than their tight lips. Though Virginia blamed her father for deadening all their emotions, the deadness might have come from the children themselves. The main cause of mental illness in the fictional Septimus Warren Smith is his inability to respond to the death of the person whom he had loved most in the world. Virginia could never forgive herself this frozen time that followed her mother's death, and this was one source of her sickness, to stick at this time.

It was at this point that Stella, aged twenty-eight, emerged as a figure of importance to the children, not only as a substitute mother but also because, it seems, she managed to break the stagnant state. She quickened them by her very sacrifices to the common 'tyrant', her stepfather. Pale, hiding her tears, she evoked some feeling in the younger children, some chivalric devotion that was real and therefore enlivening. And they were further revived by vicarious pleasure in her romance with Jack Hills.

We see Stella, through Virginia's 1897 diary, taking up the mother's mantle: scrubbing Virginia and Adrian, attending their retarded sister, Laura, at Earlswood, visiting the workhouse. Her paleness was for a long time the only sign of the ill-health that she carefully hid. She secured clothes allowances (£40 and £25 each from their tight-fisted father) for her younger sisters. She gave Adrian a microscope when she left to be married. 'We depended on her as thoughtless men on some natural power', Virginia said.

Virginia Woolf described Stella in *To the Lighthouse* (where she appears as Prue) and in her memoirs in two ways. She was obedient, with a dignified not submissive obedience. She called up images of whiteness and purity: 'She reminded me always of those large white flowers—elderblossom, cow parsley, that one sees in the fields in June. . . . Or again, a white faint moon in a blue sky suggests her. Or those large white roses that have many petals and are semi-transparent. She had beautiful fair hair, growing in horns over her forehead; and no colour in her face at all.' In the summer of 1894 she rejected her foremost suitor, Jack Hills, against her mother's wishes. That night the children heard her crying in the next room. 'Marry, marry', urges the mother in *To the Lighthouse* and promises that happiness will be assured. Stella was no longer in her first youth. She had many suitors but had resisted marriage because of a deep attachment to her mother.

Virginia thought of Jack as a 'tenacious wire-haired terrier'. He would sit through his Sunday visits 'worrying his speech as a terrier a bone'. She saw that Stella must have respected him, but to 'meet him face to face, as one capable of the supreme gift of all, needed as Stella found, prolonged consideration and repeated rejection. He satisfied so many requirements, but the sum of all he gave did not need love to reward it. After her mother's death, however, Stella became far less exacting, as indeed she lost interest in her fate . . . Jack was persistent as ever . . .'. Many years later Vanessa told her son, Julian, that Stella, who had refused to marry while Julia was alive, died because she could not live without her. Virginia, too, may have sensed Stella's morbid attachment to the memory of her mother.

'Did mother know?', Virginia asked when Stella announced her engagement.

'Yes', Stella murmured.

Virginia took out her resentment on Jack, to whom she referred in her diary as Stella's 'poor young man'. When urged to accompany the couple (as chaperon) to Bognor she wrote: 'I have been in a dreadful temper all day long. . . . Cannot protest *too* strongly against going.' On 13 February 1897 she said: 'Another week of drizzle in that muddy misty flat utterly stupid Bognor (the name suits it) would have driven us to the end of the pier and into the dirty yellow sea beneath.' When Stella went away on honeymoon, Virginia broke her own umbrella in half and went to bed 'very furious and tantrumical'.

t) Perhaps her irritability was also a sign of anxiety for Stella's health. Stella had had rheumatic fever as a child. During the mourning period she had grown whiter and whiter in her black dress. There had been what was called a chill in the innards at Christmas 1896. Late in February 1897 Virginia accompanied her to see Elizabeth Garrett Anderson (the first woman doctor in England). Stella dismissed her trouble as mere 'fidgets' (the family term for nerviness) but Virginia noted in her diary that Dr Anderson had kept Stella a long time. She must have been aware that only something Stella wished to keep private would have prevented her from going to Seton, the family doctor. On 5 March another visit to Dr Anderson is recorded. Stella was, again, evasive: 'She did not say anything new.'

That spring Virginia witnessed several street accidents that became the focus for her increasing nervousness. Virginia's mental health deteriorated as Stella became plainly ill, the doctors plainly baffled. When doctors made reassuring noises, she wrote in her diary on 4 May: 'This is most satisfactory but I am unreasonable enough to be irritated—.' On 9 May her lessons were stopped on doctor's orders. Quentin Bell notes that during the summer of 1897 Virginia's health and Stella's were in some way connected and ascribes this to the normal friction between adolescent girl and surrogate mother. But the diary shows that the sick eldest sister and the worried youngest one found comfort in each other's company. When Stella was stronger they went each afternoon for slow carriage drives around the Serpentine in Hyde Park. When Stella grew worse, in July, she lay on the sofa with Virginia at her feet and they spent hours talking 'of everything'. Stella would not allow Leslie Stephen to take Virginia away. She slept in Jack's dressing room, opposite Stella's bedroom. 'I had the fidgets very badly', she wrote of the night of 14 July, '& she [Stella] sat with me till 11.30—stroking me; till they went.' Next morning 'she came in to me before breakfast in her dressing gown to see how I was. She only stayed a moment; but then she was quite well. She left me, & I never saw her again.'

The pregnant Stella died three days later after what seems to have been a bungling decision on the part of two new doctors, Broadbent and Williams, to perform the then fashionable operation for peritonitis. She was buried by her mother's side and on 24 July Virginia writes that 'Jack took Nessa & me to Highgate to see Stella's grave. . . . It was covered with dead flowers—.' Her diary admits to 'terrible' rage followed by inertia and depression.

Virginia retold Stella's story four times at different stages of her life: in her 1897 diary, in the 'Reminiscences' of 1907-8, in 'A Sketch of the Past' (June–July 1939) and, in fictional form, in *To the Lighthouse*. There, in 'Time Passes', the eldest daughter, Prue Ramsay, is likened to an evanescent spring which acquiesces in the fertilizing activities of bees and gnats. The fiction uses the passive form in speaking of her fate: 'Prue Ramsay . . . was given in marriage.' A chorus of 'people' figure in her story: 'people' said her marriage was fitting and, when she died that first summer in some illness connected with pregnancy, 'people' spoke again: it 'was indeed a tragedy, people said. They said nobody deserved happiness more.'

Prue's brief spring represents one hopeful moment in this blank passage of Time, a romantic hope that it is possible for the human spirit to revive with this delicate, wakeful nature. The small rain of spring seems to carry some knowledge of human sorrow. Against this burgeoning of hope and trust, Prue suddenly dies. Prue has injected some order and peace in which the imagination has briefly stirred to a sense 'that good triumphs, happiness prevails'. Her death, then, is nature's impersonal betrayal.

'I shrink from the years 1897-1904—the seven unhappy years.' So wrote Virginia Woolf in her final memoir. 'Mother's death: Stella's death. I am not thinking of them. I am thinking of the stupid damage that their deaths inflicted.' Stella's death, especially, was to have two effects on the course of her life: it set off her hunger for women's love and it set off a pattern of mental breakdowns.

Her need of women's love was encouraged, too, by the growing distrust of men. She still worshipped her father and was jubilant when he unbent, but this only whetted her appetite. Throughout her life there remained an unslaked eagerness for approval and liking so that she would approach adult relationships, particularly with women, with demanding intensity. She tended to conduct her friendships—with Violet Dickinson, Victoria Sackville-West, even with her sister, Vanessa—in the style of her lost tie with Stella, a mix of chivalric crush and immature clinging, and while such emotions might be perfectly appropriate to a girl between the ages of thirteen and fifteen, they can be rather silly in an adult. In her earlier relationship with Stella's friend, Violet Dickinson, from 1902 to 1907, Virginia was still young and bereaved and it was natural that the older Violet should console and cheer. Violet, born in 1865, was the daughter of a Somersetshire squire and grand-daughter of Lord Auckland. When her mother died in 1893 she was taken up by Julia. 'My Violet', as Virginia called her, seems to have been one of those warm, comfortable women to whom people turn in trouble. It was a 'romantic friendship', an innocent love. Miss Violet Dickinson was thirty-seven when she befriended the twenty-year-old Virginia, large (she was six foot two), high-spirited, harum-scarum, immensely sympathetic, indispensable to her many friends—the first and kindest of the strong women to whom Virginia looked for petting and cherishing.

In the autobiographical fragment, Virginia traced her mental fragility to her state of mind in 1897. Her mother's death, she said, had been a latent sorrow, not fully felt. But Stella's death two years later 'fell upon a different substance—upon all that extraordinary unprotected unformed unshielded yet apprehensive, anticipating fabric' of an awakening consciousness. There must have been a strange detachment in Virginia when Julia died. But in 1897, with her day-by-day closeness to the failing Stella, her emotions were 'forced' into being: 'I remember saying to myself this impossible thing has happened:—as if it were . . . against the law, horrible, as a treachery, a betrayal—the fact of death. The blow, the second blow of death, struck on me tremulous, creased, sitting with my wings still stuck together, on the broken chrysalis.'

5. *The Question of Madness*

I N September 1897 Virginia Stephen first fought a wish to die. 'This diary is lengthening indeed', she wrote, 'but death would be shorter & less painful.' During October and half of November she did not write at all, for one grey day seemed much like another. 'Life is a hard business', she scribbled into the void, 'one needs a rhinoceros skin—& that one has not got!'

At fifteen Virginia needed some answer to the cruelty of fate and this her sister gave her: 'Nessa preaches that our destiny lies in ourselves. . . .' She resolved to follow 'the scar to the end' and then to fling the diary into a corner to be obliterated by 'dust & mice & moths & all creeping crawling eating destroying creatures'. The disintegration of 1897 was eventually recomposed, in 'Time Passes', as the chaos and decay which nearly blots out the Victorian family. The Victorian house is brought, symbolically, near to ruin.

In her final entry, on 1 January 1898, Virginia summed up her awakening to her life's bleak prospect:

Here is a volume of fairly acute life (the first really *lived* year of my life) ended locked & put away. And another & another & another yet to come. Oh dear they are very long, & I turn cowardly throughout when I look at them.

This was the first of five breakdowns as well as minor disturbances between 1897 and 1915.[*]

In May 1904, following her father's death, Virginia had a complete breakdown. She was twenty-two. That summer she threw herself out of a window and was nursed back to health—very quickly, it seems, within three months—by Violet Dickinson. Violet, prescribing fresh air and friendship, was more successful than any of the later nurses, which may have had to do less with her patient's emotional attachment than with the simple fact that Violet had a knack, according to Virginia, for saying the right thing.

'Those awful headaches made one ache oneself for her', Violet told Vanessa.

---

[*] Some signs of mental illness preceded Stella's death. In October 1896 Stella's diary records taking Virginia to see Dr Seton and 'Father in a great state'. She was disturbed again in the spring of 1897.

Virginia said that this breakdown was 'not unnaturally' the result of suffocating emotions for her father during the last years of his life, a mixture of that longing she had first shown at thirteen, when she had opened her arms, and, at the same time, a healthy young woman's revolt against her father's oblivious dominance. During the last nine months of his life, when she knew he was dying, there were remorseful outbursts of devotion.

'There is no-one more lovable', she declared to one friend after another.

In the 'black summer' of 1910 Virginia's mental health was again threatened though, judging by her witty letters, she was in no sense mad. In July and August she spent six weeks at Burley, a private nursing home in Twickenham which specialized in patients with nervous disorders. This was her first experience of a sanatorium, the threat of which would later drive her to attempt suicide. Her letters recount anecdotes of being shut up with the tiniest of minds. In this the staff were indistinguishable from patients. A nurse told her that 'the old Queen the Queen mother & the present Queen represent the highest womanhood. They reverence my gifts, although God has left me in the dark.' She told her sister that to escape this, 'I shall soon have to jump out of a window.' Jean Thomas, the director, was 'always culminating in silent prayer'. She abhorred the phoney religious atmosphere—the staff 'always wondering what God is up to'—and the inexplicable ugliness of the house decorated in mottled green and red.

It is remarkable that, shut up in such a place, Virginia was still able to exercise her wit. 'Miss Bradbury', she told her sister, 'is the woman you saw out of the window & said was homicidal. I was very kind with her at dinner, but she then put me to bed, and is a trained nurse.' She was able, too, to joke about insanity: 'I feel my brains, like a pear, to see if its ripe; it will be exquisite by September.'

It seems incomprehensible that, despite lucid protests against Twickenham, her doctor, Sir George Savage,* could think of nothing better than to send her back for insomnia in 1912 and again in 1913, when she sank once more into depression. This time, she emerged suicidal. On 9 September 1913, she saw two new doctors,

---

* Savage was one of the leading men in his field. In the course of his career, he was Physician-Superintendent of the Bethlem Royal Hospital for the mentally disturbed, President of the Medico-Psychological Association of Great Britain, and Examiner of Mental Physiology, University of London. He was also joint editor of the *Journal of Mental Science*.

in the morning Dr Maurice Wright and in the afternoon the distinguished Dr Henry Head, and both prescribed a return to Twickenham. She went home, took an overdose of veronal, and very nearly died.

This was the longest of all the breakdowns, particularly if, as Quentin Bell suggests, the breakdown of 1915 is to be seen as a continuation. During both episodes Virginia remained more resistant than in 1904 to nursing and treatment. In October 1913 she was installed in George Duckworth's house, Dalingridge Place, near East Grinstead, Sussex. It was unimaginative, to say the least, to make her once more the helpless dependant of the man who epitomized sexual exploitation and social power. She improved by the end of the year on her return to her Sussex house, Asheham, but felt patronized by her nurse, Ka Cox, who had an irritating quack-quack in her voice as though she were trying to impress people with her busy beneficence. She was broad-cheeked, her face long-drawn and pale. Virginia called her Bruin to convey her thickness and said, 'I don't think I was ever at my ease with her.'

With a relapse in February 1915, she lost self-control. Incoherent, sometimes screaming, she babbled wildly until she lapsed into a coma. Yet it is extraordinary that even this nightmare, the worst of her life, was not without a mental advantage. 'Rashness is one of the properties of illness—outlaws that we are', she argued later. To her, illness could be an act of release: 'what ancient and obdurate oaks are uprooted in us by the act of sickness.' Concealed by 'the cautious respectability of health', there lay 'a snowfield where even the print of birds' feet is unknown. Here we go alone, and like it better so.' Septimus Warren Smith, the fictional madman in *Mrs. Dalloway*, is aware (in the more revealing detail of the manuscript) that 'a naked soul looking at emptiness has its independence' and he has 'the desire to test it further', if necessary by death. He has a vision 'of flight, on & on, an escape, as if the door one fell against, opened'.* In another vision he is 'the first man who had crossed from life to death. . . . I go & come through the waters'. He sees himself as an explorer, like Darwin, on behalf of humanity and does not drown in the usual way, simply passes through 'a green mist'. Telling himself that he has passed 'through' death, he is tossed on to a further shore '& for the first time in the whole world, the dead were alive. . . . I have passed through death, he said. I am the first to

* Cancelled line.

cross.' Others will follow: '& now, through evolution, a few of the living have access to this world'.*

This is recounted as a madman's ludicrous fancy but it grew from the writer's own receptivity to the voices of the dead and her recurring attraction to water.

Miss Thomas announced that Virginia's mind was 'played out' and persuaded her family that not only her mind but her character had permanently deteriorated. But the doctors and nurses, who believed there could be no full recovery, were wrong. She began to improve and by November 1915 was quite 'sane'. The twenty dark years were over and the fertile stretch of her life began.

There can be no pat conclusions about Virginia's illness, but what she herself has to tell in novels and diaries (including the juvenile diaries) does help. Her diaries require imaginative assent to a view of herself which in some ways contradicts her reputation for being fragile and nervy. She inherited her father's spartan toughness, could tramp endless miles, and, on journeys, put up cheerfully with daunting conditions. In 1906 at Olympia in Greece she found bugs in her bed. She simply swathed herself from head to foot in a mosquito net, squashed them hourly between one and four, and, in the early morning, distracted her mind with the *Christian Herald*. She thought nothing of the mice which habitually scampered across her bed in the Sussex countryside and rather relished the thought that *Mrs. Dalloway* paid for the luxury of an indoor lavatory. But more revealing is the diaries' repeated claim that she generally enjoyed a remarkable level of happiness: 'I think perhaps 9 people out of ten never get a day in the year of such happiness as I have almost constantly . . .'. She would keep up 'a kind of vibration' for long spells; then, quite abruptly, the vibration would stop.

To be vibrating in response to impressions was to enjoy, she believed, a state of illusion. Not to vibrate was to see reality: 'Things seem clear, sane, comprehensible, & under no obligation . . . to make one vibrate at all. Indeed, it's largely the clearness of sight which comes at such seasons that leads to depression.' Bounding responses may make living possible but they have nothing to do with clarity, like the clarity of Eliot when, himself near to breakdown, he saw London as a waste land, or like the clarity of

* Cancelled line.

Virginia's conclusion that 'one's lowest ebb is nearest a true vision'. And then, she carefully noted, the appetite for sensation would slowly revive and, once again, one would 'vibrate'.

She suggests that what a depressed intelligence sees may not be unrealistic, merely unendurable. In that state, we are awake, as Eliot shows in *The Waste Land*, to our customary oblivion. Septimus Warren Smith is awake to his incapacity to feel and to others' mental tactics of evasion (his boss, Brewer, regrets that his geraniums were ruined in the war). Smith's doctors cannot hear in any sophisticated sense of the word, and his failure to communicate becomes so urgent that he can no longer contain his outward conduct. His unendurable thoughts are, first, that 'it might be possible that the world itself is without meaning' and, second, that human beings, in the mass, 'have neither kindness, nor faith, nor charity beyond what serves to increase the pleasure of the moment'.

There are few clues to Virginia's own thoughts during her bouts of illness in 1904, 1913, and 1915. She stopped writing at these times and witnesses saw only misconduct which she was quick to acknowledge. It is not possible to know to what extent her distorted behaviour was caused by organic illness, to what extent by constant drugs (she spoke of the 'humiliation & dissolution' felt after a sleeping draught), or how far her behaviour was an exposure of distortions forced upon women by their society. 'The blight which fell upon each girl at the outset of her life', Ray Strachey explains, 'was more insidious and even more irresistible than its compulsory emptiness. For there was a belief strongly held by men and women alike that it would be unnatural, wrong, and, moreover, impossible for any female to do or say or think anything worth serious consideration.' According to John Stuart Mill, half of a woman's faculties were subjected to hothouse development while the other half—her intellect and agency—were stunted with packs of ice. The mental specialist, Dr Maudesley, published an influential article in 1874 in which he argued that, although women had now proved they could benefit intellectually from higher education, by so doing they inevitably destroyed their bodily health and made themselves incapable of 'performing their functions as women'. Savage, in his *Insanity and Allied Neuroses* (1884, enlarged in 1907), which became the standard medical text on the treatment of the mentally ill, advised against the education of 'the weaker sex' for, he said, if a 'promising girl is allowed to educate herself at home, the danger of solitary work and want of social friction may be seen in conceit developing into insanity'.

Accordingly, George made his well-meaning but crass efforts to turn his rebellious half-sisters into society ladies. George, with his job as private secretary to Austen Chamberlain,* typified for Virginia the obstinate climbers who ran the country. He is re-created as the proper, thick-headed Hugh Whitbread in the Westminster setting of *Mrs. Dalloway*. After the 1904 illness, the sisters moved to a home of their own. George was snubbed, and Virginia wrote exultantly to Violet: 'And now we are free women!'

Biographers taking up the question of madness have looked for genetic causes. On the Stephen side there was a strain of nervous instability. Leslie Stephen went in for what he termed 'Berserker Fits' which were explosions of fury against evasion of fact, hollow sentiment, respect for current idols, and unintelligibility. His father, Sir James Stephen, was 'the most nervous, sensitive of men'. His friends feared to suggest criticisms, not because he resented advice but because he suffered so much from blame. Virginia Stephen inherited this extreme sensitivity to opinion. She inherited, too, like her brother, Adrian, a quick sense of degradation. Adrian remarked at the end of the first world war that it positively frightened him to see people's faces on Hampstead Heath, 'like gorillas', he said, 'like orang-outangs—perfectly inhuman—frightful' and he poked his mouth out like an ape.

People or material things could assume for Virginia a sinister aspect or an extraordinary beauty. Her prose follows the movement of her response: inspection and recoil, or inspection and radiance. In the fictional case of Septimus Smith, she showed such responses blown up by madness so that there is a strange blend of insight and distortion.

Her fictional suicides, Septimus and Rhoda (in *The Waves*), suffer from mental isolation. She demonstrates through these characters the most terrifying experience she herself knew, which is to lose communication with the world outside one's mind. Septimus Warren Smith feels like a 'relic straying on the edge of the world, this outcast who gazed back at the inhabited regions, who lay like a drowned sailor, on the shore of the world'. This is what 'breakdown' meant to her, not so much collapse (Septimus deliberately *enacts* collapse as a distress signal), but thought so

* A Conservative MP, and Chancellor of the Exchequer 1903–6

rapid that language, the main route of communication, became incoherent. Here, if anywhere, is the link between Virginia Woolf's madness and creativity. In 1931, when she wrote the climactic final pages of *The Waves*, she felt the proximity of madness as her thoughts flew ahead and her reason stumbled after. She recorded this experience immediately in her diary:

I wrote the words O Death fifteen minutes ago, having reeled across the last ten pages with some moments of such intensity & intoxication that I seemed only to stumble after my own voice, or almost, after some sort of speaker (as when I was mad). I was almost afraid, remembering the voices that used to fly ahead.

'Voices' sounds bizarre, but if one substitutes 'thoughts' it is comprehensible enough. She explained that the under-mind of a writer works at top speed while the upper-mind drowses. Then, after a pause, the veil lifts and there is the subject, simplified and composed. It is important to distinguish, as Charles Lamb does, between the flights of great and small wits.* It is quite possible for people of small wits to have such an experience—it happens in dreams—and one knows instantly on waking how futile it has been. But the madman, living in mental isolation, is incapable of judging the quality of his ideas. Septimus orders his wife to take down his portentous messages which, for him, represent enormous feats of condensation but they are, unfortunately, quite banal: universal love, he says. There is no death.

In Virginia's case, the line between madness and creativity is harder to draw. Her worst episodes—in 1904, in 1915, and finally in 1941—were invariably heralded by voices which spoke to her alone. There are only hints of what was said. In 1904 she heard King Edward VII defiling the language; in 1915 the voice of her mother. She told Violet that voices told her to do 'all kinds of wild things'. Whatever she heard early in 1941 was so unendurable that she committed suicide. In the absence of any real facts (for her husband recorded only physical symptoms: how she slept, how many pounds gained or lost) and in view of the inadequacy of psychiatry in those early days either to diagnose or to help her, her illness will remain a mystery.

In part, her madness seems to have been an escape into the past. She recalled having at Hogarth House, Richmond, after her

---

* 'On the Sanity of True Genius', 1826

marriage, 'some very curious visions in this room . . . lying in bed, mad, & seeing the sunlight quivering like gold water, on the wall. I've heard the voices of the dead here. And felt, through it all, exquisitely happy.' For another part, where voices were her own racing thoughts, she experienced, it seems, a mental isolation that was essentially constructive. But when the voices were those of power, they sealed her off in a destructive isolation. She survived such episodes by temporary capitulation: making her mind blank and resigning herself to a vegetable state of total passivity. In *The Waste Land*, Eliot projects a consciousness assaulted by the voices of society, but that mind saves itself by dismissing society, in fact the whole of civilization, as 'Unreal' and therefore doomed. Like a prophet, he gives total authority to alternative supernatural voices who speak through thunder. Virginia Stephen, in contrast, was an heir of Victorian rationalism. It was her very commitment to society that made her so vulnerable to its voices. Yet even at her most abject, when she lay forbidden by doctors to read or write, she would make up phrases and stories and, she said later, 'all that I now, by the light of reason, try to put into prose (I thought of the Lighthouse then, . . . and others, not in substance, but in idea)'.

As a child Virginia had purple rages. Rages of early childhood vent, of course, the frustrations of the pre-verbal stage. Words are an alternative to rage. Yet, even at later stages of development, and particularly in the case of a woman, it is often hard to find adequate words for complex states of mind. Each communicatory gesture has a private residue and the private connotations for each of us modify 'standard' English. Virginia Woolf's fictional women and children hoard private connotations because their scope for public discourse is limited by their inferior status. In the opening page of *To the Lighthouse*, six-year-old James Ramsay, silently cutting out a refrigerator at his mother's knee, already commands a range of private definitions and emotions. (The refrigerator, for instance, is 'fringed with joy'.) Later in the novel, the adolescent James and his sister, Cam, witness their father's intemperate moods and, though outwardly they are silent, inwardly they are raging. They demonstrate a vast gap between inner and public expression. The linguistic impasse in *To the Lighthouse* reflects Virginia's own status as a girl at the turn of the century. Her sister, Vanessa, who resisted their father utterly, found a simple solution in rebellion. In his lifetime she preserved a stony imperviousness to his words; after his death she threw over his respectable Kensington for a free life devoted to art in Bloomsbury. Virginia could not so easily discard her father's language—he had permanently shaped her mind and tastes—so that the constant friction of inner perception against standard expression is one aspect of her mental suffering.

At any controversial point in a conversation, an alarm bell would ring, she said, resulting in 'a strong desire to be silent; or to change the conversation', to talk about trivia, the family servant or pet. Mitchell A. Leaska has pointed to the name she chose for the Victorian family in *The Years*, the Pargiters, so called because they were trained to parget or cover over deep wells of feeling. Virginia herself did this with practised ease. In 1906 after Thoby's death from typhoid she elaborated on his progress in encouraging letters to the typhoid-stricken Violet. On 5 December she reported that Thoby (then two weeks dead) was flirting with his nurses, and on 12 December had him pointing out to his doctors 'the virtues of a mutton chop'.

The code of incommunicativeness had innumerable shades. The charade described above is a weird act of consideration. The code would often take the form of decent reticence, for Virginia a mark of a civilized person—in 1906 her travel diary approves signs of reticence in faces in the streets of Constantinople. But the code could also stifle the truth. In her youth she could not speak of being fondled by her half-brothers because their credit was such that no adult would have believed her. ('What awful lives children live!' says Martin to Rose, who has tried to cut her wrists, in the 1908 section of *The Years*. 'Yes', Rose agrees. 'And they can't tell anybody.') And by tacit agreement, the Stephen children never spoke of Julia and Stella. By the time Virginia reached adulthood, then, she was adept at evasion. Once, when Ottoline Morrell confessed that her diary was devoted to her inner life, Virginia opened her eyes wide and declared flatly that she herself had no inner life.

If a stranger came into the room while she was writing her first novel she would hide it and pretend to be reading letters. In her last novel, Miss La Trobe, writing plays in 1939, is regarded by the village as a bit of a freak. Speculating on the fate of a woman born to write in the sixteenth century, Virginia believed that she would have been so thwarted and pulled apart by contrary obligations that she 'would certainly have gone crazed, shot herself, or ended her days in some lonely cottage outside the village, half witch, half wizard, feared and mocked at'. Had she survived, what she wrote would have been deformed, and would anyway have gone unsigned.

That refuge she would have sought certainly. It was the relic of the sense of chastity that dictated anonymity to women even so late as the nineteenth century. Currer Bell, George Eliot, George Sand, all the victims of inner strife as their writings prove, sought ineffectively to veil themselves by using the name of a man. Thus they did homage to the convention, which if not implanted by the other sex was liberally encouraged by them (the chief glory of a woman is not to be talked of, said Pericles, himself a much-talked-of man) that publicity in women is detestable. Anonymity runs in their blood.

For Virginia to expose herself by publishing in her own name was an agony which now requires some historical imagination. 'Is the time coming', she wrote just before submitting her second novel, *Night and Day*, to Duckworth in March 1919, 'when I can endure to read my own writing in print without blushing & shivering & wishing to take cover?'

Through fiction alone was she able to expose what lay in the recess of her mind. In *The Voyage Out* the undefined promise of Rachel Vinrace, finding no platform of action in society, is submerged in fatal hallucinations. In the opening of the manuscript of 'Times Passes' we enter a 'sleeper's' mind. The sleepers 'acted in the depths of night a drama unseen' while listeners pace the dark chambers to receive, in the folds of their cloaks, a half-murmur or a cry. It is a drama of communication fraught with difficulties: hands are raised, now to clutch an idea, now to ward off another. In the end the sleeper finds in the listener the secret sharer of her deeds and of the 'senseless wild laughter' which would frighten the waking world. 'To each a sharer; to each thought completeness; & in this knowledge content.' What Virginia Woolf could not verbalize, she communicated only to ghostly sharers so that her inner life might well seem, at times, unreal. Her fiction was the sole bridge between this ghostly mental existence and the waking world, and she always feared that her private thoughts, nurtured in such unspeakable isolation, would appear ridiculous in the arena of public discourse. 'Suppose one woke & found oneself a fraud?' she wrote in her diary soon after the publication of *To the Lighthouse*. 'It was part of my madness—that horror.'

I do not want to imply that there was not something wrong with Virginia. Whatever the diagnosis—Leonard Woolf called it manic depression—her illness must have had some biochemical base which was not understood. What I have tried to show is that there are aspects of her illness that are open to explanation and, beyond that, even in madness, hers remained a particular, rare mind. Our language has, as yet, no term for madness which is not demeaning. The Stephen family would toss off phrases like 'Oh you know very well the Goat's mad' and she herself would cheerfully allude to the times she was off her head. This candour does not disguise the blankness of these phrases. They reinforce the isolation of the mentally ill by placing the entire onus for breakdown on the sufferer. But in Virginia Woolf's own fictional case-study of Septimus Warren Smith, sufferer and society share responsibility, though doctors blame him alone, particularly his resistance to their definitions of normality.

Virginia herself drew a distinction between a solitude that is potentially creative ('slipping tranquilly off into the deep water of my own thoughts') and a debilitating state of withdrawal following impulses of aversion. Her abundant imaginative energy would suddenly flag. 'And I do not love my kind', she admitted at such a time. 'I detest them. I pass them by. I let them break on me like dirty rain drops. No longer can I summon up that energy which when it sees one of those dry little sponges floating past, or rather stuck on the rock, sweeps round them, steeps them, creates them. Once I had a gift for doing this, & a passion, & it made parties arduous & exciting.' In 1925 she noted such a failure of emotional energy when her old friend, Madge Vaughan, died. They might have buried a faggot of twigs. 'Rustling among my emotions, I found nothing better than dead leaves. . . . Oh detestable time, that thus eats out the heart & lets the body go on.'

This is a common feeling. Certainly one does not usually connect it with mental disturbance, yet the failure of emotional energy *can* appal. It is the earliest symptom of derangement in Septimus Warren Smith. When his officer–mentor, Evans, is killed in the first world war, 'the appalling fear came over him—he could not feel'. Smith's feelings have been blunted by four years of war and he might be excused, but he retains too much integrity to console himself with the sham identity of decorated hero which has been willed on him by authorities: military officers, doctors, and

politicians. Stubbornly, he sticks to his conviction that war has
made him a brute. His conduct becomes more deranged when
Evans haunts him. He is filled with shame beyond the normal
range, with self-disgust. In the early hours of the morning his
prostrate body wakes to its degradation. In the aftermath of the
war he had married an Italian, Lucrezia, without loving her. His
sense of crime is carried over from the war. He sees no artificial
distinction between the organized aggression that destroyed the
man he most revered and the random callousness of any Tom or
Bertie in civilian life, their starched shirt fronts 'oozing thick drops
of vice'.

A sane Virginia Woolf can detect in Smith's failure of feeling
a symptom of madness. But when she herself broke down in 1915
she had no insight into unexpected flashes of cruelty in her diary.
A long line of imbeciles outside Kingston offended her, shuffling
creatures with no forehead or no chin, an imbecile grin or a
suspicious stare. 'It was perfectly horrible', was her curt comment.
'They should certainly be killed.' Her attention was then caught
by a fruit stall. 'We bought a pineapple for 9d', she added
triumphantly.

It is curious to see the swift link between the gentility of
'perfectly horrible' and the blank savagery of her conclusion.
A beautiful, clever woman, she was condescending to the unbeautiful or stupid, and could be, in private, annihilating.

There is a recurring pattern to her bouts of madness. The diary
entries for 1915 and 1941 show, just before collapse, a phase of
studied mundaneness, preceded by—and sometimes interspersed
with—a Swiftian hatred of the human race. The great English
detectives of human nature, Chaucer and Austen, maintain calm
detachment, no matter how repulsive the object of their contempla-
tion—a merchant, a pardoner, a Mrs Norris. Virginia admired
Chaucer and Austen, but many of her own quick portraits in her
letters and diary are crueller, less precise. Wit strains into hilarity.
Human figures becomes grotesques.

In 1915, after attending a concert in the Queen's Hall, in Langham
Place, then London's main concert hall, she wrote: 'I begin to
loathe my kind, principally from looking at their faces in the tube.
Really, raw red beef & silver herrings give me more pleasure to look
upon.' And so to the next day: 'I do not like the Jewish voice; I do
not like the Jewish laugh.' There was no attempt to control the

irrational malice. It arose from her jealousy of her sister-in-law, who managed to publish stories while earning her living as a secretary.

In the third to last entry in her diary before the breakdown she wrote that the winter seemed 'to have lost all self control'. Loathing was followed at the very last by attempts at mundaneness, the featureless conduct of the indisputably normal. The last entry is studiedly placid, as the last entries in 1941. She bought a blue dress in a department store for 10*s*. 11*d*. Then a sudden escape of strained hilarity: she almost burst out laughing to see an old suitor, Walter Lamb, at Dover Street Station, in frock coat and top hat, fresh from lunch with an MP's wife and oozing satisfaction.

A too-facile scorn for her kind was part of Virginia's illness, and also fear of ridicule. Any passing criticism of her work or person drove her to what she called black despair. She would go to bed 'like a diver with pursed lips shooting into oblivion'. In *A Room of One's Own* she points out that the indifference of the world which Keats and Flaubert and other men of genius found so difficult to bear was, in the woman's case, not indifference but hostility. 'The world did not say to her as it did to them, Write if you choose; it makes no difference to me. The world said with a guffaw, Write?'

She tended to dramatize the inevitable disappointments that attend high aspiration, much as her father had done. But where Leslie Stephen was ready to be placated with praise and sympathy, his daughter fell into real depression. In a dramatic letter of June 1911 she described to her sister how all the devils came out, hairy black ones: 'To be 29 & unmarried—to be a failure—childless—insane too, no writer.'

The warning signs of madness were headaches, insomnia, tingling veins, and light-headedness. When she was 'jangled' by visitors or over-stimulated by fiction, she would have to 'dandle' her brain, that is take to bed and stop writing for at least three weeks. Her symptoms and treatment are well known but it is not easy to decide about the course of illness in two matters: her refusal to eat and the conduct of the doctors.

Discussing Dr Bradshaw's cures in the manuscript of *Mrs. Dalloway*, Virginia Woolf wrote sarcastically that 'Milk is the great standby, with raw eggs beaten up in it taken every hour, oftener if possible.' Roger Poole suggests that when she put on three stone more than her normal weight in 1915, she did not gain it by the patient spoonful but was coerced, if not force-fed (standard treatment, according to Savage) by four nurses whom she resisted, for the only time in her life, with physical violence. But were doctors to let her starve? And how were they to cope with her spiritual rebellion against the enchainment of the flesh? 'Disorder, sordidity and corruption surround us', she wrote in *The Waves*. 'We have been taking into our mouths the bodies of dead birds. It is with these greasy crumbs, slobbered over napkins, and little corpses that we have to build.'

Virginia's suicide attempt in 1913 immediately followed visits to doctors. The hopeless meddling of consultants—Dr Fergusson, Sir George Savage, Dr Henry Head, Dr T. B. Hyslop, Dr Maurice Wright, Dr Maurice Craig—is distilled in her fictional portrait of a Harley Street nerve specialist, Sir William Bradshaw. (The name probably came from the Bradshaw lecture to the Royal College of Physicians, given in 1922 by Dr Craig.) The eminent doctor has the tables turned on him as, with relentless penetration, the novel diagnoses his diseased mentality.

What she privately called the 'Dr. Chapter' in *Mrs. Dalloway* amounts to a manifesto against the medical profession. Her characterization of Sir William discerns the coercive discourse of power behind the cant of duty and family. This discourse of power connects Harley Street with Westminster, and it is this dominant order that Septimus Warren Smith finds he has fought four years in the trenches to preserve, not the plays of Shakespeare. The status quo is guarded by Sir William, a son of a tradesman who flaunts a photograph of his wife in court dress. To him, Dalloway society is the acme of normality and he impresses its code on the weak, the sick, the rebellious.

Septimus Smith *is* sick and in desperate need of help but there is ample justification for his aversion to Bradshaw: the doctor's bland refusal to hear what Smith tries to say; his imperviousness to truth outside the narrow dogmas of his class and profession; the hypocrisy with which this man, who has the crudest conception of madness, avoids using the word; the very accents of condescension which preserve his safe distance from his patient. 'We have had our little talk', says Sir William.

The only person who appears to help Septimus is his wife, who genuinely cares for him, who listens to what he says and respects his eccentricity. Although she is an uneducated woman, a maker of hats, her natural good feeling enables her to perceive that this doctor is, as Mrs Dalloway puts it, obscurely evil. Ironically, just before Septimus kills himself, his wife recalls him from the abyss by reawakening his sense of humour. They laugh together over the absurd hat ordered by their landlady's daughter. There is also an ironic contrast between the residual humanity of the failed Smith marriage and the warped proprieties that make the Bradshaw marriage such a public success. Where Septimus laments how far his impulsive union has fallen short of the marriage of true minds, such a notion would never enter Sir William's head. For him, marriage is an arrangement which best promotes a man's rising status, and the wife's reward is to rise in tow. He has drained his wife of any agency beyond that which expresses loyalty to him. 'Once, long ago, she had caught salmon freely: now, quick to minister to the craving which lit her husband's eye so oilily for domination, for power, she cramped, squeezed, pared, pruned, drew back, peeped through.'

Since doctors are the official prescribers of normality, Virginia Woolf examines how, precisely, they define mental illness. In *Roger Fry* she reports on a lecture given by one of her doctors, T. B. Hyslop, on the first Post-Impressionist exhibition in 1910. He gave his opinion that 'the pictures were the work of madmen. His conclusions were accepted with enthusiastic applause'. In *Mrs. Dalloway* the fictional GP, Holmes, simply does not believe in mental illness; he writes it off as 'funk'. The specialist, Sir William, takes the opposite position on mental illness, but his notion is equally thin. He regards abnormality primarily as a form of radicalism, a social danger to wipe out. When Smith repeats the word 'war' interrogatively, the doctor notes a serious symptom in his 'attaching meanings to words of a symbolical kind'. Like Virginia's specialists, Sir William insists that Smith is dangerously ill and must be shut up in a sanatorium where there are to be no ideas and no contacts until the patient comes to heel:

Sir William not only prospered himself but made England prosper, secluded her lunatics, forbade childbirth,* penalised despair, made it impossible for the unfit to propagate their views until they, too, shared his

---

* VW was forbidden children on the grounds of her mental health. This remained a long-standing grievance, for she excelled with children and often wished for her own.

sense of proportion—his if they were men, Lady Bradshaw's if they were women (she embroidered, knitted, spent four nights out of seven at home with her son). . . .

All intemperate questioning of Sir William's creed spends itself in the Harley Street consulting room. The very clocks of Harley Street 'counselled submission, upheld authority'. And if some obdurate patient will not endorse the sanctity of family, career, honour, and courage—in short, the good of society—he can rely on his Home in Surrey which 'he remarked very quietly, would take care . . .'. The secret vice of this man is diagnosed: it is to stamp indelibly in the sanctuaries of others the image of himself.

When Septimus kills himself he waits until the last possible moment. He does not want to die but Holmes, Bradshaw's agent, is coming to take him away. Septimus knows that suicide is tiresomely melodramatic. It is not his idea of tragedy, merely the only means of escape from the indignity of brutes with red nostrils snuffing into the secret places of his mind.

This story of madness and suicide, often told from within the mind of the sufferer, is an imaginary case-study put together from personal experience. 'I am now in the thick of the mad scene in Regents Park', she wrote in her diary. 'I find I write it by clinging as tight to fact as I can. . . .' She concluded that normality, what Bradshaw called a sense of proportion, was an arbitrary notion, arrived at by the consent of generations of practical men. She concluded, further, that the symptoms of madness are to be found in responses too common to strike one as they ought: emotional inertia, loathing of one's kind, psychological as well as physical brutality. Her case suggests, first, that in some measure society, with its arbitrary norms, may be implicated in the individual breakdown. It is not surprising that, in Virginia's youth, norms of military aggressiveness and ineffectual ladyhood seemed to distort human capacities. Her case suggests, too, that up to a certain point diseased emotions are part of the common rage.

Vanessa said that her sister could 'give one the most extraordinary sense of bigness of point of view. I think she has in reality amazing courage & sanity about life.' Through Septimus Smith, she explored the nature of madness. Through the figure of dim old Mrs McNab, caretaker of the Ramsay home, she asks, what is sanity? And, again, common assumptions evaporate. Mrs McNab is 'witless' by society's standard and even by her own. She is uncommunicative, uneducated, and simply goes on in the minimal way of Wordsworth's leech-gatherer. To live is no more than to exist; when such creatures die they cease to be. Yet, although she is witless, some primitive resilience comes out in snatches of an old music-hall song that console her during the routines of cleaning. She knows no politics, yet she deprecates the war and gets on with work. One point of this portrait is to ask whether, for all her oblivion, Mrs McNab is not saner than such educated young men as Andrew Ramsay who rush off to the front to be killed. Andrew is schooled in his Victorian father's fantastic dreams of heroism but dies knowing nothing about daily life as it is known to working women.

'Madness' or 'sanity', like all such defining terms, are absurd simplifications. To enclose anarchic experience within a verbal category is no way to understand it. The most subversive element in Virginia Woolf's work—more so than her challenge of notions of madness and sanity—is her challenge of the category *per se*. Her prose moves back and forth with deliberate hesitation. She once said that for her life was like a novel by Henry James and, at one time, she had his photograph on her writing-table. She followed James in her search for fullness of definition and in her sense that any judgement worth having is hard won. This receptivity to fact and to its moral and psychological nuances was offset, in company, by holidays from fact, the flights of fancy that could froth or turn cruel. It coloured her social manner but not much of her fictional work, which spurted from the sort of madness that may be explicable. She told a friend that in 'the lava of madness' she found her subjects: 'It shoots out of one everything shaped, final, not in mere driblets, as sanity does.' She prolonged her apprenticeship so that this volcanic matter might be cooled and shaped by an educated intellect. This rational instrument was the result of a rigorous but unconventional training.

6. *A Woman's Education*

'SHE always said that she had had no education,' Vanessa Stephen said of her sister, 'and I am inclined to agree with her if by education is meant learning things out of books.' But if Virginia Stephen was denied the advantages of a proper education, she was given, in a random way, an ideal training for becoming a writer.

What kind of education makes a writer? She herself observed that the training of writers is less definite than a training in music, art, or architecture; for a writer, reading, listening, talking, and leisure are all as important as formal instruction. The inadequacy of the ordinary processes of education is a commonplace, but difficult to analyse. T. S. Eliot suggested that it is because 'these processes consist largely in the acquisition of impersonal ideas which obscure what we really are and feel, what we really want . . .'. There is an obverse to Virginia Stephen's plaints of deprivation, a witty diatribe which turns the tables on the intellectual pretensions of her brother's Cambridge friends: 'There is much to be said surely for that respectable custom which allows the daughter to educate herself at home, while the son is educated by others abroad.' To submit to such an artificial influence as Cambridge scepticism, she argues, must sap the son's natural responses while the daughter's remain unaffected.

The earlier women writers provide a curious test case. Since women were not until the mid-nineteenth century given an academic education, it is easier to trace what kind of learning — or lack of learning — was useful to them. When George Eliot became her father's housekeeper in 1836, she learnt languages in her spare time. In the case of the Brontës, two facts in Mrs Gaskell's biography are immediately suggestive: her opinion that they had no children's books; and that they saw no women — for, after the death of their mother, when men visited that remote parsonage, they rarely brought their wives. In the case of Virginia and Vanessa, there were insistent exemplars of womanhood, not least their mother, and they had the usual training in female accomplishments. At boring dancing classes with Mrs Wordsworth they would spend as long as they dared in the lavatory. But what mattered was

Virginia Stephen's extraordinary informal education between the ages of thirteen and about twenty-eight.

It is impossible to overestimate the advantage of being 'born beneath green shades', as one of her characters puts it, born, that is, to the life of the mind.* She grew up surrounded by books and with the sound of good talk in her ears. Too much can be made of her social as opposed to her intellectual privileges. Throughout her life she flirted with aristocrats but they merely charmed her as gambolling creatures, a little under-endowed with brains. Her real allegiance was to the serious, literate, conscience-bound middle class. When she was sent into frivolous Edwardian society, she would sit in a corner, reading a book. She acknowledged an awkwardness amounting to 'shame' over too much parade of feminine beauty. 'I inherited some opposite instinct', she noted, something spartan, ascetic. 'I am almost inclined to drag in my grandfather — Sir James [Stephen], who once smoked a cigar, liked it, and so threw away his cigar and never smoked another. I am almost inclined to think that I inherited a streak of the puritan, of the Clapham Sect.'

Virginia Stephen, like E. M. Forster, was an offshoot of what Noel Annan has called England's intellectual aristocracy, a group which had its origins in the first decade of the nineteenth century in the Clapham Sect. At first few in number and attracted to one another by a common hatred of slavery, these men were able to move between the worlds of intellect and government. Sir James said that their purpose in manning pulpits, in writing, in Parliament, was to wage war 'against every form of injustice which either law or custom sanctioned'. The usual view of Virginia is of her distance from public issues but 'by nature', she said, 'both Vanessa and I were explorers, revolutionists, reformers'.

James Stephen (their great grandfather), a lawyer of democratic sympathies, spent part of his life in the West Indies. On a visit to

---

* Meanwhile the Mind, from pleasure less,
  Withdraws into its happiness:
  The Mind, that Ocean where each kind
  Does streight its own resemblance find;
  Yet it creates, transcending these,
  Far other Worlds, and other Seas;
  Annihilating all that's made
  To a green Thought in a green Shade.

  Andrew Marvell, 'The Garden'

England in the winter of 1788-9 he sought out Wilberforce and offered to supply evidence of the abuses of slavery. In 1800 he married Wilberforce's sister, who was said to spend all but £10 of her income on charity and was often to be seen parading in rags and tatters. The Stephens and the Wilberforces lived at Clapham Common, in the company of Macaulays, Thorntons, and others, a coterie under the aegis of the rector of Clapham, John Venn, another of Virginia's great grandfathers.* Although, in the course of the nineteenth century, the evangelical creed was abandoned by their descendants, the habits and tones of Clapham were handed on: a contempt for shams and cant and a strong distrust of the worldly-wise. The Claphamite in Leslie Stephen deplored, above all, 'sordid motive or blunted sensibility'. He said that 'it is not from want of human feeling so much as from want of imaginative power that we are generally so dead to the sorrows and sufferings of the great mass of our fellow-creatures'.

Thomas Clarkson's sketch of James Stephen records an unusual combination of energy and sensibility. The evangelical, with less formal education than his more famous descendants, 'had, in an eminent degree, that . . . glowing ardour of soul, which lies at the root of all eloquence; he was gifted with great industry, a retentive memory, an ingenuity that was rather apt to err by excess than by defect'. His imagination, a little unchastened for severe taste, coloured his feelings and recollections. His son, Sir James Stephen, was said to be 'a man of exquisitely sensitive nature'. The latter's son, Leslie Stephen, recalled how their mother had warned them that Sir James was '"without a skin". . . . He [Sir James] had, as he said in a letter, "a morbidly vivid perception of possible evils and remote dangers."' His granddaughter, Virginia Stephen, has often been slighted for sensibility as for some kind of hothouse preciousness, but the same strain in her forebears is precisely what made them such able public servants, Sir James Stephen as the Colonial Under-Secretary (Mr Over-Secretary Stephen, he was called) who drafted the Abolition Bill in 1833, Leslie Stephen as an editor of incorruptible standards. Mill insists that sensibility, though often dismissed as womanish, is, when united to strong purpose, the material of great orators, preachers, and diffusers of

---

* LS's mother, Jane Venn, was the daughter of John Venn and granddaughter of Henry Venn, whose _Complete Duty of Man_ was accepted by all Claphamites as a classic exposition of evangelical theology.

moral influence. As she grew older Virginia was 'surprised and a little disquieted by the remorseless severity of my mind'. With unshakeable purpose, she was to put out unpopular pamphlets against war and the suppression of women, and against the suppression of the common reader by pretentious experts.

Clapham tradition shows a persistent concern for education and the Stephens had the most developed ideas of what education means. Virginia summed up her father's teaching in this way:

> To read what one liked because one liked it, never to pretend to admire what one did not—that was his only lesson in the art of reading. To write in the fewest possible words, as clearly as possible, exactly what one meant—that was his only lesson in the art of writing.

Nothing enraged him so much as verbal pretension or the routine bray—he used to draw owls and donkeys on the flyleaves of books. Sir James said, with pride, that Clapham had no intellectual coxcombry: 'The true Claphamite will know how to separate the pure ore of truth from the dross of nonsense to which the prophets of his time give utterance.' In a lecture on the right use of books in 1853 he warned against the pretensions of the new handbooks to render all knowledge accessible to all readers. He had too democratic a sense of human ability to accept that the growing body of literate Englishmen should feed on the kind of instant pap that disqualifies people for the vigilant, humble, persevering use of intellectual powers. When Leslie Stephen was courting Julia in 1877, he discussed women's education and argued, with some vehemence, against dilettante accomplishments. 'It makes me angry sometimes to see how people are twisted', he said. 'I hate to see women's lives wasted simply because they have not been trained well enough to take an independent interest in any study. . . .' And so it came about when Vanessa and Virginia grew up, the one studied art, the other Greek, with professional thoroughness. And if Virginia Stephen secretly nursed ambitions beyond anything her father had imagined, the very existence of the Stephen educational tradition probably fortified the long apprenticeship which she imposed on herself before presuming to be a novelist.

Leslie Stephen's influence on his daughter seems to me to lie less in whatever formal instruction she got from the retired don in his library and less in the liberty he allowed her in her reading, than in more intangible, informal communications: his adventurousness (more evident in his walks and climbs than in his writings); his eye for truth; his vigilance in its defence; his sensitivity as a reader. He remained to Virginia as a voice declaiming English literature as though he were its spokesman: 'as he lay back in his chair and spoke the beautiful words with closed eyes, we felt that he was speaking not merely the words of Tennyson or Wordsworth but what he himself felt and knew. Thus many of the great English poems now seem to me inseparable from my father; I hear in them not only his voice, but in some sort his teaching and belief.'

Sitting with one leg curled round the other, twisting his lock of hair, Leslie Stephen would read to his children during the one and a half hours which they spent in the drawing-room in the evenings. He read prose on nights in the week, poetry on Sundays, and Milton's 'On the Morning of Christ's Nativity' on Christmas night. Thirty-two volumes of the Waverley novels are what Virginia chiefly remembered, together with Jane Austen and Hawthorne. Virginia's ear was trained, from an early age, to the native rhythms of English. As a professional writer she recognized that it was 'getting the rhythm' in writing that matters. 'Could I get my to-morrow morning's rhythm right—take the skip of my sentence at the right moment—I should reel it off; . . . it's not style exactly—the right words—it's a way of levitating the thought out of one—.'

At the same time reading, like listening, is a very difficult skill. A child can be taught the mechanics; an adolescent to identify images and allusions; but the leap of imaginative accord cannot be taught, I think—only demonstrated. She learnt, from observing her father, that reading could be a kind of action. 'He read, she thought, as if he were guiding something, or wheedling a large flock of sheep, or pushing his way up and up a single narrow path; and sometimes he went fast and straight, and broke his way through the thicket, and sometimes it seemed a branch struck at him, a bramble blinded him, but he was not going to let himself be beaten by that; on he went, tossing over page after page.' Another such energetic reader was Lady Strachey. She read 'with fire and ardour', Virginia recalled. 'She carried on . . . the passive act of reading with something of the vigour with which she strode the streets . . . or tossed her head high in a shout of laughter.' In an early version of *The Voyage Out* she shows the physicality with which an authentic scholar, Mr Ambrose, engages with a text: 'First he looked comfortable, and stroked his thighs; then he looked intent; by degrees innumerable fine lines came into his face, ripening it to the likeness of a pencil drawing. His eyes saw something noble close to him, which could only be seen by looking very steadily. Communication was now established; and an intense stillness was in the room where the Greeks were.'

Virginia first managed this communication at the age of thirteen while reading aloud to her sister from Palgrave's *Golden Treasury*, as they lay in the grass behind the Flower Walk in Kensington Gardens:

I opened it and began to read some poem. And instantly and for the first time I understood the poem. . . . It was as if it became altogether intelligible; I had a feeling of transparency in words when they cease to be words and become so intensified that one seems to experience them; to foretell them as if they developed what one is already feeling.

She had the queer sense there, in the long hot grass, 'that poetry was coming true'.

When Virginia's mother died, her father took up her education. He taught her for the next two years, from the age of thirteen to fifteen, every morning. Lessons were in his study, on the fourth floor. In one autobiographical fragment she describes this room in loving detail: the high ceiling of yellow-stained wood; the complete editions of English and French classics—twenty, thirty, or forty volumes—bound in red calf; the rocking-chair, covered in American cloth, in which her father would lie with his feet off the ground, with a board across the arms and on it a china inkstand. Minny Thackeray's portrait by Watts hung over the fireplace and leaning against the bookcase in a corner stood a stack of rusty alpenstocks. The three long windows looked over the roofs of Kensington to St Mary Abbots.

Leslie Stephen's gifts were an acquired taste. He was not a crowd-pleaser like his wife. His calibre could be apparent only to an older child capable of detaching the gentleman in the library from the moody domestic tyrant. In *To the Lighthouse*, as Cam sails with her father on that long-delayed voyage of enlightenment, she feels a growing zest for the promised beacons of the mind: questions about ancient civilizations and great men. An autobiographical section, cut from the manuscript, recalls the humble intellectual hunger with which Virginia had haunted her father's library, and 'all the questions, wild, rapid, heterogeneous' which piled up in her thoughts. Though she did not venture to speak, she listened to her father talking between puffs of pipe smoke to other learned old gentlemen, and she 'made a collection of little odds & ends they had said'.

Why was she dumb? Why could she not share her ambitions or even show her privately written essays to her father (except for one on the Elizabethan voyagers)? Another, called 'Religio Laici', proved that man has need of a God, though the God was described in process of change. Other unshown essays were 'A History of Women' and a history of her own family. The humble passivity of the attitude recorded in *To the Lighthouse* is apparently contradicted by the diary of 1897 which tells of frequent conversations each morning around the Round Pond in Kensington Gardens. He was not alarming then but simple and confiding. His silences, though they might last from the Pond to Marble Arch, were companionable as if he were thinking half-aloud about poetry, philosophy, and people. Leslie Stephen must have been exemplary in the tutelary relation of don to student. He was delighted to direct her reading and to draw out her responses. Her reserve came from his seeming unawareness of her proximity to his own high gifts. She craved her father's recognition and approval, yet he never drew her to him. Virginia had reason for wariness. There was in Leslie Stephen a characteristic blend of contradictory attitudes towards women's learning. In theory, there was to be no double standard (though he sent only his sons to school and Cambridge). In practice Leslie could not restrain his irritation at the unexpected obtrusion of a woman's ideas. Virginia noted how his niece, Katherine Stephen (later Principal of Newnham College, Cambridge), was snubbed at lunch for presuming to be an intellectual. When he met the novelist, Olive Schreiner, at Clarens in 1887 he was charmed by her black eyes but her critical talk 'riled' him. No, despite excellent reports of the *African Farm*, Miss Schreiner, he told Julia, 'is not my kind of young woman'. In principle, Leslie Stephen wanted his daughters to exercise their talents to the best professional standards; in practice he seems to have taken it for granted that no proper woman would encroach on male preserves. He dreamt of his son, Thoby, as Lord Chancellor; his daughter, Ginia, was to be an author— 'that is a thing for ladies'.

There are clear pictures of two periods in Virginia's education, at fifteen and twenty. In April 1897 Leslie Stephen noted that 'Ginia is devouring books, almost faster than I like—'. Her leather-bound diary shows her almost entirely wrapped up in books, nineteenth-century biographies, novels, and histories, Lockhart's *Life of Sir Walter Scott* and Macaulay's *History*, about which she spoke with a certain extravagance. Hawthorne, especially, was 'dearly beloved'. Her father was contemptuous of novelists who merely reflected workaday life with servile fidelity, and he taught Virginia to admire 'fountains of poetic interest' which Hawthorne could discover in a prosaic scene. Some of Stephen's praise of Hawthorne helped, perhaps, to create his daughter's fictions: Hawthorne's 'mean between the fanciful and the prosaic' and his psychological fascination for 'the borderland between reason and insanity'. Hawthorne's ghosts exist in the twilight of the mind, never too obtrusive, never quite dispelled, but controlled by a delicate sense of humour. Later, Virginia said that to the Americans, to Hawthorne and Henry James, 'we owe the best relish of the past in our literature, not the past of romance and chivalry, but the immediate past of vanished dignity and faded fashions'.

While Nessa went to drawing classes and Stella to the work-house, Virginia was reading. The very casualness of what amounted to daily tutorials with her father in Kensington Gardens was, I think, the clue to their success. Such discussions were simply a part of daily life. Life *was* literature: the conversations which literature sparked and the proximity of the writers themselves. Strolling together along the Parade at Brighton in April 1897 (they were there while Stella was on honeymoon), Leslie Stephen told her stories of her hero, Macaulay, 'and other old gentlemen whom he had known'. He could recall the alarming parties of George Eliot where one had to be ready to discuss metaphysics or the principles of aesthetic philosophy. He remembered how, at Freshwater, Julia Margaret Cameron would scold Tennyson for his little vanities.

During her fifteenth year Virginia carefully recorded her reading. In January, while she was absorbing Carlyle, her father took her to see Carlyle's house in Chelsea.

Jan. 29, 1897

... Went over the house with an intelligent old woman who knew father and everything about him—. We saw ... C's sound proof room, with double walls—His writing table, and his pens, and scraps of the manuscripts—Pictures of him and of her everywhere. Took a hansom home.

Leslie Stephen's injunctions filter through the diary: the second
volume of Froude's *Carlyle* is to be read slowly, 'and then I am to
reread all the books that he has lent me'. Obviously, her father was
applying the brake, insisting—as old Sir James might have done—
on a thorough, not too effortless reading.

Virginia's reading seems to follow no course but was directed, as
she was later to advocate, by natural appetite. 'I finished Scott', she
noted on 24 February 1897, 'and father has given me the *Essays in
Ecclesiastical Biography* [by Sir James Stephen] which will do me
for some time—.' During the morning stroll on 10 March she
remarked that the *Essays* were done with 'and most boldly
suggested Mr Lowell's essays'. That month she read also Lowell's
poems, Pepys's *Diary*, Carlyle's *Life of Sterling*, Coleridge's *Life* by
James Dykes Campbell, *Felix Holt*, and *Silas Marner*. In April she
read Macaulay's *History*, *Wives and Daughters*, Lamb's *Essays*, and
Barchester Towers. In May, while Leslie read aloud nightly from
Godwin's *Caleb Williams*, she was reading Carlyle's *French
Revolution*, and *The Scarlet Letter*. In June she read a life of
Cromwell and, in July, the works of Charlotte Brontë. In August
she took up *Adam Bede* and Leslie Stephen's *Life of Fawcett*.* The
diary peters out from September under the impact of Stella's death,
but it is curious to note how, during the ups and downs of Stella's
last months, the habit of reading did not abate. In fact Virginia held
to it—particularly to Macaulay—as to a rock.

It is quite easy to reconstruct from the diary a sample day in
Virginia's life at fifteen. It would begin with the morning walk
followed by two hours of instruction in classics—some Livy or two
Greek exercises. She might, alternatively, do a little German with
Stella. Later in the morning she and Stella might go shopping to get
stuff for the drawing-room chairs or, more often, visit the National
Gallery. In the afternoon there might be visitors for tea and Leslie
Stephen would come down and cause confusion by throwing
biscuits under the table for the dog which Nessa would attempt to
rescue with her feet. Some evenings the sisters would walk up to
Hyde Park Corner through the gardens to see 'the drawing room
ladies' go by in white satin.

Five years later we have a brief glimpse of another 'orgy of
reading'. At the age of twenty she filled notebooks with the names of

---

* This is a selection. For a complete list of books read Jan. to June 1897, see *QB* i,
pp. 50–1.

great writers in order of merit and with lists of books she had read or planned to read. After Leslie Stephen brought her Hakluyt's *Voyages* from the London Library she devoured the Elizabethans (she mentions in particular Spenser and Webster). Then she read Browning, Shelley, and Congreve; all of Peacock and Austen's novels two or three times, all Meredith, all Ibsen, and a little Shaw. She engaged in 'stupendous arguments', often with Thoby, in which the Greeks were pitted against the moderns, romance against realism, Racine against Shakespeare.

Her lists included no contemporary writers. Meredith, Hardy, and James were, by then, established classics. No man of her generation influenced her, she said, as a Carlyle or a Tennyson or a Ruskin had influenced their contemporaries. And as there was no acceptable giant, to her mind, she decided to have nothing to do with smaller men. She would stay with the classics 'and consort entirely with minds of the very first order'.

Virginia Stephen was now a young lady who had firmly to escape from the gossipy downstairs world of 'pure convention' to the exalted upstairs world of 'pure intellect'. There Leslie Stephen would be, swinging in his rocking-chair, pipe in mouth. He was old and deaf. Slowly he would become aware of his daughter's presence. He would rise, put her book—it may have been Dr Johnson—back on the shelf and 'very kindly' ask her what she had made of it. Then he might remark that Jane Carlyle had written the best letters in the language and hand the volume to her. 'For some time we would talk and then, feeling soothed, stimulated, full of love for this unworldly, very distinguished, lonely man, I would go down to the drawing room again. . . .'

Leslie Stephen was Virginia's first and most enduring intellectual model. He not only shaped her tastes, especially for biography, but she would also watch him writing and the very format of her drafts follows his: the brief clauses, punctuated by semicolons, pile up, adding a new observation, a new nuance to the basis of the sentence. Their minds pressed on towards exactness of statement, a final judiciousness. She picked up her father's reverential glow and unexpected transitions from sentiment to humour. But the clue to Leslie Stephen's deepest influence on his daughter's writing may lie not in his professional work but in more intangible demonstrations:

his brave and intransigent nature and, oddly enough, his unorthodox tramps.

Thomas Hardy, too, saw Leslie Stephen essentially in his passion for the crags and snow-fields of the Bernese Oberland. Hardy, travelling in Switzerland in 1897, spied in the gaunt peak of the Schreckhorn a semblance of his friend:

> Aloof, as if a thing of mood and whim;
> Now that its spare and desolate figure gleams
> Upon my nearing vision, less it seems
> A looming Alp-height than a guise of him
> Who scaled its horn with ventured life and limb. . . .

F. W. Maitland, who belonged to the band of Sunday Tramps, recalled how Stephen stalked 'like fate' across the moors through the mist and blinding rain. He was a forty-mile-a-day man who was said to have covered the country like compasses over a small-scale map. His contemporaries stress qualities of character that fitted him to be a leader of expeditions: his nerve on the summits; his grim perseverance; his directional instinct so sure that, as Maitland claims, he seemed to his followers to subdue space and time to his will.

Virginia, like her father, grandfather, and great grandfather before her, was a walker. A year after her father's death, she returned to his favourite ground in Cornwall and, in the Cornwall diary of 1905, describes her awakening taste for 'solitary tramping'. 'A great distance of the surrounding country have I now traversed thus and the map of the land becomes solid in my brain.' The idea was to discover, without signposts or maps, those secret places which the walker might make his point of pilgrimage.

In the Cornwall diary, ten years before the publication of her first novel, lies buried the strange origin of her most experimental work. As Virginia's Woolf's novels were to follow the uncharted paths of the mind's free movement, so this diary records how she would step aside from the high road at St Ives and trust to innumerable footpaths, 'as thin as though trodden by rabbits', which led over hills and moor in all directions. As though she were tracking a metaphor for her future work, she followed natural paths which ignored artificial boundaries. The padlocked gates and farm walls were deceptive barriers for, when she climbed over, the path would continue quite happily. In this way, she found a covert but massive network of tiny paths, in reality unobstructed which, she wrote, 'keeps the land fluid, as it were. . . . The pedestrian then should sketch his path with a free hand, & trust that he will find some little hidden line to guide him.' She was a strategist like her father who was said to have 'weird powers of devising ever new ways between point to point'. By imitating her father's pastime, she came upon a structural principle which was fulfilled in the 1920s with a plot that ignored the signposts of birth, marriage, and death in order to find those unlooked-for moments that shape our lives. As early as 1905, tracking her individual way across the gorse where there were only grey farms, she noted that 'for the walker who prefers the variety & incident of the open fields to the orthodox precision of the high road, there is no such ground for walking as this'.

In the *DNB*'s postscript Leslie Stephen said he was impatient of the kind of research that seemed incapable of fruitful conclusions. The success of his daughter's novels was to depend on their conclusions where she would justify the mind's keen ramble by some astonishing find.

The Cornwall diary voices the curiosity and exhilaration of those who push through uncharted territory in the face of the elements. 'Twice these walks were taken in the teeth of heavy rain storms', she wrote. 'I walked, it seemed, toward the very fount of the torrent, up among the grey hills. Both times it swept like driving smoke across the sea, and all the cheerful shapes and colours evaporated.' As she ploughed through dense mist to take her bearings from Knells monument she diverted herself by reciting verses as her father would have done: 'A blinding mist came down and hid the land. . . .' She reflected how easily she might share the fate of Wordsworth's Lucy Gray who was lost in a storm 'upon the lonesome wild'.

In *To the Lighthouse*, Virginia pictured her father as a spare, desolate stake. Leslie Stephen's vigilance was another attribute which might not be learnt from an expensive education. As a child she was confronted by a mind not in itself innovative but a guardian of the truth and a marker—like a lighthouse—in the obscuring flood of ignorance. He was oddly blind to ordinary matters, as, for instance, his children's feelings; but for the extraordinary, she said, he had an eye like an eagle's:

It was his fate, his peculiarity, whether he wished it or not, to come out thus on a spit of land which the sea is slowly eating away, and there to stand, like a desolate sea-bird, alone. It was his power, his gift, suddenly to shed all superfluities, to shrink and diminish so that he looked barer and felt sparer, even physically. . . .

From her father, Virginia absorbed the fierceness with which the empirical mind pits observed truth against established paradigms. In *A Room of One's Own* she said that to sacrifice a hair on the head of one's observation, or a shade of its colour in deference to some Headmaster with a silver pot in his hand 'is the most abject treachery, and the sacrifice of wealth and chastity which used to be said to be the greatest of human disasters, a mere flea-bite in comparison'.

In an article called 'The Modern Essay' she remarks her father's intellectual courage in contrast to the modern journalist who, because he secretly fears his readers, masquerades as one of them— and draws out of harm's way any precious feeling or thought that might be damaged by contact or anything sharp that might irritate their skin. These paltry journalists, she wrote contemptuously, 'are as far removed from the extravagant beauty of Walter Pater as they are from the intemperate candour of Leslie Stephen'. He taught her that writing, if it is to have the permanency of Bacon, must have, for its backbone, 'some fierce attachment to an idea'.

Virginia saw her father as a model of the Cambridge analytical mind. He taught that 'the one thing that can spoil the social intercourse of well-educated men living in great freedom from unnecessary etiquette is a spirit of misplaced zeal'. He regarded Cambridge as blessedly free from the religious fervour of nineteenth-century Oxford. Cambridge men, he said, 'did not deny the existence of the soul; but knew that it should be kept in its proper place. It should not be unduly stimulated in early years, but kept in due subordination to the calm understanding occupied with positive matters of fact.' When Leslie Stephen's faith gave way, he suffered none of the doubts and regrets of Tennyson and Arnold; simply felt 'relieved of a cumbrous burden'. The points at which he had touched Christianity had been purely moral and these he took intact into his new life: his contempt of self-indulgence, his adoration for tenderness of heart, his pity for suffering.

Virginia had, according to Leonard Woolf, a down-to-earth, 'granitic' mind. All the Stephens, he said, had a 'lapidary' way of expressing opinions, which reminded one of the Ten Commandments engraved upon tables of stone, even when they were only telling you that it would rain tomorrow. The weakness in Virginia Woolf's work lies less in the direction of cloudiness than on the other side, a literal-mindedness that can be wilfully obtuse. If her more cutting caricatures (the kind she tossed off in her letters) are probed, there is a certain mundaneness masquerading as liveliness. Her childlike alertness, that made her so fiercely true, made her also, at times, insensitive and callow. In 1906, when she visited St Sophia in Constantinople, her diary blankly ridicules its un-English customs. She is baffled by disorderly worship and the turbaned figures moving about in a manner that seems to her too easy to be religious.

Influenced as she was by her father, did she in any way resist his teachings? Or were there things he could not teach her? While she accepted the pieties of Cambridge rationalism, she did resist its methods. Leslie Stephen was compelled to be 'always logic-chopping'. Given a thought to analyse, a thought of Mill, Bentham, or Hobbes, his mind would be acute, concise, clear. But to his daughter the narrow concentration of brainwork was 'crippling'. Her father in old age had 'no conception of what he himself did and said; he had no idea what other people felt'.

Her ridicule of Mr Ramsay, forcing his way by laborious logical deduction through the letters of the alphabet to bash his head in frustration at R, is intended as a critique of the education which attaches prestige to intellectual feats. She implies a definition of intelligence which includes certain qualities that have traditionally had no official sanction. These qualities are to be found typically in her female characters not because they are limited to women but because women have, for so long, escaped formal education.

When she mocks Mrs Ramsay's naïve trust that knowledge of square roots, the French system of land tenure, and the current definition of the character of Napoleon will uphold civilization, she is questioning the status of the theorizing intelligence. Beside this she places Mrs Ramsay's humble observation that the conditions of the working classes in Victorian London might be marginally less horrifying if there were proper drains and the milk did not arrive brown with dirt. She defines the educated intelligence primarily by its penchant for fictions; the uneducated by its quick grasp of fact. She wrote that 'our facts give us really so much the more material for our imaginations'. Two contradictory facts can coexist: say Mr Ramsay's imperviousness to his child's longing to sail to the lighthouse and, at the same time, his attunement to his wife as they read together. The prose, oscillating between contradictory facts, may appear inconsistent to some readers, but it is a strenuous effort to contain the whole truth.

Mr Ramsay's thinking is strictly compartmentalized. If one compartment is unproductive he closes it off and tries another so that his thinking is abrupt and programmed. It is as though there is a different slot in his mind for each experience, emotion, or thought to which he responds separately. The old perceptions of Mrs Ramsay, Lily Briscoe, and Cam, on the other hand, hold fast while new perceptions impinge on them. This stretching vessel of the mind is, if anything, a more demanding mode of intelligence, in its acute attentiveness, than the narrow trajectory of logic, but it still lacks status.

Mr Ramsay's logic and Leslie Stephen's 'logic-chopping' are, though, later caricatures and not strictly fair to the father whose writing, say, on *Gulliver's Travels*, shows a remarkable grasp of the subtleties and contradictions of Swift's misanthropy. His prose is, in fact, much like his daughter's in that, far from rushing to glib conclusions, it samples all the nuances of the whole truth. Both father and daughter conform to Mill's model of a mind with capacity to assimilate conflicting truths. Their minds reach for generalization but it must be hard won.

Virginia Woolf's final view of her father in her 'Sketch of the Past' was even harsher than in the *Lighthouse*. Only in her youthful 'Reminiscences' do we get a fair impression of the peculiar stimulus of his paternal presence. There she tells how he set his daughters free from grief in the summer of 1895. They spent that summer at the Isle of Wight in the low bay at Freshwater in an atmosphere of lush plants, hot rooms, and silence, choked with too-luxuriant feelings, so that they had at times a physical need of fresh air, something bracing, even abrasive. This their father gave them. Suddenly, on a walk, he would brush aside convention 'and show us for a minute an inspiriting vision of free life, bathed in an impersonal light. There were numbers of things to be learnt, books to be read, and success and happiness were to be attained there without disloyalty.' He suggested they use sorrow to quicken other feelings that remained. 'Beautiful was he at such moments',

Virginia recalled, 'simple and eager as a child; and exquisitely alive to all affection; exquisitely tender.'

By the end of her father's life, she no longer needed his guidance. Schooled in self-education, she went on devouring books. 'Books', she said in 1903, 'are the things I enjoy—on the whole—most.' She packed Shakespeare and the Bible for her summer vacation in excited anticipation 'that all that thickness of paper will be passed through my mind'. She looked to the country to provide the leisure appropriate to the 'big books', but was strangely beset by humility. 'I read—then I lay down the book—& say—what right have I, a woman, to read all these things that men have done?' Perhaps her bookish appetite was all the sharper for her sense that to commune with the greatest minds was a privilege.

I feel sometimes for hours together as though the physical stuff of my brain were expanding larger and larger—throbbing quicker & quicker with new blood—& there is no more delicious sensation than this. I read some history: it is suddenly all alive, branching forwards & backwards & connected with every kind of thing that seemed entirely remote before. I seem to feel Napoleon's influence on our quiet evening in the garden for instance—I think I see for a moment how our minds are all threaded together—how any live mind today is of the very same stuff as Plato's and Euripides'.

She sensed a 'common mind' binding poet, historian, and philosopher: 'I feel as though I had grasped the central meaning of the world, & all these poets & historians & philosophers were only following out paths branching from that centre in which I stand.' Then she opened her Greek text to translate and had to acknowledge its 'indifference' to her pretensions. Then, again, she went tramping and the physical movement would free her mind once more.

Openly, she expressed envy of Thoby's training. He was then at Trinity College, Cambridge and afterwards would go to the Bar. 'I don't get anybody to argue with me now', she wrote to him, 'and feel the want. I have to delve from books, painfully and all alone, what you get every evening sitting over your fire and smoking your pipe with Strachey etc. No wonder my knowledge is but scant. There's nothing like talk as an educator I'm sure.' Yet she had her father to talk to, not the same as a contemporary, but probably better. So she built up the plaintive, self-deprecating image while privately she fattened herself on the 'big books' and consorted only with minds 'of the first order'.

The training which Virginia Stephen received from her father was supplemented from 1902 by Janet Case, one of the first women to pass through Girton College, Cambridge, who gave her the only systematic tuition she ever had and introduced her to the feminist cause.

When Thoby had come back from school for the first holidays he had told his younger sister the story of Troy as they had walked up and down the stairs: 'I felt he was shy of telling it; and so must keep walking up and down . . . and he told me about the Greeks, fitfully, excitedly.' In October 1897, Virginia began, at fifteen, to attend intermittently Greek and history classes at King's College, London. At eighteen, she wrote to her cousin, Emma Vaughan, in June 1900: 'Greek . . . is my daily bread, and a keen delight to me.' In October that year she began private lessons with old Clara Pater (the sister of Walter Pater) in an atmosphere of Persian cats and Morris wallpapers, but these lessons proved too undisciplined. Miss Pater was replaced by Miss Case, who refused to allow her to seize the sense of a sentence, ignoring grammar. She was to go back to the beginning. She began a new regime, studying alone each morning in her bedroom—the old night nursery—where Case taught her and where she was shaping a 'central private life' pinpointed by the Greek lexicon which always lay open on Stella's green and brown writing table and by the manuscript books, the 'surreptitious' sketches and essays of her self-imposed apprentice-ship. A fragment of autobiography recalls that

half the room was literary; half washing and dressing. To encourage my vanity—for I dressed badly—George gave me the swinging glass that I still have. Seven pound ten it cost, & he hoped I should learn to take care of my looks. Dresses hung on the door; & there was the old nursery cupboard, reeking with medicine bottles. George I think, had the room papered for me; and added I think a new fireplace. I was given a deep wicker chair for a birthday present; & there I would sit, between tea & dinner, withdrawn from the house reading until Gerald or Adrian or George or perhaps Jack, or it might be father on his way up to the study tapped & came in;—The mornings, from 10 to 1 I spent entirely alone. . . . There I sat, reading Greek. . . .

By July 1901 she had gone through the *Antigone* and *Oedipus Coloneus* and was in the middle of the *Trachiniae*. She announced to Thoby with pride that she not only admired Sophocles, she could enjoy him. Her notebooks contain her translations, summaries, or notes on Greek and Latin—the Satires of Juvenal; the 4th Georgic ('the song Virgil made, while Caesar was conquering & making laws. Lovely!'); the *Ion* of Euripides; the *Ajax* of Sophocles; *The Frogs* of Aristophanes; Plato's dialogues, the *Phaedrus* and the *Symposium*—and a record of a detailed study of the *Odyssey* which she began in Greece in 1906 with the first four books and completed on 15 May 1908. For Virginia Stephen, as for the classically educated young men of her generation, the Greeks provided a touchstone of beauty and truth. In an early typescript of *The Voyage Out* she wrote that intimacy with the Greeks had made Mr Ambrose 'terribly hard upon the living. He knew when they spoke the truth; he knew when they were stupid.' The Greeks, she wrote in a later essay, face up to 'a sadness at the back of life' which they do not try to mitigate 'and it is to the Greeks that we turn when we are sick of the vagueness, of the confusion, of Christianity and its consolations, of our own age'.

Virginia saw her teacher, who was twenty years older, as one of the pioneers of women's emancipation, but the kind who worked in the background: 'a counsellor rather than a champion, listening to the theories of youth with a little chuckle of merriment, opening her beautiful veiled eyes with a sudden flash of laughter'. During the worst of the tyranny in Hyde Park Gate, Janet Case taught her how to hold on—with spunk and humour. When Case came to stay at her rented house at Firle in Sussex in the summer of 1911, Virginia blurted out the story of George's assaults. Case's outrage supplied a secure point of judgement. Virginia's letters to her teacher were less frivolous than to most of her other correspondents. When Case was dying, in March 1937, she wrote: 'please know and understand with what affection I always think of you. How unhappy I was, and how you helped me, and still do, dear Janet. . . .'

Virginia herself tried teaching between 1905 and 1907 at Morley College, an evening institute for working people in South London. In the early typescript of *The Voyage Out*, she recorded the impressions of a middle-class lady who ventures into an area of London where there were no hansom cabs and discovers that 'this was the city of the poor'. The lady is somewhat encouraged to pass a building put up by the London County Council for night schools but 'it was very gloomy'. In Virginia Stephen's report of July 1905 she complained that the organizers of Morley College preferred the safety of mediocrity. The Principal, Mary Sheepshanks, had suggested that she might hold a little social evening or pass on a little English grammar, but she argued (like her grandfather) that the newly literate should not be fobbed off with sham learning. She insisted on a proper course in English history, even though only three pupils came. She wanted to give them a solid overview which would serve as a foundation for further study rather than the 'disconnected fragments' offered by the college curriculum. She commented indignantly on a proposed course on the French Revolution: 'Eight lectures dropped into their minds, like meteors from another sphere impinging on this planet & dissolving in dust again.' So useless would eight lectures be to pupils who had no power to receive them as part of a continuum. Virginia soon abandoned Morley, but her interest in the shape of English history, particularly the shift from one age to another and the unobserved part played by women, was to find its way into many of her writings, 'The Journal of Mistress Joan Martyn', *To the Lighthouse*, *Orlando*, *The Years*, *Between the Acts*, and *Anon*.

'By the way, I am going to write history one of these days', Virginia Stephen wrote to Violet Dickinson in May 1905, 'I always did love it; if I could find the bit I want.' That summer she 'solidly read and annotated 4 volumes of medieval English'. A year later the brief but revolutionizing historical piece was done.

Virginia spent her August holiday in 1906 at Blo' Norton Hall, a moated Elizabethan manor house in East Harling, Norfolk. She wrote gaily to Violet that, as she tramped the countryside, leaping ditches and scaling walls, she was 'making out beautiful, brilliant stories every step of the way'. 'The Journal of Mistress Joan Martyn' is the story of Rosamond Merridew's researches into the land-tenure system of medieval England. Roughly half the manuscript is about Merridew's views on history and her search for old documents. The other half presents the contents of a journal, written in 1480, which she finds at Martyn Hall, set a few miles from Blo' Norton Hall.

What is the ideal historical document is the implied question behind the story of Merridew's find. What is the line of a woman as historian? What importance have women in the history of England?

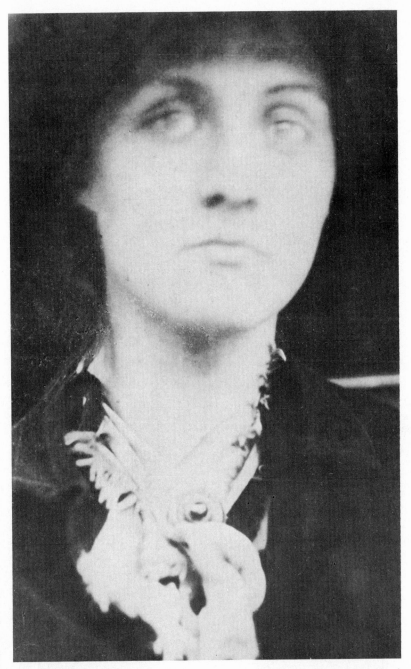

'She alone spoke the truth. . . . That was the source of her everlasting attraction.'
Julia Duckworth, *c.*1865–6

Julia Stephen reading with her children, *c.*1894

Julia Stephen and Stella

The journal recounts Joan Martyn's life over the course of one year, her habits, thoughts, fears, motives, and expectations. In short, it brings into historical view an obscure young girl who is taking on the duties of womanhood during the wars of the Roses.

The document displaces attention from the civil wars to a girl reading Lydgate aloud to distract her family from fear. Later, when it is too dark to read, she listens to their 'dreadful stories' of the state of the country, the plots, the battles, and 'the bloody deeds that are going on all round us'. These 'dreadful stories' will come, in time, to be what we call history but they are peripheral to Joan's busy, orderly day. Only at night, when gusts come in through her bedroom window and lift the tapestry on the wall, does she think of men in armour, and then with horror. 'My prayer last night was', she writes, 'that the great gates might hold fast, & all robbers & murderers might pass us by.'

Joan confesses that she is entranced by the romances of an anonymous singer who shelters for a night in Martyn Hall. Inside his yellow manuscript 'knights and ladies moved undimmed, to the unceasing melody of beautiful words'. Yet she is drawn inexorably to the challenges of real life, to a suitable marriage with good Sir Amyas where she will fulfil not romantic dreams but 'my proper work as a woman'. As marriage approaches, she begins 'to understand how much of my time will be passed in thoughts which have nothing to do with men or with happiness'. She looks forward to bearing children and to watching over the crops and herds and to keeping accounts in her husband's absence. Like her mother before her, she will bolt the door against vagabonds rampaging outside her walls. 'Within doors', she muses, 'I shall store up fine linens & my chests shall be laden with spices & preserves; by the work of my needle all waste of time & use will be repaired & renewed.'

From her strong mother, whose cheek is coloured like a healthy winter apple, Joan picks up this vocation for nurture, preservation, repair, and renewal. 'It is a great thing to be the daughter of such a woman', Joan writes earnestly, '& to hope that one day the same power may be mine. She rules us all.' Joan's account of a fictional mother of the fifteenth century—whose eyes are deep and stern and whose 'thought & watching' have cut noble lines on her brow— prefigures, in part, the strong maternal figure of Mrs Ramsay.

But Joan's mother also lives by a national dream which she confides to her daughter. A responsible dream, not one of power, it has nothing to do with the legal ownership of land which is passed down the male line:

> And she went on to expound to me what she calls her theory of ownership; how, in these times, one is as the Ruler of a small island set in the midst of turbulent waters; how one must plant it & cultivate it; & drive roads through it, & fence it securely from the tides; & one day perhaps the waters will abate & this plot of ground will be ready to make part of a new world. Such is her dream of what the future may bring to England; & it has been the hope of her life to order her own province in such a way that it may make one firm spot of ground to tread on at any rate. She bids me hope that I may live to see the whole of England thus solidly established.

Here, Virginia Stephen imagines the ancestors of the makers of England, obscure women who pass their unnoticed code of preservation from mother to daughter. Our historical dependence on unhistoric acts is an idea that she took from George Eliot: 'that things are not so ill with you and me as they might have been, is half owing to the number who lived faithfully a hidden life, and rest in unvisited tombs.' Joan's journal is a document which her male descendants assumed to be insignificant. And this is where Miss Merridew comes in: if such a historian does not exist, she must be invented, a deliverer advancing to the rescue of some stranded ghost of the past. She is a professional counterpart to Virginia Stephen who, with this history, called her authorial role into being. The centre of history is not the legal document or the muddled vicissitudes of the wars of the Roses but the woman left alone in her citadel, who kept order as a matter of course, who kept anarchy, so far as she was able, at bay.

Miss Merridew carries to its logical conclusion a suggestion made by Sir James Stephen when he was Professor of History at Cambridge. He said that medieval historians might as profitably study Chaucer as legal records. In short, the contemporary story is the historian's prime document. Virginia Stephen goes further to suggest that, if contemporary stories do not exist, they must be imagined.

In the course of her future career, Virginia Stephen would repeatedly take up the challenge of a woman's portrait of a woman. Another line of development radiates from this story. At the end of her career, she would return to the piquant vanishing figure of the anonymous poet. In her last work, *Anon*, she would reach out

through the oral poet to an obscure faceless audience, to call out
a spontaneous communal response lost to the modern reader.

The most important influence in Virginia Stephen's life in the five
years between the death of her brother, Thoby, at the end of 1906
and her engagement to Leonard Woolf in 1912 was her sister's
husband, Clive Bell. Bell was the first to take her writing seriously.
He made an ideal adviser for an acutely modest young woman who
needed, above all, recognition. Leslie Stephen, had he lived, would
have undermined his daughter's ambitions, so she thought. Later
on, Leonard Woolf, too, for some reason, could not be shown work
in progress. Perhaps, for all his practical support, he was too
abrasive. Clive Bell's manner was perfect: warm and enthusiastic,
he encouraged her latent gifts as part of a long flirtation which they
began in 1908. 'We talked. We vibrated in sympathy. We billed
& cooed. Rosy lights shone on his cheeks. Our intercourse was very
gay, vibrant, like that of stringed instruments.' 'My dear Virginia',
Clive wrote on 7 May 1908, 'I suppose I shall forfeit all my
reputation for self-confidence and character when I say that, on the
top of Rosewall, I wished for nothing in the world but to kiss you.
I wished so much that I grew shy and could not see what you were
feeling; that is what happens always. . . .'
    After Vanessa's marriage in 1907 Virginia had felt diminished by
her sister's status of wife and mother. 'Seriously nature has done so
much more for her than for me', she wrote to Bell in May 1908. He
took 'infinite pains' to thaw her out and, later that summer, she felt
able to own her secret aim: 'I think a great deal of my future', she
wrote, 'and settle what book I am to write—how I shall re-form the
novel . . .'. When they spoke of her writing he praised it 'sufficiently
to give his strictures a good deal of force'.
    Where Leonard Woolf was, initially at any rate, attracted to
Virginia Stephen as to a work of art, Clive Bell liked her for her
human qualities, her fun and originality. She was, he said, 'the
gayest human being I have known and one of the most lovable'.
His letters continually reverted from frivolity and teasing to
affirmations of her promise. He saw her one June evening, sitting on
a bench at Hampton Court 'with soft deep eyes, and in their depths
the last secrets of things'. She wore a white muslin dress and
floating over it a long white ghost-like cloak, a broad soft straw hat,

and a broad streamer. 'That day', he told her in February 1909, 'I half guessed at what you, perhaps, and a few great poets have half known.' Years later, in 1917, he confirmed this impression: 'You have got to put down what goes on in Virginia's head and I have never doubted—you know I haven't—that what goes on there is about as exciting as anything in the world.'

In his own way, Clive Bell had something to teach her. He introduced her to more sophisticated reading. His first letter in 1907 directed her attention away from the Victorians to the French: 'Have you read Mérimée "Letters à une inconnue" (exquisite) . . . or "La duchesse bleue" by the first snob in Europe,—George Duckworth always excepted—Monsieur Paul Bourget? Have you read "Liaisons dangereuses", the most indecent work of genius that I know and one of the greatest? . . . When last did you reread La Bovary?'

With the advent of Bell, Virginia Stephen knocked up against a more worldly, more masculine point of view: 'you who are as feminine as anything that wears a skirt (I forbear a more scientific classification) are too much of a genius to believe in your own sex— or in ours either.' He teased her with anti-feminist remarks ('the average woman is inferior to the average man'); at the same time exhorted her to write something about women 'before your sharp edges get blunted in the bed'. In his flirtatious way, he fortified her independence. 'My dear Virginia', he wrote, 'to-day I saw a full, rich, ear of barley, spared somehow by the reaper, standing alone in the middle of its stubble, and so I thought of you.' There was a real modesty behind his boastful worldliness, and a real generosity. He owned that, compared with this sheltered virgin, his experience was second-hand: 'I just go on fingering the smooth outside. . . .' He had a loud voice, but it was never overbearing, like Leslie Stephen's. Its characteristic note, said a friend, was one of high expectation and shared enjoyment.

Later, Virginia was influenced by Leonard Woolf's disapproval of Clive Bell and began to speak with fond derision of his vanities and love affairs. But this belies the bracing effect Bell had in the years before her marriage. Bell picked over the initial drafts of her first novel with mock 'horror'. To make use of such words as 'solid' and 'block' to give a sense of matter is irritating, he told her. Imaginations, too, must they shimmer always or be quite so often 'shadowy'? Yet he praised her characterization of the worldly

Dalloways: 'them you have stripped quite naked at all events, I am stunned & amazed by your insight.' He responded, too, to the muted element in Virginia's first heroine: 'Rachel is, of course, mysterious & remote, some strange, wild, creature who has come to give up half her secret.'

Virginia Stephen matured late in comparison with other writers. She was held up by bouts of illness. She deliberately drew out her education, reserving as samples of excellence only the greatest writers, in particular those of ancient Greece. During her twenty-year apprenticeship she had to take in her father's precepts and then move beyond them, seeking a model in her own mind. She had, too, to liberate herself as a woman from Victorian habits of self-deprecation. Perhaps her greatest problem in becoming a writer was to overcome her modesty, the fear of public exposure (a fear for which the founding of her own Hogarth Press in 1917 was to provide only a partial solution). In the middle years of this long transitional stage Clive Bell was an essential catalyst, for he gave her confidence, both as a woman and an artist, to seek independence from established norms. In May 1908 she confessed to him that she was generally bored by drawing-rooms and much excited by private thoughts: 'Then you come . . . and tell me that what I think is the thing; and my head spins—I feel above the Gods. . . . As it is, I bid fair to become a prophetess, with only one worshipper.'

7. *Setting Out*

'WE need not always be thinking of posterity', Virginia Stephen remarked to Clive Bell in February 1909. This self-rebuke reveals for an instant the extent of her aim. Publicly, she mocked herself as the helpless, awkward, scatty dependant of her elder sister. She liked to expand on the 'agony' of shopping for 'one forced as I am to keep my underclothes pinned together by brooches'. Yet, in writing, she was enviably self-disciplined. She was vastly ambitious. Her aim was no less than to 're-form' the traditional novel, the traditional biography, and the traditional treatment of character so as to capture, she told Clive, 'multitudes of things at present fugitive'.

When George Eliot looked at the blundering lives of women, she concluded that, as long as their potentialities could not be determined with any accuracy, their social lot must remain in question. 'Meanwhile', she said, 'the indefiniteness remains . . .'. Virginia Stephen's first novel, *The Voyage Out*, reiterates this question. ' "It's awfully difficult to tell about women," [St John Hirst] continued, "how much, I mean, is due to lack of training, and how much is native incapacity." ' The novel doubts whether it will be even remotely possible to coax its heroine, Rachel Vinrace, into the light of inspection. Virginia Stephen launched herself on a problem passed on by George Eliot in whose heroines she saw 'the ancient consciousness of woman . . . for so many ages dumb' brim with 'a demand for something—they scarcely know what—for something that is perhaps incompatible with the facts of human existence'. Rachel Vinrace cannot take a novelistic place in English society; she cannot survive, that is, the undefined possibilities of her growth. Patterned after the *Bildungsroman*, the novel swerves suddenly near the end: there is no knowing what Rachel could be because she evolves in a way that is perhaps incompatible with the facts of existence.

This is a stern outlook, not to be aligned with straightforward hopes of women's rights. All Virginia's positions were to be too subtle for classification. Her sense of madness, womanhood, and, later, marriage, all contain their zones of silence which reverberate with unstated suggestion. Intellectual appetite must round out the woman's point of view, she said, thinking of George Eliot. 'She must reach beyond the sanctuary and pluck for herself the strange bright fruits of art and knowledge.' Yet, 'clasping them as few women have ever clasped them, she would not renounce her own inheritance—the difference of view'.

Virginia Stephen's initial efforts at creative writing were, predictably, overwhelmed by the bright fruits of art and knowledge. She was intimidated by the achievements of Austen, Meredith, and Hardy, and dared not write with the mind until she perfected her eye. Her Hyde Park Gate diary (1903) and her travel diary (1906–9) were filled with high-flown descriptive exercises. Her first abortive chapter for a novel was written immediately after Leslie Stephen's death while the family recuperated at Manorbier on the Pembrokeshire coast. The chapter's flatness may be due to Virginia's grief. It is a routine attack on the manners of good society. Plain Hester Fitzjohn turns down handsome Roger Brickdale under the influence of her uppish family. However disgruntled by good society (to which she was still subject), the author appears equally disgruntled by the imagined alternative, Brickdale, the nice young man of mild vanity and little brain. His looks suggest Hawthorne's faun-like Donatello but, alas, he turns out to be a tame faun after all.

Virginia Stephen first moved from imitative exercise to the woman's 'difference of view' in the summer of 1906 when she imagined a model ancestress in Joan Martyn and her mother. From there she went on to her first and possibly most brilliant portrait of her own mother in the 'Reminiscences' of 1907–8, a series of elegiac portraits of the family, still dominated, as in life, by Julia Stephen. The daughter picked out prompt wisdom as her mother's prime trait: 'every deed and word had the bright, inexorable, swift stamp of something struck clearly by a mass of hoarded experience.'

The two model mothers led Virginia Stephen to history and biography as a source of other models. She admired Jane Carlyle, particularly, for a gift in common with Julia Stephen: a quick eye for the essential in character 'which is creative as well as critical, and, in her, amounted to genius'.

The problem of every biography is to see distinction, not just achievement, and to recognize distinction demands certain qualities in the biographer: decided morals, firmness of mind, and generosity of surrender. The biographic reviews that Virginia Stephen wrote in her twenties show a fully formed set of values. She valued Jane Carlyle's common sense in the face of pretentious bores, her stern check on self-analysis in the presence of her husband's overweening self-absorption, and her keen sympathy for the poor, the sick, and the genuinely unhappy. She liked, too, Charlotte Brontë's solitary resilience and passionate craving for liberty. She criticized Shelley for his veering attachments. Sense, sympathy, honesty, strength of feeling: these were her exacting standards by which character should be judged.

Her biographic reviews between 1908 and 1910 may read like spontaneous, idle shots at motives, conduct, and phases in a lifespan that may seem, from a historical or political or learned view, quite peripheral. But she was developing a biographic theory that was to be crucial to her development as a novelist. She examined the hidden moments and obscure formative experiences in a life, rather than its more public actions.

Her brief portrait of Elizabeth I, in December 1909, concentrated on the formative phase exclusively. She asked herself what kind of girlhood led to that inscrutable figure, equipped with a complete armour of coldness, who rode through London to her coronation at the age of twenty-five. She imagined 'a very precocious and somewhat priggish child' and how Elizabeth, at fourteen, learnt to subdue her passions when her feeling for Thomas Seymour was exposed to inquisition by a council of noblemen. It was then, in the retreat at Hatfield, that vanity drove her to excel in the only direction now open to her, scholarship. Precocity, self-control, intellectual vanity: Virginia Stephen immediately touched the hidden fact at the centre of character, ignoring the pomp and flourish that would attract Strachey (in *Elizabeth and Essex*, 1928) and refusing to define a woman, as Strachey does, by her lover.

Again, with Lady Hester Stanhope, she stressed the formative phase. Both Virginia Stephen (in June 1910) and Strachey (later) were amused by Lady Hester's advance on the East in 1812 and 1813, in male clothes, astride her horse. Strachey's traveller is no more than a ridiculous eccentric, flourishing all the manners of power without power itself. He filled gaps of understanding with gorgeous oriental clothes. But Virginia wanted to know what drove Lady Hester abroad. Where Strachey dwelt on the grandeur of her three years in the home of her uncle, William Pitt, Virginia Stephen

saw, from Lady Hester's account of her triumphs, that she must
have made herself disliked:

With scanty education but great natural force, she despised people
without troubling to give them a reason for it. Intuition took the place of
argument, and her penetration was great.

Real powers fermented in Lady Hester. 'If you were a man, Hester',
Mr Pitt would say, 'I would send you on the Continent with 60,000
men, and give you *carte blanche*; and I am sure that not one of my
plans would fail, and not one soldier would go with his shoes
unblacked.' Since there was no scope for her in England, she
indulged her fantasy of power abroad and 'drove herself as near
madness as one can go by feeding a measureless ambition upon
phantoms'.

Biography was the point of departure. Virginia Stephen began,
in the biographic portrait, to hint her discovery of states of mind
so muted that they almost defied expression. She was no longer
imitative; she spoke in her own voice, with humorous concern, and
approached her subject with a kind of attentive passivity. In 1909
she followed up *Joan Martyn* with a new experiment in fictional
biography. It is a fictitious review of a biography of an imaginary
Victorian spinster, Miss Willatt. A curious exercise, 'Memoirs of
a Novelist' is not a great work, but it provided a theoretical base for
her experiments in fiction. She wished, she said, 'to write a very
subtle work on the proper writing of lives. . . . It comes over me that
I know nothing of the art; but blunder in a rash way after motive,
and human character . . .'. Running to seventeen pages, 'Memoirs'
is longer than her usual biographic review, and the first fiction that
she thought good enough to publish. It was to be the first of a series
but, to her chagrin, Reginald Smith, editor of the *Cornhill* (her
father's journal), turned it down.

Miss Willatt was a writer who died in 1884. Her books now lie on
the topmost shelves of seaside libraries.* One must take a ladder to
reach them and a cloth to wipe them off. Virginia Stephen
deliberately picked an unpromising subject, a not very appealing
woman whose talents were less than minor. (Miss Willatt thought it

---

* Miss Willatt possibly derives from the Miss Willett of Brighton, mentioned in '22 Hyde
Park Gate', *MB*, pp. 144, 150, who was 'moved to write an Ode comparing George
Duckworth to the Hermes of Praxiteles—which Ode my mother kept in her writing table
drawer'. Brighton would provide the link with the seaside library.

indecent to describe what she knew—her family—so 'invented Arabian lovers and set them on the banks of the Orinoco'.) Miss Willatt so fits the type of silly romantic spinster that she makes the greatest possible demands on her biographer's powers of discernment.

It is at once clear that her fictitious biographer, Miss Linsett, has no powers of discernment. She dwells on the balls of the 1840s, unaware that a large, awkward creature like Miss Willatt would have wished to hide her body. Miss Linsett obscures her further with platitudes: tender regrets at the death of her father. Virginia Stephen (as fictitious reviewer) dismisses this twitter:

> Happily, there are signs that Miss Willatt was not what she seemed. They creep out in the notes, in her letters, and most clearly in her portraits. The sight of the large selfish face, with the capable forehead and the surly but intelligent eyes, discredits all the platitudes on the opposite page; she looks quite capable of having deceived Miss Linsett.
>
> When her father died (she had always disliked him) her spirits rose . . . .

Miss Linsett makes the father's death in 1855 the end to one chapter and Miss Willatt's move to London the beginning of the next. In other words, the biographer's plan depends, whenever possible, 'upon changes of address', which confirms the reviewer's suspicion that she 'had no other guide to Miss Willatt's character'. What Miss Linsett misses is the decisive moment in the life: Miss Willatt's sudden decision, at thirty-six, to give up the sham of philanthropy for writing.

Miss Willatt's work among the poor provokes long accounts of charitable societies. Digression, like platitude, is the result of a biographer's inability to discover what is interesting about a writer's life which is without public action. Other typical fillers are the pedigree (Miss Linsett takes thirty-six pages over the family's history, 'a way of marking time during those chill early pages') and the slow approach to the grave. Again, the narrative slackens to a funeral pace. Miss Linsett lingers with relish over the excruciating details of her subject's last illness and leaves her buried in extraneous detail.

With this satire on literary biography, Virginia Stephen bounced herself away from a stale tradition much as Austen's early satire, 'Love and Freindship', cut off the sentimental novel. She satirized superfluous detail that could blur the crucial moments of a life.

Clive Bell told her, 'Do not think I was so blinded by its brilliance that I failed to see that, perhaps, you had discovered a new medium peculiarly suited to your genius.'

She satirized also the type-casting of women. Miss Willatt is imprisoned in the spinster slot and, though the reviewer can glimpse a live woman, flawed, ambitious, restless, and intransigent, she cannot rescue the rest of Miss Willatt's story—for such women, in the past, 'have been rolled into the earth irrecoverably'. And here, Virginia Stephen circles a potential subject, the obscure middle-aged woman.

Miss Willatt represents the lives of the obscure who, in the absence of fair records, will have to be imagined against overwhelming odds. Miss Willatt also represents a fictional tradition. She acknowledges the inevitable debt to Charlotte Brontë and George Eliot 'for they disclosed the secret that the precious stuff of which books are made lies all about one, in drawing rooms and kitchens where women live, and accumulates with every tick of the clock'. No life, then, is too narrow for the material of fiction. This view licensed Virginia Stephen to draw on her own limited experience for her first full-length fiction, 'Melymbrosia'—later called *The Voyage Out*—not only the superficial details of her travels to Portugal and Greece in 1905 and 1906, but her knowledge of death and mental suffering, and her strange unfolding through a home education. The heroine, Rachel Vinrace, is a young woman of twenty-four who gazes from a ship into the dim recesses of the sea as into a mirror of an unfathomable self. Down there lie the black ribs of wrecked ships and the 'great white monsters of the lower waters'. Rachel feels 'like a fish at the bottom of the sea'. She is surfacing slowly in the course of the novel and then dies before her shape is clear. In this way, *The Voyage Out* dramatized the problem 'Memoirs' proposed: how to recover what has been lost to sight in human nature.

'Virginia Woolf' emerged as novelist through writing *The Voyage Out*. It was begun early in 1908 and not published until 1915. The fact that she rewrote the book so many times (she left evidence of five drafts, burnt several more) suggests her uneasiness. She wanted to transform the novel in ways that now seem quite consistent with contemporary experiments in modern art but which were for her, in 1908, solitary ambitions. Her letters touch on her idea of an art that could 'shape infinite strange shapes'. She

wanted her writing to be judged 'as a chiselled block', she told
Clive, so that it could live disconnected from its author. She dared
to make Rachel featureless so that she might take shape as an
abstraction—of what is unknown in human nature—as Mrs
Ramsay, later, appears on canvas as a triangular purple shape.

'My boldness terrifies me', Virginia told Clive at the outset of this
experiment. But she veered between daring and the decorums of
traditional fiction. She felt the obligation to 'animate' her narrative
with multiple events, which was counter to her inclination to give it
'the feel of running water', the unbroken interior stream of her later
novels. Another challenge was to transform the autobiographic
sources, her obvious links with her heroine. The solution, again,
called for novelistic convention: going abroad, changing places, as a
standard provocation to development. Rachel Vinrace takes her
voyage out to an exotic South American shore, as remote as possible
from her sheltered, monotonous life in Richmond.

In *The Voyage Out*, Virginia Stephen adapted her theory of
biography to fiction, to find in Rachel's random life a definitive
shape and to follow, in her obscure case, what is fugitive in the
mind. This is the bold, autobiographic aspect of the book, the
treatment of Rachel as an oddity who is yet representative of
something latent in human nature. I shall look at what Virginia
Stephen drew from her own experience and at the ways she could
or could not transform it. Virginia Stephen wrote this book, not
Virginia Woolf,* and, in summing up her long apprenticeship, it
offers a remarkable account of a young spinster's uncompromising
and yet elusive state of mind.

Rachel Vinrace is not an exact self-portrait but Virginia Stephen
drew many details from her own situation: the uneasy innocence of
a girl growing out of a Victorian childhood, motherless, oppressed
by a shuttered existence, socially awkward, without formal education, ignorant and afraid of men, but fiercely guarding a sense of
freedom—these thoughts, unfolding casually in 'Reminiscences',
led to a novel about a young woman *en route* from London to Santa
Marina, a popular resort for the English middle classes. There,
Rachel is given a room of her own by an aunt, Helen Ambrose. As
Rachel begins to measure herself by new women—her truth-telling
aunt, Ibsen's Nora or Diana of the Crossways—she meets a

---

* VW did finish off two drafts after her marriage (in Aug. 1912) but the changes were not
drastic.

novelist, Terence Hewet, and they fall in love. From Santa Marina there is a further voyage up a tropical river, a continuation of Rachel's voyage of discovery. After this last expedition Rachel, who has by now shown herself to be a person of mysterious promise, comes down with fever and dies.

Although the voyages are given this remote setting, Rachel's education follows Virginia's own. Rachel has had the fragmentary education of most well-to-do girls in the late-nineteenth century but the 'one great advantage' was that their education 'put no obstacle in the way of any real talent'. Rachel has been left free to play the piano for hours and hours. In company she appears rather indolent and nebulous but, in the privacy of her music-room, she has practised like a fanatic, taught herself, and indulged in 'dreams and ideas of the most extravagant and foolish description'.

Rachel is encased in a set of English characters like an embryo in a shell. She has a poetic suggestiveness compared with the surrounding characters who are immediately recognizable as dons, wives, the eldest daughter of the parsonage, the imperious lady. These fixed characters began as 'bare passages of biography' which were not meant to remain in the text. The young author told Vanessa that the socialite on board ship, Clarissa Dalloway, was Kitty Maxse almost 'verbatim'. 'Never was there such an improvident author—' she groaned that first summer, 'Flaubert would turn in his grave.'

Terence Hewet is given the exact background of Clive Bell, the improbable son of a fox-hunting squire. The aristocratic Mrs Flushing with her exotic clothes is rather like Lady Ottoline Morrell. The beautiful aunt, Helen, is modelled on Vanessa. Her husband, the scholarly editor who hands Rachel books when she visits his study, groans aloud in uncongenial company, and takes 'wonderfully long' walks, has obvious traits of Leslie Stephen. And the lofty Cambridge don, St John Hirst, is an unsympathetic and rather envious portrait of Lytton Strachey.

The idea of a voyage went back to a fantasy recorded by Virginia in the cryptic 'Warboys' diary of 1899, when she would have been seventeen. This seems to have been a secret diary for it is written in a minute, almost unreadable hand on pages pasted into an eighteenth-century book, *Logic or the Right Use of Reason in the Inquiry after Truth*, by the Revd Isaac Watt, DD. On 7 August 1899 she wrote: 'I must now expound another simile that has been rolling

itself round in my mind for many days past. This is that I am . . .
bound on some long voyage. . . . I have taken with me after anxious
thought all the provisions for my mind that are necessary to the
voyage.' The spur to this fantasy came from Hakluyt's *Voyages of
the Elizabethan Seamen* which she had read in 1897. 'Since the time
of Elizabeth', she wrote in *The Voyage Out*, 'very few people had
seen the river, and nothing had been done to change its appearance
from what it was to the eyes of the Elizabethan voyagers.'
Something of Sir Walter Ralegh's description of the inland shores
of the Orinoco goes into the novel—the plains twenty miles in
length, the grass short and green as in an orderly park, and the
grazing deer.* Different people wrote the *Voyages*, she said in a
later review, 'but they have the same outlook . . .—an attitude of
mind, large, imaginative, unsated'. This outlook Rachel shares.
'. . . Seen through their eyes, the world appears fresh and flowing,
unexplored, and of infinite richness.'

Rachel's voyage to the new world makes it possible for her to
escape Edwardian England and a life hemmed in by well-meaning
aunts who warn her not to play the piano so seriously in case she
spoil the shape of her arms. England, receding into the distance,
looks like a small, shrinking island 'in which people were imprisoned'. But all too soon English power boards Rachel's ship in
the shape of the politician, Mr Dalloway, backed always by his
sweetly winning wife. From the deck of the *Euphrosyne*†, Dalloway,
who sees all action as 'fight', hails the appearance of the Mediter-
ranean fleet, 'two sinister grey vessels, low in the water and bald as
bone, one closely following another with the look of eyeless beasts
seeking their prey'. The character of power is epitomized by the
banality of the Dalloways who have travelled briefly in Spain in
order to understand how peasants live. The safety of the Dalloway
travels, in which the pair barricade themselves behind the bland
platitudes of a ruling class, contrasts with Rachel's passive exposure
when, later, she drifts, almost without volition, up the dark river.

Mr Dalloway claims to read Jane Austen but condescends to
her as 'the greatest female writer we possess'. Clarissa Dalloway
employs 'our beloved Jane' to take her husband's mind off the

---

* Gillian Beer suggests another source in *The Voyage of the Beagle* in 'Virginia Woolf and
Prehistory', *VW: A Centenary Perspective*, ed. Eric Warner (Macmillan, 1984).

† The name of the ship was a coterie joke. *Euphrosyne* was the title of an undistinguished
collection of poems by Lytton Strachey, Clive Bell, Leonard Woolf, and others, published
privately in 1905.

important affairs of the manly world ('the guns of England') by drawing him into what she calls the 'quaint, sprightly and slightly ridiculous world' of a woman. There is a marvellous satiric scene in which Mrs Dalloway lulls her husband to sleep by reading aloud the scathing opening pages of *Persuasion*, an introduction to a very vain man. Rachel, like the independent heroines of *Howards End*, is temporarily beguiled by practical efficiency of power. Her attraction to Richard Dalloway is checked only when he kisses her. The kiss itself is heady, but she is appalled by the thought of herself as prey, pursued by idle appetite. Rachel has a lurid vision of hunched women playing cards in a tunnel under the Thames who will reappear in the delirium of her final fever. Here, Virginia Stephen could not transmute life into art. Rachel's response is excessively fevered, for Dalloway is not much of a threat. It makes sense only in terms of Virginia's fear of her half-brother who, masked by respectability, would prowl by night and pounce. We can follow, through Rachel, Virginia Stephen's analysis of the way a natural response is frozen. Lying in her cabin later that night, Rachel, with the instinct of a terrified animal, plays dead. 'Still and cold as death she lay, not daring to move . . .'.

Later, in a draft version, she confesses to Hewet that she is permanently handicapped: 'I shall never never never have all the feelings I might have . . .'.

The draft also explains the tunnel. Rachel realizes that it is sexual fear that has stunted the lives of women. In draft there is more outspoken anger at the 'creeping hedged in' lives of Victorian girls, 'driven cautiously between high walls, here turned aside, here plunged in darkness . . . made dull and crippled—her life that was the only chance she had, for ever'. Later, Eleanor, an intrepid traveller in *The Years*, thinks in 1917: 'When shall we be free? When shall we live adventurously, wholly, not like cripples in a cave? . . . She felt not only a new space of time, but new powers, something unknown within her.' The drama of this woman's life, like Rachel's, is in breaking free from the enclosures of the Victorian sitting-room. But where Eleanor will manage to make life 'a perpetual discovery', her predecessor, Rachel, cannot forget the proximity of the cave.

The Voyage Out has an anti-male bias and even Terence Hewet, fat and self-indulgent like Clive Bell, with 'a wonderful power of making [Rachel] daring and confident of herself', is not exempt.

Early on, Clive criticized the sharp contrasts between the sexes, 'the subtle, sensitive, tactful, gracious, delicately perceptive, & perspicacious women, & the obtuse, vulgar, blind, florid, rude, tactless, emphatic, indelicate, vain, tyrannical, stupid men'. Absurd, said Clive, also bad art. Virginia, who was submissive to all other criticisms of the novel, rejected this one: 'Possibly, for psychological reasons which seem to me very interesting, a man in the present state of the world, is not a very good judge of his sex . . .'.

When dons talk academic shop, the women on board ship leave the room as soon as they decently can. Virginia's informal education alerted her to cerebral sterility. Mr Pepper can translate Persian poetry into English prose and English prose into Greek iambics but he is a thorough bore. An Oxford don, Mr Elliot, descending a South American mountain on his donkey, calls out to the Cambridge don: ' "Who writes the best Latin verse in your college, Hirst?" ' Hewet explains to Rachel that it compensates them for their drudgery if they are taken very seriously: if they get appointments and offices and bits of ribbon and degrees. Suddenly, 'the masculine conception of life' turns into view as a curiosity which has stamped itself on all we see, on law courts, parliamentary debates, and war. ' "What a world we've made of it!" ', Hewet exclaims.

This judgement is set, at two points, in the contemporary political context of women's struggle for the vote. ' "My good creature, you're only in the way where you are" ', Mr Dalloway, MP, admonishes a suffragette outside the House of Commons. ' "You're hindering me, and you're doing no good to yourself." ' Later a teacher, Miss Allan, who earns her own living, supports a hopeless brother, and has lines of responsibility on her face like those of an elderly man, hears from her sister that ' "Lloyd George has taken the Bill up, but so have many before now, and we are where we are".'

Virginia Stephen is not without sympathy for the cause but, to her, the potential strength of women is less in public rights than in their very remoteness—enforced, of course, but ingrained by habit—from the cynicism of power. The Victorians' ideal of womanhood was a sheltered innocence and Virginia, interestingly, does not entirely reject it. She rewrites the Victorian ideal, asking whether it would be feasible for a grown-up to retain innocence without the old disability of ignorance. Such a creature would, naturally, present as a random oddity of evolution. And if such a creature did come into being, could it survive? The novelist spies Rachel like Darwin or like some watcher of the skies. The novel is couched in the metaphor of exploration and the silence of discovery.

Hirst inspects Rachel with the coolness of a pseudo-scientist: ' "Does she reason, does she feel, or is she merely a kind of footstool?" ' Hewet's curiosity is more that of the genuine scientist. He is not only excited by the unknown but has a knack for discerning the unknown in the familiar. ' "There it was going on in the background, for all those thousands of years, this curious silent unrepresented life. Of course we're always writing about women— abusing them, or jeering at them, or worshipping them; but it's never come from women themselves." ' In Chapter 16, Hewet poses a series of questions to Rachel which swing a multitude of obscure lives into view: lives of women of forty, of unmarried women, of working women, of women who keep shops and bring up children. ' "One knows nothing whatever about them".'

It is in Chapter 16, where greatness is required, that the book falls short, for Hewet's questions invite bold answers from which Rachel holds back. The book moves towards a climactic definition of what such a woman might be—to be foiled by Rachel's unsure muteness. It is plausible enough, but muteness itself is not interesting, and the thoughts that surge behind her silence remain sadly half-formed. The young writer, at this demanding point, could not separate herself from her heroine; could not, that is, allow Rachel Vinrace some measure of articulation denied to Miss Virginia Stephen constrained by the tea-table manner of Victorian ladyhood.

Terence's first question is: how do you spend your day? The answer, in Rachel's case, is easy: she plays the piano. But she is so offhand that Terence passes on to his next, more provocative question: what does she think of men? Does she laugh at them or does 'the humbug of male dominance' make her blood boil?

This provocation effectively silences Rachel, but she thinks of her aunts 'who built up the fine closely woven substance of their life at home'. What her aunts 'do' cannot be framed in plausible terms:

She reviewed . . . their minute acts of charity and unselfishness which flowered punctually from a definite view of what they ought to do . . .; she saw all these things like grains of sand falling, falling through innumerable days . . . and building up a solid mass.

Hewet's third question, 'were you happy?' brings back sexual fear. Here, again, Virginia Stephen blends with her heroine in agonized evasion. There is something to say which cannot, yet, be said. Rachel does manage to convey to Terence that beside sexual abuse all other facts about women's lives pale into insignificance. Terence wins Rachel's confidence, at this point, by not deriding her. ' "I can believe it," he said. He returned her look with perfect sincerity.'

    The novel contrasts the mutedness of Rachel to the volubility of Evelyn M. Evelyn is the feminist who craves what men want and models herself on the warrior, the empire-builder, and the glib political activist in search of modish targets—for her, alcoholics and prostitutes are not people but causes. Her mind is dull and imitative; her inflated interests are as pathetically banal as Mr Dalloway's. Evelyn M. is clearly diagrammed at the beginning of a century in which it becomes fashionable to support equal rights for women, assuming, of course, that women will replicate the power structure, its thinking and language. The loud Evelyn places herself in the advance guard of the envious, sycophantic feminism which Virginia Stephen derides. Through the muted Rachel she posits a different fate. *What* exactly is to surface she cannot say, but sees in Rachel a character who is not imitative. And, to back Rachel, there are the matter-of-fact actions of the obscure, of Helen Ambrose and even the Richmond aunts, 'building up' the fabric of life, embroidering, reading aloud, nurturing. When Helen sits sewing, she takes an exemplary posture quite different to heroic statues:

With one foot raised on the rung of a chair, and her elbow out in the attitude for sewing, [Helen's] own figure possessed the sublimity of a woman's of the early world spinning the thread of fate—the sublimity possessed by many women of the present day who fall into the attitude required by scrubbing or sewing.

The autobiographical basis for Rachel Vinrace was only a starting-point for an imaginative character whose career was to be more adventurous than Virginia's own. The ship itself is a metaphor for Rachel: 'She was more lonely than the caravan crossing the desert', more mysterious, sustained by her own resources.

Virginia Stephen launched Rachel into an area of imaginative possibility: not what she herself was or what her biographic subjects had been. Rachel is an unacknowledged musician of unknown potentialities. Hewet, too, though drawn in part from life, is a figment of imagination: an endearing possibility. More optimistic than Rachel, he balks at her proposition that the sexes ' "should live separate; we cannot understand each other; we only bring out what's worst" '.

At first, Terence does not find Rachel attractive, but he comes to realize that, though her face varied from plain to passionate, she was always the same 'because of the extraordinary freedom with which she looked at him, and spoke as she felt'. For him, love begins with an exchange of unaccustomed honesty. He thinks: 'You could say anything—you could say everything, and yet she was never servile.'

Rachel's love is awakened earlier when Hewet and Hirst offer to share their books: 'her mind dwelt on them with a kind of physical pleasure.' Though Hewet is far from chaste—his friends teasingly call him 'Monk'—Rachel has no thought of fear. She repudiates all common forms of love chasing about the hotel—genital urgency and vanity and security—for an idea as yet unexplored: ' "What is it to be in love?" she demanded after a long silence; each word as it came into being seemed to shove itself out into an unknown sea.'

The novel is most imaginative when it leaves society behind and takes Rachel on a dreamlike journey into the heart of the jungle and then follows her mind, through illness, into death. The blend of poetry and shock in the last third of the novel is its great achievement though, as Louise DeSalvo suggests, each time it was completed, the author, too, plunged into illness.

The second phase of Rachel's journey, into unknown territory, removes her from the last bastion of Edwardian England, the hotel at Santa Marina. The novel now turns into allegory as the voyage out extends to a voyage inland, up the dark river, to view primitive lives in the depths of the jungle. Rachel goes partly out of her ingrained passivity before the wishes of her group and partly because, as Hewet tells her (in an early typescript), ' "You really want to know." '

She agrees: ' "Everything. Every thing. Not only human beings." '

As they sail up-river, Hewet reads aloud from Whitman's 'Passage to India':*

> O secret of the earth and sky!
> The Reckless soul, steering for the deep waters,
>   risking ship, and our lives
> O my brave soul!
> O farther, farther sail!

The six voyagers seem to drive 'into the heart of the night'. As in *Heart of Darkness*, their spurious habits fall away but, in contrast with *Heart of Darkness*, there is no dreadful intuition to be seized: the novel seems to refrain from judgement and simply to wait, its attention poised. This sustained act of attention may be irritating to readers used to action and conclusion; others will appreciate the honesty of the incomplete result. It is perhaps momentous enough to recognize, as a scientist, the vast tracts of the unknown. The shock of this perception comes through a bold ploy which Virginia Stephen developed for this novel and which she retained in her most experimental works: she injects silence into the narrative, letting her own medium of expression—words—fail.

On board the steamer the voyagers enter a dreamlike silence, staring into the 'deep gloom' of the unbroken spaces ahead. Men and women sleep on deck, but they are 'curtained from each other by the darkness'. Terence recognizes the irresistible force of his feeling for Rachel when he is bemused by her physical proximity but cannot see her. Carried along the current of feeling into the primitive darkness, he loses his stable image of Rachel. 'He was drawn on and on away from all he knew, slipping over barriers and past landmarks into unknown waters as the boat glided over the smooth surface of the river.'

For Terence and Rachel there is no set pattern of mutual discovery. When they extend their journey with a solitary walk in the jungle, they seem to disappear into the silence that guards the heart of this novel. This is not to be mistaken for a Victorian evasion. They do clasp and kiss, she rests against him, but this is a formal seal, peripheral to the elusive quickening of feeling which seems to come and go and rush them on. Terence tries out the conventional phrases and Rachel, in a drugged way, echoes them:

* In the earlier typescript of the novel. This is a far from accurate quotation, no more than VW's rough memory.

'We are happy together.' He did not seem to be speaking, or she to be hearing.

'Very happy,' she answered.

They continued to walk for some time in silence. Their steps unconsciously quickened.

'We love each other,' Terence said.

'We love each other,' she repeated.

The silence was then broken by their voices which joined in tones of strange unfamiliar sound which formed no words.

Unspeakable love is edged with dead words.

Back at the hotel, the machinery of mating is then set in motion. 'Love' is trivialized by the clichés of well-wishers and Rachel finds it impossible to sustain the pure sense of union. Rachel's barely stated resistance to having tea with Mrs Thornbury, to Evelyn M.'s definitions of happiness, and, finally, to Terence himself, is somehow connected with the sickness that follows. And the failure of diagnosis is connected with a profound ignorance of the nature of the patient.

Diagnosis must begin with the fact that Rachel was a musician. Until her engagement she was self-contained in her music, on board her father's ship happily absorbed in Beethoven's Opus 112 (the cantata, 'Meeresstille und glückliche Fahrt'—'Calm Sea and Happy Voyage'), then contained, again, in a room of her own in Helen's villa. The room, the music she made there, was the fount of what Emerson calls 'the sense of being which in calm hours arises . . . in the soul'. But now she loses her privacy. Hewet asks her to stop playing because he wishes to talk. He reads aloud from *Comus* and words like 'curb' and 'Brute' loom distorted with connotations for Rachel not meant by Milton. She hears of the virgin, Sabrina, who drowned herself and became immortal, 'Goddess of the silver lake'. At that point, Rachel's fatal headache begins.

Rachel's strange sickness takes her to join deformed women in their tunnel under the sea. She has no wish to see Hewet. When he kisses her, she sees, in her delirium, a woman's head sliced off with a knife. Her mind, detached from her body, lies curled up at the bottom of the sea and only comes to the surface to bid Hewet goodbye.

Virginia Stephen's experience of madness became, in this way, a fable of the submerged woman. Rachel must die: her undefined spirit can find no habitation in marriage but continues to reverberate beyond her particular lifespan. Her hallucination called for a new form of narrative that was to develop into the modern novel of the 1920s and 1930s.

The Cornwall idea recurred on a visit to Italy in 1908. Provoked by the static symmetry of a fresco by Perugino, she opened her diary and wrote the following words as though her experiment was already done: 'I attain . . . a symmetry by means of infinite discords, showing all the traces of the mind's passage through the world; achieve in the end, some kind of whole made of shivering fragments; to me this seems the natural process; the flight of the mind.' At the end of *The Voyage Out* she first put this theory into practice.

With the break in rapport between Rachel and Terence, the narrative abruptly fragments. The finale is a series of discords as Rachel's hallucinating consciousness wrenches her from the momentum of the wedding-bell plot. In the last chapter the tourists at the hotel recompose themselves after Rachel's death, fortified with chatter and chess, but it is only a mechanical harmony. In the preceding chapters, Virginia Stephen has displaced the mechanical continuity of action for psychological continuity, exposing, in her case, what lies beneath the stream of association and habit which gives Sterne and Joyce their narratives. She reaches for that intermittent life of feeling which is the source of all genuine action and which, if ignored, corrupts and deadens.

The other peculiar feat is to suggest what cannot be said. This, Terence tells Rachel, is to be the subject of his future work:

> 'What novels do you write?' she asked.
> 'I want to write a novel about Silence,' he said; 'the things people don't say. But the difficulty is immense.'

Many readers will not 'hear' what George Eliot called 'that roar which lies on the other side of silence'. Where George Eliot used 'the secret of deep human sympathy' to unlock the lives of the obscure, Virginia Stephen followed them with a slow-paced silence, pausing whenever she sensed an unvoiced intent. *The Voyage Out* offsets the groping novelist, Hewet, and the inarticulate Rachel against an articulate, sharply marked English community. Rachel, still in the making, knocks against an ex-MP, a don, a doctor with the crust of definition upon them.

What form of speech is not an echo? At one with Terence, Rachel echoes him, palely, in the jungle. At odds with him, her only recourse is a non-verbal form of communication: she replies to the questions of her lover, the novelist, with the virtuosity of her music. Terence wants to try out his notes on womanhood for his novel, for example, 'Every woman . . . an optimist, because they don't think.'

Rachel said nothing. Up and up the steep spiral of a very late Beethoven sonata she climbed, like a person ascending a ruined staircase, energetically at first, then more laboriously advancing her feet with effort until she could go no higher and returned with a run to begin at the very bottom again.

Terence, oblivious, presses her to say what, for women, corresponds to the term 'honour'.

Attacking her staircase once more, Rachel again neglected this opportunity of revealing the secrets of her sex. . . . It seemed to be reserved for a later generation to discuss them philosophically.

Rachel's elusiveness can get a bit exasperating—after all, it may signify nothing but vagueness—but her author took this risk in order to show that whatever the given language cannot express will float away, undefined. This is brought to the reader's attention when Rachel cannot reply.* To inflict a discordant silence is deadly from Rachel's point of view. It signals her withdrawal although, in other such cases, withdrawal might more plausibly terminate in frigidity or estrangement than in death. In her own life, Virginia Stephen was to find another solution. From the moment of her engagement to Leonard Woolf, in 1912, they would invent a private language that would ease communication across barriers of background and sex.

Although she completed two drafts of *The Voyage Out* after her engagement, they were the last of numerous drafts and not much affected by the new relationship. The drafts show no major change except that characters were made to talk less, less about love and less about the exploitation of women. By playing down Helen Ambrose and deepening the silence around Rachel, she made her odd heroine even more pre-eminent.

Rachel is a risky tease to the reader. She presents the same sort of challenge as Fanny Price in *Mansfield Park*, a woman of intrinsic stature who invites ready-made categories: she appears passive,

---

* VW plays up a similar crisis of abandoned translation in *To the Lighthouse* when, at dinner, Lily Briscoe refuses for a moment to reply to the academic's need to relieve his vanity.

malleable, and pitifully lacking in the animation which we expect
from heroines. Rachel does not look in the least like a heroine. Her
face lacks colour and 'definite' outline. Her author dared to make
her faceless, inarticulate, incompetent, and, except for her music,
inactive to the point of indolence. She is not merely unformed; she
is the epitome of indefiniteness.

Rachel seems blurred because she is fixed on a social structure
that is unreal to her, 'reality dwelling in what one saw and felt, but
did not talk about . . .'. Using anonymity as cover and freed by
humility, her restless intelligence stirs but is too unconventional to
risk exposure on the platform of action. She lurks obscurely
beneath the sea. Her affinity is for imagined monsters of the deep
who 'would explode if you brought them to the surface, . . .
scattering entrails to the winds'.

Through Rachel, Virginia Stephen managed to sum up the
identity that had emerged over the twenty years of her apprenticeship. She was an explorer out of Hakluyt, but of the foreign parts of
the soul. As she went through the motions of tea with Aunt Mary or
Kitty Maxse, her life was shaping itself in her imagination as a
voyage out. 'The sea is . . . more congenial to me than any human
being', she confided to Clive in 1908. To all appearances stricken by
mental illness, she was, like Rachel, a deep-sea creature. Yet, unlike
Rachel, she came to the surface. She broke free of convention and
made a new life in Bloomsbury.

Virginia found it difficult to act. She needed the leadership of her
more Bohemian sister. After Leslie Stephen's death, Vanessa acted
decisively. She dislodged their accumulated possessions from Hyde
Park Gate, detached the four desirable members of the family from
the Duckworths, and found a new home for them on the other side
of London. They left the solid red brick of Kensington for the
superb fadedness of Bloomsbury. Bloomsbury was a sequence of
squares, stretching from Bedford on the west to Mecklenburgh on
the east, from Gordon and Tavistock on the north to Bloomsbury
on the south, each square with its own character, yet all of a piece,
symmetrical, urban, and once the haunt of writers and artists. The
move meant to the sisters a dramatic break with Victorian stuffiness
for, in Bloomsbury, they gathered round them a coterie of talented
young men just down from Cambridge—including Lytton
Strachey, Maynard Keynes, and E. M. Forster—who blended
friendship and freedom of mind. Bloomsbury outspokenness

helped Virginia to overcome the problem of modesty in the years immediately following her father's death when she still measured her writing by his resistance to female presumption. One night in April 1908, she dreamt that she was showing the manuscript of her novel to Leslie Stephen, and he snorted and dropped it on the table. 'You don't realise the depth of modesty in to which I fall', she told Clive Bell. She turned Silence to effect in her novels but, initially, it was a weakness, the temptation not to speak at all.

If 1897 was the crucial year for the forming of Virginia Stephen's mind and character, 1907–9 were the formative years for her as a writer, with 'Reminiscences' the turning-point. That unfinished memoir of her childhood, her parents, and Stella, brought her up against the 'arrow-like speed' of the single life 'and its tragic departure'. Recurring personal tragedy, which had silenced her diary in 1897, was given a measure of expression in 1907. She found a theme for her novels in life's perpetual waste and repair. As her mother's ghost revisited her imagination, gliding very erect in her old shabby cloak with her level, large-eyed gaze, Virginia Stephen saw how she might show the past to be at once domestic, over-familiar, and yet extraordinary, elusive. Her confronting death, here, for the first time, after Thoby's sudden death in November 1906, lies behind the questions framed in later novels: what is the structure and purpose of our truncated existence?

Her writing brought her into the company of women of the past. Her memory was stirred by her mother in the 'Reminiscences', by Elizabeth I and Hester Stanhope, Jane Carlyle, Charlotte Brontë and George Eliot, until she came to see the character of great women behind her own writing; other imagined women, Joan Martyn or Miss Willatt, passing in the silence of obscure lives behind her own life.

The apprenticeship years were also the most experimental in her career. Her innovative ideas for the modern novel can be traced back to theoretical statements in unexpected places: in the Cornwall diary of 1905, where she trod out the stream-of-consciousness novel to come, and in the travel diary where, in 1906, she conceived of an art that would blend delicacy of treatment with strength of form. Arriving at 6 a.m. at Constantinople, she saw St Sophia 'like a treble globe of bubbles frozen solid, floating out to meet us. For it is fashioned in the shape of some fine substance, thin as glass, blown in plump curves; save that it is also substantial as a pyramid'. The light of a butterfly's wing on the arches of the cathedral, she says later in *To the Lighthouse*; a frame which could be ruffled with a breath but which could not be dislodged with a team of horses.

Another repository for Virginia Stephen's theory was a review of 1905 where she considered the difficulty of the autobiographic mode: 'Confronted with the terrible spectre of themselves, the bravest are inclined to run away or shade their eyes.' One type of evasion was garrulous subjectivity, a mere verbal dribbling; another type of evasion was sham impersonality when the writer pretends to 'an oracular and infallible nature'. Her distinction between cheap egotism and the stress of genuine self-scrutiny was basic to the kind of fictional autobiography that she developed in *The Voyage Out* and *To the Lighthouse*, with their authentic emotional detail. Her model of honesty remained her father with his 'intemperate candour'.

Through genuine self-scrutiny, Virginia Stephen created a new kind of heroine, easily defaced, therefore faceless and, because we cannot *see* her, we can hear her breathe, and faintly, far-off, pick up her elusive note. After her father, the captain of the ship, leaves her with the sisterly, unconventional Helen, this note first sounds—a strange note, to Hewet's detective ear, as she and Helen look out of the window at night into the dark garden of the foreign villa. They speak in broken sentences like people in their sleep. Their snatches of memory, in low, inexpressive tones, barely break the night's silence. 'Very gentle their voices sounded, as if they fell through the waves of the sea.'

In the process of writing her first novel, Virginia Stephen brought herself to the surface and worked out an idea of love. She thought that a couple might come to know each other not through word or deed (which crumble into banality) but, intuitively, in the silent self. This was her unspoken pre-condition for marriage, which she undertook at the age of thirty as she completed the novel. The years 1905–15 took Virginia through a long, secretive, and sickly incubation but they also marked the beginning of a new active phase in her life. She moved to Bloomsbury. She married. She published. In what way did she translate her solitary convictions into action?

THE LIFE COMPOSED

I come to shape here . . . the story of my life and set it
before you as a complete thing.

The Waves

8. *Freedom and Friendship*

B y the end of her apprenticeship, Virginia Stephen had framed her life as an experiment in which she would live as freely as a circle of like-minded friends permits. The deliberate way that she chose her milieu, her working habits, her home, her mate is mirrored in the way that she composed her works, coming down on moments of rapport, beauty, and insight, and flying determinedly past any stale design for success and happiness, whether it be the conventional marriage or the wheeling and dealing of the literary market-place which she called the Underworld. Bernard, the writer in *The Waves*, wishes, he tells his reader, 'to give you my life'. It is a composed life, like those of his five distinctive friends, composed in each case around an unobtrusive but repeated phrase—'a limpet clinging to a rock' or 'the nymph of the fountain, always wet'— which gives the distinctive life its internal coherence. Compared with this, the set design of standard biography is, says Bernard, 'a convenience, a lie' because it does not see, beneath the platform of public action, the half-finished sentences and half-discernible acts on which the real life turns. Virginia Stephen's passion for biography came from her father but, by the time she wrote her satire on standard biography, as early as 1909, she surpassed him in originality.

She meant to become a writer, and for a young woman of her generation to take up a profession or art (she later explained in her first polemical piece on the position of women), she had to make a dash for freedom. It meant not only a break with the family circle but with accepted notions of womanliness and decency. This divergence, she went on, was 'a species of torture more exquisitely painful, I believe, than any that man can imagine'.

Whatever Bloomsbury meant to others, for her it was a revolt against Hyde Park Gate. Her various memoirs, her diary-essays of 1903, and her Bloomsbury diary of 1904–5 help to explain the conditions that made home intolerable and how drastically, in the sisters' eyes, they were changed by their move to Bloomsbury. It is clear from Virginia's repeated comments that her Bloomsbury friends were important not for their thoughts but, at first, for an atmosphere of mental freedom. Later, when she built them up in her imagination, they were to become more important as a rudimentary source for *The Waves*, which explores the relation of six people who form a lifelong coterie.

As *To the Lighthouse* composed a final view of Virginia Stephen's childhood in the first stage of this biography, and as *The Voyage Out* set the seal on a young woman's search for knowledge in the second stage, so the climax of the third stage is *The Waves*, in which the mature novelist was to formulate the classic outline of the significant life.

October 1904 marked the beginning of a new life. Virginia Stephen, aged twenty-two, no longer had to look out on old Mrs Redgrave washing her neck across a narrow street. She looked out on trees which seemed to fountain up in the middle of Gordon Square. More important, she now had a separate work-room with a very high desk where she would stand to write for two and a half hours each morning. She stood, she claimed, to be even with Vanessa who complained of standing for hours at an easel, but the posture may have suited the seething energy that she inherited from her father. Just before lunch she liked to 'dash' down the Tottenham Court Road, poking into old furniture shops, and then to loiter in old book shops in Oxford Street. Everything was to be changed, she recalled in the Memoir Club essay, 'Old Bloomsbury': painting and writing would come first; they would drink coffee after dinner instead of tea at nine; they would do away with Victorian red plush and elaborate Morris wallpaper, wash their walls with plain distemper and furnish their tall, clean, rather cold rooms in white and green chintz. Vanessa resurrected their great aunts' Indian shawls, draped them over chairs and tables, and their colours took on a barbaric richness against the white walls. The Watts portraits of their parents were displayed and, in the hall, a whole row of Mrs Cameron's photographs of their mother opposite photographs of Herschel, Lowell, Darwin, Tennyson, Browning, and Meredith. After Vanessa's marriage in 1907, Virginia and Adrian Stephen moved to the derelict elegance of Fitzroy Square with its fine Adam façades. There, the eighteenth-century houses had become lodging-houses, offices, nursing homes, and small artisans' work-shops. The Stephens were the only inhabitants to have a house to themselves complete with family cook, maid, and dog.

The sisters now planned their day around work, and their bonding—which had once been a conspiratorial necessity—became now a fertile basis both for their experiments in art and for their new group, giving that group its domestic character as their brother's friends shifted from male-dominated Cambridge into a feminized setting dominated by two original and determined women.

Of the sisters, Vanessa was the more overtly daring. She flaunted bawdy talk (as Adrian observed in 1909) and, at a party in 1911, shook off all her upper clothing as she danced. She declared to Sydney Waterlow that she wanted to form a circle on the principle of complete sexual freedom.

Virginia appeared to follow. When Vanessa took a lover, Roger Fry, in 1911, Virginia bathed naked with Rupert Brooke in the river at Grantchester. That year Virginia set up house with a number of bachelors (including Leonard Woolf) at 34 Brunswick Square and, when George Duckworth protested its impropriety, Vanessa retorted pertly, on her sister's behalf, that the Foundling Hospital was handy. The sisters had African dresses made of printed cotton. They dressed themselves as Gauguin pictures and careered round Crosby Hall at a ball to mark the end of the second Post-Impressionist Exhibition in 1912. But, as the years passed, it became obvious that this flaunting of rebellion did not wholly engage Virginia, who proved more concerned with mental than with sexual freedom.

Julia Stephen had upheld womanly acquiescence with all the attraction of her monumental character. It was her clumsy replacement, George, who had provoked rebellion by the force with which he had driven his sisters into the marriage market. From his point of view, George was simply carrying out the ethos of their Pattle family in which the hereditary strain of female beauty was sold to the highest bidder. Virginia noticed how their aunt, Virginia Pattle, put her daughters through tortures, compared with which 'the Chinese shoe is negligible', in order to marry them to aristocrats. Virginia, still in the schoolroom, was held by the spectacle of her sister dressed in white satin like a potential peeress, yet concealing beneath the blue enamel butterfly in her hair 'one passionate desire—for paint and turpentine'. Soon it was the younger sister's turn to undergo the season and, in an agony of shyness, to be sent off in a hired hansom cab, with straw on the floor, to a ball at one of the great London houses where she would know and speak to nobody all evening and stand, crushed by the crowd, against a wall.

Duncan Grant, who first met Virginia during what she called 'the Greek slave years', said that she would resist an unforeseen introduction with an expression of blazing defiance and a few carefully chosen banalities. Once, when George took her to dine with a pair of aristocratic dowagers, she confounded polite conversation with a torrent of Plato. In one of her funniest satiric pieces, '22 Hyde Park Gate', she recalls that disastrous evening when the dowagers were outraged first by the impropriety of Plato and, later, by grunting sexual intercourse staged by French actors at the theatre, while she, playing up her set role of virginal bewilderment, overheard George and the Countess of Carnarvon (ex-Vice-Reine of Canada and Ireland) kiss discreetly behind a marble pillar.

Although Virginia was ignored, like Vanessa, at balls and concluded that she, too, must be a social failure, she was able to be more detached. In her diary description of 'A Garden Dance' (30 June 1903) she noted that a stout lady bade them welcome 'with a smile which had spent itself on fifty others & would have to do duty for one hour more to come'. The crush was such that only very few could waltz in the centre of the room and even these looked 'like flies struggling in a dish of sticky liquid'. She watched the ladies flow out of the windows and roll in cascades of lace and silk down the garden slope: she could make of it 'a French painting' and, when she got home, matter-of-factly turn to a book of astronomy on her bedside table. Since she was anyway in the position of observer she preferred to watch a dance in Queens Gate from the safety of her own bedroom window, wearing her nightgown open and her hair tumbled on her forehead. She could see the dance floor as 'a farmyard scattered with grain on which bright pigeons kept descending'. Or, when the musicians dashed into a waltz, 'it was as though the room were instantly flooded with water. After a moment's hesitation first one couple, then another, leapt into mid-stream, and went round and round in the eddies.'

Virginia was never, as was Vanessa, wholly disenchanted with society. Her anger was directed more specifically against George.

'Kiss me, kiss me', George terminated all argument. She felt like an unfortunate minnow shut up with a turbulent whale.

All mention of George Duckworth in her letters and satires

Virginia, aged ten, inspects her parents at St Ives

Virginia Stephen realized
that, to Leonard Woolf,
she seemed remote and
self-contained 'like a hill',
1 May 1912

Virginia Woolf and Lytton Strachey at Garsington, 1921

dismissed him lightly as a fatuous snob but in her last breakdown, the doctor reported, she said that she was haunted by George Duckworth whom she had 'evidently adored'. If this is true, it would explain her blaming George for earlier breakdowns. George, as his sisters' first 'lover',* exerted some power over Virginia when he would invade her bedroom—to comfort her, he later explained to Dr Savage, for the illness of her father. Here is her version in '22 Hyde Park Gate':

> Sleep had almost come to me. The room was dark. The house silent. Then, creaking stealthily, the door opened; treading gingerly, someone entered. 'Who?' I cried. 'Don't be frightened', George whispered. 'And don't turn on the light, oh beloved. Beloved—' and he flung himself on my bed, and took me in his arms.

It is impossible to know what truly happened. After Julia and Stella died and Leslie Stephen withdrew, an adult offer of emotional warmth—however uncontrolled and ill-judged—may have been irresistible to a girl like Virginia. George was thought very handsome and his combination of sensual lips and considerate manners made him the pet of society ladies. In any case, his mastery as effective head of the family, his age (he was thirty-six, his sister twenty), her dependence (he had a thousand pounds a year, she fifty) backed his overtures. George, she said, had been 'in a position to press his mould tight upon us'.

When she came down in a new evening dress, George would look her over as if she were a horse in a ring. 'Go and tear it up', he said once, in a rasping, peevish voice, spying in some ingenious detail a defiance of social standards.

George was a stickler for correctness. He wore a 'slip' during the day, a sort of under-waistcoat, providing white edges to the neck-opening of the waistcoat proper. He remained a virgin until his marriage. His manner was that of 'the good boy whose virtue has been rewarded'. George's combination of lurking desire and propriety led, predictably, to conflicting signals. Though he fondled his sister by night, by day he ridiculed her appearance and spoke of her as 'the poor goat'.

The hypocrisy of George was the hub of Virginia's troubles. She

---

* 'Yes, the old ladies of Kensington and Belgravia never knew that George Duckworth was not only father and mother, brother and sister to those poor Stephen girls; he was their lover also.' (*MB*, p. 155).

came to fear that sexual love would always be connected with contempt and so to her idea of marriage as 'a very low down affair'. That George Duckworth was furtive and absurd did not mean that he was not dangerous. In *The Voyage Out*, Virginia Stephen joked about the Duckworth danger to a girl's voyage of discovery: the ship's captain remarks that the most dreaded of navigational perils is said to be *Sedgius aquatici* which, to the layman, is 'a kind of duck-weed'.

Under the circumstances Virginia retained a fair spark of optimism. There is hope of a better kind of love in *The Voyage Out* and she was able to make an interesting marriage. Yet, possibly, the taint of George was never quite eradicated. It came back oddly after George's death in the late 1930s. In *Between the Acts* the mature Isa imagines herself and the secretly loved farmer Haines 'like two swans. . . . But his snow-white breast was circled with a tangle of dirty duckweed', in other words, a demeaning sexual tie. The intelligent and sensitive Isa is similarly tied to a stockbroker, Giles Oliver. At the end of the novel, Giles makes a comic effort to placate Isa for his infidelity with the offer of a ready-peeled banana which she refuses coldly. Yet under the spell of the family tie Isa will continue to succumb: her resistance is an ephemeral drama between the acts of lovemaking.

To go back to Virginia's expression of defiance in 1903, the last year at Hyde Park Gate, there was not only her sense of social failure and sexual abuse, but also the female 'mould' which George pressed upon them. Complete animation was not wanted. Victorian women look like eggs: round, featureless, smooth. There are the much-reproduced Beresford photographs of Virginia in 1903 looking exquisitely lifeless. Another, back in 1901, shows her slight, expressionless, frozen in her white dress, contemplated by a masterful George. In her unpublished 'Thoughts upon Social Success' Virginia Stephen defined the normal woman, in the summer of 1903. This woman specialized in one branch of learning: social skill. She lived solely in the evening: the dinner bell, striking eight, called her into existence. What did she talk about? This, to Virginia, was 'the ultimate mystery'. The synthetic creature evades the eye of her own sex: 'If I come by she is silent', she observed, 'she folds all her petals closely round her.' In 1908, in Perugia, she observed a pretty English girl whose trade mark was an 'invariable' simplicity and sweet temper. She thought how a generation of

Victorian mothers had bequeathed these attributes to their daughters and pitied such poverty of self-conception: 'Old mother nature is not a skinflint; human beings might soar very high.'

Virginia Stephen's idea of freedom was straightforward and practical: a small income of one's own and a room of one's own, just enough money and privacy to free the mind. Margaret Schlegel, E. M. Forster's independent heroine, says bluntly that one cannot have independent thoughts without independent means. Virginia later declared that women had failed to distinguish themselves until the Victorian age because, by law, their incomes were controlled and their privacy swallowed by domestic demands.

So much has been made of the Bloomsbury Group that gradually collected around this feminine core at 46 Gordon Square and 29 Fitzroy Square. It has been described in terms of an ideology derived from the Cambridge philosopher, G. E. Moore (by Maynard Keynes) and in terms of its variety of astonishing characters (by Quentin Bell) but for Virginia Stephen her new friends were at first only a prop to her new freedom to plan her life.

The sisters were not at first Bohemian, but they caused murmurs because they no longer bothered to dress for dinner or to entertain in a formal way. What they liked was what Virginia called 'shabby crony talk' with Thoby's friends till two or three in the morning, fortified by whisky, buns, and cocoa, in their large, ground-floor sitting-room with Gurth, the sheepdog, as sole chaperon.

It was not the intellects of Thoby's friends that so delighted the Stephen sisters; it was a freedom of speech which would have been unremarkable on the staircases of Trinity College, Cambridge, but to which these women were totally unaccustomed in the presence of young men. Virginia recorded in her diary for 8 March 1905 how, on returning from Morley College, she 'found Bell, and we talked about the nature of good till almost one!' The event is marked by a rare exclamation (another follows her first cigarette with Lady Beatrice Thynne). Part of the charm of the regular Thursday discussions that followed was their austere abstraction: their subjects were 'good' or 'beauty' or 'happiness' or 'reality'. But they were free to be ordinary if they liked, to talk about the weather or the dog. There was not a rarefied atmosphere of self-conscious brilliance, simply a feeling that acute intelligence was present even if unexpressed. Thoby's friends criticized his sisters' arguments as severely as their own and, as they did so, all the encumbrance of appearance and behaviour which George had laid upon them seemed to melt away. 'Never have I listened so intently to each step and half-step in an argument', Virginia said. 'Never have I been at such pains to sharpen and launch my own little dart.'

The unlovable woman was always the woman who used words to effect. She was caricatured as a tattle, a scold, a shrew, a witch. Particularly in the Victorian age women felt the pressure to relinquish language, and 'nice' women were quiet. Mrs Ramsay smiles at her husband silently. Her only speech to him is in answer to *his* needs. She can speak freely only in the darkest hour of night to another woman, the odd Lily Briscoe. Bloomsbury broke down the ideal of feminine silence. There was eventually no subject, not even what they earnestly called 'copulation', that was not freely discussed in mixed company. Thoby Stephen's Cambridge friends were amazed by the boldness and scepticism of his two sisters.

'You might have discussed the qualities of my inmost soul or body without making me blush and Virginia is equal to saying anything to anybody's face', Vanessa told Roger Fry when he joined their circle.

Vanessa was the more eager of the two. Having been more responsible than Virginia, and having had the burden fall on her at eighteen of running the enormous Hyde Park Gate establishment, she tried all the more determinedly to protect her right to paint. She had also been less obviously gifted than her younger sister (her father had praised her beauty but had made rather caustic remarks about her 'random splotches'). In other words, Vanessa needed the Bloomsbury Group more than Virginia. For her it was more exclusive, more a barricade against society. Virginia, by contrast, came to revel in certain society. A distant relative, Octavia Wilberforce, likened her social skills to those of a first-class tennis player who can catch up with the most erratic or difficult ball.

Needing Bloomsbury less, Virginia participated with reservations. It is curious to compare her criticisms of her friends as they were with what she made of them, following Thoby's outlines, in her imagination. She saw at once through the pretensions of Saxon Sydney-Turner, Clive Bell, Strachey, and Walter Lamb. They implied, she remarked in 1906, that tomes of gigantic significance, as yet 'unprintable', reposed in their desk drawers—tomes which, she could predict, would never appear. She noticed that they liked to crown certain authors with the epithets 'supreme' and 'astounding' but if the public showed signs of appreciating the same things, they quickly transferred their praise to some more obscure head. She teased Thoby's friends for being 'pale, preoccupied & silent' as though during their three years at Cambridge 'some awful communication had been made them, & they went burdened with a secret too dreadful to impart'. Their regard for their own abilities was 'the last illusion that is left to them'. Leonard Woolf's autobiography projects a Virginia Woolf deeply influenced by his Cambridge set, but her initial comments were sarcastic—she was merciless in her ridicule of their poems—and her early work, both the unpublished fiction and the theoretic reviews, showed her independent development. 'To dwell upon Bloomsbury as an influence', she later told a prospective critic, 'is liable to lead to judgements that . . . have no basis in fact.'

Among Virginia's papers there is a cutting fictionalized portrait of Saxon Sydney-Turner as the prodigy of learning who suggests genius but fails to perform. Saxon's friends were dazzled by his prodigious memory for obscure fact; Virginia was less impressed by feats of brain. She asks, practically, what this clever bachelor did with his life—for its obscurity hid no unseen usefulness.

The same practical attitude—what Clive Bell called her 'Victorianism'—made her impatient of artiness. Bell should have been at the Bar, she would say, only half-joking; Duncan Grant should have been a soldier; Lytton Strachey should have been an Indian civil servant.

For Lytton Strachey, 'the Goth' (Thoby Stephen) was the pinnacle of creation. In December 1904 he was introduced to 'the Visigoths', Thoby's sisters. 'On Sunday I called at the Gothic mansion', he wrote to his friend, Leonard Woolf, 'and had tea with Vanessa and Virginia. The latter is rather wonderful, quite witty, full of things to say . . .'. He found her wildly fanciful. Strachey's talk, in his peculiar exclamatory counter-tenor, was of being 'shattered', of life being 'too fearful'. He presented to Virginia the 'slightly stingy appearance' of someone who lacked warmth and could not afford to be generous. This was to produce (in *Eminent Victorians*) 'that metallic & conventionally brilliant style which prevents his writing from reaching, to my judgement, the first rate'.

It is important to distinguish the two strong Stephen sisters and the men whom they eventually married from the 'paleness' of Old

Bloomsbury.* 'Excessive paleness is what I think worries me most', Strachey wrote to Leonard Woolf as an undergraduate. 'The Taupe [E. M. Forster] in his wonderful way I imagine saw this about me, and feeling that he himself verged upon the washed-out, shuddered.' The 'Gothic' Stephens were quite different from the Cambridge waterspiders of John Maynard Keynes's celebrated description: 'I can see us . . . gracefully skimming, as light and reasonable as air, the surface of the stream without any contact at all with the eddies and currents underneath.'

These pale, skimming young men were miraculously re-created in Virginia's imagination as, during school holidays, Thoby had used to re-create boys at Evelyn's preparatory school and boys at Clifton College, Bristol. She thought about these boys whom she had never met 'as if they were characters in Shakespeare. I made up stories about them myself.' It became a shared fiction, like the nursery stories. 'We talked of them by the hour', she recalled, 'rambling about the country or sitting over the fire in my bedroom.' When Thoby went on to Cambridge he told her of Clive Bell, a mixture between Shelley and sporting squire; of Lytton Strachey, a prodigy of wit who had French pictures in his room and a passion for Pope. He told her, too, of the trembling Jew, Leonard Woolf, who dreamt one night that he was throttling a man and dreamt with such violence that when he woke up he had pulled his thumb out of joint. Virginia was at once 'inspired with the deepest interest':

When I asked why he trembled, Thoby somehow made me feel it was part of his nature—he was so violent, so savage; he so despised the whole human race. . . . Most people, I gathered, rather rubbed along, and came to terms with things. Woolf did not and Thoby thought it sublime.

Naturally, when she met unimpressive-looking mortals, she was disappointed. And then, perhaps out of loyalty to Thoby's memory, she gradually built up his friends again in her imagination. By 1925 they were so interwoven with her sense of her own existence that she admitted to herself 'if 6 people died, it is true that my life would cease: by wh[ich] I mean, it would run so thin that though it might go on, would it have any relish? Imagine Leonard, Nessa Duncan Lytton, Clive, Morgan [E. M. Forster] all dead.'

She re-created Lytton first as the misogynist don in *The Voyage*

* VW associated paleness with homosexuality. In 1925 she comments in her *Diary* (iii, p. 10) that 'the pale star of the Bugger has been in the ascendant too long'.

Out and later, as she grew more fond of him, as the exquisitely cultivated but limp William Rodney in *Night and Day* and then, finally, as the brilliant, cutting Neville in *The Waves*, whose fretting ambition and eccentric homosexuality find an ideal refuge in Cambridge. Another of the Cambridge set, E. M. Forster, became in her imagination a pale blue butterfly. 'I used to watch him from behind a hedge as he flitted through Gordon Square, erratic, irregular, with his bag, on his way to catch a train.'

Durability and imagination, these are the two irreducible conditions of proper friendship as defined in *The Waves*. Six friends live in one another's generous imaginations. They are continually being created in the way Shakespeare created the beloved of his sonnets. Thoby had been a reserved young man, and Virginia pursued his unknown ghost through two novels, trying to deduce Jacob from his room, Percival from his friends.

The missing Thoby, Lytton's pinnacle of creation, remained the presiding genius of Bloomsbury, in the same curious way as in *The Waves* the dead, magnificent Percival remains the focus for the lives of his six friends. *The Waves* is the story of a set of friends who do not let marriages, jobs, and other differences interfere with friendship. It celebrates friendship not as it actually was but as it might be. Despite Virginia's reservations, the Bloomsbury Group was special enough, in its lifelong loyalties, to allow her to imagine an ideal and to write a kind of lyric poem: an ode to Friendship that was also an elegy to Thoby. 'I had him so much in my mind', she said to her sister when she finished the book. 'I have a dumb rage still at his not being with us always.'

The original group was an extension of the Stephen family and retained a domestic character (as distinct from the frivolous, scandal-ridden Bloomsbury that emerged after 1910 with the advent of Ottoline Morrell, Slade painters like Dora Carrington, and the Newnham College 'neo-pagans'—Marjorie Strachey and Ka Cox of the circle of Rupert Brooke). Quentin Bell says that it was cemented in common grief for Thoby's death, which broke down barriers between his friends and sisters, who were all passionately attached to his memory. For the Stephen sisters to marry Thoby's friends, Clive Bell and Leonard Woolf, for Virginia initially to consider Lytton Strachey, was to link themselves imaginatively to Thoby. Lytton Strachey wrote to Leonard Woolf in Ceylon:

May 24th, 1907

The grandeur of him!—Isn't it enough to make one go about in sackcloth
& ashes for the rest of one's days—, to treat life as a valley of desolation . . . .

Virginia used to wander about London, reciting Stevenson's 'In
Memoriam F.A.S.':

> You alone have crossed the melancholy stream,
> Yours the pang, but his, O his, the undiminished
> Undecaying gladness, undeparted dream.

Her private grief was distilled in 'Sympathy', an unpublished
meditation on death encased in a veneer of fiction. The name
Humphrey Hammond appears in the death column. It shocks a
friend, casually glancing at *The Times*. He sees the body 'male and
unyielding stiff' and eyes 'with the young man's look of resolution'
closed. Worse, the friend recalls half-framed thoughts that now will
not be known. And with this awakening to the final unknowability
of the dead comes a deeper loss: 'when I think of him I scarcely see
anything of him. . . . There is the yellow armchair in which he sat,
shabby but still solid enough, surviving us all; . . . but he is
ephemeral as the dusty light which stripes the wall and carpet . . . .
The sun stripes a million years into the future, a broad yellow path;
passing an infinite distance beyond this house and town; passing so
far that nothing but sea remains.' Seeds of the two novels are here:
the fragmentary story of Jacob who leaves only a room to speak for
him and the story of Percival whose sudden end draws his friends to
mark the divide between mortality and timeless nature.

The point of 'Sympathy' is that death should stir the imagination
in this way and, also, remove barriers between living and dead: 'The
simple young man whom I hardly knew had, then, concealed in him
the immense power of death. He has . . . fused the separate entities
by ceasing.' He leads his friend mentally to the water's edge. 'Must
I go back?' the bereaved one asks as the roar of traffic sounds across
a gulf. Buses conglomerate, the clock strikes midday. 'No, no.'

Virginia Stephen speaks most directly through this refusal. For
her, death tears off the veil of existence so that grief, for all its
depression and even madness, brings the clarity essential for her art:

How death has changed everything, as, in an eclipse of the sun, colours go
out. . . . Death lies behind leaves and houses and the smoke wavering up. . . .

So, from an express train, I have looked upon hills and fields and seen the man with the scythe look up from the hedge as we pass, and lovers lying in the long grass staring at me without disguise as I stared at them without disguise.

In the end, it turns out that the Humphrey who died was someone else. The morning post brings a letter inviting the friend to dinner at Humphrey's house. Almost disappointed, the friend is forced to relinquish his dreams of death as the letter flings him back upon the banalities of dinner, business, and moving house.

Virginia Stephen despised indiscriminate ephemeral ties which she calls in one manuscript 'the ramshackle jerrybuilt houses run up, here & there, called friendships, called loves'. The strength of the Bloomsbury Group lay in the fact that it was bound by no aesthetic rules as were the 'Men of 1914', Pound, Wyndham Lewis, Joyce, and Eliot. It lived on affection. This is the difference too between Bloomsbury and other modernist groups, Hemingway's or Sartre's, which conducted a café life that was, by contrast, studiously anti-domestic and anti-sentimental.

In 1919 she noticed the wider hypnotic attraction that Bloomsbury was beginning to exercise, the source of which was a Victorian confidence in the social bond that lingered on in Bloomsbury and may account for so much Bloomsbury nostalgia. It may be as relics, not as the avant-garde, that their attraction persists.

It is often thought impossible to state what Bloomsbury stood for since the Group had no formal basis. But it did share certain values. The Stephens, Strachey, and Forster were descendants of the Victorian intelligentsia: they made much of friendship and manners and, though manners were deliberately changed, they were carefully observed: slouching instead of deportment, cigarettes instead of kid-gloves, free speech instead of modest blushes. Virginia always remembered but never practised her mother's parting injunction to 'hold yourself straight, my little Goat'. When Leonard Woolf came upon the Group in 1911 he was struck by how they sat: 'Harry saw silent figures lying back in their chairs and Camilla very still, one hand hanging loosely unclasped over the arm of her chair, looking down so that her eyes seemed closed.' This became Virginia's characteristic posture, almost insolently indolent. Silence would never have been tolerated for a moment in the drawing-room at Hyde Park Gate where the sisters were schooled to keep conversation flowing. At the Victorian dinner table in *To the*

Lighthouse, Lily Briscoe has to renounce her experiment of not responding to a vain academic. Lily resents the price women must pay for domestic harmony. 'She had not been sincere.' This was the Bloomsbury code: to speak the truth.

Bloomsbury practised a polite disregard of worldly opinion. It had a strong sense of the ridiculous and applied it to such conventionally serious subjects as the British Navy, the Empire, glory, and power. This is the precise note that Virginia Woolf's work shares with the Bloomsbury Group. She ridicules the circus trickery of Tansley's academic ambitions and the boastful-little-boy heroics that incite men to battle. She is mildly astonished by the pretensions of the MP and Harley Street. Adrian Stephen spoke to Vanessa Bell of being a 'spectator', not in the sense of being an outsider himself but 'almost everyone else seems to be outside any life that is worth living'. Forster uses the word 'saved' for those of his characters who do not give way to social tyrants.

Bloomsbury's calm assurance that it stands out against a philistine world ruled by fools sets readers on edge from the 1930s to the present day but, as Noel Annan insists in his excellent essay on Leonard Woolf, their political attitudes *were* admirable. If the public is now more sceptical of the necessity of proclaiming the superiority of the white race and its right to rule colonies, some credit, says Annan, must go to members of the Bloomsbury Group. Policies for the African colonies, framed by Leonard Woolf for the Labour Party between the wars and considered then too advanced, became the commonplaces of Macmillan in the 1960s—but, grumbled Leonard, implemented far too late.

The great influence on Virginia came not from any writer in the group but from her sister. Apart from their practical reciprocity they were, in a more subtle way, co-workers. And if the sisters were, indeed, the foundation of Bloomsbury, it is fitting that it was Vanessa Bell who finally painted the group's portrait, just as her sister immortalized the group in *The Waves*.

Vanessa Bell's covers for her sister's books were attractive in design and colour but inappropriate. Their wavering lines and tranquil, drooping tulips give no hint of the witty, incisive mind inside the covers. Yet when Vanessa Bell turns to people, in particular to women, her work quickens. There are two superb paintings in the Tate, a 1914 portrait of her husband's mistress, Mary Hutchinson, looking like a flat-browed yellow reptile, and a symbolic work, *Studland Beach*, painted in 1912, the year after she broke free from marriage. On a bare, hot beach sit a few figures. Two backs in the foreground are, to judge from 1911 photographs of a family holiday at Studland, Dorset, Virginia Stephen and Vanessa Bell's son, Julian. The figures huddle in two groups, bundled into obscuring clothes and hats, but in the middle of the canvas there stands a woman about to enter a changing booth on the edge of the sea. Her hair is already loosened and her arms bare. A lone, pillar-like figure in her sturdy severity, she has turned her back on the curved crouchers close to the sand. She is dominated only by the white changing booth which surrounds her as a frame.

There are two experimental paintings of women where Vanessa Bell shares her sister's view with uncanny exactitude. ('Do you think we have the same pair of eyes, only different spectacles?', Virginia once asked.) *The Tub* (1917) makes the same kind of break with artistic tradition as Rachel Vinrace. *The Tub* presents a woman's view of the nude. The woman's body is round and long-limbed, but the focus of the painting is her downbent, introspective face as she finishes off her plait. Her nudity is not a display but a stripping-away. Behind her there is a large, empty tub, so placed that one looks directly at its bottom. It awaits the woman, an empty vessel which she must fill, yet she lingers, thinking.

Writing of Vanessa Bell's *Portrait of a Lady* (1912), Richard Shone remarked 'a certain unemphatic air of mystery'. But this is no beguiling Mona Lisa whose mystery is spurious, part of her equipment. The mystery comes partly from a face shadowed by ornamental hair and partly from the unguarded expressionlessness, as though the artist has caught the woman in a moment of unstudied repose just as Virginia Woolf was to catch Mrs Ramsay as the beam of the lighthouse hits her. The eyes of Vanessa Bell's Lady are unseeing. Her mouth is unsmiling—not sad, not inviting, not composed in any communicative act. It is simply closed. The mystery lies in the firmly closed lips, the inward-looking eyes, the slight hunch of the body, a picture of unspoken intelligence which is perfectly complemented by characters such as Mrs Ramsay and Isa Oliver. Both sisters play up the gap between the silent, placid, decorous conduct and the inward mental action.

Duncan Grant always painted Vanessa Bell as a formidable presence. In a 1916-17 portrait of her in her farmhouse, Charleston, she gazes past the viewer, open-eyed, at some person or event off the canvas. Although the pose is reclining, here is no passive madonna: her expressiveness is startling, concentrated in the latent determination of an arm flung across the back of the earth-brown sofa and the almost mesmeric force of judging blue eyes. The warm tones of flesh and sofa are balanced against the cool tones of her eyes and the soft long dress, the tones of cold, sunstroked waters in the still hollows of rocks. Vanessa's body does not repose on the sofa. It is poised like an animal's on guard to defend its territory. The curves of her cheeks and lips glow with pulsing life. There is an unmistakable air of strength—the woman nobly planned to warn, to comfort, and command.

In 1916 Vanessa Bell rented Charleston in Sussex as a refuge for pacifists where they could do legitimate farm work. Life at Charleston is said to have been a comic mix of happy improvisation for any number of visitors together with middle-class props, the cook, the governess, good books, and good manners. The two houses that the sisters leased near Lewes reflect their differences. Virginia's choice, Asheham House, is lonely and buried, and reached by a path through a wood. It has an air of mystery, with its pointed Gothic windows and myriad small panes. At Charleston, Vanessa opened her home as a protector, like her mother. At Asheham, Virginia tramped alone, like her father, and wrote.

Within the charmed circle of Bloomsbury and at Charleston, Vanessa Bell presided, painting or sewing in her impregnable pool of calm, and round her the sister darted, her niece recalls, 'like the dragon-fly round the waterlily'. Virginia Stephen put something of her relation to Vanessa into that of the enquiring Rachel and her free-thinking aunt, Helen Ambrose in *The Voyage Out*. The very names Helen and Rachel suggest a contrast of Greek and Biblical figures: Vanessa's statuesque splendour; Virginia eager, impulsive, searching.

The most interesting portrait of Vanessa was painted when she was sixty-three, a full-length study by Duncan Grant in 1942. It is easy to connect that face with that of the child of two in 1881 in whom Leslie Stephen saw, behind the mother's beauty, something of himself, 'grave & rather sarcastic I think'. Her hands folded on her crossed knee seem passive and decorous but it is unmistakably the posture of a watcher. The form, surrounded by a rich cloak, by a great curving chair where she sits in state, a Victorian screen and curtains, suggests the layers and folds of formality out of which, at the very centre of the canvas, there rises the long neck, the pointed chin, the narrow fingers, the ridge of the black-covered knees and the black-pointed toe. Here, Grant pared away Vanessa's charms to reveal a consequential Victorian character with the initiative to shed false roles and beliefs however deeply ingrained by training and custom.

Virginia once delivered 'Nessa's curse on marriage' to a prospective bride. When Vanessa's husband strayed to her sister and others, she remade her family with Duncan Grant, without excluding Bell and her first, rather too dominating lover, Roger Fry. Vanessa never divorced Clive Bell, but lived with Duncan Grant, tolerating his active homosexuality, to the end of her life. Ottoline Morrell saw Vanessa's character 'like a broad river, not worried or sensitive to passers-by. She carries along the few barques that float with her on her stream of life, her two sons [by Bell] and daughter [by Grant], but the sea towards which she flows is her painting, above all the thing which is of importance to her.' Virginia, as novelist, was more drawn to passers-by, ranging more widely in both the society and street life of London. When Sydney Waterlow dined with the sisters in December 1910 he noted this essential difference: 'Vanessa icy, cynical, artistic; Virginia much more emotional & interested in life rather than beauty.' Virginia was more demanding and expressive in her relationships, her finger on their pulse. Leslie Stephen once commented on Vanessa's 'odd little misgivings . . . as to doing anything demonstrative'; her sister always twitted her on her emotional evasion and Vanessa admitted that 'when she is demonstrative I always shrink away'. Vanessa was Virginia's leader into freedom. But for love Virginia Stephen looked to the other activist in her life, Leonard Woolf.

9. *The Trial of Love*

VIRGINIA WOOLF shaped fictional lives which ignore such formal signposts as weddings. In none of the six lives related in *The Waves* does marriage play more than a peripheral part. What part had marriage in her own life: did it affect her thoughts and values, did love matter or did she choose in Leonard a practical civil servant, willing to order her existence and nurse her through illnesses?

Another way of putting this question is to start from the fact that writing was the centre of Virginia Woolf's life. Did her marriage bear on her writing or was it peripheral? It is obvious that Leonard Woolf propped the outer structure of her career: he established a press to publish her works; he kept unwanted visitors at bay; he read final drafts and made just comments. But did he affect that self that his wife reserved for her work?

Leonard Woolf revealed nothing about his marriage after an ill-judged novel, *The Wise Virgins*, in 1914. His official account in the third volume of his autobiography was packed with elaborate digressions. His no-nonsense manner was not designed to inform but to give the illusion of information. In truth, he tells nothing of the living relationship, producing instead precise dates of meetings, stylish descriptions of his wife's clothes, and fact-filled, though not very telling, records of her post-marital breakdowns of 1913 and 1915. Behind the profusion of almost obsessional detail there is a decided silence. From the time that Leonard moved into Virginia Stephen's household in Brunswick Square in December 1911, which is the time that he decided to pursue her, he kept certain entries in his diary, which are anyway not very revealing, in a code made up of Tamil and Sinhalese characters. Virginia had a less guarded, more socially secure nature but she, too, was loyal enough not to talk about marriage.

The only real clue lies in the letters they wrote to each other, meant for no other eyes. Leonard's are unpublished; Virginia's scattered so thinly over multiple volumes that their collective character is lost. But if that small correspondence is read as a unit, it reveals a passionate and strange union, locked in its own vocabulary, that must be seen in its own terms. The basis of their union was

Leonard's imaginative willingness to share a playful, private vocabulary.* The first use of what was to become an elaborate drama appears in a love-letter which Leonard wrote from Cambridge on 24 May 1912: 'I hope the Mandril went to its box early and isn't worried by anything in the world.' Five days later, Virginia declared her love. They became engaged on 29 May 1912.

Why marry Leonard Woolf? There were other suitors, Cambridge men like Sydney Waterlow, Edward Hilton Young, Walter Lamb, and Walter Headlam (a Greek scholar and Fellow of King's), whose backgrounds were more familiar, who were less harsh, less poor. But Leonard's appeal was a special kind of awareness of women which he has summed up himself: 'I have always been greatly attracted by the undiluted female mind, as well as by the female body.' He meant a gentle, sensitive mind, not necessarily intellectual, but quite elusive. 'It is not easy to catch it or bring it to the surface', he went on. 'I think I have taught myself gradually to be interested in what women say to me and to listen attentively . . . for in this way you get every now and again . . . a breath of this pure, curiously female quality of mind.' To feel this quality was to him a romantic pleasure.

This attitude made it possible for Virginia to consider a novel marriage. Her criticism of traditional marriages, of the Dalloways and, later, of the Olivers, and her sarcastic view of modern lovers consuming each other with dull automatism ('There are the public gardens intersected by asphalt paths. There are lovers lying shamelessly mouth to mouth on the burnt grass'), issued from her insistence that marriage should not warp the character or become automatic. In a pre-engagement letter to Leonard, on 1 May 1912, she trod back and forth between doubt and hope. She admitted to marriage having the usual attractions for her—companionship, children, being busy '—then I say By God, I will not look upon marriage as a profession'. Her attitude recalls her mother who refused to marry without 'proper passion'. Marriage, Virginia told Leonard, must be 'everything': love, children, adventure, intimacy, work. The letter ended on that adventurous note: 'We both of us want a marriage that is a tremendous living thing, always alive,

* The use of a private vocabulary was a Hyde Park Gate custom though there it was a matter only of the odd word. The habit is extended in the relationship of the Stephen sisters and in the earlier ('Dolphin' and 'Peak') letters of Vanessa and Clive Bell but only the Woolfs were to extend a private vocabulary into an elaborate drama.

always hot, not dead and easy in parts as most marriages are. We ask a good deal of life, don't we? Perhaps we shall get it; then, how splendid!'

Virginia married late, at the age of thirty. She had refused to compromise on the mutual awareness of her parents or on the excitement of Stella's betrothal. She remembered reading at fifteen Fanny Burney's diary behind the folding doors of the Hyde Park Gate drawing-room and glowing in response to a love-letter she had, by chance, seen. 'There is nothing sweeter in the whole world than our love', Jack had written.

'There's never been anything like it in the world', she had repeated when Stella came to kiss her goodnight.

And Stella had laughed gently and said: 'Oh lots of people are in love as we are. You and Nessa will be one day.'

Stella's betrothal awoke in Virginia an idea of ecstasy that would be 'extraordinarily enduring'. It was connected with respectable engagements. Unofficial love, she said later, never gave one the same feeling. Then, when Virginia was in her early twenties, this idea of love was confounded, first by George and then by Jack Hills himself.

Jack was the first person to speak openly about sex to Virginia when he visited one day in Fitzroy Square, soon after Vanessa's marriage in 1907. He told Virginia that men 'had' women incessantly.

'But are they—', she hesitated, 'honourable?'

Jack laughed. He assured her that sex, for a man, had nothing to do with his sense of honour. 'Having women is a mere trifle in a man's life', he explained.

Virginia was shocked. She had believed that the same standards applied to men as to women. She had thought that all men, like her father, loved one woman only. She decided that men were dull dogs; they could no longer 'illude' for her. Out of sympathy with mere appetite, as she now saw it, she found imaginative refuge in women like Violet Dickinson and Vanessa who allowed her the kind of imaginative play that excited her affections. With Violet she played the pet: she was Violet's Sparroy (a mix of sparrow and monkey), her Kangaroo, her Wallaby. With her sister she was more physical—the 'Apes' were eager to be stroked and kissed. Our age is so alert to sexual deviation that it is hard to see this behaviour in the less self-conscious context of its own time. All Virginia Woolf's novels show men and women whose education has sensitized them to their own sex and left them ignorant of the other which is not to be known but conquered. In *To the Lighthouse* Paul Rayley is sadly unfit for marriage in that his ability to respond to a woman's feelings is undeveloped, so accustomed is he to indulge his own. When Lily Briscoe looks at Paul in the heat of his conquest, love seems 'the stupidest, the most barbaric of human passions'. Paul's laugh of triumph foretells the unscrupulousness of possession. Lily flinches for the newly engaged Minta Doyle 'exposed to those fangs' and is thankful that she has her work. 'She was saved from that dilution.'

It is easy to misunderstand Rachel's response to Dalloway or Lily's to Rayley as passionlessness but it is nothing more than disappointment. It is disappointing for a young woman to find out how far the instincts fall short of the odes sung to love. 'Women, judging from her [Lily's] own experience, would all the time be feeling, This is not what we want; there is nothing more tedious, puerile, and inhumane than love.'

It is not then surprising that Virginia should have held out so long against marriage. David Garnett first saw her, very thin and beautiful, dressed as a Valkyrie at a fancy-dress ball in aid of Women's Suffrage. A fiercely self-protective virginity had hardened in her during the 'seven unhappy years' following Stella's death. Yet Clive Bell detected, he told her on her twenty-sixth birthday, the gleam of 'emerald sleeping passions'.*

'Shall you kiss me tomorrow?' she wrote to Vanessa in 1908. 'Yes, yes, yes!' In 1909, on holiday in Bayreuth, she wrote: 'There are bullocks here, with eyes like yours, & beautiful trembling nostrils.' Again to her sister, 'How pleasant it would be', she wrote from Asheham to Charleston on 24 October 1916, 'to roll on the downs together, & the Ape would steal kisses from the most secluded parts!' With Vanessa, and later with Leonard, she caricatures her intent amorousness as that of a set of apes or a mandrill (the ugliest and most ferocious of primates).

From about the time of her sister's marriage and as her young need of Violet abated, she began to consider the possibilities of love, first in literature, then in actuality, with men quite different from

---

* 'Yellow and Green', a rondeau written 'to A.V.S.' and dated 25 Jan. 1908. CB wrote of
Eyes where blithe fancy's sparks contest
With sombre moods of rich unrest,
And emerald sleeping passions gleam.

the politely overbearing types whom she would have met, in the
normal course, at society balls with George. When she read the
letters of Mérimée to an unknown woman, which were written over
thirty years, she noted in her travel diary of 1906 an instance of
continuous talk and understanding which rang a new note to her
ear: 'If you could hear these two voices speaking together it would
not be a dulcet sound, or a loving sound, or a passionate sound that
they would make in unison; but it would be something sharp and
curious, something . . . not to be forgotten.' Perhaps she put this
sound into the honest talk of Rachel and Terence. 'You feel perfect
faith in a man who tells a woman her motives and her faults', she
mused. 'A man & a woman, then, may come so near, and stay so
near, and keep always just so much distance between them, — and
draw nothing but profit, apparently from the alliance.'

In the love of Wordsworth and his sister she noted another
instructive relationship. Wordsworth's attraction, in Dorothy's
words, lay in a 'violence of affection, which demonstrates itself
every moment of the day, in a sort of restless watchfulness which
I know not how to describe, a tenderness that never sleeps'. The
twenty-six-year-old Virginia Stephen quoted these words in a
review and added: 'Their companionship, so equal, so simple, and
so sincere, continued throughout their lives . . ., every letter hints at
the exquisite relationship.' Between 1906 and 1908 she theorized
about a relationship between a man and a woman that should be
equal, intense, honest, and lasting.

The problem that was immediately apparent was that not even
literature, let alone life, offered many suitable candidates. 'There
are such beings in the World perhaps,' Jane Austen cautioned her
niece, 'one in a Thousand, as the Creature You and I should think
perfection, Where Grace & Spirit are united to Worth, where
Manners are equal to the Heart & Understanding, but such a
person may not come your way. . . .' In *Night and Day* the old
Victorian aunts wish that Tennyson had written 'The Prince'—
a sequel to 'The Princess'. 'I confess', says Mrs Cosham, 'I'm
almost tired of Princesses. We want some one to show us what a
good man can be. We have Laura and Beatrice, Antigone and
Cordelia, but we have no heroic man.'

In the years between the death of Thoby in 1906 and the
reappearance of Leonard Woolf in 1911, she came closest to
marrying Lytton Strachey. Tall, with very long and beautiful

hands, he would stalk elegantly across a lawn under a white sunshade lined with green and fold his long legs into a deck chair. His velvety brown eyes were full of expression. 'Oh I was right to be in love with him', Virginia thought. 'It is an exquisite symphony his nature when all the violins get playing . . . so deep, so fantastic.' His mind was 'softest to impressions, least starched by any formality or impediment'. He seemed to understand 'from the sight of the tail what the whole body of the thought is in one's mind'. Lytton was infinitely 'supple'—'my dear old serpent', she called him—but she found him a little low in tone and a little too careful in assembling his comforts. The invalidish Lytton would, she later recognized, have 'repined a little if one had broken free'.

Just before Lytton proposed to her, Virginia tried to tease him into vigour with one of her fictions: 'So I think of you as a kind of Venetian prince, in sky blue tights, lying on your back in an orchard, or balancing an exquisite leg in the air', she wrote on 20 November 1908. Early in 1909 Lytton proposed but, even as he spoke the words, he shrank from contact. Virginia saw, sympathized, and the next day released him. Lytton then wrote to Leonard Woolf in Ceylon suggesting that Leonard take his place.

August 21st, 1909

Your destiny is clearly marked out for you, but will you allow it to work? You must marry Virginia. She's sitting waiting for you, is there any objection? She's the only woman in the world with sufficient brains; it's a miracle that she should exist; but if you're not careful you'll lose the opportunity. . . . She's young, wild, inquisitive, discontented, and longing to be in love.

Leonard, who had only seen her two or three times, took up the challenge with alacrity. 'Do you think Virginia would have me?' he replied. 'Wire to me if she accepts. I'll take the next boat home.'

Virginia made no move. She hardly knew Leonard, and it had to be a joke. Two years later Leonard returned to England, was at once invited to dinner by the Bells, and there he met Virginia. Leonard had sardonic features with narrow lips turned down at the corners. His brilliant light-blue eyes would fix, as he listened, with a severe intensity of expression. With his big nose he looked like a young hawk and when laughter filled his eyes it was as though the hawk rose in the air. A pipe-smoking man who had what was known in Cambridge as 'a good mind', he was addicted to logical argument.

The slight trembling of his head and hands gave the impression not of infirmity, but of the vibration of a powerful intellectual machine.

Leonard, like Virginia, had reached his thirties without falling in love. But in his case, flirtations and coupling, what he called 'healthy vice' as opposed to sodomy, had left him contemptuous of desire. In one unidentified paper he spoke of the swift corruption that falls when hopes are satisfied. 'Women seem to me absolutely the abomination of desolation, in Ceylon at any rate', he had written to Strachey in 1905. In 1907 he had rationalized his lack of feeling: 'I am beginning to think it is always degraded being in love: after all 99/100ths of it is always the desire to copulate, otherwise it is only a shadow of itself, and a particular desire to copulate seems to me no less degraded than a general.' The obverse of his passionate temper was a harsh puritanism. He used to lie on the seaweedy sands of the lagoon at Jaffna, petting an eighteen-year-old girl, 'Gwen', all the time despising her cow eyes that could never understand what he said.* For both Leonard and Virginia, only understanding could save love from ridicule. For both, falling in love was an imaginative act in two stages: first composing characters of each other, then drawing these characters together in a playful drama not unlike the elaborate courtship rituals of beasts.

It is curious to compare Leonard Woolf in reality with the way that Virginia Stephen came to align him with her brother. In reality, he was a Jew. He was quick in everything: in intelligence, in practical matters, in temper. He was relentlessly moody: his diary entry for 11 December 1911 is just one word: 'gloomy'. He was fussy, along the whole gamut of fussiness: meticulous in his work, a stickler for correctness to the last halfpenny, an obsessive list-maker (he would, for instance, note down each day how many words he had written and add them up); above all, he was watchful of health. Some of his later letters to Virginia are funny mixtures of endearment and fuss ('Has Cascara acted?' If not, 'you must get Liquor Paraffin *at once*').

I don't think that Virginia took in fully the character of Leonard Woolf except to register that he seemed foreign and that she disliked his suburban family. Oddly enough, she decided that Leonard reminded her of Thoby 'not only in his face', although

---

* In his second novel, *The Wise Virgins*, LW was possibly drawing on his experience with 'Gwen' in his characterization of the seductive but mindless suburban girl, Gwen, whom Harry marries despite his love for a wise virgin.

they could not have been more unlike: Thoby, a strapping blond with bland, classical features; Leonard, thin, dark, tense. This fantastic identification of Leonard and her brother, though, made it possible to take Leonard, without much knowing him, into the hallowed family circle. Maybe, also, Leonard appealed to the high-minded Clapham strain, stronger in Virginia Stephen than in any surviving member of her family. As a child Leonard had heard his father quote from the prophet, Micah, 'What doth the Lord require of thee but to do justly, and to love mercy . . .'. The Armenian massacres and the Dreyfus affair had shaped his vigilant social conscience that, in the face of human cruelty, was constantly filled with despair. On Leonard's return to England he took up the cause of socialism not because he thought it would be effective but, as Noel Annan puts it, he hoped that occasionally some act, by some lucky chance, would diminish cruelty, ignorance, and injustice and that at least it was the duty of every man to go on striving for this against all odds. He never struck heroic attitudes—he was coolly rational on platforms, in committees, in his political journalism—but his layer of cynicism protected, as it often does, the idealistic reformer.

The two men most important to Virginia appear quite different: Leonard Woolf, a strenuously efficient ex-civil servant who answered every letter the day it arrived; Leslie Stephen, emotional and intuitive, whose letters reveal a civilized notion of manliness: 'Every man ought to be feminine,' Leslie Stephen wrote, '*i.e.*, to have quick and delicate feelings; but no man ought to be effeminate, *i.e.*, to let his feelings get the better of his intellect . . .'. There was a delicacy in her father that was grounded in self-confidence. It is unlikely that Virginia met with this among the men of her own generation, not in Bloomsbury, and probably not in her husband—though his ardent letters show a closer approximation to Leslie Stephen than one may otherwise imagine.

Leonard's initial image of Virginia Stephen was in one way idealized and conventional. He saw her as a fine English lady, remote, not wishing to be touched. He had first seen her at the age of eighteen or nineteen in Thoby's rooms at Trinity, demure in a white dress, carrying a parasol, looking 'the most Victorian of Victorian young ladies', yet he noted there was a look at the back of the eye of this quiet beast, intelligent, hypercritical, sarcastic, 'a look which warns you to be very, very careful'. As Leslie Stephen had first seen her mother from a worshipful distance—she had seemed to the modest young don about as approachable as a Sistine madonna—so, to Leonard, the Stephen sisters had seemed as exquisitely aloof as the temple of Segesta in Sicily which had taken his breath away as he rounded a bend in the road. This aesthetic view was not much changed eleven years later when he returned from Ceylon. In *The Wise Virgins*, his *roman-à-clef*, the Jewish suitor from Richstead (Putney) sees in Camilla (Virginia) the purity and coldness of hills and snow. In another, private fancy he approached her like a Syrian wanderer visiting Olympus.

Leonard as Thoby; Virginia as fine lady: these unlikely images that a man and a woman concoct as the basis for a relation hardly fit them for marriage. They stake out the distance that Leonard Woolf and Virginia Stephen had to overcome. But what made their union unusual was the way they came to supplant unlikely images with dramatic new ones.

'No woman was ever nearer to her mate than I am', Jane Eyre concludes. '. . . We talk, I believe, all day long.' Virginia and Leonard Woolf first discovered their compatibility in this way. Soon after her engagement, Virginia wrote to Madge Vaughan (on whom she had once had a crush) that she had only known her betrothed six months 'but from the first I have found him the one person to talk to. He interests me immensely, besides all the rest.'

He found now that Virginia was no longer the aloof girl he had met at Trinity College. Though she was still rather silent, he noticed how 'the spring of a fantastic imagination' seemed to bubble up 'from strange recesses'. It made him catch his breath as on a mountain when suddenly the wind blows. Her mind appeared 'so astonishingly fearless' that it made his pulses beat. There was no fact that she would not frankly touch. It made life seem to go quick and, at the same time, it made him feel protective. He thought: 'I am always frightened that with her eyes fixed on the great rocks she will stumble among the stones.' When she spoke, her eyes, large like her mother's and grey-blue, lit up, but in repose her expression was pensive and girlish. She was not conventionally beautiful—her face was too long for symmetry and she was thin—but she had a kind of awkward boniness with its own grace.

After their marriage on 10 August 1912 they spent their first days at the Plough Inn at Holford, Somerset, near Alfoxton House where William and Dorothy Wordsworth stayed in 1797-8. 'We've seen nothing of the Quantocks [the hills], except great shapes of mist', Virginia wrote to Janet Case, 'but we've walked to the top of them, and now we sit over a fire and read novels like tigers.' She ate delicious meals, with cream and chocolates. Her good spirits were undaunted by steady rain in Somerset, by mule-back journeys and dirty inns in Spain (where they went next), by a rusty iron cargo ship to Italy, and by the mosquitoes which interrupted 'the proper business of bed'. She was more matter-of-fact than most virgins to discover the transports of sex a bit overrated. 'Why do you think people make such a fuss about marriage and copulation?', she asked Katherine Cox. 'Why do some of our friends change upon losing chastity? Possibly my great age makes it less of a catastrophe. . . . I might still be Miss S.' She was making an ambiguous statement, easily mistaken for a confession of sexual failure but holding a certain note of relief that her being had not been overcome. Still mistress of herself, she could yet declare, in a combined letter from Venice on 28 September 1912, that a basis for compatibility had been achieved: 'We've talked incessantly for 7 weeks, and become chronically . . . monogamic.'

Before their engagement they had forged a private language that both created and preserved their secret world. During the course of the marriage her thoughts, whenever she was away, seem to have homed to Leonard and she would hasten back to their delicious discourse. 'I like continuing our private life, unseen by anyone.' Her best short story, 'Lappin and Lapinova', is about honeymooners who concoct a wild rabbit language. It tells of the success and failure of marriage on the strength of its verbal drama—the woodland adventures of a splendid hunter rabbit and a rare white hare with dangling paws—for the drama enables the prosperous, stuffy Ernest Thorburn and his playful orphan wife, Rosalind, to cross the distance of fortune and temperament:

They were the opposite of each other. . . . He ruled over the busy world of rabbits; her world was a desolate, mysterious place, which she ranged mostly by moonlight. All the same, their territories touched. . . .

Thus when they came back from their honeymoon they possessed a private world. . . . No one guessed that there was such a place, and that of course made it all the more amusing.

To others their love-play would appear childish. But as long as it lasted it ensured continued intimacy and a share in each other's development. King Lappin became 'an animal of the greatest character; Rosalind was always finding new qualities in him'. And when Rosalind dangles her sewing in her paws, her eyes big, bright, and a little prominent, he suddenly sees 'the real Rosalind', whom she promptly identifies as Lappin's strange mate, the elusive Lapinova. In their play, Lappin always protects Lapinova from the Squire and the poacher, her domineering in-laws who wish to trap her. They wish to subdue her to their regimented drive for gain, which is their substitute for living. But, in time, Ernest reverts to type: he tires of the new drama and turns from sporting with Lapinova to hunting her. Even before he nabs her, the elusive spirit of Lapinova has vanished. The body she leaves behind is 'stiff and cold'.

Leonard and Virginia made up their own fable of beasts. The first hint appeared in a pre-engagement letter of Leonard's, dated 29 April 1912. At that time when their future hung in balance— a hair's breadth seemed to separate Virginia from falling in love or turning away—Leonard owned to 'many beastly qualities', especially lust. In January he had told her: 'I am selfish, jealous, cruel, lustful, a liar & probably worse still.' Now again, in desperation, he fell back on frankness, not cynically, but as if a nasty fact might wake in her some feeling—even if it be dislike—that would at least answer his vehemence.

He repeated, deliberately: 'I have faults vices beastlinesses but even with them I do believe you ought to marry me & be in love—'.

From this there arose a game between two 'beasts'. One was a great variegated creature, sometimes a lovely Bird with ornate plumage and given to exotic courtship display, but most often Virginia was a Mandrill, a large, fierce West African baboon, whom they also called 'the great Brute'.* This Brute took into her service an insignificant mouse or Mongoose (Leonard), otherwise dubbed the 'grey Goose'. The imposing creature then conceived a ridiculous passion for her unattractive servant with his thin, flea-ridden body.

In exchanges between Leonard and Virginia there was not one note of tepid compromise. Virginia brought to their intimacy a sense of fun and a nonchalant audacity. In December 1913, when

---

* This appears to be a development of VW's character as half-monkey, half-bird, 'Sparroy', which she had assumed with Violet Dickinson. An earlier French nickname was 'singe', meaning ape or mimic.

Leonard left Asheham for London to arrange to vacate their
Clifford's Inn rooms, she wrote the following invitation:

> Asheham House,
> Rodmell,
> Lewes,
> Sussex.

Immundus Mongoosius Felicissimus, I could write this letter in
beautiful silver Latin, but then the scurvy little heap of dusty fur could not
read it. Would it make you very conceited if I told you that I love you more
than I have ever done since I took you into service, and find you beautiful,
and indispensable? I am afraid that is the truth.

Goodbye Mongoose, and be a devoted animal, and never leave the great
variegated creature. She wishes me to inform you delicately that her flanks
and rump are now in the finest plumage, and invites you to an exhibition.
Kisses on your dear little pate. Darling Mongoose.

> Mandril

'Beloved,' wrote the Mongoose on 31 October 1917 (while
lecturing on International Government to a number of Co-
operative Societies in Lancashire and Cheshire), 'I adore . . . every
feather on your magnificent form.'

His 'sweetest Mistress', it seems, took the initiative. She would
boldly book her servant for one hour of 'antelope kissing'.
Sometimes she put on-stage 'the marmots', high-mountain mice.
'Come along marmots', she wrote on 4 October 1929, 'and do your
jublimmails'.* In *Orlando* lovers invent 'a cypher language' to
convey a complicated state in a word or two.

While the Mandrill conducted courtship, the Mongoose was
given to uncontrollable outbreaks of 'scarlet fever', a disease to
which his miserable body was much prone. The Mongoose always
feared that his 'Mistress Mandril' would dismiss him; she most
certainly would if he ever told her a lie for it was his honesty that
had compelled her to admit him 'into service'.

Although they shared this third-person private language, their
accents were distinctly different. The Mandrill's accents were
reassuring—she does love every hair of his fleasome body. The
accents of the Mongoose were absurdly emotional.

* The editors of the *Letters* have thus deciphered this almost illegible word. It is equally
impossible to know what marmots implied but, according to Jean O. Love, p. 154, Leslie
Stephen comments jokingly in a letter to his wife that no doubt she would like him to play the
marmot and sleep the winter away (28 Jan. 1894).

'My sweetest Mandy', he wrote on 27 July 1913 while Virginia was forcing herself to endure a rest cure at hateful Twickenham, 'if it weren't so late I should sing you a Mongoose song of joy which begins

> I do adore
> I do adore . . .

I shall think of you tomorrow as a brave beast lying quietly in its straw & cheering its dear self from time to time by remembering that.'

At the end of the first year of marriage he begged to be taken into service for another: '—& if you'll only let him grovel before you & kiss your toes, he'll be happy'. At this time Virginia was on the brink of breakdown, yet they had forged a humorous rapport that carried them through their troubles. The urgent, coercive accents of the suitor, Leonard Woolf, pursuing the remote Virginia Stephen were dispelled by her sense of fun.

'Will you really take me in your arms & kiss me' he demanded on 12 March 1914 when he was away, visiting Strachey and then his sister, Bella. 'Mandy darling, I love you, I love you.' And two days later: 'I kiss you, dearest One, in imagination & worship you, Mandril Sarcophagus Rarissima.'

It was during this brief separation as Virginia recovered from her post-marital breakdown in 1913 that Leonard's letters first carried a note of almost surprised confidence. 'There is no doubt of one thing, beloved, & that is that we do suit each other in some amazing way.' He wrote again from Lytton Strachey's home 'The Lacket', near Marlborough:

Sometimes in the last few days I've thought it may be a bad thing to love anyone as I love you—but I don't really believe it can be—only it cuts one off in some odd way from the rest of the world. Listening to Lytton & Norton I sometimes almost hugged myself to think what you are to me & I am to you—they seemed so wandering & incomplete & everything so thin to them & to me—everything with you in it—so rich. All this morning I walked by myself in the woods, & for hardly a moment could I think of anything but you, it was just as if I had dropped back two years to the time before you took me into your service & I was down there on Exmoor. I want so much from you, dearest one. . . .

When Strachey praised Virginia's handwriting as the most 'eminent' he had seen, Leonard allowed himself a proprietory touch of smugness: 'I think sometimes he is rather jealous of your old Mongoose.'

Virginia sounds consistently her playful self in the letters. It is the doggedly rational Leonard Woolf who was changed within the circle of this love. Virginia ignored his hardness and, through the game, encouraged the passionate honesty of 'my rapid bold Mong'. To have one's best side elicited is very satisfying; it is the source of the high morale that resounds through this marriage. When Saxon, Leonard's college room-mate, visited in 1914 while Leonard was away, he told Virginia that theirs was the best marriage he had seen. Virginia herself confirmed this in her diary at the end of 1919: 'I daresay we're the happiest couple in England.'

In the beast dramas the characters allowed themselves to reverse roles and the servant became 'Master'. The great Brute, moping in her pet's absence, would lose her usual command: she would remember him in his white nightgown, shamelessly kiss his pillow, and cry in bed. 'It will be a joy to see Master tomorrow', she wrote after their move to Monks House, Rodmell, in 1919. 'The furry little beasts send their love.' It was in his capacity as Master that Leonard Woolf was able to superintend his wife's health. There is a contract drawn up before Leonard's departure for a Women's Co-operative Guild meeting in Birmingham in 1914 which shows with what tact and humour his restrictions were imposed:

I, Mandril Sarcophagus Felicissima, var. rarissima, rerum naturae simplex, (al. Virginia Woolf) swear that I will on June 16, 17 & 18

1. Rest on my back with my head on the cushions for a full half hour after lunch

2. Eat exactly as much as if I were not alone.

3. Be in bed by 10.25 every night & settle off to sleep at once

4. Have my breakfast in bed

5. Drink a *whole* glass of milk in the morning

6. In certain contingencies rest on the sofa, not walk about the house or outside, until the return of animal illud miserrimum, mongoosius communis

7. Be wise

8. Be happy

This contract was flourishingly signed by 'Mandril' on the appropriate days.

In the past there have been men and women who have understood the skills of courtship, but can such skills be combined with mature feeling? There is a glimpse of such a possibility in the verbal play of Beatrice and Benedick or of Elizabeth Bennet and Darcy. And here, in the Woolf letters, is a relationship in which desire is subject to friendship and in which interest endures. This was possible only for two people who had the capacity to go on developing. Their beast drama was their means of drumming up character and tending the nuances of their commitment. They were far less free than others in their set. They were miserable apart. Their letters constantly expressed flatness and longing. 'It's so frightfully tame without you', Virginia complained at the end of October 1917. Saxon was keeping her company at Asheham but, indecisive and inarticulate, he seemed like a tame pussycat 'after my own passionate & ferocious & entirely adorable M'.

Virginia Woolf's marriage was crucial to her not so much for the practical reason of Leonard's protection nor for the literary reason that he provided, as did her parents, subject-matter for her work, but because marriage itself presented a complementary challenge to becoming an artist: to be creative in private life. She presents the case of a writer who believes that creativity must not be reserved for work. Her letters to her husband show how imaginatively her marriage was composed, how much verbal skill went into its daily conduct. Obviously, the marriage was infused with Virginia's flair for characterization. What is less obvious is Leonard's contribution — not to the woman, now, but to the artist, in particular to his wife's sense of just action.

In Virginia Woolf's mature fiction, just feeling, not reason, is shown to be the basis of just action, and the more just the feeling, the more humane the action. To her, action was a practical act of loving kindness, like Mrs Ramsay knitting a brown stocking for the lighthouse keeper's boy who has a tuberculous hip. What the world calls action—legal, imperial, belligerent, or economic action—is disregarded as worthless and worse, so much strutting and mouthing. Leonard Woolf's first novel, *The Village in the Jungle* (begun in 1911), sets out this premiss which his wife took up. It is about the failure of a court case to uncover the integrity of a Sinhalese peasant, Babun. The accused, in turn, cannot comprehend British justice which ends his life. The trumped-up charges brought against Babun by fellow-villagers are the result of his refusal to sacrifice his social-outcast wife, Punchi Menika, to the debt collector, Fernando, who wishes to sleep with her. The absolute devotion of Babun and Punchi Menika is incomprehensible to all the villagers whose actions are habitually dictated by worldly calculation. Leonard Woolf shows how rare in the jungle of Ceylon, as elsewhere, is the man who can sustain integrity of feeling as the basis of action. Ironically, it is this very man that the British public-school magistrate, understandably ignorant of a remote jungle village, condemns. The rare love story is buried by cheap court-room fiction as, eventually, Punchi Menika is literally buried by the ever-encroaching jungle. The jungle dominates the book, both in its terrible power to obliterate the clearings and as a metaphor for the obfuscation of justice (as in Dickens the London fog shrouds Chancery). Leonard Woolf also shows through one simple tale how impossible it was for British rule, however well intentioned, to penetrate the jungle of the ruled, how superficial that rule was and, in a way, absurd. In short, *The Village in the Jungle* proved that the Colonial Service had just lost one of its most thoughtful magistrates.

Babun has the sensual dignity of Gauguin's paintings. Leonard Woolf contrasts the routine, exploitative sensuality of the village villain and that of the noble savage with his tenderness and family devotion.

Though Virginia and Leonard Woolf agreed on the futility of public action, Leonard's sensuality never touches his wife's work. In *To the Lighthouse* she describes the preliminary drama as the Ramsays read together. In *The Waves* Louis and Rhoda are lovers, but their love is reported, not enacted. In *Between the Acts* Isa Oliver and a neighbouring farmer cherish a secret attraction which will never be acknowledged. Where Leonard recounts the physical act of surrender, Virginia dwells on a subtle rapport. Here is the difference between the Woolfs, and the source of their early troubles.

In an early unsigned review of the Carlyles' love-letters, Virginia perceived that 'the more we see the less we can label' and again, 'the further we read the less we trust to definitions'. To see this marriage on its own terms, it is essential to emphasize the rapport that was called into being through words and to isolate, as subsidiary, a terrible period of trial from 1912 to 1915, what Virginia later called the 'prelude' to the marriage proper.

The autobiographic detail in her novels suggests, repeatedly, a deep distrust of men. Lily Briscoe is drawn by Paul's signal fire: 'Some winy smell mixed with it and intoxicated her, for she felt her own headlong desire . . .'. But at the brink of imaginary surrender she notices how the splendid fire 'fed on the treasure of the house, greedily, disgustingly, and she loathed it'. The unusual rawness of Lily's emotion suggests how closely Virginia Woolf was registering her own mingled responses. She believed that her mother had been consumed by marriage and perhaps this is what the Virgin Queen felt, drawn to courtiers, but unable to forget her mother's death and the deaths of successive stepmothers. Coldness is no explanation for this complex state of mind. In a draft of *The Voyage Out*, Rachel experiences, with Dalloway's kiss, a sense of subjection: 'I remember looking at his hand. It takes one back to prehistoric times'.

While Leonard responded readily to Virginia's verbal play there was, he discovered, a guard against his own initiative which he met with demanding vehemence. And on his side, too, there was, I suspect, some mental resistance. There is no hint in Leonard's autobiography of the self-questioning that a new wife's breakdown might reasonably provoke. During Leonard's six years in Ceylon, Virginia had romanticized him, on the basis of Thoby's anecdotes, as a misanthrope, trembling with suppressed feeling, who shook his fist at civilization and disappeared 'into the tropics' perhaps never to return. She never considered that suppressed feeling might tell against her or her kind.

In the early years of marriage, Leonard's sense of his Jewishness smoulders through the pages of his fiction: his second novel, *The Wise Virgins*, and his tale 'Three Jews'.* 'Three Jews' is a series of portraits of Jews in various stages of assimilation, moving down the social scale to the least assimilated, an old blackbird of a cemetery keeper, rocking backwards and forwards and looking up sideways with a wrinkled forehead. The cemetery keeper is poor, seedy and lonely, yet he has turned away his promising artistic son because that son married a Christian servant. Leonard was a rational atheist who had married out of the tribe. In this tale his persona, the

* 'Three Jews' with VW's 'The Mark on the Wall' was publication no. 1 of the Hogarth Press in 1917.

assimilated Jew, sipping tea at Kew, feels an irrational nostalgia for the old code that forbids intermarriage. Leonard Woolf was examining not the old faith itself but the hot energy and indomitable strength that issued from it so that a Jew might be very low in the world yet remain indifferent to misfortune.

Virginia eventually came to understand this. Louis, like the other figures in *The Waves*, is a type, not an exact portrait, but through Louis, who speaks with an Australian accent, his friends understand what it feels like to be an alien, to strive for acceptance and to rebel against the very adaptation for which one has striven. It comes as a surprise that the super-successful Louis, ringing the world with his ships, should choose the unworldly Rhoda as his soulmate and mistress. They meet in a City attic, like Leonard and Virginia in Clifford's Inn. Rhoda, too, is a type—far from an exact portrait of the author—but the outcast basis for their union may show Virginia's sympathetic identification with the alien in Leonard which she had gained in twenty years of marriage. But at the time she married him, his assertiveness, far from overwhelming her, had the opposite effect. She waited. She drew back.

'I'm half afraid of myself', Virginia confessed to Leonard in a letter of 1 May 1912. 'I sometimes feel that no one ever has or ever can share something—It's the thing that makes you call me like a hill, or a rock.' Leonard repeated this image, 'like hills with virgin snow on them', in *The Wise Virgins*. In this version of their courtship he had the artist, Camilla Lawrence, refuse the suburban Harry Davis because she would be one of Hakluyt's adventurers: 'Her life was an adventure, the joy of roving among experiences that were ever new under the shifting and changing of chance.' She would swing from being half in love 'to the extreme of wildness and aloofness'.

For Virginia to be half in love was promising, as her letters to Leonard frequently suggest, but Leonard, caught up in the urgency of his own desires—he admits in a letter of 29 April that they were growing 'violent'—could not wait for her feelings to match his own. The lover in *The Wise Virgins* wants 'a certain fierceness of love, mental and bodily . . . a flame that shall join and weld together'.

Leonard found Virginia 'extraordinarily gentle' the day he first kissed her on the cliffs near Birling Gap, Eastbourne. She told him afterwards that she felt 'no more than a rock'. When her mother had confessed her 'deadness' to Leslie Stephen, her father had taken no undue alarm. But Leonard could only see that something in Virginia seemed to rise up against him and his only recourse was to vent desire in a yet more deafening roar, calling repeatedly on God to bear witness.

Leonard did admit to shutting her off with a wall of words, on the other side of which she sat 'so dear & beautiful'—and unapproachable. Leonard was swinging from the extreme of contempt for sex to the other extreme of grand passion. It would be hard for any woman to find in such attitudinizing a human habitation. Mill said that it is so difficult for men to realize the subtler differences between the sexes because women who are worth knowing (as opposed to stupid women) have given little testimony of their thoughts and feelings. To know a woman truly, a man must be not only a competent judge, but of a character so sympathetic in itself, and so well adapted to hers, that he can either read her mind by sympathetic intuition or has nothing in himself which makes her shy of disclosing it. 'Hardly anything', Mill insists, 'can be more rare than this conjunction.'

Leonard met Virginia's silence with highly articulate reproaches, taking the entrenched line that if a woman does not respond there must be something wrong with her. He cast her as the cold maiden in his analysis of 'Aspasia' (her name in his diary)* during their courtship.

'I am in love with Aspasia', he wrote. 'When I think of Aspasia I think of hills, standing very clear but distant against a cold blue sky; there is snow upon them which no sun has ever melted & no man has ever trodden.' The effect of the lengthy rapture that follows is to distance the woman as a natural phenomenon, perhaps as heartless as nature itself.

Leonard gave this to Virginia. 'She read it slowly', he noted, while he gazed in pleasure at her face and hair before the fire. She sat silent for some time.

'I don't think you have made me soft or lovable enough', she said finally.

What is clearly ominous in the Aspasia paper is Leonard's delight at the prospect of 'battling' against the cold and the snow. There follows a high-flown fantasy about the 'romance' of the virginal woman with her horror of sordid feelings. 'If they touched her she would go mad as some women go mad at the touch of a caterpillar.'

---

* Aspasia, a hetaera or courtesan in fifth-century BC Athens, was the highly educated companion of Pericles.

Virginia said that, with a small turn, he could hate her.

Their first weeks of marriage, from Virginia's point of view, proved an unlooked-for success. Her letters were contented, almost placid. And then the tone changed suddenly in a letter to Ka Cox from Saragossa, Spain, on 4 September.

Leonard shall not see this, she told Ka, namely that she found the climax immensely exaggerated and that twinges of anger were 'at once visited upon my husband'. These unexpectedly disloyal comments immediately follow the apparently casual information that Leonard, sitting opposite, was writing the first chapter of *The Wise Virgins* and must, I think, be seen in the context of this angry book.

In *The Wise Virgins*, Harry Davis (the name Davis came from a branch of Leonard's family) is torn between a stupid passionate girl, Gwen, who seduces and eventually marries him, and the classier Wise Virgin of Bloomsbury, Camilla Lawrence, who admires and likes him but who is constitutionally incapable of physical love. Harry, a passionate Jew, taunts the *habitué* of Bloomsbury, Trevor Trevithick:

I admire your women, your pale women with their white skins and fair hair, but I despise them. . . . There's no life in you, no blood in you. . . . Your women are cold and leave one cold—no dark hair, no blood in them. Pale hair, pale souls, you know.

The Wise Virgins was patently a reproach to Virginia. The only extenuation allowed her was that she was the product of an effete milieu. In *The Wise Virgins* Camilla is allowed to be 'very affectionate' and to wish for 'soft things and strokings' and it is mystifying why, to Leonard, such natural wishes should be dismissed as manifestations of 'virgin snow'.

I doubt that Leonard showed her actual passages from the book, and it cannot be known how much he told her, but I think she discovered, at least, that Leonard was disappointed in her and proposed to make a fuss. He intended to announce his disappointment in print. Leonard went on honeymoon with an idea that a woman is dormant until awakened by sex. He wrote of Camilla Lawrence that 'it was not in her, a woman and unmarried to know the want'. The problem with the sleeping beauty myth is an unfortunate obligation on the prince abruptly to awaken and on the princess to *be* awakened. Virginia, with no fairy-tales in her head, did not demand too much. But for Leonard it was all or nothing, and he became anxious and hurt.

On their return from their honeymoon they went rather solemnly to Vanessa for advice on orgasms. Vanessa was vastly entertained by the unexpected confidence. She boasted her own prowess and disparaged her sister as incurably frigid. Leonard grasped at this. The reproach in *The Wise Virgins* turns on a chapter called 'Katharine's Opinion of her Sister'. Katharine warns Harry that even to attempt to wake Camilla would be fraught with danger to them both.

Virginia had proposed a view of herself as a sexual failure while still very young, at the time of her sister's marriage, and repeated it over the course of her life to her fiancé and to various friends, Gerald Brenan in Spain, Vita Sackville-West, and Octavia Wilberforce. But she was so much a creature of ironic nuance that it is well to be wary of taking her statements at face value—that she was an uneducated woman, a poor writer, often 'rejected [as reviewer] by the *Times*': all these statements were self-deprecating poses which ironically guarded some very ambitious plan. Could the sexual failure, too, be a pose?

The main problem is how to reconcile the passionate and growing intimacy of the Woolf letters—reading the letters alone one would think her invitations to love delightfully candid—with Vita's report that Virginia Woolf had said that sex was a failure and soon abandoned. The truth lies buried in what women did not say, in the fiction of female frigidity to which Virginia herself submitted, and in her two successive breakdowns which followed the marriage.

Whatever the truth, it must include Leonard. His sister, Bella, who read *The Wise Virgins* at the height of the crisis, wrote to him bluntly on 12 August 1913: 'The fact is you have dipped your pen in pessimism & it sticks to everyone. . . . In him [Harry] I trace all your less pleasant characteristics. . . . In fact he appears such an ill-mannered cub that I wonder anyone put up with him for two minutes.' In one rare analysis of Leonard in her diary Virginia mentions 'his curious pessimistic temper: something deeper than reason, strangling, many coiled, that one can't deal with. Influenza has exactly the same effect, liberating the irrational despondency which I see in all the Woolves, & connect with centuries of oppression. The world against us &c.' *The Wise Virgins* is the book of a man who has missed the point and is simply stamping in frustration. Harry/Leonard blames himself only for what he cannot help, his Jewishness, and throws it in the face of the cold maiden:

We [Jews] wait hunched up, always ready and alert, for the moment to spring on what is worth while, then we let ourselves go. You don't like it? I see you don't; it makes you shrink from me—us, I mean. It isn't pleasant; it's hard, unbeautiful.

Defiantly, Harry dissociates himself from the pleasant, idle inhabitants of the Lawrences' country house where he is spending the weekend. His need to *do* things, he explains further to Camilla, is a sort of artistic feeling. 'To feel people moving under your hands or your brain, just as you want them to move. . . . Then of course we get an acquired pleasure in the mere operation of doing things, of always feeling oneself keyed up and absolutely alive. . . . You don't like my picture of us? But you must admit that our point of view implies imagination?'

Camilla responds with sadness. 'She distinctly did not want him to be like that.' And at that moment the charm of her presence has never been so strong.

Leonard Woolf does not give a fair definition of Jewish character—for in traditional Jewish society the opposite type predominates, the unworldly scholar and teacher—but it contains some truth about himself. Harry Davis is said to have a stern face and gloom in the drooping corners of his mouth. He bears a look of discontent, almost of suffering that, he imagines, both draws and repels Camilla:

She liked his sensibility, his vigour, and his violence; she liked his hardness, and it repelled her; the sombreness of his mind and his yellow face repelled her.

So he makes his face into an immovable screen which is unaffected by passing thoughts and spends time ruminating on the eternal discomfort of the universe.

Harry announces to Camilla that he will not change for her, but Camilla reassures him that she likes him as he is. Gently she touches him on the arm and laughs, and Harry relaxes as he notices the point of light which dances in her eyes.

Lytton Strachey suggested delicately to Leonard Woolf that he had failed to see the virgin's point of view: 'And didn't she desire it? Why aren't we told?' He thought the analysis, at a crucial point (when Harry succumbs to the all-too-willing Gwen), simply stopped. Strachey said with impressive tact that it was not clear how superb Harry and Camilla were meant to be nor could he see the inevitability of Harry's furious despair and lapse into cynicism. He advised Leonard to leave the book for six months and turn to something else.

Virginia Woolf's diary recalls a bitter skirmish in 1913. This suggests that the trials of that year were not exclusively to do with the publication of her first novel. It is not possible to say exactly how much she knew of *The Wise Virgins* at the time of her first post-marital breakdown, but Leonard was in the middle of it in April 1913 when her headaches began. He completed it in June 1913, the month during which she became so depressed that in July she had to enter a home. When she emerged from Twickenham in August, Leonard took her back to the Plough Inn where they had spent the first happy days of their honeymoon. The trip was a disaster. She left Somerset in an openly suicidal state and on their way back Leonard was in terror that she would throw herself from the train. She claimed the entire burden of 'fault', for how was she to deny Leonard's newly completed book which fixed her image as sexual failure?

Leonard persisted that she was going through one of her inexplicable periods of madness, another unanswerable position. She denied that she was mad but could not articulate the source and nature of her injury. Only once at Twickenham, when she offered separation, did he invite any blame: 'dearest one', he wrote on 3 August 1913, 'if I *have* done anything wrong to you & which has displeased you, you would tell me, wouldn't you? I do adore you so, Mandy, that I would do anything to change any beastliness in myself, if I knew how it had shown itself.' There is no evidence of what followed except a typically brief entry in Leonard's diary on 30 September 1913, that Virginia 'confessed' to him. What she confessed he does not say, but it may not have been very much for it brought no relief. She was, he noted, 'v. violent in night'. Possibly she loved Leonard so much that she had to protect at all costs his self-esteem. When she broke down in 1904 there was less need of loyalty to George and she did speak of him to Dr Savage, to her sister, to Janet, to Violet, but this was marriage.

The second phase of the breakdown began in February 1915, two weeks after Virginia finally read *The Wise Virgins*. The night before, Leonard had read 'Three Jews' aloud to her and Janet. The next morning there was a quarrel. Then, between tea and bedtime, Virginia read the whole novel. She was determined to see it in the best light—after all, their code of truthfulness obliged her to allow Leonard to voice his opinions—but she thought parts of the book 'very bad'. Her breakdown is usually ascribed to fears for *The Voyage Out* which had been held back but came out finally in March. What Leonard did not say is that his book, too, was delayed. Yet once Virginia seemed better, he went ahead with publication. It was accepted by Edward Arnold on 7 February 1914 and came out in October. All Bloomsbury responded with just distaste. It is a closed-minded book, inferior to *The Village in the Jungle*, but Leonard never understood why it failed. The outbreak of war killed it dead, is his sole, curt comment in his autobiography.

Leonard Woolf shaped himself as a man of reason—an admirable self-image but, in his case, too rigidly sustained to admit any lapse. He was temperamentally incapable of remorse. His correspondence with his family and publisher in 1913-14 shows an unyielding obstinacy in the face of strong criticism. It is as though two irreconcilable states coexisted in Leonard, passionate devotion to his wife and a cold refusal to modify his opinions. His love was to prove the stronger and more durable emotion and this he seemed to know. It was as though he was saying, without words: let me do this and then be perfectly happy. To rewrite, he told Bella, would have been mental torture. For this brief period, then, his own mental relief was his first priority.

In late May 1915 Virginia turned against Leonard and for about two months refused to see him. Leonard continued to do his best by his own lights which was to defer to medical advice which, from a later perspective, was stupidly firm in its ignorance and which Virginia rightly distrusted. Before praising Leonard, we might compare Lamb's protective tenderness for his mad sister or Virginia's fictional Rezia Warren Smith who comes to distrust the glib doctors attending her mad husband.

How, after this, did Virginia come to accept Leonard again? Her diary was abandoned for the duration of her illness. In any case it almost never explores her attitude to her husband. To observers, she simply recovered, against all expectation. But that recovery must have turned on some hope of healing their differences. In August 1915 Leonard was allowed to take her for drives or in a Bath chair to Kew. In October she gave him a copy of Dostoevsky's *The Insulted and Injured*, inscribed 'A Memory of the grand treat; Brighton'. For his part, Leonard saved the marriage by his response to the beast game and by affirming constantly an emotional commitment that lay deeper than their differences: 'You can't realise', he wrote on 13 March 1914, 'how utterly you would end my life for me if you had taken that sleeping mixture successfully or if you ever dismissed me.'

All question of conditional love now vanished from their letters. Leonard was given control of her health which he exercised with minute thoroughness. One day he slipped into the Richmond branch of the Co-operative Society and came home carrying a large paper parcel. While they had tea, he unpacked two enormous pairs of thick woollen combinations for Virginia with long legs, long sleeves, and an array of buttons. His gift was met with dismissive laughter. Another night, when Virginia stepped out to see the stars, the impact of their strangeness was muffled by Leonard's calls that she would get cold. She submitted willingly for the most part to what seemed, at times, unnecessary fuss. In return, I imagine, Leonard agreed to play the beast game on Virginia's terms, whatever they were.

Virginia disagreed with Arnold Bennett when he remarked that the horror of marriage was its dailiness which rubs off all the acuteness of love. She admitted that, say, four days out of seven did become automatic 'but on the 5th day a bead of sensation (between husband & wife) forms, wh. is all the fuller & more sensitive' for the customary days on either side.

'How lovely is the privacy of those to whom the world has given so much strife', Virginia Woolf wrote of Louis and Rhoda in the first draft of *The Waves*. Although Louis and Rhoda were never exact portraits of the Woolfs, the first, more autobiographic draft gives the rationale for a very strange and, in its own way, 'constantly passionate' union. Louis, despite his impregnable air, is an alien who fears men in tailcoats and finds consolation in poets. This is why Rhoda comes to him. 'And I suppose that the simplest & tenderest things that have been said in our time, were said in his top room . . . when the kettle boiled over.' Rhoda, though herself acutely vulnerable, is the nurturer, not the nurtured, in this relationship, for Louis is burdened by cosmic suffering. Present pleasures are (in the first draft) 'purpled with the shadows of dungeons, & tortures, & infamies practised by man upon man'. His ironical manner is meant to distract from his 'shivering and unhappy soul'. To this Rhoda responds. The manipulator she eventually rejects, for Louis is also 'formidable, bony, harsh & sardonic'.

The beast letters and, on one occasion, her diary suggest that although Virginia Woolf projected an image of herself as sexless, there were times, at least, when marriage gave her some sort of physical pleasure. On 10 November 1917, after a dispirited day together, they recovered their 'illusions' in the evening, before the fire, and were 'going merrily till bedtime when some antics ended the day'. No other couple so long married, she remarked in the diary on 28 September 1926, could reach and keep so constantly their own level of intimacy.

The imagery of Virginia Woolf's novels deplores those attributes of masculinity that are least attractive to women: aggression, egotism. Mr Ramsay is a brass beak or an arid scimitar when, obsessed with his own needs, he cannot imagine a woman's. The imagery of *To the Lighthouse* also connects the impersonal brutality of war with sex and both with the anarchic power of nature. During the war, waves mount one another and lunge in their 'idiot games' until it seems that all the world is tumbling 'in brute confusion and wanton lust'. But the wanton destructiveness of war may be counterbalanced by the controlled creativity of artists. In the same way, the image of brutal sex is counterbalanced by well-conducted union:

So, unhesitatingly, without fear or reserve, at some moment of culmination when all separation is over, except that delight of separation— which is consciousness of mixing—bodies unite; the human love has its gratification.

This sentence, left out of *To the Lighthouse*, compares the bliss of such union with that of artistic creation. The latter is more complete only because it is less transient:

Even while the arms are locked, or the sentence married in the air with complete understanding, a cloud moves across the sky; & each lover knows, but cannot confess, his knowledge of the transience of love: the mutability of love . . . .

A robust energy keeps surfacing through the invalidish regimen that Leonard imposed. More than praise, she decided, she would prefer to have £3 to buy rubber-soled boots for country walks. When she married she fully expected to have children, exclaimed happily over Violet's gift of an old cradle, and up to April 1913 was still talking hopefully of her 'brats'. The decision to have no children was taken on Leonard's initiative.* She liked to wander about naked in the early mornings at Clifford's Inn in Fleet Street where she and Leonard first took rooms. And she relished the sight of Leonard giving earnest advice to their charlady from his bath:

'And your husband, Mrs. Worsley—now what Society is he insured in?'—'A postman? O well—they must give him a rise then after 5 years, in the Naval Reserve too'—and all this with Leonard naked in his bath—Mrs. W. leaning on the W.C. door looking at him.

She had an unashamed interest in the body. 'We were kept awake till 4 this morning by mice in our bedroom', Virginia scribbled in one of her typically expansive letters to her sister. 'At last Leonard started to make his bed, & a mouse sprang out from his blankets, whereupon he had a wet dream—you can't think what his sheets are like this morning—.'

However the Woolfs resolved their differences, the important fact is that from about 1917 they came to find in each other 'divine contentment'. Virginia used these words to describe their reunion after Leonard's trip to Manchester in November 1917. Examining her feelings in his absence, she came to the conclusion that 'one's personality seems to echo out across space, when he's not there to enclose all one's vibrations'.

Leonard took the night train from Liverpool to Euston on 2 November and the next morning she lay awake from five till seven listening for his step. At eight, just as her expectation was beginning to flatten, Leonard suddenly appeared at her door and words flowed between them: 'things kept oozing out; sudden silences & spurts; divine contentment at being once more harmonious.'

Leonard steadily won her respect as a political speaker and as a champion of the Women's Co-operative movement. His style, she noticed approvingly during a speech to the International Group at the 1917 Club, was very clear yet with the right degree of passion to

* In January 1913, five months after marriage, LW consulted five medical authorities on the advisability of having children. On the basis of conflicting advice a decision was at this time postponed. VW must have abandoned hope of children during the 1913–15 breakdowns.

be interesting. She approved, too, his unpretentious manner with women, and wrote in her diary: 'No-one except a very modest person would treat these working women, & Lilian [Harris] & Janet [Case] & Margaret [Llewelyn Davies], as he does. Clive, or indeed any other clever young man, would give himself airs; & however much he admired them pretend that he didn't.'

She could now observe Leonard's gloom with calm detachment. Once, walking in Richmond Park on a cold grey afternoon in January 1915, she tried to cheer him up with praise when he shouted a peremptory 'Stop', and they walked on in silence. 'There's no arguing with him', she concluded in her diary. If she showed a preference for her family he was liable to turn 'stony' or 'cut up rusty'. He never bothered to conceal his resistance to her excursions into society but she came to find his harshness bracing. 'I think the worse of you for ever', he would say sourly when she accepted an invitation from Ottoline Morrell. 'L. may be severe; but he stimulates', she reflected. 'Anything is possible with him.'

The last breakdown of the twenty dark years came at the beginning of Virginia's marriage to Leonard Woolf, whose difficult task it was to fill the gap left by the dead past of her youth. More difficult, the divisiveness of dishonest sexual convention that remained in each as a Victorian residue was sharpened by her intelligence and her growing determination to be true to her nature. One bit of the Victorian residue, though, helped them overcome their differences: their trust in good feeling itself and a rock-like commitment to the marriage bond. They were bonded in deed by their exuberant beast game which somehow developed and flourished through their worst times. Ten years after the break-down in which she would not see Leonard, she claimed him as the hidden core of her life and the source of her freshness:

I snuggled in to the core of my life, which is this complete comfort with L., & there found everything so satisfactory & calm that I revived myself, & got a fresh start; feeling entirely immune. The immense success of our life, is I think, that our treasure is hid away; or rather in such common things that nothing can touch it. That is, if one enjoys a bus ride to Richmond, sitting on the green smoking . . ., airing the marmots, . . . sitting down after dinner, side by side, & saying 'Are you in your stall, brother?'—well, what can trouble this happiness? And every day is necessarily full of it.

Divine contentment, not tame nursing, shaped the authorial character who came into being in the spring of 1925 when her two greatest books, *To the Lighthouse* and *The Waves*, came to mind. After a holiday at Cassis that spring, Virginia wrote in her diary: 'L & I were too too happy. . . . Nobody shall say of me that I have not known perfect happiness, but few could put their finger on the moment, or say what made it.' She fell back on Othello's words as he meets Desdemona after their separation on a stormy voyage:

> If it were now to die,
> 'Twere now to be most happy, for I fear
> My soul hath her content so absolute
> That not another comfort like to this
> Succeeds in unknown fate.

10. *Counter-history*

To become a post-war artist, Virginia Woolf had to come to terms with the first world war, and she did so in a strange way. She devised a counter-history in which war is not the centre-piece but a vacant period through which time rushes, while home-makers and artists —the creators of civilization—sleep. In 'Time Passes', the second part of *To the Lighthouse*, there are seasons and colours—autumn trees appear as 'tattered flags', an explosion on the horizon colours the sea red—but, strangely, there are no people, only reports of the dead, given in brackets. What is left out—blurred emotions, battles, gore, and political justification—is by that deliberate omission acutely judged. This was far from withdrawal, as many assume, from public events; it was a critique of what histories and newspapers accustom us to define as memorable. In January 1916, reading *The Times* at breakfast, she wondered 'how this preposterous masculine fiction keeps going a day longer'. In need of truth, she distanced war so as to focus, from the angle of anarchic nature, on unseasonal loss of life. Voices of young men and women at the end of the Victorian age chatter late at night at the Ramsay door—Andrew's voice and Prue's—voices which, like those of Thoby and Stella, will not be heard again. It might have been a night like any other, and the Ramsay children and their guests retire to bed, but the night quickly becomes metaphoric, an engulfing darkness of war: 'One by one the lamps were all extinguished.'

Catherine Morland, the untutored heroine of *Northanger Abbey*, pities the deluded historian who fills up great volumes with 'the quarrels of popes and kings, with wars or pestilences, in every page; the men all so good for nothing, and hardly any women at all—it is very tiresome: and yet I often think it odd that it should be so dull, for a great deal of it must be invention'. For Virginia Woolf, too, the unnoticed acts of most ordinary people on an ordinary day, what they think and feel, are as much history as the wheelings and dealings of a small class in power. 'If you object that fiction is not history', Virginia Woolf wrote later, 'I reply that though it would be far easier to write history—"In the year 1842 Lord John Russell brought in the Second Reform Bill" and so on—that method of telling the truth seems to me so elementary, and so clumsy, that I prefer, where truth is important, to write fiction.'

A civilization, Steiner says, depends on understanding its history through imaginative records. 'We remember culturally', he says. 'The landscape composed by the past tense is . . . differently coded by different cultures.' History 'is an instrument of the ruling caste' for whom war has always been a drama of supreme importance. In 'Time Passes', Virginia Woolf rewrites history to show war as a time when the constructive energies of our species sleep. In Hardy's 'The Roman Road' there is a similar refusal of the militaristic bias of history in favour of those small common events which engender not heroic postures and inflated emotions but strong natural piety for one's native land.* The professional historian makes fictions of 'Helmed legionaries, who proudly rear | The Eagle'—a remote and artificial fantasy compared with the act of a mother guiding an infant's steps along the ancient road. In the same way, Virginia Woolf counters the heroics of Mr Ramsay's rendering of 'The Charge of the Light Brigade', with the composure of Mrs Ramsay knitting and reading. She subdues barbarity and chaos as she reads to her child while her husband, reciting his intoxicating platitudes, cavorts on the periphery of her solid field of action.

Mr Ramsay dreams of receiving no less than a dozen spears into his body. Thrilling to Tennyson's idealization of military disaster, he blunders about the garden of his safe, seaside villa. Shouting ' "Boldly we rode and well" ', he nearly knocks over the artist's easel as he races off 'to die gloriously she supposed upon the heights of Balaclava.' And a few minutes later, as the artist, Lily Briscoe, and the scientist, William Bankes, are making a friendship based on mutual respect for order and good sense, Mr Ramsay breaks in on them with a glaring report that ' "Someone had blundered." ' This comic dream of valour links the Crimea with the disasters of the first world war.

Virginia Woolf took physical courage for granted and admired

* See also Edward Thomas, 'This is no Case of Petty Right or Wrong':
> Two witches cauldrons roar.
> From one the weather shall rise clear and gay;
> Out of the other an England beautiful
> And like her mother that died yesterday.
> Little I know or care if, being dull,
> I shall miss something that historians
> Can rake out of the ashes. . . .

intellectual courage, but 'courage' in warriors was, to her, a deceptive term of value, like 'glory' and 'honour', because it could license stupid brutality. In the 1917 episode of *The Years*, Sara recoils from her cousin 'in his mud-coloured uniform, with his switch between his legs, and his ears sticking out on either side of his pink, foolish face . . .'. The idea that soldiers are not worthy of public record, that they are wretched interruptions to the continuum of civilization, harks right back to the summer of 1906 when she put the fitful vicissitudes of the wars of the Roses at the periphery of historical record and constructive domesticity at the centre.* In other words, she posits a history that might emphasize continuity more than change as, in her chronicle, *The Years*, the continuity of the family links Victorians and Moderns and as, in her pageant of English history in *Between the Acts*, Chaucer's pilgrims weave a perpetual backdrop to every age.

At the centre of history, she implies, are the acts of the obscure between the acts of kings and warriors. In place of the failed first world war ideal of military heroism, she brought out a different sort of spunk in obscure, old Miss Parry, a Victorian relic in *Mrs. Dalloway*. Miss Parry's relations had ruled India, but she retained 'no proud illusions about Viceroys, Generals, Mutinies—it was orchids she saw, and mountain passes, and herself carried on the backs of coolies in the 'sixties . . . an indomitable Englishwoman, fretful if disturbed by the war, say, which dropped a bomb at her very door, from her deep meditation over orchids . . .'. Miss Parry with her intrepid curiosity, Joan Martyn or Mrs Ramsay with their skills in natural happiness become incidental in times of war. In 'Time Passes' human faces disappear and, in one round of seasons, years are swallowed. The only visible person—and she looms larger in the manuscript—is Mrs McNab who bobs up after the war, emblematic of persistent life. This 'caretaking woman' is a comic saviour for she and her crony, Mrs Bast, 'stayed the corruption and the rot; rescued from the pool of Time that was fast closing over them now a basin, now a cupboard; fetched up from oblivion all the Waverley novels and a tea-set one morning'. The true saviours lurch and grumble. Bonneted, toothless but humming, they contemplate 'the magnificent conquest over taps and bath' and 'the more arduous, more partial triumph over long rows of books'. An antidote to patriotic emotions of cultivated hatred, Mrs McNab

* See 'The Journal of Mistress Joan Martyn', pp. 86-9.

croons forgiveness. In the draft, her song trickles out as though 'a channel were tunnelled in the heart of obscurity & through the rift . . . there issued peace'.

So, at the end of the war, old crones repair the Ramsay home, the abandoned, rotting bastion of Victorian culture, and then the artist, Lily Briscoe, returns to paint a remembered picture. The activities of the old crones and the artist are reciprocal in that they are the preservers of the past. As the crones sift the Victorian relics, so the modern artist sifts those qualities of the age that must be preserved, from the clutter of outworn beliefs that may safely pass into oblivion. In the wake of the war, Virginia Woolf was doing precisely this.

Her counter to history, her interest in the lives of the obscure, was rooted in her pre-war writing but was now to find its perfect expressive form. The originality, the self-evident modernity of the post-war novels, lay not in subject so much as in a new distorted design. She achieved this by exploiting subjective time against mechanical time. In her novels, time expands lingeringly over memories or time contracts when an empty epoch, like the war, flashes by, or time stands still in moments of what Joyce called 'epiphany' and she termed 'moments of being'.* But to understand, first, the affront to historical narrative, it is essential to see in her resistance to war an outrage so complete that, taking a line more extreme than anti-war poets, she refused to treat war at all.

An oblique comment on war does appear in several of her works: it points always to the damage to character. In *Mrs. Dalloway* she studies the effect of four years of brutalization on an individual soldier who is suffering the delayed guilt of insensibility.† In *Between the Acts*, written at the beginning of the second world war, she looks at a stain on the immaculate shoes of an English country gentleman (he has stamped on a toad): it marks nothing logical in his case, simply the awakening of the crudest war-fever, stirred by reports of German offensives.

Married to Leonard Woolf, she was well aware of the rationale for pacifism in the first world war and for belligerence in the second, yet she concentrated on what is common to all wars: the improper emotions to which patriotism gives licence.

Her nerve, at least, if not her precise position she got from her father. Leslie Stephen was disgusted by the 'vulgar brag' of

---

* She derived the phrase, possibly, from Hardy's *Moments of Vision* (1917).
† Cf. Wilfred Owen's 'Insensibility'.

patriotism. 'Nobody can accuse me of yielding to that weakness', he liked to declare loudly in Victorian society, and he relished looks of solemn disapproval mixed with bewilderment.

Virginia Woolf's dismay with the war came from a love of country deeper than patriotism, which is appalled to see one's countrymen degraded. In October 1918, with the end of the war in sight, she was confounded when *The Times* publicized a proposal for yet another season of killing in order to carry the war into Germany and there, she added sarcastically, 'imprint a respect for liberty in the German peasants'.

National rejoicings with victory on 11 November made her wonder 'whether any decent life will ever be possible'. To celebrate on 19 July 1919 there were processions of generals and tanks amidst almost continuous rain. Londoners 'sleepy & torpid as a cluster of drenched bees' crawled over Trafalgar Square. Would they ever own up that they 'saw through it'—saw, that is, that there was nothing to celebrate—or were they too docile, a herd of animals? She was touched only by disabled soldiers and sailors at the Star and Garter, a Home at the top of Richmond Hill. They lay 'with their backs to us, smoking cigarettes, & waiting for the noise to be over. We were children to be amused.'

The breakdown of 1915 together with the chasm of war and its melancholy aftermath necessitated a period of healing which, for Virginia Woolf, meant renewed ties with the past. The past contained 'treasure' that must be discovered and preserved. In *Jacob's Room* the moor literally hoards treasures: Betty Flanders's darning needles, Roman skeletons, and all the dead who cry aloud from their tombstones. Leonard Woolf has described the benign influence of their home, Hogarth House, in Richmond: 'Unconsciously one was absorbed into this procession of men, women, and children who since 1600 or 1700 sat in the panelled rooms, clattered up and down stairs, and had planted the great Blenheim apple-tree or the ancient fig-tree. One became part of a history and of a civilization by continuing in the line of all their lives.'

Night and Day, Virginia Woolf's second novel, was conceived in 1916 at Wissett (a farm in Suffolk that Vanessa was trying to manage with Duncan Grant and David Garnett). The novel revived a picture of the pre-war intellectual aristocracy, epitomized and questioned by Katharine Hilbery, granddaughter of an eminent Victorian poet. The character of Katharine was modelled on Vanessa: her dependence on reason, her silent stoicism, her secret commitment to mathematics, an equivalent to Vanessa's painting and, like that, in conflict with a Victorian sense of responsibility as the daughter at home. Katharine is drawn into the contrasting lives of the new woman, the idealistic political worker, Mary Datchet, and of the abrasive solicitor, Ralph Denham, rising out of an ugly, graceless suburban household which yet, as Katharine perceives, seethes with vigour.

The Hilbery house is set in Cheyne Walk, Chelsea, where George Eliot lived and, later, Henry James. There, art and prosperity mingle to make a stable civilization. But it has become too precious, exclusive, mannered, the kind of milieu that cherishes the rather effete, correct, second-rate writer, William Rodney, to whom Katharine, almost automatically, becomes engaged. Katharine's silent uneasiness is the focus for Virginia Woolf's light ridicule of the pre-war intelligentsia: of the endless ritual teas, the pink ribbons on the dinner table, and the ever-present relics and never-to-be-finished memoir of grandfather. Eventually, as Katharine's discomfort deepens into wordless futility, she is driven to reject Rodney for the ungentlemanly but life-giving Denham.

When *Night and Day* came out in 1919, Katherine Mansfield, reading it for review, condemned it as decorous and old-fashioned. There was no novelty: no attention to the war and no evidence of modernity. But *Night and Day*'s interest lies precisely in its continuity with the Victorian novel. The ordeal of consciousness, developed by George Eliot and Henry James, was, for Virginia Woolf, a starting-point for the novel of the future where, as she put it in 'The Mark on the Wall' (1917) her plan was to follow the mental track of 'modest mouse-coloured people' who had, lurking in them, a sense of a 'romantic figure' as opposed to 'that shell of a person which is seen by other people. . . . Those are the depths [novelists] will explore, those the phantoms they will pursue, leaving the description of reality more and more out of their stories. . . .'

'The romantic figure': I propose that Virginia Woolf's celebrated modernity was, in some ways, a jaunty overlay and am stressing her unbroken ties with the nineteenth century. Her scheme above suggests a wish to blend into the novel that extension of the self through the kind of dreamlike reverie to be found in Romantic poetry. She differed from the Romantics, though, in discarding the pretensions of the great soul for the 'mouse-coloured' person, a nondescript old woman in a third-class carriage or a housewife ordering the fish, and located the Romantic drama, the awakening to a moment of sublimity, in the domestic scene. This is the source of Virginia Woolf's continuous appeal to most readers: not the experimentalism that intellectuals admire, but her repeated demonstration that the most humdrum domestic actions, knitting a brown stocking, or dishing out the *bœuf en daube*, or sewing a dress for a party, could spark moments of romantic enlargement, just as a mere mark on the wall sends the writer's mind racing on different tracks, on the history of the house and its occupants, or on the question of death and after. The writer deflates herself comically when the mark is revealed as a snail: here is the modern discord as the reverie crashes upon, say, the appearance of morning tea. In *Between the Acts*, Mrs Swithin, day-dreaming of the prehistoric monsters who once roamed rhododendron forests in Piccadilly, 'elephant-bodied, seal-necked, heaving, surging, slowly writhing, and, she supposed, barking monsters . . .' casts on Grace, putting down the morning tray, 'the divided glance that was half meant for a beast in a swamp, half for a maid in a print frock and white apron'. 'Batty', the servant thinks, yet the hallucination holds for there is, in fact, a connection between Grace and prehistory, if only we could see it.

At the same time as she planned her version of the romantic reverie, she cultivated the image of an 'up-to-date woman' (so, she hoped, she struck a shrinking Forster). She practised the modish tone of mocking hilarity, at its peak in her post-war letters. She watched Mrs Clifford's mouth 'open like an old leather bag, or the private parts of a large cow'.* Her cousin, Emma Vaughan, had 'a blankness in the eye which is precisely that of a toad glutted with large moths'. Rather idly, she wooed people, wanting love and attention, at the same time reserving herself behind a mocking surveillance of others' weak spots, using her annihilating wit not judiciously, as Austen to educate, but callously, to expose. The manuscript of *Mrs. Dalloway* commends 'a cool waiting wit, which flickered upon the air like the tongue of a lizard'. She began to see herself as 'the spectator of the public, never part of it'.

This brittle modernity was bolstered with advanced essays and

---

* Mrs W. K. Clifford (d. 1929), a prolific writer and journalist, had been a friend of VW's parents. VW called her a hack (*Diary*, i, pp. 254 and 255 n.).

sketches, 'An Unwritten Novel' and 'Modern Fiction', and a startling rejection of the 'and then . . .' narrative of *Night and Day* for the collage of broken impressions that makes up the portrait of a young man in *Jacob's Room* (1922). Although I do not want to slight the novelty of her experiments, her work could be seen from another view as backward-looking. Her true originality is not merely technical but lies in the heroic perversity of her sense of history. For, despite the prevailing mood of cultural despair in which inevitably she shared, she contrived in her post-war novels to build a resonant past. Her fictional biography of the promising Jacob, whose course of development is blotted out by the war, was continuous with earlier work, with the biographic view of history in 'The Journal of Mistress Joan Martyn' and with the elegiac impulse in the 'Reminiscences'.

To Virginia Woolf, in an elegiac mood, life was 'but a procession of shadows' destined for death. 'God knows', she exclaimed, 'why it is that we embrace them so eagerly, and see them depart with such anguish, being shadows.' Such anguish for Thoby compelled her 'sudden vision' of the solidity of his memory. Could she transform shadow into the substance of a young man reading in a chair in his room? Could she confer on Thoby the enduring aesthetic form of statues whose backs the sculptors had left unfinished? In *Jacob's Room* she devised a form of imaginative biography which refused deceptive fullness of definition. This, she hoped, would give to biography the formal restraints of a suggestive art.

One way of transmuting memory into art was to recast Thoby in the figure of the lost generation of the first world war. Her particular war memorial disregards the usual props of angels, battledress, and gun and sets up, instead, an image of natural manhood, nurtured by seas, suns, moors, friendships, and loves, rather like the dead comrade of Owen's 'Futility' who is defined not by the gory area of war but by scenes of his past, infused with the poet's purest emotion, a sublime pity.

Jacob's Room excludes the scene of his death but the whole book forecasts it. With the mention of Jacob's surname, Flanders, in the first sentence and with the recurring discovery of the poppies he has pressed between the leaves of his Greek dictionary, there is the ghostly, advancing echo of the famous war poem:

> In Flanders fields the poppies blow
> Between the crosses, row on row . . . .

As a child on a beach Jacob is drawn to an animal's skull: 'Clean, white, wind-swept, sand-rubbed, a more unpolluted piece of bone existed nowhere on the coast of Cornwall.' Later, the skull is found in his room, hung above his bedroom door. Like Hamlet, Jacob is destined to contemplate mortality before his time. Many years after *Jacob's Room*, in Virginia Woolf's last portrait of her brother in 'A Sketch of the Past', she alluded to the last words Fortinbras speaks over Hamlet's body: 'Had he been put on, he would have played his part most royally.'*

Jacob passes mysterious and barely visible through a sea of interchangeable faces. These faces, drawn in brief, hard outline, are, ironically, less memorable than the shadowed Jacob, who is given his enduring form by the emotion he has provoked. This elegiac longing is curiously at odds with the ostentatious modernity of the collage of faces who come cheap, and fall away, together with the routine fictions that fill their minds. By contrast, when Jacob will cease to be, Cornwall, Cambridge, London will contain the impress of his invisible spirit, just as his father, Seabrook, endures as part of nature. So Virginia Woolf conferred immortality on her brother. In the midst of drafts of essays, in about 1922, she jotted down a design for his tombstone, using Catullus' elegy for his brother who died near Troy, a familiar inscription but especially appropriate for Thoby who died of typhoid contracted abroad on a visit to Constantinople:

Julian Thoby Stephen

[1881–1906]

atque in perpetuum frater
ave atque vale.

All through *Jacob's Room* his biographer talks directly to the reader: we two push ourselves forward—busy, agog, distractable—while our subject slips out of sight. The would-be biographer is vibrating 'at the mouth of the cavern of mystery, endowing Jacob Flanders with all sorts of qualities he had not at all . . . what remains is mostly a matter of guess work. Yet over him we hang vibrating.' The biographic obsession is comic in its futility. The biographer confides the struggle to do an imaginative portrait from scraps of

---

* Cf. *Hamlet*, v. ii:

> For he was likely, had he been put on,
> To have proved most royal . . . .

memory, fragmentary reports of friends, books fingered, scenes visited by Jacob. At moments of acute frustration, when the biographer finds the room empty, its occupant gone, in other words ungraspable, the reader is invited to share in his creation.

It is to be a modernist portrait. This much the biographer directs. We are not to draw Jacob's features but to give him a significant form, as people who had loved him had built an image, like Fanny Elmer who recognized him in the statue of Ulysses in the British Museum. The reader is given little help. The biographer supplies only the barest outlines: he spent his childhood at Scarborough; he was educated at Cambridge; he worshipped the Greeks; he smoked a pipe, sat by fires, exchanged small talk. He seems to have the qualities of a hero; the way people of all backgrounds are drawn to him for no particular reason suggests a leader in the making. His blend of simple-heartedness and worldliness promises responsible action. But what exactly Jacob was to be remains a mystery. The deliberately fragmented narrative with its curt sentences, its tantalizing glimpses—Jacob lying on his back in Greece—forces the reader to share in the biographer's effort and failure. What is so impressive is this honesty about failure. Jacob's biographer refuses to content herself with the usual stories, the Tom Jones story of the young man who couples with the plausible flirt, Florinda, or becomes besotted with an idle married woman on tour. Jacob does perform the Tom Jones routine and others, but we sense that whatever is silently furled within him would have bypassed banality with the passing of youth.

In *Jacob's Room* elegy finds a new expressive form in the gaps and silences of broken prose which confront loss repeatedly. The elegiac poem—'Lycidas', 'Adonais', 'In Memoriam', 'When Lilacs Last in the Dooryard Bloom'd'—is consolatory. It covers the dead with verbal extravagance and so, tacitly, consents to the deepening shades. But Virginia Woolf demonstrates how to be inconsolable. She will not let Jacob go. She is always after him, following this track or another—his sail to Durrant's home in Cornwall, his tour to Greece and Constantinople—waiting with faithful patience for his telling biographic moment.

Yet two problems remain. The counterpoise to the unknowability of Jacob is the comic drama of a writer in pursuit of a subject. This drama (forecast in 'An Unwritten Novel' published in July 1920, three months after this novel was begun) cannot sustain a whole book unless the writer becomes a character like, say, Tristram Shandy. The narrator is pathetic but should have been much more pathetic if she were not to seem half-invisible. In theory, Virginia Woolf planned to make herself 'a wall' for the book but, in the writing, was too guarded. She used her voice more boldly in *The Voyage Out* which gives it an impact that, I think, *Jacob's Room* lacks.

The other problem rose directly out of the haste for modernity: the book's treatment of the myriad people who glanced at Jacob, but did not *see* him. Given their brash, instant visibility, they should hit the eye with the hilarious jolt of the crowded caricatures in Eliot's post-war poems or with the deflating humour of Katherine Mansfield. (Both were published by the Hogarth Press in 1918 and 1919, samples of advanced writing.) But the casual modern thrust of derision never quite brought out the best in Virginia Woolf. Her opinions became rash to the point of prejudice. She had neither Eliot's lethal strike nor the worldly-wise affections of Mansfield. She herself feared that *Jacob's Room* might come to appear 'sterile acrobatics'. In the mean time, though, she was developing her own kind of portrait in the great diary: that searching lighthouse beam that was her mother's gift.

This diary, begun in the midst of the first world war and ending abruptly with Virginia Woolf's suicide in the midst of the second, was her most sustained counter to history: a private document of her times.

After the war, Virginia Woolf went up to London more frequently, sometimes to parties and concerts, but often simply to lope the streets. She was now on the scent of people and scenes, of multitudinous impressions which she sealed hot in her diary. She used to arrive from Richmond at Waterloo and cross the Thames by the Hungerford footbridge from which she saw the grey-white spires of the City. With the observant eye of Defoe, she examined old women selling matches '& the draggled girl skirting round the pavement of St. James' Square seemed to me out of Roxanna or Moll Flanders. Yes, a great writer surely to be thus imposing himself upon me after 200 years.'

One bright night with a fresh breeze, she was returning on the top of a bus to Waterloo when she spied a blind old beggarwoman against a stone wall in Kingsway, holding a brown mongrel in her arms as she sang aloud shrilly for her own amusement, not begging. Her reckless jollity seemed 'much in the spirit of London'. This resilient creature reappears in *Jacob's Room* and *Mrs. Dalloway*, and inspires the last unfinished work, *Anon*. 'Then the fire engines came by—shrill too; with their helmets pale yellow in the moonlight. Sometimes every thing gets into the same mood; how to define this one I don't know. . . . Nowadays I'm often overcome by London; even think of the dead who have walked in the city.'

After the early-war breakdown, she began the diary again in October 1917 at the same time as she reviewed a 'book of memories', the posthumous volume of Henry James's autobiography. 'The Old Order', her celebration of James's monument to his age, suggests her reciprocal wish to hoard memory as a kind of 'savings'. In her novels she wished to transform memory into art; the diary complements this with the wish to transform memory into a social document that would, in time, speak with the breath of a vanished age. She shared with James a relish of the past: both were most entirely in their element in the act of recollection. James's memories, Virginia Woolf wrote, are yet more wonderful than the novels. In the same way, some readers will justifiably prefer Virginia Woolf's diary to her novels, for hers is one of the great diaries.

On 8 February 1926 she spelt out her aim: 'At 60 I am to sit down & write my life.' The diary was to be 'rough material' for 'that masterpiece'. Rereading the first accumulations on 20 April 1919, she saw, looming ahead, 'the shadow of some kind of form which a diary might attain to. I might in the course of time learn what it is that one can make of this loose, drifting material of life.' Her diary was like a deep old desk into which she could fling a mass of odds and ends: lightning sketches of the great, rows with the cook, broodings over her next book and, always rising to the surface, the dates of Stella's engagement, her mother's death, her father's and Thoby's birthdays. Her most insistent memory was the summer of 1890, St Ives, the sound of the sea at night, the children running in the garden. In March 1921 she wanted to 'go down to Treveal & look at the sea—old waves that have been breaking precisely so these thousand years'. In old age she would come back, she hoped, '& find that the collection had sorted itself . . . & coalesced, as such deposits so mysteriously do, into a mould, transparent enough to reflect the light of our life, & yet steady, tranquil composed with the aloofness of a work of art'.

In defining the exact nature of this diary, it is helpful to look at preceding diaries and their motives. Starting in 1897, again in the summer of 1899, and again in the winter of 1915 there was a commitment to regularity which is alien to the confessional diary, content to respond to mood. She kept grim details at bay. ('It's enough to live one's disagreeables without writing them.') Nor is there, surprisingly in view of Leonard Woolf's earlier extracts, *A Writer's Diary*, a vast amount about her work. The diary's main concern was continual portraiture. In none of her novels do we get such a profusion of faces. Virginia Woolf was a supreme noticer, not just of her circle. She observes, for instance, that German prisoners during the first world war, stacking corn at the back of Asheham, 'whistle a great deal, much more complete tunes than our work men'.

There was always a string of portraits on the walls of her mind. Death brought out the best portraits, extended elegies. When Kitty Maxse died in October 1922, Virginia Woolf decided to make Mrs Dalloway the centre of a full-scale novel. She recalled how Kitty got engaged at St Ives and, again, was tugged back to the summer of 1890: 'I keep going over this very day in my mind.'

In the first years of the diary the portraits are physical. Her cousin, Katherine Stephen, now retired from Newnham College, was 'strangely unaccented' in South Kensington. She sat 'all of a piece, white, unjointed with a mute sagacity', saying that on her deathbed she would order the charwoman to burn the neat row of her diaries from 1877. Vita Sackville-West looked 'like an over ripe grape in features, moustached, pouting, striding on fine legs in a well-cut skirt'.

Another form of record was the scenario. There is an exact report of a conversation with Bertrand Russell who told her that to write mathematics is the highest of the arts. 'God does mathematics', he claimed. There is a scenario of Eliot and his wife, Vivienne, taking tea in 1923 when the Woolfs were setting up the type of *The Waste Land*. Vivienne struggled pathetically to enter into this literary scene in her capacity as loyal supporter to the coming poet, but was too over-dressed and powdered, too anxious to puff Eliot's reputation.

In 1919 and again in 1923 Virginia Woolf tried out a series of portraits of friends, a quick penetration of a hidden self which became the major methodological link between the diary and the novels. Here, she put into practice what she had noted in 1917, the Jamesian attention to 'the shadow in which the detail of so many things can be discerned which the glare of day flattens out'. Her attention to shadow is only occasional in the diary but when it does happen, the insight is stunning. 'How he suffers!' she thought when Eliot came to tea in 1935.

> Yes: I felt my accursed gift of sympathy rising.... Suddenly T. spoke with a genuine cry of feeling. About immortality: . . . he revealed his passion, as he seldom does. A religious soul: an unhappy man: a lonely very sensitive man, all wrapt up in fibres of self torture, doubt, conceit, desire for warmth & intimacy. And I'm very fond of him—like him in some of my reserves & subterfuges.

And, again, in 1940, the diary points through Eliot's 'bronze mask' to the penitent martyr: 'An inhibited, nerve-drawn; dropped face— as if hung on a scaffold of heavy private brooding.'

When Virginia Woolf went to Golders Green to sit with Mary Sheepshanks in her suburban garden, she 'beat up the waters of talk . . . so that life mayn't be wasted'. She castigated herself if she did not catch every drop in the bowl of the diary. If eleven days went unrecorded it was a 'lapse'. She wrote: 'life allowed to waste like a tap left running.' Her diary had another use: deliberately, it retains 'life' untransmuted into art. She did not drop life for art quite so quickly as the cerebral young man of 'La Figlia che Piange'. Her diary spurts all the time, bathing her with scenes. Her proximity to life and her responsiveness were so unflagging that she had no need to generate feeling like Yeats through the actor's mask, or, like Eliot, to break agonizingly through a crust of comfortable deadness.

Fiction was 'the finished article', the diary was 'the raw', and the one was, in some indirect way, dependent on the fertility of the other. Her work depended on keeping that fount of life going so that, instinctively, she had to resist Leonard's wish to tuck her up at home. Virginia Woolf saw that 'to be as subtle as Henry James one must also be robust; to enjoy his power of exquisite selection one must have "lived and loved and cursed and floundered and enjoyed and suffered", and, with the appetite of a giant, have swallowed the whole'.

The flying hand of the diary, faster than a typewriter, set it all down after tea. She enjoyed the rush and indiscretion. The act of writing was like the sweep of a brush. Nobody was too insignificant or indecent to make her own. Each sentence is invested with the whole fling of her intelligence, throwing out, at its swiftest, incredible felicities of phrase. It is all strenuous and of a piece with her Victorian energy that could take in teas and dinners, hop on buses and trains, and yet have a rigidly regulated working day in which every half-hour had its use. Yet if she lived indefatigably, recorded hugely, had an enormous, sustained, increasing appetite for life, there remained, as she noted in James, 'something incommunicable, something reserved'. This is the 'aloofness and loneliness of the artist's life' which enters the diary only in passing.

It is essential to define the diary not only by its long-term motive, which is to see it as a distinct work, or to see it below the fiction as a practice-ground for portraiture, but also to place it in the day-to-day conduct of a writer's career. I think that the diary built up a kind of base (the press was another) from which Virginia Woolf could move between the otherwise irreconcilable night and day which she describes in her novels. From the swivelling base of the diary she leaps out into Bloomsbury or swings easily the other way into the anonymity of the writer's life.

Virginia Woolf assumed that hers was not a real diary because, from the start, it banished 'the soul'. The diary waves us aside from the strange, unpredictable thoughts that surface, it seems, in the novels alone. Fiction was her repository of the soul's truth, not the diary where she exercised the skills of observation. There she analysed Eliot, Keynes, Ottoline Morrell, but the people who mattered most were excluded. Leonard and Vanessa cross and recross her field of vision but her attention will not settle on them, except for trivial exchanges: servant problems and the question, at the end of 1923, of a move back to London.

As well as a record of social history, the diary was also a practical measure: a fortification on the perimeter of the private life looking out into the arena of public life. Behind this fortification, a distinctively post-war artist was emerging from the facelessness of the apprenticeship and the deranged face of the prelude to marriage. Rereading the diary in December 1919, she marked the change: 'I'm amused to find how its grown a person, with almost a face of its own.'

11. *Inventing the Artist*

THE face forming in the diary of 1919 was that of a high priestess of the modern novel. Virginia Woolf's entry for 24 January 1919 commends a 'new departure' to match a Post-Impressionist movement or a printing press. 'We Stephens', she assured herself, 'had the initiative, & the vitality to conceive & carry our wishes into effect because we wished too strongly to be chilled by ridicule or checked by difficulty.'

Between the low-point of what looked like incurable madness in 1915 and the triumphant publication of *To the Lighthouse* in 1927, Virginia Woolf remade herself as a modern artist. E. M. Forster, in an essay on the anonymity of great art, said that artists have two personalities, one public, one private, and that art comes from the obscure depths. Virginia Woolf developed a mercurial public manner—she called it 'doing my tricks'—at Bloomsbury parties. With a little encouragement she threw off words like a musician improvising. Her voice seemed to preen itself with self-confidence in its verbal facility as she leant sideways, a little stiffly in her chair, to address her visitor in a bantering manner. She confounded strangers with wildly fictitious accounts of their lives or shot malicious darts at friends who, the night before, she might have flattered outrageously. Good readers often say that they cannot bear Virginia Woolf. Some mean, I think, that her public manner affected her work. I see it in her unresolved attitude to the gushy side of the London socialite, Mrs Dalloway, and, later, throughout the frothy *Orlando*, a fictional biography of her aristocratic new friend, Victoria Sackville-West.

But to go back to Forster's two personalities, what is important about Virginia Woolf is her serious core. At a certain moment, she admitted, 'I see through what I'm saying and detest myself; & wish for the other side of the moon . . .'. This dark side, the subject of this biography, is hardest at this stage of her career to discern. The public personality outstares her. But the core is always there, in her marriage and in her best work which is never gushy, mercurial, malicious but poetic and searching, and protected, in a sense, by the glittering carapace of the public act.

In short, there is a gap between the sociable Virginia Woolf of Bloomsbury and even the businesslike Virginia of the diary and the experimental novelist. She put all the private force of feeling into the novels; the diary and letters, on the other hand, were tossed off with effervescent nonchalance.

The letters had a different place in Virginia Woolf's career. With their flights of fancy, their impetuosity of address, their exaggerations and mockery, the letters were like her talk. She spoke easily, in a pure, idiomatic English, with enquiring passion tempered by humour. Her eyes lit up with animation and curiosity. This fantastical queen of Bloomsbury, so visible, so often recalled in the Bloomsbury memoirs of the 1960s and 1970s, has been emphasized at the expense of the writer, far more difficult to know, often invisible, and almost the opposite in character, not fanciful, not cruel, but tenderly attentive to the recesses of character. The letters are, for the most part, flamboyant performances, delirious antics, at once amusing and irritating as the relentless sprightliness with which Tristram Shandy guards his vulnerable self, a victim of crushing circumstance. She worried about 'dullness' in her letters to her sister because, here, she is an entertainer. Stephen Spender contrasted Keats's and Lawrence's letters, which speak out of the centre of their being to those of their friends, with Virginia Woolf's letters which create a character for herself which speaks to the characters she creates for her correspondents. Spender adds that the letters read like fiction. Her correspondents (with the exceptions of Leonard and the dying Jacques Raverat*) were divided into intimates and butts who, at a moment's caprice, changed places. 'And I don't like my own letters', she owned to Raverat. 'I don't like the falsity of the relationship—one has to spray an atmosphere round one. . . .' Written with the kind of brazen, offhand candour that is not very intimate, the letters were not a serious mode of communication but, as Virginia commented to her sister, a routine social gesture, reverting to the habits of ancestors who wrote daily and at length. 'Let us consider letters . . .', she interposes in *Jacob's Room*. These efforts to relay news and make appointments will fade. How committed she was to immortality! It consoled her to think

---

* Raverat, a Frenchman, studied mathematics at Cambridge and married a 'neo-pagan' friend of VW's, Gwen Darwin. After that he became a painter. VW wrote him marvellous letters which he found consoling during his illness. She also sent him the proofs of *Mrs. Dalloway*, which his wife read him during his last days.

that Byron and Cowper did also turn 'from the sheet that endures to the sheet that perishes'.

Criticism, on the other hand, brought her back to the anonymity of art. In an unpublished introductory chapter for 'Reading', her early idea for *The Common Reader*, she held by Chaucer's advice to

> Flee fro the prees, and dwelle with sothfastnesse,
> Suffyce unto thy good, though it be smal.

In the summer of 1923, when she started writing *Mrs. Dalloway*, all need for praise dropped away. 'I feel as if I slipped off all my ball dresses & stood naked—which as I remember was a very pleasant thing to do.' 'Nakedness' was the condition to which she always returned, 'the backbone of my existence'. A month later she called for courage to speak out without mincing and when she came to the terrible doctor, Sir William Bradshaw, she promised herself, at the top of her manuscript, the relief of honesty. True to her promise, she left the attack on the doctor unchanged. She felt fairly free of foreign influence '& this I must prize, for unless I am myself, I am nobody'.

In 1922–3 Virginia referred frequently to her age—she was now in her forties—and to an acute sense of time passing: 'I feel time racing like a film at the Cinema. . . . I prod it with my pen.' She became more aware of the passage of the lifespan and the opportunities offered by its different stages. She saw forty to forty-one as an age of choice: either one spurs faster or one flags. Watching friends like Desmond MacCarthy and Lytton Strachey lose their freshness, she was determined to risk more, to live more stormily. Her diary testifies to the way that she created her life. It was not a background to her work, it was a creative work itself.

She beat up her sense of change by planning a move to London and spurred herself to new candour with a portrait of a madman. Septimus Warren Smith was to be more 'close to the fact' than Jacob. She would venture into the unexplored caves behind madness, going back in time. And all the while, the diary threw up seeds of books that lay yet far off in the future. 'What happened between Chaucer and Shakespeare?' This question, tossed out in 1923, was the seed of *Anon*, begun in 1940.

'Often now I have to control my excitement', she said on 13 June 1923, 'as if I were pushing through a screen; or as if something beat fiercely close to me. What this portends I don't know. It is a general sense of the poetry of existence that overcomes me. Often it is connected with the sea & St. Ives.'

In search of new stimulus for writing, Virginia and Leonard Woolf moved, in March 1924, from Richmond to 52 Tavistock Square in Bloomsbury. Vanessa decorated their rooms with rough trellises, wavy lines, two-handled vases, guitars, fans, and floral motifs. In the basement, they re-established the Hogarth Press and Virginia Woolf wrote in an adjoining store-room, which had once been a vast billiard-room, with great bales of books, each containing 500 copies, strewn like sandbags around her. The room had a skylight and a damp stone floor which made the books give off a smell of mildew. Leonard said that when she wrote a protective skin or integument insulated her from her squalid surroundings. She wore a blue overall and steel-rimmed glasses and sat hunched in a distended wicker chair with a board across its arms to which she glued her inkstand, in imitation of her father. A home-rolled shag cigarette drooped from her lips, her hair hung over her forehead.

'It is a mistake to think that literature can be produced from the raw', she told herself. 'One must get out of life . . .', not be Virginia Woolf scattered and gregarious, but 'very, very concentrated, all at one point'. After too much society, she would rock herself back into literature primarily through exercise in the open air and then by reading. Her working life established itself upon this act of oscillation. Back in London, in reach of people, this oscillation became more rapid and all the more fertile for being controlled. She seethed if talkative young Robert Graves (a Hogarth author) overstayed tea-time hours and if her noisy sister-in-law, Karin Stephen, descended on their country home, Monks House, with children in tow. For they interrupted the renewing, daily flow of *Mrs. Dalloway*. If people continued to sap her attention rather than nourish it, she would withdraw into the impenetrable silence of ill-health. 'Something happens in my mind. It refuses to go on registering impressions. It shuts itself up. It becomes a chrysalis. . . . Then suddenly something springs.' Illness, or threatened illness, could itself be a source of fertility, a dangerous final resort, shedding the layers of being—the well-bred lady and the shabby Bohemian—to reinvent from the bedrock of minimal existence.

'My only interest as a writer lies, I begin to see, in some queer individuality.' Through her diary Virginia Woolf invented a more effective view of herself than *The Voyage Out*'s image of sunken monster. In the entry for 2 January 1923, she suggested 'an image of forging ahead, alone, through the night: of suffering inwardly, stoically; of blazing my way through to the end—& so forth'. This romantic dream served to beat up her persistence and sense of adventure. As a young woman in 1903 she had realized that 'London itself is an unexplored land'. She returned to London in 1924 as a mature writer, 'owling' the alleys of the City, taking her voyage out to Regent's Park or the parties of the West End. Finishing *Mrs. Dalloway*, she was sure that her talent was on the rise. If her rival, Katherine Mansfield, had gone on, 'people would have seen that I was the more gifted—that wd. only have become more & more apparent'.

Leonard has explained that, when Virginia Woolf wrote, she was holding three states in balance and that all three had their place in the plan of her day. On long afternoon walks before tea she thought out her books with enormous care in a state of drifting rumination. Wandering in Holborn and the Charing Cross Road or on the downs and water-meadows near Rodmell, Sussex, she made up lines for the next morning's stint. In this state in which her art took shape, she is, next to illness, least accessible. We might see her best in the dreaming Rhoda who flies through darkness, tolerating doubt and uncertainty, to find the essential forms of human nature. This state appears also in a bust by Stephen Tomlin. Her face is rough-hewn, inchoate, but the large, owlish eyes are single-minded, staring, as though fixed on something invisible.

Virginia had highly developed social skills and managed to domesticate her strangeness as lovable English eccentricity which was so at home in Bloomsbury. Frances Partridge describes her acting the cracked Englishwoman, with an old felt hat on top of her head, hurling her bowl with wildly waving arms. She wore either dowdy or original outfits of her own devising. Once, she decked herself in a summer cloak of grey crinkly silk which made her look, she told her sister, like a young elephant. But when she drifted through the streets without disguise, rapid, staring, entranced, bystanders tended to laugh. Her unaffected strangeness made them uneasy.

In the mornings, when Virginia Woolf wrote fiction, she was in a different state, of concentrated passion. Twice, Leonard uses the word 'volcanic' for the depth of her abandon. Later in the morning or in the afternoon, when she typed a new draft, she became as coolly detached as when she wrote reviews and essays. Leonard could tell from the depth of the flush on her face as she came in to lunch whether she had been at fiction or criticism.

At this time, she gained complete confidence in her judgement of books: 'nothing shakes my opinion . . . —nothing—nothing . . . I think myself infallible.' Her judgements were accurate because she could surrender to a book on its own terms. She was a great reader because she could forget her own enterprise in total attentiveness to the words of others. With the exception of a few essays on the art of the novel, her criticism was not a by-product of her private workshop. She was also omnivorous and took in every period of literature and history with an unflagging curiosity about the obscure as well as the famous. Though her reviewing (primarily for *TLS*) was constant and prolific—it was one source of income— she always made quite separate reading lists of anything that would, at that moment, appeal to curiosity or refresh and nourish the mind. The lists, then, are rather an odd jumble, for she believed that we should read as children do, following natural appetite, not a programme.

Bold in judgement, Virginia Woolf abjured self-assertion. She never concerned herself with reputation. Nor was she a preacher like Pound, Eliot, Wyndham Lewis, and Lawrence. She saw that in England the public 'is a very suggestible and docile creature, which, once you get it to attend, will believe implicitly what it is told for a certain number of years'. This docile relation she did not want. Her aim, like her father's, was to induce independence of mind. She therefore avoided the deadening effect of 'definitive' studies and chose rather the brief, more provocative form of the essay. Her criticism has an air of spontaneity (the fruit, in fact, of numerous drafts) as though she were opening up free debate. The second-rate works of a writer, she suggests, offer the best criticism of his masterpieces. '*Middlemarch*', she declares, 'is one of the few English novels written for grown-up people.' And what draws us back to the Greeks is that 'the stable, the permanent, the original human being is to be found there. . . . These are the originals, Chaucer's the varieties of the human species.'

Virginia Woolf may be less immediately arresting than her more

portentous or dogmatic contemporaries, but her criticism may wear
better because its judgements have the intent playfulness of dis-
interested reading. Though the tone is determinedly light, she
performs the most difficult of critical feats, extracting the essence
of Austen or George Eliot or the Brontës in five or ten pages. Where
an academic tome interposes itself between writer and reader,
saying, in effect, the only route is through me, the Woolf essay
invites the reader to a direct and energetic response. It infuses the
reader with agency.

But if Virginia Woolf did not preach from a lofty eminence,
neither did she disarm. Her reader was a travelling companion who
was nudged, amused, teased with opinions that shook comfortable commonplaces about men and women, about the novel and
history, about the plot of our lifespan. Deliberately, she broke the
barrier between writer and public, inviting the reader to become
a co-worker:

In your modesty you seem to consider writers are of a different blood
and bone from yourselves. . . . Never was there a more fatal mistake. It
is this division between reader and writer, this humility on your part,
these professional airs and graces on ours, that corrupt and emasculate the
books which should be the healthy offspring of a close and equal alliance
between us.

Her chief critical effort was the rescue of the common reader
from a variety of passive states: insensibility, humility, deference
to experts. She had two other large ambitions. Following James,
she wished to establish the novel as a form of great art. With
her celebrated essays, 'Modern Fiction' and 'Mr. Bennett and
Mrs. Brown', and the even finer 'Narrow Bridge of Art', she
became in the 1920s the foremost spokeswoman for the modern
novel.

Her other aim was to establish a woman's tradition, recognizable
by its circumstances, subject-matter, and its distinct problems (the
age-old confinement of women in the domestic sphere, the pres-
sures of conformity to patriarchal ideas, and worst, the denial of
private income and privacy). *A Room of One's Own* charted this vast
territory with an air of innocent discovery which itself sharpens the
case against induced ineffectiveness and ignorance that for so long
clouded the counter-history of women.

'Am I a fanatical enthusiast for work like my father?' Virginia Woolf asked herself in 1926. In *The Waves* a lady writes at a table in the garden while a gardener sweeps the leaves. This could be a literal picture of Leonard and Virginia at Monks House or an image of their reciprocal effort as writer and practical man. Both were avid workers, every day of the week. Virginia Woolf also worked hard for the press, reading manuscripts and appearing in the Bloomsbury basement to set up type, sometimes in bedroom slippers and a nightie with a great tear down the side. For Leonard it was a Jewish tradition that unremitting work, 'in the sweat of one's brain as well as one's face, is a proper, even a noble occupation for all the sons of Adam'. Leonard Woolf had a determined idea of what his wife should be. He backed the worker and productive friendships (with Katherine Mansfield and Vita Sackville-West), discouraged society friendships (with the Garsington set or Margot Asquith), and tried to wean his wife of her occasional wish for adornment. She did like beautiful clothes but had to brave many a party 'spartanly "on principle" as the marmots would say'. When she spotted a blue Victorian dress one day in Brighton, Leonard advised her not to buy it.

'Why?' he would wail if crossed. 'Absurd!'

What she called Leonard's 'fiery harshness' (he would certainly deny this, she added) never really touched her, but his temperament seemed, at times, the opposite of her own. He was a Puritan, a disciplinarian. Her social side opposed his 'Spartan' control.

'Surely we should get more from life than we do,' she pleaded. Her social side could not be entirely reprehensible. 'It is a piece of jewellery I inherit from my mother—a joy in laughter. . . . Moreover, for my work now, I want freer intercourse, wider intercourse—. . . . I might know people.'

If his wife defied him and, say, kicked up her heels at a nightclub, Leonard's shoulders stiffened to sharp points. He would sit, not saying anything, looking glum.

But when Leonard forced her to give up a party, she would think: 'Never mind, I adore Leonard.' There was always a delicious alternative: to sit in a dressing-gown in front of the fire, smoking and talking to Leonard. He plucked out her 'thorns' and encouraged the truth.

'But my God—', she exclaimed, 'how satisfactory after, I think, 12 years, to have any human being to whom one can speak so directly as I to L!'

Leonard rebuked snobbery as well as frivolity, but he exercised no restraint on snobbery in the case of successive friendships with Katherine Mansfield and Victoria Sackville-West, both of whom touched Virginia Woolf's vanity as she took on the image of modern novelist.

It is usual to comment on Virginia Woolf's attraction to women, but it is well known that neither case remotely matched her love for Leonard. Her friendship with Katherine Mansfield, between 1917 and 1923, was essentially professional: she was fascinated by the fierceness of Katherine Mansfield's commitment to her 'precious art'. At their closest, their talk was 'disembodied'. The quite different tie with Vita, whom Virginia Woolf met at Clive Bell's in 1923 and who promptly fell in love with her, is harder, from Virginia's side, to define. Quentin Bell and Nigel Nicolson are properly cautious about using the word 'affair' for, though Virginia liked to stroke Vita's hair as she sat at her feet, she did not warm to physical demonstrations (Vita claimed that they went to bed twice) and managed, over the years, to convert Vita to a 'warm-slipper' friendship. She admired Vita's highborn image, her 'pendulous rich society face, glowing out under a black hat at the end of the smoky . . . room, very ancestral & like a picture under glass in a gallery'. She liked, too, Vita's bountiful presents but what mattered, above all, was Vita's modesty as a writer: she simply revelled in another writer's unqualified adulation.

Katherine Mansfield, on the other hand, was not a devotee: she was an equal and in her lifetime appeared the more talented Modern. After a dinner party in 1917 Virginia retired into huffy gentility: 'We could both wish that one's first impression of K.M. was not that she stinks like a—well civet cat that had taken to street walking [she only means scent]. In truth, I'm a little shocked by her commonness at first sight; lines so hard & cheap.' All the same, she was intrigued by the evasiveness of 'the inscrutable woman'.

Their short relationship was marked, as Virginia Woolf put it, by slides and arrests. For months they would not see each other— Katherine Mansfield was often abroad—but when they did meet, they would come 'to an oddly complete understanding'. In March 1919, Virginia was relieved to find that Katherine's hard composure was much on the surface and in April noted, again, how swiftly their minds moved together.

'And then we talked about solitude', Virginia reported in May 1920, '& I found her expressing my feelings, as I never hear them expressed. Whereupon we fell into step, & as usual, talked as easily as though 8 months were minutes. . . . I feel . . . a queer sense of being "like"—not only about literature. . . . I can talk straight out to her.'

Virginia said: 'You've changed. Got through something.' The other woman was speaking as though subterfuges were no longer necessary.

Katherine then told of her loneliness at Ospedalletti (on the Italian Riviera), where she had gone for her TB the previous winter, and of her crisis of despair following her husband's Christmas visit when, facing death, she had to accept how far Middleton Murry's support, emotional and physical, fell short of her needs. She described, too, her stone house with caverns beneath it into which the sea rushed. Virginia Woolf may have stored up this picture for *The Waves* where, in the last phase of the storyteller's life, the oncoming tide sweeps through the caves as he comes to artistic maturity in the face of death.

That summer of 1920 their friendship was at its peak. Virginia saw that 'a woman caring as I care for writing is rare enough I suppose to give me the queerest sense of echo coming back to me from her mind the second after I've spoken'.

She said: 'My own character seems to cut out a shape like a shadow in front of me.' Katherine Mansfield thought this self-preoccupation bad. 'One ought to merge into things', she said. The waves of conversation seemed to scatter them, then fling them together.

Characteristically, Virginia admired the most memory-ridden of Katherine Mansfield's stories, *Prelude*, a frieze of scenes from her New Zealand childhood, written after her beloved brother, Chummie (Leslie Heron Beauchamp), was killed in 1915. There was the same elegiac motive when Katherine Mansfield said of her brother: 'I hear his voice in the trees and flowers, in scents and light and shadow. Have people, apart from these far-away people, ever existed for me?' She wanted to seal their shared past 'because in my thoughts I range with him over all the remembered places'. Virginia Woolf's elegiac novel of childhood, *To the Lighthouse*, may have been inspired, in part, by *Prelude*. Mrs Ramsay, like *Prelude*'s mother, Linda Burnell, soothes family crises, charms and placates her husband, yet is inwardly remote, craving solitude.

Both writers, too, stressed women's rapport: Helen and Rachel, Mrs Ramsay and Lily Briscoe, and, in *Prelude*, Kezia and the grandmother. Alone on the veranda, Linda Burnell speaks to her mother 'with the special voice that women use at night to each other as though they spoke in their sleep or from some hollow cave'.

This was 'the only writing I have ever been jealous of', Virginia admitted. *Prelude* was the Hogarth Press's second publication in 1918, after the Woolfs' own *Two Stories*, and the first book they sent to reviewers. Virginia Woolf set up the type and bound it herself.

Yet, too often, she spoke of Katherine Mansfield ungraciously as a rival who wrung surprising concessions. She deliberately sent her an 'insincere-sincere letter' when *Bliss* was praised in *TLS* in December 1920. In March 1922 she again spewed jealousy over *The Garden Party and Other Stories*: 'Ah, I have found a fine way of putting her in her place. The more she is praised, the more I am convinced she is bad. . . . She touches the spot too universally for that spot to be of the bluest blood.'

Yet their work was all the time converging on similar positions: Katherine Mansfield wished to elicit the muted woman, to do away with the nonsense of power and to attend to the tremendous trifles. She, too, saw the funniness of these trifles. No one could make Leonard laugh so much as she sat on the edge of a chair telling stories with 'not the shadow of a gleam of a smile on her mask of a face'. Later, nursing her lungs at the Villa Isola Bella at Menton, she missed Virginia, she confessed, in a special way: 'I wonder if you knew what your visits were to me—or how I miss them. You are the only woman with whom I long to talk *work*. There will never be another.'

Early in 1923 Katherine Mansfield died. At once, Virginia Woolf set down the more just and sympathetic portrait that death often provoked. It recalled one of her last visits to 2 Portland Villas on Hampstead Heath:

Everything was very tidy, bright, & somehow like a doll's house. At once, or almost, we got out of shyness. She (it was summer) half lay on the sofa by the window. She had her look of a Japanese doll, with the fringe combed quite straight across her forehead. Sometimes we looked very steadfastly at each other, as though we had reached some durable relationship, independent of the changes of the body, through the eyes. Hers were beautiful eyes—rather doglike, brown, very wide apart, with a steady slow rather faithful & sad expression. . . . She looked very ill—very drawn, & moved languidly, drawing herself across the room, like some suffering animal.

Katherine disconcerted Virginia because she reflected the dark side of Virginia's moon. In this sense, their friendship, though so brief and erratic, was more serious than the much-publicized 'affair' with Vita who adored her more surface attributes: the beautiful, frail, sensitive figure of the coming artist. Virginia, in turn, responded to reputation: at the very time that she planned to live 'stormily', she befriended the hedonistic Vita who was endlessly susceptible to women, greedy for the present moment—she described herself as 'ravenous for life'—and judged others in terms of being 'highbred' and 'mettlesome'.

Orlando: A Biography (1928) celebrates Vita as an aspiring writer who, as a dauntless aristocrat, persists from the Elizabethan age to the present, first as a man, then as a woman. A promising plot, but this is not one of Virginia Woolf's searching fictions. It is a pageant of social postures, gorgeous clothes, and all the artifice of sex roles played to the hilt and encased in a thick layer of glamour. When Vita read *Orlando* she wrote to Virginia Woolf on 11 October 1928: 'I feel like one of those wax figures in a shop window, on which you have hung a robe stitched with jewels.'

The best scenes in *Orlando* are when Virginia Woolf forgets to flatter Vita and evokes eighteenth-century London, particularly an imaginary meeting with Pope. For a moment, glamour is put to one side, as Orlando contemplates the visible and invisible aspects of the poet. As she and Pope ride in a coach through the sparsely lit town, Orlando perceives alternately a great mind, invisible in darkness; then, lit up, an unbearably awkward presence.

Where Katherine Mansfield was 'like', Vita's attraction was based on difference, her confident worldliness the antithesis to Virginia Woolf's introspection. This attraction may have been encouraged by Vanessa's opinion that her sister had 'Sapphist tendencies' (offered at the time that Virginia was flirting outrageously with Clive Bell). Through Vita, and through *Orlando*, Virginia Woolf built up a self-image which never quite rings true: Vita gave her the illusion that she was joining in the gay abandon.

Their silliest exchanges were over Potto's* 'scandalous' behaviour one day—it was during the writing of *Orlando*—on a sofa at Long Barn. Shrieks and giggles followed and the ardent platitudes of romance rolled easily off Vita's lips. Potto behaved like a queen with a courtier: she milked Vita shamelessly for compliments, promised favours, simulated rashness, hinted archly of (non-existent) lovers, and pretended grief over Vita's supposed neglect. Her increasingly facile letters were pumped with a monotonous gush that is quite different from her resounding 'echo' of Katherine Mansfield, with its note of surprised stimulation, or, later, with Ethel Smyth, her confessional candour with its note of surprised relief. Compared with Vita, Virginia's sighs were put on, as though she were trying out a category and, as usual, not quite fitting it.

If Vita could not excite passion, she did provoke the idea of androgyny. While writing *Orlando* and *A Room of One's Own*, between 1928 and 1929, Virginia Woolf toyed with the notion of an ideal composite of opposite sexes. But such a composite, as exemplified by Vita, was based on social stereotypes of masculinity and femininity and Virginia Woolf, at her most searching, questioned these in favour of natural attributes as yet obscured. Her flirtation with androgyny was short-lived.

A Man Ray photograph of Virginia Woolf with jutting profile, red lipstick, and shorn hair projected an image of bold modernity, as did the jaunty 'affair' with Vita. In *Mrs. Dalloway*, Peter Walsh, who has been in India from 1918 to 1923, returns to find that 'every woman, even the most respectable, had . . . lips cut with a knife. . . . there was design, art, everywhere'. Publicly explicitness, flamboyance replaced shadow but, in Virginia Woolf's novels, attention to shadow deepened. *Mrs. Dalloway* and *To the Lighthouse* explore madness, memory, people such as Septimus Warren Smith and Lily Briscoe who are haunted by the past. To give this shadow-life the defining shape of art, she followed characters' minds as, repeatedly, they came to rest at a certain point in their past.

Composing *Mrs. Dalloway*, Virginia Woolf resolved on a process of 'tunnelling'. She wanted to dig 'caves' behind her characters, to enter that silent life that the first three novels simply circle as unknown—unknown, that is, to Rachel, Katharine, and Jacob.

* 'Potto' was Vita's nickname for VW.

With Mrs Dalloway and Septimus, she chose maturer people, burdened by memories and themselves able to explore the connecting caves behind the public images of hostess and war veteran, setting off the sane restricted exercise from the insane reckless one.

Virginia Woolf thought the most cogent criticism came from Lytton Strachey, who found Mrs Dalloway disagreeable and limited and complained that, as the writer set it down in her diary, 'I alternately laugh at her, & cover her, very remarkably, with myself.' The portrait may not entirely cohere but, as Virginia Woolf moved from a detached, mocking view of Mrs Dalloway into the shadows of her past, she brought herself closer to artistic maturity. If she were to become a great novelist, she had to learn, as Katherine Mansfield had advised, to 'merge' with someone alien to herself (or her sister or brother, the family sources of the first three novels). And if she were to transcend the modish disillusion of the post-war period she had, as Forster had urged, to create a lovable character.

The initial problem was how to express through a lovable figure her disgust with the literary society of the early 1920s with its 'hidden satire, gorging of pate de foie gras in public, improprieties, & incessant celebrities'. She admitted a certain fascination for the 'slippery mud' of Garsington, the Oxfordshire home of Lady Ottoline Morrell, in which soil were planted young men 'no bigger than asparagus'. 'A loathing overcomes me of human beings', she went on, ' — their insincerity, their vanity — A . . . rather defiling talk with Ott[oline] last night . . . & then the blend in one's own mind of suavity & sweetness with contempt & bitterness. . . . I want to give the slipperiness of the soul. I have been too tolerant often. The truth is people scarcely care for each other.'

She speaks here in exactly the terms of Septimus Smith who thinks that people 'have neither kindness, nor faith, nor charity beyond what serves to increase the pleasure of the moment'. The madman does not appear in Virginia Woolf's first plan for the novel, in her manuscript of *Jacob's Room*, on 6 October 1922. Her first idea was a short book of six or seven scenes grouped around Mrs Dalloway but done separately, beginning with 'Mrs. Dalloway in Bond Street' and ending with 'The Party'. On 6 October she was still preoccupied with the 'party consciousness'. Then, she revised the idea drastically in her diary on 14 October to bring in the madman and, with him, her own loathing. Suddenly, she had the idea of a novel that could balance contradictory attitudes to society: 'I adumbrate here a study of insanity & suicide: the world seen by the sane & the insane side by side.'

With Septimus to carry the whole burden of estrangement, the author was now free to indulge the party consciousness of Mrs Dalloway. In fact, the Dalloway scenes are overblown with her slightly dubious lovability, an over-compensation for the slight sneer that occasionally may be detected. Mrs Dalloway is said to be not an exact portrait of Kitty Maxse, but fictional licence cannot cover an uncertain conception. As Quentin Bell observes, Virginia Woolf came closest to exact portraiture when she loved her subject. She did not love Kitty who, as her mother's protegée, had appeared 'the paragon for wit, grace, charm and distinction'. The earliest sketch, 'Mrs. Dalloway in Bond Street', gives a satiric edge to Clarissa Dalloway's fashionable snobbery. Clarissa thinks: 'It would be intolerable if dowdy women came to her party! Would one have liked Keats if he had worn red socks?' But then the author's own snobbery consorts with Clarissa's when an explosion in Bond Street makes shop-women cower while two upper-middle-class customers, buying long white gloves, sit bravely upright. And then, with another shift in *Mrs. Dalloway*, the author covers the hostess with her own dream: 'She had a perpetual sense, as she watched the taxi cabs, of being out, out, far out to sea and alone.'

This flighty treatment of Mrs Dalloway is passed off as 'the power of taking hold of experience, of turning it round, slowly, in the light'. Theoretically, this is a rational exercise in justice as proposed by Sir James Stephen: 'To be conscious of the force of prejudice in ourselves . . ., to know how to change places internally with our antagonists . . . and still to be unshaken, still to adhere with fidelity to the standard we have chosen—this is a triumph.' His granddaughter wanted to do justice to the world governed by Big Ben as it chimes the hours, to the regimen of politicians, their hostesses, and Harley Street. She intended to salute and, with Mrs Dalloway's final alignment with the estranged Septimus, to undercut. And, through this exercise, she would balance her own mind. 'Positiveness, dogmatism', said Sir James, 'may accompany the firmest convictions, but not the convictions of the firmest minds. The freedom with which the vessel swings at anchor, ascertains the soundness of her anchorage.' This judicious swing, Virginia Woolf did achieve briefly in the novel's climactic scene.

There is only the faintest connection between the fashionable Clarissa and the broken Smith. When Sir William Bradshaw excuses his lateness at Clarissa's party on account of Smith's suicide, she withdraws to take in the fact of death. Mrs Dalloway's awakening to fellow-feeling with a madman is no more than a moment hidden in darkness, but it transforms her. She is no longer the bright hostess in a filmy green frock, leading in the Prime Minister, for alone in that dark room she meets a self never fully acknowledged, capable of an unprecedented imaginative reach.

The first draft swings Mrs Dalloway more explicitly into Smith's camp. Watching an old woman across the way prepare for bed, she is shamed for her oblivion to the lives of the obscure. Smith presents the 'unknown' face of those who go down in 'pitiable yet heroic dumbness'.

As Big Ben strikes twelve her joy in this insight mounts to a crescendo. Then, as the outer life surges back with the sound of motor-horns and the chatter from her drawing-room, she goes back determined, as the draft puts it, 'to breast her enemy', specified here as the enforcer of normality, Sir William. It is this subversive glow that makes Clarissa so exciting to Peter Walsh when she returns.

The novel's concluding sentences ask the reader to compose Clarissa Dalloway out of the shifting scenes that reflect her existence, past and present, deep and shallow. Peter, who has always loved her, demonstrates the requisite act of composition as she comes back, through the door, to her party:

> It is Clarissa, he said.
> For there she was.

Virginia Woolf tries to sweep us via the lover's rapture into an imaginative response. But can we be sure who is there?

In the next novel, the rapture Mrs Ramsay provokes is plausible, but here, as later in *Orlando*, there is a scented adoration which is not easy to share. By contrast, the prose has a terse vigour when Virginia Woolf turns to the indomitable Victorian relics, Lady Bruton, a robust battleaxe with an inherited sense of duty, and Miss Parry, a born explorer. These eccentrics are unquestionably lovable and Virginia Woolf describes them with indulgent humour. She indulges Mrs Dalloway in a more extravagant and potentially more mocking way, the gush edged with faint satire, a residue of the satiric treatment in *The Voyage Out* and, going back further, to the

Stephen children's snide nickname for Kitty Maxse (*née* Lushington) whom they called 'Gushington'. Virginia Woolf almost gave up Mrs Dalloway, at one point, as too tinselly, then invented her memories. 'But I think', she admitted when the book was published, 'some distaste for her persisted. Yet, again, this was true to my feeling for Kitty.'

Clarissa has the familiar pathos of a woman whose face (as Mrs Richard Dalloway) is unreal. She thinks back repeatedly to her life's turning-point when, as a young girl at Bourton, she had chosen the soothing, worldly Dalloway rather than the demanding, passionate Peter Walsh, a man rather like Leonard Woolf, who values independence of mind and personal freedom above social or monetary success. Peter has never quite recovered from Clarissa's refusal: from that moment his life has been unsettled, makeshift, flirtatious, though never self-deceiving. He sees clearly that as a girl Clarissa had the kind of timidity that would harden in middle age into a prudish conservatism. This Peter defines as 'the death of the soul'.

In one of her letters Virginia Woolf said, rather enigmatically, that she had to complete the character of Clarissa with the character of Septimus. Clarissa's half-conscious withering is parodied by the madman's spiritual sickness. His attitude is fatal in that it refuses, together with society's norms, the comforting illusions and accommodations which keep us sane. We practise sanity as a matter of course; Virginia Woolf did so deliberately, and wrote *Mrs. Dalloway* from 1923 all through 1924, for the first time without interruption from illness. Through her sympathies with Mrs Dalloway she accommodated society; through Smith she demonstrated the cost of insanity—but never forgetting what sanity costs us in oblivion.

Discarding both the chapter format of the novel of event and the extreme fragmentation of *Jacob's Room*, Virginia Woolf devised here and again in *To the Lighthouse* a divided form which could define, almost diagrammatically, the antitheses of sanity and insanity, public and private, day and night, present and past. *Mrs. Dalloway* is a balancing act, borne out of the balanced life that Virginia achieved by the mid-1920s. This delicate balance is sustained, in the novel, within the strict structure of the hours of one day, from 11 a.m. to 12 p.m. The hours, designed to measure out the day of doctors and politicians, hold also more elusive interior dramas in their 'leaden rings'.

The fixity of this outer casing was emphasized in the first draft, called 'The Hours', by more attention to the six chimes that follow Smith's suicide and the twelve chimes that follow Clarissa's awakening. Virginia Woolf was transforming the novel in accordance with the aim of the Post-Impressionists, as she understood it from Roger Fry, that modern art should not seek to imitate form but to create form. The artist, in other words, invents a form to express a certain experience as Clarissa's moment of awakening finds its perfect expressive form in her midnight perspective on the fading daylight of an obscure suicide.

The revised novel plays down the hours as well as the critical perspectives of the frustrated lovers, Peter and Rezia. The effect is to draw Clarissa and Septimus forward, embedding us directly in their minds. They are united formally by the hours, more subtly by the rhythmic movement of their minds and their common preoccupation with death.

The rhythmic waves of consciousness flow through the hours as through a channel. The chimes have a deceptive finality like the full stop at the end of a sentence which is part of the rise and fall of rhythmic prose. In 1919 Lytton Strachey praised Virginia Woolf as the creator of a new version of the sentence. Her sentence is like the deep wave of the mind in repose, first recorded on the electro-encephalogram in 1924. The physiologist, Colin Blakemore, calls this the mind in its natural state, when it is receptive to impressions but unwilling to place them on preordained maps of consciousness. Virginia Woolf told Vita: 'A sight, an emotion creates this wave in the mind, long before it makes words to fit it.'

Mrs Dalloway is thus at rest as she sews her party dress:

Quiet descended on her, calm, content, as her needle, drawing the silk smoothly to its gentle pause, collected the green folds together and attached them very lightly, to the belt. So on a summer's day waves collect, overbalance, and fall; collect and fall; and the whole world seems to be saying 'that is all' more and more ponderously.

Sewing, Mrs Dalloway reposes in the involuntary rhythm of nature, most often symbolized in Virginia Woolf by the waves.

In the same way, Smith's agitated consciousness comes to rest as he trims a hat for his wife, at which point he returns to sanity (ironically, just before the doctor arrives to cart him off to a Home, which precipitates his quite rational suicide).

These parallel waves of consciousness fulfil the plan, proposed in 1917, to 'slip easily from one thing to another, without any sense of . . . obstacle. I want to sink deeper and deeper, away from the surface, with its hard separate facts.'

Virginia Woolf's sense of fact, like her sentence, transforms the traditional novel. How wonderful, she says, to discover that Sunday luncheons, Archbishops, table-cloths, and the Lord High Chancellor 'were not entirely real'. Like scientists we must redefine fact as mystery, 'crack' through the paving stone, and be enveloped in the mist. *Mrs. Dalloway* ignores the blatant fact of suicide, scorns the obtruding force of Dr Holmes, and dwells instead on the mind of a man as he trims a hat. The moment of importance, she says in 'Modern Fiction', falls not here but there. To become a work of art, she dictates in 'The Art of Fiction', the novel must 'cut adrift from the tea-table', that is, from the laborious reproduction of external detail, in order to explore hidden facts in the caves of consciousness.

At this time Virginia Woolf was reading Proust, whom she praised more than any other contemporary.* She said: 'He searches out these butterfly shades to the last grain. He is as tough as catgut & as evanescent as a butterfly's bloom.' She restates the idea of combining strict form and delicate perception in *To the Lighthouse*, but both statements repeat exactly her own idea of art as she gazed at St Sophia in 1906.

Proust's sensibility, 'so perfectly receptive', like an elastic envelope stretching wider and wider to enclose the most evanescent of memories, is described in almost the same terms as the possibility, recognized in Dorothy Richardson, of 'a sentence which we might call the psychological sentence of the feminine gender. It is of a more elastic fibre than the old, capable of stretching to the extreme, of suspending the frailest particles, of enveloping the vaguest shapes.'

It occurred to Virginia Woolf that it might be possible to give aesthetic definition to a woman's voice. It has, she said on the opening page of the first draft of *Mrs. Dalloway*, 'a vibration in the core of the sound so that each word, or note, comes fluttering, alive,

---

* VW began reading *Du Côté de chez Swann* in the spring of 1922 and continued to read *A la recherche du temps perdu* over the next few years. She believed that the French language and tradition would prevent too direct an influence.

yet with some reluctance to inflict its vitality, some grief for the past which holds it back, some impulse nevertheless to glide into the recesses of the heart'. As she and Vanessa could speak to each other in an 'inaudible way', so the voices of Rachel and Helen when they talk at night seem to fall through the waves of the sea. 'Aren't things spoilt by saying them?', Mrs Ramsay asks herself in the manuscript of *To the Lighthouse*. 'Don't we communicate better silently? Aren't we (women, at any rate) more expressive silently gliding high together, side by side, in the curious dumbness which is so much [more] to our taste than speech, with the kingdoms of the world displayed down beneath, asking no share in them?'

'I am a woman . . . when I write', Virginia Woolf concluded in 1929. In the 1920s she had developed a recognizable authorial voice, punctuated by silence or comic deflation, but always rising again like a wave surging forward. The sentence pulsates beyond the period with continued suggestion. Dorothy Richardson's 'feminine' sentence, Proust's sensibility, and Fry's claim for expressive art may have bolstered Virginia Woolf, but her experiments, if traced to their source, arose too early to be other than her own.

She may have copied minor effects from T. S. Eliot and Joyce: the modern city scene and the hours that propel the narrative. Eliot's 'Unreal City', though, has the single-mindedness of a vision, a projection of the poet's inner world of nightmare. Virginia Woolf's London, in contrast, has the multiplicity of a real city observed by a native: the dun zoo animals overlooking Regent's Park, the discreet gloss of Harley Street, the bus ride along the Strand, the lingerie department in the Army and Navy Stores, the isolated kneelers in Westminster Abbey.

The moderns never wrote anything one wants to read about death, thinks Mrs Dalloway in Bond Street. Murmuring old, comforting lines, 'From the contagion of the world's slow stain | He is secure . . .' and 'Fear no more the heat o' the sun | Nor the furious winter's rages', Mrs Dalloway, like Septimus, has a sense of posthumous existence. Mrs Dalloway can reasonably state her belief that some residue of herself will linger on in the lives of others she has known and in the scenes of her past (much as Jacob survives his death). Septimus's own sense of the dead is so obsessive that it obliterates his very existence. The dead literally visit him and he has auditory hallucinations similar to Virginia Woolf's, of birds singing in Greek 'of life beyond a river where the dead walk'. Five years after the end of the war he is still locked mentally to the fate of his dead comrades, especially to his commanding officer, Evans. He goes through the motions of living—he weds, returns for a while to the office—but cannot compose, as the writer did, a marriage, a new life.

Another subtle link between the two halves of *Mrs. Dalloway* is Smith's portentous message of altruism. Having witnessed war he wants no less than to change the world. The supreme secret, to be revealed at once to the Cabinet, is 'universal love'. Again, Clarissa in her modest way brings out the sane script. Without much fuss, she brings people together and sets youths going. This is her gift.

'The merit of this book', Virginia Woolf wrote in a notebook, 'lies in its design, which is original—very difficult.' The two halves of this design did not naturally converge. That they cohere at all was a feat of ingenuity. In her next novel, she chose to emphasize rather than minimize the divided design, in this case a more natural, chronological break between two ages, Victorian and Modern. An early notion was to put into words the pure flight of time, like a vacant corridor leading through the war into the post-war period. She called it simply 'Time Passes'.

Virginia Woolf drew an initial diagram for *To the Lighthouse* as two blocks connected by the corridor of time. In the first block Lily Briscoe begins a painting; in the last block she completes it. Why must ten years pass before that painting can be completed? Virginia Woolf combined a sense of mystery with the exactness of a curious scientist. Her sense of mystery was searching, directed, not a floating vagueness. The clear-cut, almost diagrammatic design of her greater novels frames, in each case, an experiment that leads to a resounding conclusion.

To fulfil herself as artist, Virginia Woolf had to combine the newly learnt tactics of modern art with old gifts passed on from her parents. This vital fusion took place in the final part of *To the Lighthouse*.

The long first part of the novel immerses us in the life of a Victorian family as Virginia, as a child, had been immersed. The onlooker, Lily Briscoe, first sees them in this way, close-up in their own age but, as artist, she cannot record them with total conviction

until she sees them again, after a passage of time, in the perspective
of the next age. Time has brushed like a wind through the Ramsay
home, touching a person here, an object there. Mrs Ramsay dies but
her shawl remains, a relic. The wind toys with open letters and
books, asking if they could stand the test of time. After many years,
Mrs McNab, cleaning the deserted house, recalls Mrs Ramsay
asking the cook to give her a plate of milk soup and Mr Ramsay,
lean as a rake, declaiming to himself on the lawn. These Victorians,
alive in Mrs McNab's memory, will disappear with her death. Her
random memory precedes the artist's deliberate one. In the third
part of the novel a mature Lily recalls her picture of Mrs Ramsay,
judging her now as a Modern, while the remnant of the family sails
with Mr Ramsay on that long-delayed voyage to the lighthouse.
The family are distanced mentally, physically, and historically so
as to concentrate on Lily as she transforms memory into art. The
conclusion is really about the making of an artist, the task that
concerned Virginia Woolf herself as she came to maturity in the
mid-1920s.

She said, 'I enclosed that world [of the Stephen family] in
another made by my own temperament'. She was unashamedly
subjective, ruthless now in discarding those habits of her parents
that would have no bearing on her own development, and all the
time—through Lily—sifting memory for those traits that could
define and fulfil her art.

This aesthetic enterprise was bound up with the writer's need to
lay the ghost of her mother whose insistent voice had started the
breakdown in 1915. Virginia Woolf's success as a writer depended
on her struggle to exist in her own right, in the process of which she
had finally to repossess her mother as the material of art.

In *A Room of One's Own* Virginia Woolf said that the mind 'can
think back through its fathers or through its mothers, as I have said
that a woman writing thinks back through her mothers'. In *To
the Lighthouse* she sorts the creative influence from the unhealthy
emotional grip. When she tried on her mother's puffy, black, Victorian dress, at the same time she was writing *To the Lighthouse*, was
she the creative or the haunted heir? Her face was pale and anxious,
her body too thin and awkward for the full-bodied, low-cut dress
with its feminine flounces. The puffed sleeves rose grotesquely
from her stooping shoulders. It was a dress for a figure of doll-like
uprightness, but she leant forward, her arms resting on the table

with the casual attentiveness of a woman with opinions. The disjunction was most striking in the face above the old lace frill of the collar. In Julia Stephen there was a certain calm fixity as though a madonna mask was never removed. Her daughter's face had the same kind of dignity but it was more mobile, more vulnerable, a more exposed face, yet it shared with that of the mother a watchful passivity. Haunted by a being who half-possessed her, Virginia's childlike side longed to be possessed entirely, as the hero of a James novel actually *becomes* an ancestral portrait, goes back in time to take on its very identity: 'It was for the old ghosts to take him for one of themselves.'

During the dark passage of years in 'Time Passes', the grieving mind first welcomes visitations, then casts them off, awakens to the daylight of the present. *To the Lighthouse* is popular partly because it is a triumphant book about the liberation of a woman from the past. And it is all the more triumphant for not, in the process, abrogating the past but, in a controlled and selective way, using it. It demonstrates, too, how the artist might achieve a balance between tradition and the individual talent. Instead of surrender to the ancestral portrait, she paints a new interpretative one.

The gestation of an artist was not in Virginia Woolf's initial plans. Yet Lily Briscoe came to dominate the novel. Initially, she is only one of a circle of satellites who reflect different views of the Ramsays. In the manuscript she first appears as a rather elderly spinster called Sophie, anxious, a little stupid, very pious. And then, as Mr Ramsay claims attention, it is as though Virginia Woolf hears the clichés. Suddenly she re-imagines the spinster as a young woman with professional aspirations and, with Lily's growth in stature, her view of the Ramsays becomes pre-eminent as, at the same time, she displaces them as representative of the age.

At first Lily vacillates between the extreme modesty of un-educated womanhood and the extreme boldness of the shapes on her canvas. Mr Bankes, the first Victorian to witness an abstract painting, is mildly shocked by the shape that she has given to the mother and child at the window. 'Mother and child then—objects of universal veneration, and in this case the mother was famous for her beauty—might be reduced . . . to a purple shadow without irreverence.' Lily cringes over her painting. Yet Mr Bankes supports her. What she sees may be to him entirely foreign but as a scientist he is willing to do justice to any scrupulous observation.

Lily paints a modern abstract portrait of the Victorian parents in which, finally, all extraneous detail is pared away in order to see their essential shape—a purple wedge of darkness and another less defined shape which we must imagine, say the mass of the hedge which for Mrs Ramsay 'had over and over again rounded some pause, signified some conclusion'. The artist, who is herself heir to Mr Ramsay's inwardness and to the bristling fastness of Mr Ramsay, singles out these two qualities to preserve in a precise balance in her being and her art. From the outset Lily sees the maternal shape more distinctly. The impact of the two shapes is not necessarily equal. The picture succeeds only if it is true, and Lily knows it is true only in the last line of the book as she makes her last stroke, a line down the centre of the canvas, setting off the two halves of her imaginative inheritance. On the one side is Mrs Ramsay who 'alone spoke the truth'. As Lily completes the picture, the youngest of the Ramsays, James, now a teenager, can recall how his mother used to say quite simply what came to her and therefore was a person to whom one could speak directly: 'She alone spoke the truth; to her alone could he speak it. That was the source of her everlasting attraction. . . .' From the other side of the canvas, and not to be slighted, comes Mr Ramsay's uncompromising demand that we face things as they are (he 'never tampered with a fact'), a kind of truth that comes with the courage to bear mental isolation. '"We perished, each alone"', Mr Ramsay mutters as he sails with his children to the lighthouse. As, in the first part of the book, the Ramsays' quarrel over truth is resolved in the marriage of true minds so, in the end, their artist heir will contain two kinds of truth in balance in her work.

Virginia Woolf discovered herself to be the sum of two parts; in the process of fusion a new being emerged. Yet, although this appears to have happened almost accidentally, she had, of course, a hypothesis when she formulated her experiment on 30 July 1925: 'I think I might do something in To the Lighthouse, to split up emotions more completely.' In other words, she intended from the start to break the self down into separate components, derived from father and mother, as though she were cracking a genetic code. The test would lie in putting these components together again. And as she completed the work she noted in her diary on 13 September 1926, that she had replotted a process of gestation: 'The blessed thing is coming to an end I say to myself with a groan. It's like some prolonged rather painful & yet exciting process of nature, which one desires inexpressibly to have over.'

It is curious to compare Virginia Woolf's novel about the gestation of the artist with Joyce's *A Portrait of the Artist as a Young Man* and Lawrence's *Sons and Lovers*. For Joyce or Lawrence the artist is what is left when he cuts loose from family ties and conventional ambitions. Paul Morel and Stephen Dedalus are reduced to the cutting edge of the artist's will: a dogged romantic egotism. But Lily Briscoe makes the artist an heir, evolving naturally, almost biologically, from the previous generation.

Mrs Ramsay cannot define Lily's peculiar distinction for Lily belongs to the next generation. 'There was in Lily a thread of something; a flare of something; something of her own which Mrs Ramsay liked very much indeed, but no man would, she feared.' Lily's Chinese eyes are emblematic of her foreignness to the insular taste of a Victorian, and for this Mrs Ramsay pities her. At the same time she recognizes Lily's courage not to subdue herself to the banal apparitions of male fantasy. What is latent in Mrs Ramsay, except when it flickers in response to the lighthouse signal, sees its sequel in Lily Briscoe. But in Lily the individual flare is so intransigent that Mrs Ramsay turns away.

Lily is watching Mr Ramsay, Cam, and James sail away across the bay, and it seems pointed that the decisive last line is drawn at the very moment that the Ramsays land at the lighthouse. 'I meant *nothing* by The Lighthouse', Virginia Woolf wrote cryptically to Roger Fry. 'One has to have a central line down the middle of the book to hold the design together.' At a distance the lighthouse looks romantic, a 'misty-looking tower with a yellow eye that opened suddenly and softly in the evening'. Close-up, when the Ramsay children arrive there under the philosopher's direction, they see bare reality: a tower like a spike 'stark and straight' and washing spread on the rocks to dry. Looking at the spike James Ramsay thinks:

> So that was the Lighthouse, was it?
> No, the other was also the Lighthouse. For nothing was simply one thing. The other Lighthouse was true too.

In the midst of writing the book, Virginia Woolf wrote in her diary: 'I think I will find some theory about fiction. . . . The one I have in view, is about *perspective*.'

Far off or close-up, various characters look at the lighthouse and the artist, watching them, marks their point of enlightenment. Mrs Ramsay is receptive to the beam at a distance; her enlightenment comes suddenly, as a flash. Mr Ramsay, on the other hand, must make a laborious journey to the lighthouse. He is not really drawn to the lighthouse, but goes in homage to his wife. The lighthouse marks the point from which he is able to recall and see *her*. And as he gazes at her with true perspective, from across the bay, he closes a triangle, the emblem of Mrs Ramsay. The lighthouse beam had nourished her, she had nurtured her husband, and then at last he undertakes the journey with James, which she had so desired, to the lighthouse.

The closer the characters draw to the lighthouse, the closer Lily comes to artistic enlightenment. Lily's modesty does not hide the fact that, though she might be impervious to mere fame, she is bent on immortality—at any rate for her subject. For this high aim, perspective is essential but not enough.

First, Lily must accept the necessity for distortion. If she is to make an immortal portrait, she must not see the Ramsays in multitudinous detail, as when she was immersed in their lives, but must discard the facets of Mrs Ramsay which would turn to dust—her indulgence of power, her refrain 'Marry, marry'—and enlarge on her selflessness and truth, those rare qualities which Lily must perpetuate.

Second, Lily learns how to exercise feeling. She learns to love her subject not spontaneously but deliberately: 'One must keep on looking without for a second relaxing the intensity of emotion, the determination not to be put off, not to be bamboozled. One must hold the scene—so—in a vice and let nothing come in and spoil it.' Looking up, Lily is engulfed in memories; looking down, she steadies her mind. The feeling must be exactly right. Lily fumbles in her love for Mrs Ramsay, trying to turn the focus so that she lights up clearly. The difficulty is that the closer she draws to her subject, the more its presence overwhelms her. At once, Lily's brush falls. Instead of controlling her subject, she is wrung by death's separation. Then suddenly Mrs Ramsay sits, knits with a flick of her wrist, and allows Lily's idea. 'It became a miracle, it became an ecstasy that she had lived. It stayed there before her while she painted. . . .' This, in first draft, is Lily's moment of vision. When she draws the last brush stroke, the steps are empty, the ghost has departed, but Lily has caught her.

Virginia Stephen was thirteen when her mother died. She was forty-four, exactly Lily's age, when she completed the draft of *To the Lighthouse*, and during all those years her mother had haunted her. 'I could hear her voice, see her, imagine what she would do or say as I went about my day's doings', she recalled. And then, when this novel was done, she no longer saw Julia Stephen nor heard her voice. By giving shape to memories, she was able to command her parents' gifts, reject their mistakes and, so, invent herself as artist.

12. *Specimen Lives*

THE year 1926 marks a change in Virginia Woolf's career, though outwardly its surface was unbroken. 'No biographer', she told herself, 'could possibly guess this important fact about my life in the late summer of 1926; yet biographers pretend they know people.'

The change was as momentous, in its own way, as the series of family deaths that, between 1895 and 1906, had closed off childhood as a buried well of memory. *To the Lighthouse*, completed in first draft in September 1926, had reopened that well and drawn out its store. It ends with an artist who has faced the past and composed it to advantage, with a mounting sense of her powers. But no sooner had Virginia Woolf come to full tide than she sank into depression. She woke one morning at about three to face, quite without warning, a gigantic wave that seemed to swell, crash, and spread out over her. Shocked and baffled, she could yet say, wryly: 'I am glad to find it on the whole so interesting, though so acutely unpleasant.' She knew that this was not illness but some sort of vision, not the artist's vision of her own powers, but something beyond the self, in the natural universe. She glimpsed a fin passing far out amidst the waste of waters, some mighty submerged creature which she must stalk through her own gloom. *The Waves*, begun three years later, in 1929, and completed in 1931, is the strange result of this encounter.

The Waves is the story of multiple lives that run a parallel course and meet at defined points. It traces lives from childhood to middle age, against the backdrop of the timeless universe, the sea and the sun. The book is markedly diagrammatic in its outline: nine episodes in the course of six lives, linked by impersonal interludes describing the flow and ebb of the tide in the course of one day. The fixing of the book's structure is an attempt to defamiliarize lives and to see them as phenomena of nature. Virginia Woolf's diary remarks her own perpetual sense 'of my own strangeness, walking on the earth . . . of the infinite oddity of the human position'.

This is the book about which she said least, even in the privacy of her diary. At no time were the two levels of her consciousness more distinctly separate than during the gestation of *The Waves*. The articulate, witty surface of her mind, so publicly effervescent in her family and Bloomsbury, tossed off *Orlando* and *A Room of One's Own* as though she were exercising fancy and logic while deliberately holding back the more searching activity of her mind till its discoveries grew 'gravid' and 'impending'. It is hard to know what went on in the wordless depths as she stalked the fin between 1926 and 1929.

One clue to what she was after is the fact that she pored over Wordsworth's long autobiographic poem, *The Prelude*, soon after her abortive attempt to launch her first draft. On 22 August 1929, she made a note of lines in which Wordsworth comforts himself that his attention to inner as opposed to external event will not be scorned by those

> Who, looking inward, have observed the ties
> That bind the perishable hours of life
> Each to the other, and the curious props
> By which the world of memory and thought
> Exists and is sustained.

She resolved to follow only the internal lines of development in six lives, the unfolding of character, mind, and soul.

It is still unclear why Virginia Woolf saw *The Waves* as a complement to the *Lighthouse*. Where *To the Lighthouse* was a story of individuals, ultimately a story of one individual, *The Waves* played down human differences. 'I am not concerned with the single life but with lives together, thinking them into one story', she wrote in her earliest stretch of the first draft of *The Waves*, on 2 July 1929. When she restarted the first draft on 4 September she opened with the same words. Initially, the six voices sound undifferentiated: simply the rhythmical sound of the general human voice, declaring its normally unvoiced perceptions. This is one facet of the strangeness of *The Waves*: there are no characters, as we understand them, only voices. And there are no chapters, so that we may hear the unbroken rhythm of the six voices as they recount their lives. Their rhythm is made to synchronize with the continuous rhythm of the waves which bring the six to the shores of existence and suck them back afterwards. Virginia Woolf did not set out to write about six lives but about the classic course of human life. She wanted to make the blood run like a torrent from the beginning of life to its end.

In *To the Lighthouse* she fixed on the way an artist might compose herself from a dual endowment, supplied by the parental figures of the previous generation. Until she was forty-four, Virginia Woolf searched for identity as a writer and *To the Lighthouse* brought that search to fulfilment. Almost at once she swung round, facing now not the sources of her life, but its surge towards termination. As a sense of private fulfilment in the spring of 1925 presaged *To the Lighthouse*, so a disconcerting blank, eighteen months later, presaged *The Waves* as she faced the second half of her career.

Her sudden gloom at the age of forty-four is seen in *The Waves* to mark the onset of middle age, a wretchedly vacant phase in the life of Bernard, a storyteller. But he learns that without that phase he could not develop further. Bernard, too, speaks of a fin, an emblem of the as yet unknown being that slices for a moment the blank horizon of his mind.* In fact, his depression proves, in the end, a sign of his potential stature to be called out with age. This, in short, was what the fin portended. Virginia Woolf had to write the book in order to understand and overcome her own depression. She had to see how it fitted into the pattern of the lifespan. The autobiographic detail of depression was a late insertion—in the second draft—and the fin even later: it appears only in the final draft. *The Waves*, then, was its author's own means of renewal after stasis. Bernard, locked in middle-aged deadness, observes the involuntary quickening: 'But observe how dots and dashes are beginning, as I walk, to run themselves into continuous lines.'

Virginia Woolf, like the other great Moderns, had a long creative life by comparison with the Romantic poets. The Moderns, taking a longer life for granted, felt the need to go on developing. Hardy's and T. S. Eliot's solution was to change their genre (Hardy from the novel to poetry, Eliot from poetry to drama). Virginia Woolf, like Yeats, made growing older a subject. In the years preceding *The Waves* she was dismissive of her growing fame and concerned only that her quick responsiveness—the shock-receiving capacity— should not atrophy: 'At 46 I am not callous', she reassured herself in

---

* VW may have taken the fin image from Ishmael's masthead meditation in *Moby Dick* (ch. 35) where the waves seem to harbour every strange, half-seen, gliding thing that eludes definition, 'every dimly-discerned uprising fin of some undiscernable form'. VW mentions *MD* in 'Phases of Fiction' (1929), repr. *CE*, ii. She first read it in Feb. 1922 (*Diary*, ii, p. 161). Another possible source is the Cornwall diary, Monday, 14 Aug. 1905: 'To-day we did what we have long promised ourselves to do on the first opportunity, that is we hired a fishing boat & went for a sail in the bay.' The sea at St Ives had a dull surface that day until the calm was broken by their sailing into a school of porpoises.

1928, 'suffer considerably; make good resolutions—still feel as experimental & on the verge of getting at the truth as ever.'

To read *The Waves* is to confront a strange diagram. This diagram of the human lifespan and of six people who move along its track is set out with an almost scientific detachment. 'Draw a little apart', she wrote in 1926, 'see people in groups, as outlines, and they become at once memorable.' Her diagram poses a set of questions which are answered in the long final section of the book, and the conclusions suggest how best to approach the experiment. For the unprepared reader the first hundred pages can be as baffling as an unknown code. But once the code is cracked, the whole experiment has a brilliant simplicity.

The Waves asks what shape lifespans have in common and, if there were a classic shape, whether its crucial marking-points necessarily coincide with the biological markers of birth, growth, mating, and death.

To find the common contours of six lives Virginia Woolf synchronizes them—the six are exact contemporaries—and removes the obscuring clutter of biographic trivia. We are not told where Rhoda lived or with whom Jinny flirted at her first ball. Instead, she takes cross-sections of the lives at nine points in their span. Her method at each stage is to examine nature under a particular angle of the sun and to let that dictate human parallels. The italicized nature interludes link the stages of human development so that they may be considered as part of a continuum. Virginia Woolf also blends stage into stage by an overriding rhythm that takes its rise, at dawn, from the ocean's waves and pulses like the blood from end to end.

Six children—Bernard, Susan, Jinny, Neville, Louis, and Rhoda—are brought together in one garden within reach of the sea. The sea is Wordsworth's immortal sea which brought us hither. Rhoda, in particular, is still swept by 'the mighty waters rolling evermore' as she rocks water in a bowl. The waves roll towards the shore as the children wake at dawn as though they were waking to the world.

Their speeches are so strange that some readers shut *The Waves* after the third page. What we expect to hear from children is a quaint imitation of adult discourse. Instead, Virginia Woolf bestows roundness and explicitness on pre-verbal thoughts. Assuming that the authentic person is to be found in the unuttered rather than the uttered thought, she devised a language in which the lonely unversed mind can formally declare itself. Impressions pour from each mind in quick succession. Each of the six is endowed with Wordsworth's 'sense sublime' that rolls through all things. Their imaginations sever them from lessons so that they are able to make their own worlds, in Wordsworthian terms 'to be'.

But to express the intersection of personal memory and impersonal sublimity, Virginia Woolf would have had to have been Wordsworth himself, and the anxiety is evident in her initial poetic straining. She actually called the first stage 'Prelude' in the first draft. She had great trouble beginning the book—the manuscript, even when she got going, is a thicket of abortive phrases—and her view of the early stages of development is rather derivative (of the Romantics) and conventional (demarcated by school, college, and adulthood). It was only in the fifth cross-section, when the six come to maturity—the particular challenge for the author herself at the time of writing—that she became wholly original. Still, the account of childhood gains interest as the six differentiate.

The children know one another as states of being attached to objects. The incisive Neville wields his knife. The sensuous Jinny eyes a crimson tassel with gold threads. The seething Louis fastens his grey flannel trousers with a snake belt. Rhoda, the dreamer, rocks her bowl of water, the vessel of her imagination; the petals she floats in it are dreams voyaging out. She has an obvious affinity with Virginia Woolf, who often recalled sailing boats on the pond in Kensington Gardens. One winter day her Cornish lugger sailed perfectly to the middle of the pond and then sank suddenly.

'Did you see that?' Leslie Stephen cried, striding towards her. Weeks later, in the spring, a man brought up the boat in a dredging net. In great excitement Virginia claimed it.

The first cross-section of the children's lives is taken at the moment they are jarred into separateness. One day, when they are in the bath, their nurse, Mrs Constable, raises a sponge and squeezes rivulets of sensation down their spines. With that casual baptism, each is encased in flesh. Jinny kisses Louis among the ferns. Susan, watching, is awakened to the lifelong drama of desire and rejection. She cries and Bernard consoles her. All her life Susan will remember the delicious bond forged by Bernard's comfort.

Like Wordsworth, Virginia Woolf wanted to uncover those hidden moments that dominate memory and shape development:

> those first affections,
> Those shadowy recollections,
> Which, be they what they may,
> Are yet the fountain light of all our day. . . .

The next cross-section of the six lives is taken at school. As the school train puffs off, they are (in the second draft) launched 'into England'. They appear in acquiescent postures: in chapel listening to the headmaster's sermon or, with arms binding their knees, they sit on the edge of the playing-field, listening to the tap of cricket bats. They sit locked in a ring of opinion.

Heaven lay about them in infancy; now the prison-house of social forms begins to close upon growing boys and girls. The six take up the burden of existence as a task that might be questioned but a question they can allow only at the periphery of consciousness. Rhoda, whose imaginative purity suffers most, asks this each night, in the dark privacy of her dormitory bed. When other girls pull up their stockings, she pulls up hers, but conformity is an effort. Rhoda has the strongest sense of the futility of effort as she has the strongest sense of the inevitability of death.

Percival appears at this point. His air of contemptuous severity wins the boys' attention away from the headmaster's sermon. Handsome, good-natured Percival, the conventional schoolboy's hero, becomes surprisingly a lifelong focus for the unconventional six. Unlike them, he has no interior life. He is fixed in attitudes: a young man on horseback; eventually, a crusader on his tomb. He wins his ascendancy by a mixture of physical ease and offhand honesty. Lying with his hat over his eyes, he is shaken with a silent guffaw as he listens to Bernard's stories. His laughter sanctions them. Is he a hero simply because he *looks* like a hero to the last stage of his abbreviated life, advancing down the long, low shore of India in his sun-helmet?

Percival can be seen as a memorial to Thoby Stephen, who died when he was still something of an unknown to his sister, as her notes for her final portrait of Thoby in 1940 confirm: 'Thoby. His silence. reserve. . . . Clifton. "always the most distinguished looking boy in the school." . . . His ease and assurance. . . . His passion for the law. His gruffness . . . His manliness. . . . Protective. shy. susceptible.

. . . Ascendancy over friends. Belief in them. Reserve with us about sex. . . . Queer reserve. never discussed family emotions.'

Virginia Woolf had already made one attempt to memorialize Thoby in *Jacob's Room*. She had asked there if a young man, whose promise was not yet unfurled when his life was cut short, might be deduced from his room, and her answer was no. Like Jacob, Percival can be glimpsed in the memory of devoted school-mates, Neville and Louis, just as in real life Virginia relied on Thoby's friends, Lytton and Leonard, to bring him back to her. But in order to avoid the hopeless mystery of Jacob, she stamps Percival with an ideal character at once.

Percival evokes not the exploratory sentence of the novel but the flat statement of the epic where heroes are in one mould: 'He rode and fell in India.' The last words Virginia Woolf ever wrote about her brother, on 12 October 1940, were that he was framed to be not so much a success as 'a figure'.

Over six foot, with fine light eyes, Thoby Stephen posed for a photograph in the court of Trinity College in about 1900, a massive specimen of male solidity between the thin figures of Lytton and Leonard. Thoby was, according to Quentin Bell, a jolly extrovert Stephen like his uncle, Fitzjames (the Victorian judge), not a nervous Stephen like his father. Lytton Strachey, describing Fitz-james soon after Thoby's death, in 1907, reflects an image of Thoby: 'His qualities were those of solidity and force; he pre-ponderated with a character of formidable grandeur, with a massive and rugged intellectual sanity, a colossal commonsense.' This Johnsonian character is transposed, in the second draft of *The Waves*, to Percival in India, reading 'The Vanity of Human Wishes' with his legs over the arm of a camp-chair.

It is an easy step from Strachey's euphoric image of Thoby as 'monolithic', 'hewn out of the living rock', to Virginia Woolf's attempt at a fictional image as durable as stone. She wanted Percival to endure like the statues she and Thoby had seen on their last holiday in Greece. 'Beautiful statues', she had noted then, 'have a look not seen on living faces, or but rarely, as of serene im-mutability.' The problem with Percival is that he is a statue well before his death, and to be invited to admire a living youth in this way is like being asked to share an adolescent crush.

On the other hand, Percival does make it possible for the six friends to accommodate a dominant order, mirrored in the public school. They are therefore neither passive nor rebellious. The ideal geniality of the public order, embodied in Percival, actually encourages their moments of 'being'.

As they race in different directions on the first day of the holidays, they are thrown along different lines of action. The single-minded Susan is absolved from choice. Driven by blind homesickness that has been the sole, bitter fruit of boarding-school, her homebound train races her to a country-woman's groove. The other five, too, are allowed little play of choice; they are carried passively to their respective destinations. Neville and Bernard, as sons of gentlemen, go to Cambridge. Louis, the best scholar in the school but the son of a failed banker, goes straight to the City.

In the third cross-section, perspectives first clash as the six assert their separateness in the London drawing-room, in the College court, in the mean City pot-house, in the lonely farm field.

Craving identity, the two college men rush into imitation: Bernard loses himself in the offhand dash of what he hopes is a Byronic letter. Neville, in what he hopes is a fine frenzy, lets the words of his poem froth into foam. Rhoda and Jinny learn in the drawing-room. Debarred by their sex from the indulgent sanctuary of the College court, they are thrust on to a more exposed test-ground. At the ball Jinny wins, Rhoda, predictably, loses. She stands by silent, her staring eyes the colour of snail's flesh: green, opaque.

Virginia Woolf worked out the theory of the cross-section in the nature interlude before translating it into individual fates. The rising sun, symbol of enlightenment, '*bared her brows and with wide-opened eyes drove a straight pathway over the waves*'. The verbs suggest urgent advance: '*drove*', '*bounded*', '*raced*', '*aware, awake*'. The waves '*drummed*' on the shore like invaders.

The birds, too, define the stage. They sing in chorus as the College hearties sing their hunting-song like a torrent jumping over rocks. In the clear light of morning the birds' attention hardens on one object as they propel themselves forward. They '*plunged*' their beaks into the soft worm again and again. Their ruthless urgency readily translates into Bernard, buzzing with potency, as he plans a love letter.

With similar urgency, Neville tosses his poem into Bernard's lap and Jinny flirts late into the night. Susan, watching a cart grow larger as it comes along the flat fen, turns back to the farm as a fox to its lair, her skirt, like an animal's fur, grey with rime. She will fix on a farmer, a man in gaiters. Her expectancy, explained in the first draft, is realistic: he would be a dumb brute. But he would come home every evening. 'Then she lay in his arms.' She moves through flowers thick with pollen and flies, bent on giving herself and possessing, in return, a farm and offspring.

In their early twenties the six friends first compose themselves as a group. They gather at a French restaurant in London to create a shared memory with Percival as its focus. It is a farewell dinner for Percival who is to sail for India.

This cross-section shows the solid shape of six characters, in the direct beam of Percival's presence. In the interlude, natural objects take on full colouring under an erect sun. In the human sequel, the six sit in public view. 'Our differences are clear-cut', Jinny comments. The flourishes of personality recede as they appear graven by nature: Louis is stone-carved; Neville, scissor-cutting, exact.

In Percival's presence, they begin to rehearse the defining moments of their lives, when Mrs Constable clothed them in flesh, when Susan saw the bootboy and the tweenie in the kitchen garden and the wind blew the laundry out stiff, when Neville saw the man with his throat cut in the gutter. 'Now let us say, brutally and directly, what is in our minds', Neville suggests. Percival's approval makes the shy thought solid.

Rhoda says: 'Like minnows, conscious of the presence of a great stone, we undulate and eddy contentedly. Comfort steals over us. Gold runs in our blood.' Percival provides what patronage ideally gave artists in the past, not just gold but that confidence that frees the mind.

Percival also extends the radius of insular minds to compass the globe. Percival's physical charisma will recede into the distance, but his far-flung effort will remain a perpetual stimulus. Sitting in that London restaurant, bidding Percival goodbye, the six young Britishers see 'the outermost parts of the earth—pale shadows on the utmost horizon, India for instance, rise into our purview. That world that had been shrivelled, rounds itself; remote provinces are fetched up out of darkness.'

As the six await Percival, their differences melt. He is almost never present in the flesh; it is an expectation or memory of his presence that provokes their revelation of fraternal love. 'Here, incredible as it seems, will be his actual body. This table, these chairs, this metal vase with its three red flowers are about to undergo an extraordinary transformation.' As Percival comes to the last supper, the whole restaurant, with its swing door and cold joints, wears an air of expectation.

Fraternity is one ideal not much talked about now, compared with its companion ideals of liberty and equality. It dominated the eighteenth-century novel in France and England and the nineteenth-century American novel with its ideal partnerships, Natty Bumppo and Chingachgook, Ishmael and Queequeg, and Huck and Jim. A nostalgia for fraternity lingered in Pound's 'Exile's Letter' and Lawrence's essay on miners. It lingered most persistently in the Bloomsbury Group as a relic of the Clapham Sect, and is celebrated in *The Waves*. Love of different kinds meets round the restaurant table, though more indwelling and inarticulate — perhaps more English — than in this scene's Greek parallel, *The Symposium*, where Athenians at their festive table take turns to discourse on love. As the six friends rise to leave the restaurant, the circle in their blood closes in a ring. Their young identities pulsate too fiercely at this stage to make this circle permanent, but there is some sort of bond which they wish to hold back from the swing door that will cut it to pieces.

The swing door, opening and opening, throughout this scene invites adult readiness. They strain to go, like horses or hounds on the scent, the nerves thrill in their sides, their hair lustrous. As Percival walks out of the restaurant into public life, it is a signal for the six to enter the great city. As the sun reaches towards the zenith of the sky, their energy burns at its maximum measure: 'The yellow canopy of our tremendous energy hangs like a burning cloth above our heads.'

The fifth interlude shows a harsher nature. There is an abrupt switch from the English shore to a hot Indian plain with grey hills and dry, stony river beds. The waves, massed with energy, fall swift and hard as though the seething natural universe were a beast in chains, its energy fastened into tides, orbits, life-cycles. One word resounds, '*fell*', '*fell again*', as it leads into the rhythmic headlong energy of Percival's fatal gallop in a tournament in India and its reverberating replay in the minds of his stunned friends, thousands of miles away. The word is picked up by Neville in the abrupt opening sentence of the fifth stage: 'He fell.'

The sun rises to high noon with Percival's death. Under its level and remorseless glare, the six friends confront death. 'The death chapter', so called in the notes, is the middle cross-section. Virginia Woolf placed death in the very centre of life. In her original plan, the shock of death was to come later;* it was an inspired stroke to shift it forward. In her last notes she jotted, 'complete maturity; but with doom added'. The point at which death deals the six their first rebuff is chosen to test their mettle. If death had come earlier, as in her own life, it might have been too destructive of morale; if later, too confirmatory of the approaching end.

For Neville this is the point when the tide of life turns and starts to subside. Memory, after life's meridian, becomes life's purpose: to bring Percival back. Bernard, in turn, takes up memory as creative exercise: 'I remember, as a boy, his curious air of detachment', he muses, turning Percival into fiction.

In her notes, in the autumn of 1930, Virginia Woolf distinguished between Neville's personal loss and Bernard's humane sorrow 'which is half joy'. But her triumph was Rhoda's 'entirely visionary or ideal sorrow' which transmutes personal emotion into abstract beauty and order.

Bernard and Rhoda conduct their own funeral services, for no traditional ceremony could do justice to Percival: 'Nothing that has been said meets our case.' Bernard holds his private funeral before a blue madonna in the Italian room of the National Gallery. Rhoda conducts hers, first, at a lunch-hour concert. She realizes, as she listens to the quartet, that Percival's gift had been social order, an ideal order like that of musicians or mathematicians, who place a square upon an oblong 'very accurately', and, by their accuracy, make 'a perfect dwelling-place'. The structure of the quartet is linked, later, with Hampton Court (Wren's neo-classic palace, not the Tudor part) whose windows form squares upon oblongs. Both

---

* The death of Percival ends the first part of VW's revised plan (on 15 June 1930). Curiously, in her plan of two days earlier (see MSS. W, second draft, p. 400) death was to come *after* the sixth section, called 'Maturity', and was to be followed only by two summing-up episodes called 'Love' and 'Books', presumably in imitation of books five and eight of *The Prelude*.

music and architecture epitomize Virginia Woolf's own determination to make the form of the novel as precise as the great arts. 'The structure is now visible', Rhoda tells herself as she listens to the music. It is also all-inclusive: 'Very little is left outside.' Art so ordered, so accurate, so inclusive, is Rhoda's consolation for Percival's loss. As the music breaks over her, the sweetness of content runs down the walls of her mind, liberating reason.

Waves of music propel her to the sea. She completes her ceremony at Greenwich, the place from which all measurement of the globe begins. Standing where ships catch the tide for India, she casts a token of herself, a penny-bunch of violets, into the wave 'that flings its white foam to the uttermost corners of the earth'. So Rhoda makes what was unconscious in Percival—his heroic willingness to be spent—conscious. As her imagination feeds off him, she can cap that careless surrender to nature, Percival's reckless gallop, with the mind's complementary will to order.

In this episode the rhythm of parallel lives 'runs on a snag', as Virginia Woolf put it in her notebook. Percival's rhythm is broken artificially, his death unseasonal. 'Percival was flowering with green leaves and was laid in the earth with all his branches still sighing in the summer wind.' Rhoda's eventual death, her suicide in late middle age, has a quite different character. Death does not break Rhoda's rhythm but, like a drop that rounds and falls, she falls, inevitably, from some height.

The six friends now move forward into a future that contains their inevitable extinction. From this point, they become saturated with time, time past, time future, and the rare moment when time stands still, from which memories are made and life's pattern composed. The six share with Virginia Woolf a view of a lifespan dominated by the fact of its termination; death is for them an ever-present possibility.

The overwhelming challenge that now faces the second half of the lifespan is to find meaning in continued existence.

The death of Percival ended the first part of Virginia Woolf's plan on 15 June 1930. On 3 November 1930 she took up the plan again with what she privately called the 'Life chapter'. In the sixth cross-section, the active Louis, Susan, and Jinny come to the fore. Louis has made his life a productive regimen. Now the world's running is

Virginia and Leonard Woolf at Monks House, Rodmell, June 1926

Virginia Woolf tries on her mother's Victorian dress, May 1926

on his shoulders: he is a successful merchant, but he could be any form of ruler. Susan's life is reproduction. 'His eyes will see when mine are shut', she thinks of the soft limbs curled in a basket.

Both Louis and Susan willingly curtail their senses in order to be effective. They fall like plummets on their jobs. Jinny lacks their single-mindedness: she leaps like a mountain goat from crag to crag as she passes from lover to lover. But all three have in common the fact that, at this particular stage, their thirties, they come to the meridian of their lives.

The meridian is the high-point of agency, the sense of acting in the right place at the right time. The angle of the sun in the sky provides yet another measure—of energy—by which the passage of the six through life can be synchronized in physical terms. The high noon of physical energy does not, of course, coincide with the apex of agency. According to this sample, the majority achieve their apex *after* high noon. Bernard must wait until he is sixty-five.

Jinny, in this stage, is the wandering moth of the night. Living wholly in her body, she moves in answer to erotic signals and hears male animals rear and plunge in the forest of her senses.

'One has pierced me', she breathes. 'One is driven deep within me.' She is sheathed in moist velvet flowers.

In contrast, Louis, equipped with typewriter and telephone, scores his lines across the globe, 'lacing' different countries with commerce. His enterprise is the practical expression of a philosophic ambition: a wish to generalize. Louis's aim is nothing short of mastery; he would reduce human beings, by force of logic, to a single statement. In the mean time, he stands close to Mr Burchard, director of the shipping line and, by constructing order, makes business a counterpart to Rhoda's union of square and oblong.

At his meridian, Louis knows that he cannot afford to blink or look aside. Instead of flying off with Rhoda, he must confine his senses' pleasure to the thud of the lift when it stops at his floor, and the heavy tread of responsible feet going down the corridor of power. He must look forward not to domestic or divine bliss but, a little wryly, to status symbols.

As Louis becomes increasingly manipulative, Rhoda comes to fear his embraces. The underside of his undeflected power-drive shows sudden insecurities. He is a little too effusive in ceremony since he still craves acceptance—though he can spare no energy for rapport.

As Louis's life narrows, in this phase, to the action of a hatchet as he cuts his invincible image, so Susan's life narrows to a cocoon.

'I am no longer January, May or any other season', she says, 'but am all spun to a fine thread round the cradle.'

She no longer rises at dawn to walk the fields nor watches the stars at night. Her voice falls away from love and hate to a barely audible croon. She wants, more than anything, sleep to fall like a coverlet on these weak limbs. Life pours so abundantly from her body for the next generation that, like the birds in the interlude who are glutted with the sound of their afternoon song, Susan is 'glutted with natural happiness'.

But Neville, whose life reached its peak earlier, watches the clock ticking on the mantelpiece of his bachelor room in College and is the first to realize, 'we grow old'. Percival's death has left him barren of delight and only comforts remain: the ancient classics and conversation over a fire. The fire irradiates a friend's face, but Neville knows that the glow comes from the fire, not his feelings. Deprived of hero-worship, he can develop no mature form of love but loves in passing. His romantic attachment to Percival endures. He takes walks through London, to exercise memory, through the Park to the Embankment, and along the Strand to St Paul's. By a lion in Trafalgar Square, he revisits his past life 'scene by scene', he says, '. . . there lies Percival. For ever and ever, I swore.'

The sixth cross-section is defined by words of concentration. Susan is 'glutted' by the sound of her own croon. Louis's vast store of experience, 'packed' in his long roots, now comes into play: 'But now I am compact', he says, satisfied, 'now I am gathered together this fine morning.' The 'life' stage, itself brief, describes a brief spell of full-throttle action. It is perhaps analogous to the peak years of confidence in Virginia Woolf's own life, 1925 and 1926, when the stores of her past poured from her pen as she wrote *To the Lighthouse* with astonishing quickness.

Middle age, not youth, is the stage of extremity. At this point, Bernard, Rhoda and, momentarily, Jinny, know despair. One day while shaving, Bernard sees himself, suddenly, as a heap of old clothes. Meanwhile, Rhoda rehearses suicide as she climbs a hill in

Spain.* A wind blows this stage in. Bernard's and Rhoda's lives waver and bend.

Bernard visits his mind as a colourless place. He gives an exact description of intelligent depression, its mingled inertia and clarity. From the vantage-point of Rome, where Bernard goes to recuperate, he decides that 'London has also crumbled' just as T. S. Eliot, depressed in Lausanne, had imagined London Bridge 'falling down falling down falling down'.

Yet it is in this crumbling state that Bernard sees Virginia Woolf's fin.

'Leaning over this parapet I see far out a waste of water. A fin turns.'

The fin can only appear when the 'dots and dashes' of trained thinking blank out, leaving the mind open to shock. Bernard explains:

This bare visual impression is unattached to any line of reason, it springs up as one might see the fin of a porpoise on the horizon. Visual impressions often communicate thus briefly statements that we shall in time to come uncover and coax into words. . . . I, who am perpetually making notes in the margin of my mind for some final statement, make this mark.

As Bernard leans over a parapet in Rome, at the same moment Rhoda, on a precipice in Spain, high enough to see Africa, wonders if she should launch herself into the sea below. The waves would shoulder her under. Death, for Rhoda, is not the enemy it is for Bernard or Percival. It is a natural return to the immortal sea from which, in the rhythms of her imagination, she has never strayed. She shares the mood of the Romantic poets who would fall back on the body of nature which gave them birth. Whitman perfectly registers Rhoda's surrender when he feels the sea beckon like an old crone rocking her cradle; her waves whisper

> the low and delicious word death,
> And again death, death, death, death.

Bernard's journey marks a revolution in his easygoing existence. Rhoda's journey carries her through thoughts she has always had to a summit of negation. All her life she has secretly condemned her

---

* In the first draft this seventh episode immediately preceded the final one where Rhoda's suicide is announced. In the second and final drafts, the eighth (Hampton Court) episode intervened. This shift explains the otherwise puzzling anomaly that, *after* this suicide rehearsal, Rhoda should appear much her usual self at Hampton Court.

species for its lack of courage. She has pretended not to be surprised by lies and sycophancy. 'What dissolution of the soul you
demanded in order to get through one day', is her silent judgement.

Bernard and Rhoda on their precipice offset those whom middle
age finds in the ease of habit: Susan, Neville, and Louis. For Susan
middle age brings rest to her hungry emotions. She feels indestruct-
ibly rooted like one of her thriving trees. As she walks in the
farmyard with a grown son by her side she has reached, she tells
herself, 'the summit of my desires'.

For Jinny the prospect of physical decay comes as the shock of
her life. One day, descending the escalator to the Underground, she
sees upright bodies carried, like her own, 'down the moving stairs
like the pinioned and terrible descent of some army of the dead.'
She stands like an animal at bay, her flanks panting. Then she
emerges from the Underground, forgets, and pursues her jaunty
course down Piccadilly.

Jinny's moment of extremity in the middle of the stage links the
more sustained extremity of Bernard and Rhoda at the beginning
and end. Bernard's depression is one of the unknown modes of
being. There are no words for a world without a self, seen with
impersonal clarity. All language can register is the slow return to the
oblivion we call health, when imagination automatically recolours
the landscape, and habit blurs perception, and language takes up its
routine flourishes. 'Blindness returns', Bernard observes, 'with all
its train of phantom phrases.'

An ebbing of the tide introduces middle age. The sand, left by
the retreating tide, is smoothed and pearl-white: a blank new space
opened up for action. Middle age, with the end of the lifespan
coming into view and its manifold stages emerging, marks the onset
of the question: where do these stages lead? This is answered when
the group meets, for the last time, at Hampton Court.

In order to make their way to Hampton Court the ageing friends
have to clear away a blockage of business and domestic claims.
Bernard finds himself almost wedged in place. Their first sight of
one another with their coats and umbrellas shows them embedded
like great trees in attitudes, authority, fame, and family. Only
Rhoda remains as she always was, faceless and apart. 'Your voices

sound like trees creaking in a forest', she tells them silently. 'So with your faces and their prominences and hollows.'

The sheer difficulty of getting to Hampton Court at the same time makes it obvious that such a reunion will not happen again. But for the space of this one evening they wish to catch in one another's eyes gleams of past existence. This eighth cross-section begins with a dinner at an inn, a parallel to the fourth cross-section, the farewell dinner at the outset of adulthood. Here, reaching the point of decline, the six look back, not only at their own achievements but also at what achievements history has chosen to perpetuate.

Susan, fulfilled by daily labour, silently discounts Neville's exhibition of academic honours. Neville, chastened, decides that his real achievement is a mental net, in the making all his life, now wide enough to lift whales. Susan's achievement is her work-worn hand with its gradations of healthy colour. Bernard's achievement is fluency: he still expends verbal energy with careless expertise 'as a man throws seeds in great fan-flights'. Individually, their achievements are not momentous, but in the garden of Hampton Court they come together, an ageing generation, and ultimately make their mark, if any, together.

The eighth, like the fourth cross-section, shows the friends as a group. The palace on the Thames, the creation of many generations, is the background for the group's perspective on lives, on history, which has been the purpose not only of this book but of Virginia Woolf's whole career.

Her papers record at least ten visits to Hampton Court apart from the one just before she wrote this, on 22 October 1930, when she alluded, half-joking, to the mood of Macbeth nearing his end: 'my way of life | Is fall'n into the sere, the yellow leaf.' During her youthful visits to Hampton Court in 1903, 1913, 1917, and 1918 she had revelled in the popular pageantry of royal history. She had liked to fancy, as she went through the courts, how Henry VIII had walked there, his arm across the shoulders of Cardinal Wolsey. Here little Edward VI had been brought to die, and here Charles II had lounged with Lady Castlemaine. But, in maturity, she saw Hampton Court as a work of art, the creation of Wren. The perfect symmetry of the east front building, begun in 1689, opens out on the Great Fountain Garden with three lime avenues radiating to the horizon, in the grand manner of Louis XIV's landscape gardener,

André Le Nôtre. The garden was completed by William and Mary who planted yews in the shape of their initials. They ordered giant stone urns from Cibber and Pearce, and from Jean Tijou the magnificent wrought-iron gates at the entrances to the three avenues, and they laid out the Great Terrace beside the Thames, a straight half-mile walk: all of this is the backdrop to the reunion in *The Waves*.

As the six advance abreast, arm-in-arm, down one darkening avenue, they ask themselves how they might oppose the flood of time.

'What has permanence?' they wonder. 'Our lives too stream away, down the unlighted avenues, past the strip of time, unidentified.'

Then Jinny sees the great iron gates roll back and their childhood selves advance, against the stream of time, to meet them. There they are, singing, round Miss Curry's harmonium. There is the six-sided flower on the restaurant table when they said goodbye to Percival. As time stands still, their lifetime's love consumes the clouds of cold mortality. In that moment they see that something durable is indeed there, the sum of their lifetimes' effort. Together, the six compose one summation of the species, body, mind, and soul.

'Let us stop for a moment', Bernard says, 'let us behold what we have made. Let it blaze against the yew trees. One life.'

As childhood's sequel to their soul's awakening was a stir of sensation, so after their mature intimations of immortality, the six break apart into couples. It is with age that they feel their blindest sexual longing, like a spear of light given off by the sun as it sinks.

Rhoda and Louis, stopping by a stone urn, watch Bernard and Susan, Neville and Jinny slink over the grass and vanish towards the lake. Faintly, they overhear Susan, who has always loved Bernard, say: 'My ruined life, my wasted life', before they melt into the dark trees which seem laden with bodies, dragged down, drumming with hunger.

The couples return depleted. Susan's eyes are quenched. Jinny's yellow scarf looks moth-coloured. Neville admits to some sadness that they had yielded to desire and so broke the group 'to press out, alone, some bitterer, some blacker juice, which was sweet too. But now we are worn out.'

Their bodies are nearly used up, yet together they defy the baser facts which historians have chosen to perpetuate: their records of worthless kings and their ridiculous idea that civilization hangs on the outcome of the battle of Blenheim. The six come to see historicity as vulgar except where there is some achievement of order such as Wren's palace and its garden.

As the six pace the terrace by the river, they begin to speak as in childhood, in shorter and yet shorter sentences as though the wave-pulse of life came in briefer spurts. Their voices seem, once more, to become indistinguishable, as in earliest childhood, to merge in a chorus as the book moves towards its conclusions. The six stand immobile, like trees, against oncoming night. They begin to take on nature's silence. Bernard observes how 'silence falling pits my face, wastes my nose like a snowman stood out in a yard in the rain. As silence falls I am dissolved . . .'.

Bernard then hears the chorus of his generation 'down the river' and sees himself 'slipping away' like the others into the spinning water. This is one of Virginia Woolf's own rehearsals for her drowning in the River Ouse. 'Little bits of ourselves are crumbling', Bernard goes on. 'I cannot keep myself together. I shall sleep. . . . I am like a log slipping smoothly over some waterfall.'

Water resounds as though it were drowning Bernard's voice. Our last glimpse is his hand still clasping the return half of his train ticket to Waterloo.

Fictional lives turn on the possibilities of change, but the six people in *The Waves* do not change. In fiction, characters are transformed by experience, but *The Waves* starts from a biological premiss that the course of life is determined by endowment, in the sense not of countable genes but of more dimly felt innate attributes, always present in the species.

An even number of men and women are isolated from social context: facts about parents, class, period, formal learning, formal occupation, public achievement, status, are kept to a minimum. Instead, Virginia Woolf cuts out the contour of each of her specimens with a teasing phrase: Rhoda, with her imaginative fertility, is the nymph of the fountain, always wet; the emotional Susan is a limpet clinging to a rock; Louis, enraged, masterful, hears a beast with a chained foot stamp and stamp; Neville, with his rational intelligence, is scissor-cutting, exact; Jinny's sensual body is a dancing flame. Rhoda, the character in *The Waves* who most resembles Virginia Woolf, has her eyes fixed on the outposts of nature where statues loom. She simplifies character to contour; the clefts and ridges of faces seem to be cut from nature much as Hardy discerned the shape of Leslie Stephen in an Alpine peak.

The contour of given character cuts deeper with patterns of play and mating habits. Bernard, the writer, marries a woman whom he can take completely for granted. Neville is consumed with lascivious day-dreams. His eyes shift down the river to a young man in a punt and he begins (in the first draft) 'so to look & so to die.* to . . . crush your lips & press your thighs—'. Jinny indulges her flair for erotic power-play. Louis and Rhoda are the only real pair among the six; theirs is a marriage of true minds.

Phrases, play, and mating may be bases for classifying our species. But this classification is multiplied by six as each voice advances a different perspective.

Bernard observes people from a third-storey window, a middle distance. As a boy he is tolerant, neither hating nor revering the fraudulently majestic headmaster, lurching like a ship to his podium. Of the six, Bernard slides most easily into society's plots; at school he is prone to abandon the cutting stimulus of his friend, Neville, and go off instead with the 'boasting boys'.

In the first draft of *The Waves*, Bernard confesses: 'I have been a great many different people.' As the potential hero of a thousand plots, Bernard is malleable to the point of dampness. Something of Virginia Woolf herself went into the making of Bernard: her sociability; her verbal performances—those arias of fancy; her willingness to take on the colours of a hundred correspondents. It is her dramatic versatility that makes Virginia Woolf so elusive. In *To the Lighthouse*, she split her hidden self between the two halves of Lily's canvas. In *The Waves*, she broke down what she knew of human nature six ways so as to analyse the composite and then, at Hampton Court, she fused the six as one ideal human specimen. After *The Waves* was published she wrote to G. L. Lowes Dickinson: 'The six characters were supposed to be one. I'm getting old

---

* Neville may have in mind the opening line of Shelley's 'To Constantia, Singing': 'Thus to be lost and thus to sink and die.'

myself—I shall be fifty next year; and I come to feel more and more how difficult it is to collect oneself into one Virginia.'

It is necessary, then, to see Bernard as only one out of a potential human endowment of six though, inevitably, this one, the public performer, wins attention from the biographer (of whose future presence Bernard is intently aware).

The most constantly on show, the most likeable of the six for his geniality, Bernard is really the most nebulous, as he admits to himself in his few dark hours. He disappears in others' shapes. This is why Susan cannot hold him. 'He is gone!' she exclaims. 'He has escaped me!'

Susan is attracted by Bernard's dramatic humanity: his attentiveness to her as a child when she had wept in a passion. But that attentiveness, though irresistibly warm while it lasts, will become for Bernard, as novelist, a professional routine. Bernard eventually chooses to marry someone tamer, more ordinary than Susan—the third Miss Jones—who will want less of him. There is, in fact, very little to be had.

Unable to lend himself to Susan's passionate longing (except once), he likes to dwell on her 'safety' as she sits sewing. For him the real drama lies in his work: how is he to distinguish the true plot of a masterpiece from the many fictions? As late as middle age he keeps his choice phrases 'hung like clothes in a cupboard, waiting for someone to wear them'. Late in life he comes to the strict truth of life-writing. The problems of biography dominate his old age when it falls to him, as professional writer, to plot the lives of his contemporaries.

Where Bernard observes from a middle distance, Susan's grass-green eyes fasten intently on her close white stitches. Susan epitomizes the woman who holds steadfast to her native ground—her farm—where she must plant and nurture her offspring. Her children are netted down in their cradles like strawberry beds.

There is nothing sentimental about Susan's maternity: she knows it to be a 'bestial' as well as a 'beautiful' passion. She understands animal cries of love, hate, rage, and pain. With her set face, single-minded, sometimes sullen and 'purple', she does not want, like her schoolfriend Jinny, to be admired; she wants to give and be given, and solitude in which to unfold her possessions. Her natural domain is the kitchen garden or the corn-field, but, when the babies come, her life narrows to a pin-point of concentration. Maternity provides this creature with a field for her energy which, of all the six, she expends with the most casual abundance. She is attended by gruff, creaking, deep-voiced men and pigeons, waddling this side and that, for the grain that she lets fall from her capable hands.

In her youth Susan thinks of herself as unattractive and dowdy but in late middle age she can exult in her body which is like a well-tried tool with a clean sharp blade in daily use. She has created a sound and practical dwelling-place to shelter oncoming generations. In the dignity of her age she is like the accomplished matron in 'The Journal of Mistress Joan Martyn', who illustrates women's underrated part in shaping civilization. It is easy to underrate Susan, particularly for those who believe that interesting lives are full of event and change. But Susan's voice confronts facile agitation with the steady onward pulse of her own existence. For Susan, the waves of existence are made by the seasons. In the course of her round, she greets the same old shepherds, presides over birth and deathbeds, repairs and renews relationships.

It is curious how romance circles around the squat, homebound Susan. Unconsciously, she beguiles Bernard with her inarticulate offer of security. The glamorous Percival, hero of the Cambridge punt, prospective hero of empire, also loves her. But she refuses him. Marriage with Percival would have transplanted Susan in a paradigm of success that would have warped her. Susan, clinging to the rock of her own being, steadily refusing adaptation is, in fact, the most intransigent of her sex. She is said to have crystal, pear-shaped eyes: eyes like those the Stephen sisters inherited from their mother, from whom Virginia Woolf derived her pictures of women in strong, responsible maturity. She put something of Vanessa into her image of Susan as controlling centre of her farm and family. She saw in Vanessa's nature a strain of fierceness and possessiveness, a maternity not like that of the madonna but of the tigress or the sheepdog.

Susan clings; Jinny darts. Her darting gaze takes in and excites responses. She sees with the body's imagination and her body is always moving, like a tossed poppy, febrile and thirsty. It is through Jinny that the other five become visible.

In adolescence Jinny darts and nips like an untamed animal, but as a young woman in a ballroom she develops subtlety. Her body puts forth a frill as it basks in men's admiration. Lost in a day-dream, as she sits with her dress billowing, she meets the eyes of a sour woman who, she observes, 'suspects me of rapture. My body shuts in her face, impertinently, like a parasol.'

Jinny epitomizes the life of the body at its most exhilarating. She is not licentious. She never abuses her body but follows its rhythm precisely, from the first ball when she yields to the slow flood of the dance until, grey and gaunt, she gazes in her looking-glass at midday at the lips that always showed too much gum—and still waits in ready expectation of 'the moment'. Jinny lives for sensation, to seize the delirium of the present moment: 'she rode at the day with her breast bared.'

Despite her age, she still welcomes lovers while soberer citizens sleep: 'the squeak of trams mixed with her cry of delight and the rippling of leaves had to shade her languor, her delicious lassitude as she sank down cooled by all the sweetness of nature satisfied.' When a lock whitens on her forehead, she twists her hair to flaunt it and still rises to her door opening as on her first spring nights in London after she left school.

Jinny's succession of lovers appear not individually but at a pattern of existence: men brought into being by her quickening rhythm, her blithe nonchalance, her complete fearlessness. But this pattern, for all its excitement, is less riveting than that of Susan stuck to the farm. Susan lives rhythmically; Jinny repetitively. Too much appetite, too much body without mind or character, soon palls. Perhaps the *Orlando* side to Virginia Woolf blinded her to this, the side that was over-stimulated by glamour, style, beauty, dash; in short, Vita's elegant hoofs encased in silk stockings. Virginia's letters to Vita, pumped with manufactured excitement, may explain why Jinny's lifespan does not quite achieve the inexorability of Bernard's and Susan's. It is merely predictable.

The first three specimens—Bernard with his flowing emotions, Susan with her nurturing generosity, Jinny with her appetite—suggest an abundance of natural energy that takes different forms, but all three are *habitués* of society. The three other specimens are progressively stranger, yet they epitomize half the distinctive components of the species.

Neville's perspective is that of the detective. The enquiring beam of his curiosity will not be satisfied with anything short of conclusion. His firmness of mind is his counter to his sagging body, his fear that he is doomed to repel those whom he loves.

Neville presents an odd blend of indolence and exactness, ardour and rational scepticism, that finds its ideal haven in the Cambridge that was once inhabited by Lytton Strachey and E. M. Forster. Lying on his back, Neville floats among his friends 'like a piece of thistledown'. Intellectually, he is drawn to the Romans. With a mind like the tongue of an ant-eater, rapid, dextrous, glutinous, he searches out every twist of Catullus and Lucretius. He diverts himself further with his fantasy of naked cabin-boys squirting each other with hose-pipes on a ship's deck. He will retain a characteristic mix of goatish frivolity and donnish seriousness. Living in an all-male community which cherishes eccentricity, he is less ill at ease than he can be anywhere. The Cambridge bells ring for life. The willow 'shoots its fine sprays into the air'.

Neville has much in common with the ugly St John Hirst. But Neville has more depth of character: his ardour may spill into silly love affairs but is essentially severe. Neville exhibits the tenacious strand in a good mind: he would like 'to follow the curve of the sentence wherever it might lead, into deserts, under drifts of sand, regardless of lures, of seductions'.

Neville compares his own detective habits with the soothing repetitions of Susan's life which, in his view, blind her to evil. He detects what lies at the bottom of the heart, its obscure jealousies and desires. For Neville, each day brings its variety of delicious dangers. He sees people coiling like snakes beneath their smooth surface. Neville, in fact, enjoys the hazards of intimacy. When, in his early twenties, he hurries to the London restaurant to see Percival, he can, in the very pain of parting, mark this distinction from his friends: 'My life has a rapidity that yours lack. I am like a hound on the scent. I hunt from dawn to dusk.'

After Percival's death, the inept don seeks consolation in a lover. The lover marvels at Neville's dextrous mind; Neville marvels at 'the careless movements of your body', but he falls short of consummation, in a damp heap. It is a relief to return to the neat cat privacy of his college room to luxuriate, instead, in the severe sentences of Roman writers who will 'rebuke the horror of deformity'.

The secret of Neville's nature lies not so much in his deformities as in his consolations, chiefly his interest in the snaky people with whom he consorts and the sheer interest of his own consequent suffering. He is 'on the scent'. He sees with incisive clarity. That, he says, is what gives to suffering an unceasing intellectual excitement.

Neville, though strange, is able to adapt his diagnostic pursuits to an academic milieu, but the last two specimens, Louis and Rhoda, are ill adapted to any of society's plots. If our species were ranged along a spectrum between society and nature, Louis and Rhoda would be the closest to nature though Louis, with his anxious need to conform, does force himself into the executive mould. He pairs with the even stranger Rhoda, a creature adapted only to darkness and uninhabited places. Their love, too, like the Woolfs', is strange by public norms represented by Bernard's domesticity, Jinny's appetite, and Neville's worship. They are drawn together as conspirators. Rhoda speaks to Louis behind her hand.* They speak to each other's secret selves, and in parenthesis, when they withdraw to the distant perspective they share. For both are bent on seeing the whole human race, Louis by means of logic, Rhoda by means of imagination. They participate in the festivals that mark life's course, the party for Percival, the reunion at Hampton Court, but with far-sighted reserve. Before the sun reaches its zenith they foresee the shadow cast by its decline. They are 'withdrawn together to lean over some cold urn'.

Thoby Stephen's picture of Leonard Woolf as a man enraged by human limitations was distilled in the figure of Louis who hears the beast with the chained foot stamp and stamp. Outwardly rigid, fastidiously lifting his feet like a disdainful crane, picking up words as if in sugar tongs, Louis admits behind tight-pressed lips that his impulses are wild. His affinity is for the wild west wind and, in the sterile autumn of his life, he longs for its renewing force and regrets Rhoda. His private thought moves on the track of an anonymous medieval poem:

> O western wind, when wilt thou blow,
>   That the small rain down can rain?
> Christ, that my love were in my arms,
>   And I in my bed again!

* The gesture goes back to the first draft, MSS. W, p. 338.

Louis wills himself to confront the world's doors to success. His hand repeatedly knocks on doors for admittance, at school, in the City. The instinctive eroticism of the boy's brass snake and his hand, stroking down a stem, calls up Jinny's unwanted response. Her kiss is unwanted because Louis is locked against intrusion. His self-sufficiency, his will to control, his insistent ambition overlay his given instinct. As long as Rhoda goes on meeting Louis he maintains his public and private life, his contradictory discipline and wildness, in a saving balance. They meet in Louis's attic above the City, in the first draft, 'the most constantly passionate of us all'. The final version blots out passion to emphasize Rhoda's withdrawal from embraces. For the successful business man eventually takes precedence over the dark dreamer. The habits of dominance come to dehumanize the lover (as in 'Lappin and Lapinova'). And when Rhoda leaves Louis, his soul dwindles. He has to have recourse to public dignity, the greetings of deferential office girls, and the consolation of a typist on his knee.

If Louis has suppressed the wild impulse, he has retained his childish fascination for roots, which develops as an acute historical sense. 'Every day I unbury—I dig up', he says half-proudly, half-wearily. As a child he feels he has lived thousands of years.* He is sated in a past that goes back to Egypt in the time of the Pharaohs. Louis's prophetic imagination is forged out of Exodus and, here, the foreign origins of Leonard Woolf crack through Louis's Australian veneer: he remembers people who carried red pitchers to the banks of the Nile. There is no mention of the tables of the Law, but Louis himself is stone-like, graven, in lifelong search of a single encompassing formulation of authoritative simplicity.

Louis oscillates between extremes: violent pride is succeeded by the imitative ape whose morale cowers before dowdy women with shiny shopping-bags. A few years later, Leonard Woolf was horrified by a photograph of storm-troopers dragging a man whose fly had been torn open to expose him as a circumcised Jew. What horrified him more than the blank despair on the Jew's face were the laughing faces of ordinary bystanders. Like Leonard, Louis arms himself with a caustic manner to distract attention from his fear of

---

* Hardy attempted a similar consciousness in the boy, Father Time: 'A ground swell from ancient years of night seemed now and then to lift the child in this his morning-life, when his face took a back view over some great Atlantic of Time . . .'. (*Jude the Obscure*, Part Fifth, ch. 3.)

the jeering mass. Leonard wrote in his autobiography that by the time he had finished school he had developed a 'protective façade or carapace to conceal the uneasiness, lack of confidence, fear, which throughout my life I have been able to repress but never escape'.

Louis goes with a brand of suffering on him, the heritage of persecution: 'It is a stigma burnt on my quivering flesh by a cowled man with a red-hot iron.' Steiner has argued that the Jews were persecuted not for the given reasons but in resentment of their spiritual gift, and it seems that Virginia Woolf detected this gift in her husband, despite his atheism. When a friend, Ethel Smyth, deplored her lack of religious sense, blaming Leonard, she retorted: 'Lord! How I detest these savers up of merit . . .; my Jew has more religion in one toenail—more human love, in one hair.'

Louis throws a 'malevolent yet searching light' on men in herds. His friends feel his eye upon them, 'adding us up like insignificant items in some grand total which he is for ever pursuing in his office'. The prophetic image Leonard Woolf called up in his autobiography whenever he used the word 'despair' is matched by this image of Louis adding up the human total with a fine pen: 'our total will be known; but it will not be enough.' He and Rhoda join as secret judges, in the second draft, 'the silent people whose verdict we often craved'.

The general conclusion Louis seeks is not to be found in books but in the great metropolis of London. It means relentless inspection of urban squalor. Despite his growing affluence, he steeps himself in grimy chop-houses, chimney-pots, broken windows, and mangy cats. 'He fascinated me with his sordid imagination', Bernard relates. 'He haunted mean streets and towns where women lay drunk, naked, on counterpanes on Christmas day.'

Louis's 'unalterable' conclusion is not given but we can assume that it is not favourable from his bitter remark: 'I do not see how you can say that it is fortunate to have lived.' I think that his summing-up would have much in common with *The Waste Land*, but without any mitigating glimpses of sublimity.

Louis's puritanical severity cannot be the last word (given *The Waves'* six-fold structure of opinion) but it is not to be dismissed lightly. What is most impressive is his almost ascetic will to sacrifice most of life in pursuit of a conclusion. The effort to reduce earthly variety 'to one line' leaves him with pursed lips and fixed eyes, though suddenly they could flash with laughter. Even at school,

Louis is recognized as a scholar capable of the inspired accuracy that has something formidable about it.

To resolve the fascinating contradictions of Louis's character, Virginia Woolf treats as peripheral his props of respectability and the engagement book which keeps people at bay. She stresses rather his frown, the concentration of a man spinning a thread out of his head, which is broken by contact with others. She describes Louis with the same adjectives which she used for T. S. Eliot in her diary: Louis is 'pale', 'marmoreal'. She once remarked lightly that if she and Eliot had not been so 'sere' they might have loved each other.

Some of the external details of Louis's life came from that of Saxon Sydney-Turner, who worked for the Treasury, lived in a back room, and ate in diners. The figure is a curious composite of Saxon's outer drabness and Leonard's inner vehemence. It blends, too, the shaking Leonard and the prophetic Eliot. 'All tremors shake me', the child acknowledges, knowing himself for a potential seer: 'my eyes are the lidless eyes of a stone figure in the desert by the Nile.' With the shadow of historic persecutions upon him— 'dungeons and the tortures and infamies practised by man upon man'—he has no patience, even in his youth, for the idyll, for Cambridge. He steers away from his relaxed English friends who are coming up from the river in white flannels, carrying cushions. With that bold move he sets in motion his formidable drama of mastery, conceived against the shadow of humiliation.

Rhoda's affair with Louis is considered by their friends an aberration in two lives whose centres of interest have been hopelessly opposed. But the mystery of their tie is solved through their private voices which speak throughout the book, with only glances at public postures.

Rhoda speaks for all who are strangers to their generation. Her mind shuns the daylight in which others live and act: in daylight her imagination is broken by contact with the mean and vulgar works of man. She appears vacant, her face moony, her body, in its excruciating diffidence, hiding, dodging, disappearing. Rhoda's perspective is as distant as the moon's which casts its eerie light on the dark side of earth. The moon's beam, unlike the penetrating beam of the lighthouse, is evocative, poetic: it calls up primordial statues, what Wordsworth called 'forms':

> o'er my thoughts
> There hung a darkness, call it solitude
> Or blank desertion. No familiar shapes
> Remained, . . .
> But huge and mighty forms, that do not live
> Like living men, moved slowly through the mind . . . .

Rhoda's tie with Louis, based partly on handicaps—their awkwardness, their fear of ridicule—is more truly based on their life of dreams. 'Like Louis, I must have been a prophet', Rhoda says in the first draft, 'but I detest that masculine pose.'

Rhoda's peculiar purity defies definition. Louis stimulates his higher faculties in recoil from human flesh. Rhoda's purity is more spontaneous, a fount of spiritual energy whose

> pure spirit shall flow
> Back to the burning fountain whence it came,
> A portion of the Eternal, which must glow
> Through time and change, unquenchably the same . . . .

In the first draft Rhoda pores over Shelley in the school library. As the girl, Virginia Stephen, browsing in Palgrave, came upon 'A Dream of the Unknown', so Rhoda, leaning her arms on the desk, reads of flowers that grew near to 'the river's trembling edge':

> And floating water-lilies, broad and bright,
> Which lit the oak that overhangs the hedge
> With moonlight beams of their own watery light.

She begins to feel white and porous, fed by a fertilizing and some-times painfully irregular stream which unseals the thickness of her body, making it luminous. The draft calls Rhoda's purity 'fiery'.

Rhoda has 'gone now like the desert heat', Louis mourns. 'When the sun blisters the roofs of the city I think of her . . .'.

Rhoda's nature rises out of a point of view that Virginia Woolf dredged up from her own past: 'Life is . . . the oddest affair. . . . I used to feel this as a child—couldn't step across a puddle once I remember, for thinking, how strange—what am I?' Existence comes to her as shock, like a dark crest heaving from the sea. 'It is to this we are attached,' she says, 'as bodies to wild horses.' Where Louis is to some extent protected by his fixation on the business to hand, Rhoda is alert to the real schemes of nature from which there

is no escape. Intimations of our subjection to nature come to Rhoda
when, as a child, she makes believe that floating white petals are
boats which may founder or survive in a stormy sea.

Rhoda herself expects to 'ride rough waters and shall sink with no
one to save me'. She puts up with Louis's habitat—cranes and
lorries and indifferent faces—in part because that daylight busy-
ness is, to her, a total pretence. She takes her imaginary voyage out
in the mood of Shelley, rebellious, brave, wondering:

> my spirit's bark is driven,
> Far from the shore, far from the trembling throng
> Whose sails were never to the tempest given;
> The massy earth and spherèd skies are riven!
> I am borne darkly, fearfully, afar.

Rhoda's mental journey takes her, in the second draft, through
drifts of ice. Her phrase, 'there are icebergs in the sky' must come
from Virginia Woolf's own recurring dream of taking her way
alone into ice-fields.

Through Rhoda, Virginia Woolf explored a hidden side to her
own mind. Rhoda is obsessed with mortality from childhood, when
she rocks her petals, to middle age when she hovers on the verge of
suicide and then, as Bernard abruptly reports in the final episode,
one day simply leaps. Even Rhoda's friends have no satisfactory
explanation.

At school Rhoda's face is unreal to her when she looks in the
mirror. She says to herself, 'I am not here'. Her clothes hang on her
and hide her. Her blood will not take the jolly rhythm of dance
music at her first ball, for Rhoda beats to another rhythm, pulse for
pulse with the universe. She would joyfully beat her breast against
a storm or break on the beach with the waves. 'The livid foam is
me', she says to herself in the second draft. Her identity dissolves
so readily that she must bang her hand against some hard object,
the door of a Spanish inn, to call her body back. So in the 1930s,
Virginia Woolf would be seen to walk very slowly about the garden
at Monks House as though she were trying to remember, her servant said, and then knock against a tree. For Rhoda the reincarna-
tion, as it were, this yoking of eternal spirit to corruptible body is
always an effort. There is the temptation to diffuse herself through
nature with the kind of total surrender that would carry her effort-
lessly to the other side of death. At her funeral for Percival she

promises herself this consummation: 'Now I will relinquish; . . . now I will at last free the unchecked, the jerked-back desire to be spent, to be consumed.'

Virginia Woolf's intimates, Clive Bell, Leonard Woolf, and Ottoline Morrell, all said that she was different from other people, not in degree of cleverness like Bertrand Russell, but that she seemed a different order of being. Such remoteness in a woman, if not disguised as modesty or passivity or awkwardness, must excite ridicule, and so passers-by laughed at Virginia as she drifted along the street.

In late middle age Rhoda still has no props, no face. She slips by in shadow. Louis who alone could call her out and might, therefore, have preserved her, is now too locked in worldly interests to commune with unknown being. As darkness falls, Rhoda calls out the hidden Louis for the last time, and they sing their last conspiratorial aria, in parenthesis, as they stand, detached, gazing at the dying antics of their generation.

The submerged Rhoda is, ironically, the most memorable of the six figures in *The Waves*. Fading to a shadow in the bright light of reason, in the dark of elemental being she takes on the permanent forms of pristine nature: the moon, the remote hills, the burning desert, the waves.

Virginia Woolf drew on herself, husband, sister, and friends in order to set out this map of human nature. To compose it on the basis of six samples posed the challenge of simplification. She wanted an epitome rather than the usual fictional inventory of traits. She re-created members of her circle as prime specimens, not necessarily the best of their kind but the most full-nerved, just short of the excess that would turn epitome to idiosyncrasy. Susan is not necessarily the best possible mother, but she is entirely maternal, her body to its most delicate nerve-ends dedicated to enfolding her young.

Where the motive behind *To the Lighthouse* was primarily biographic, the motive behind *The Waves* was primarily scientific. Eric Warner saw in the six figures 'a kind of poetic algebra' where six abstractions can stand for any number. For this reason the six are given no placing surnames. Although the originals of the six could be traced to Bloomsbury, they are transformed into voices speaking for permanent aspects of human nature.

This experiment goes far back to something Virginia Woolf said about *Wuthering Heights* in 1916. Where Charlotte Brontë said with eloquence and passion 'I love', 'I hate', 'I suffer', Emily, she saw, 'was inspired by some more general conception':

That gigantic ambition is to be felt throughout the novel—a struggle, half thwarted but of superb conviction, to say something through the mouths of her characters which is not merely 'I love' or 'I hate', but 'we, the whole human race' and 'you, the eternal powers . . .' The sentence remains unfinished.

So Virginia Woolf pared away the foliage of personality to glimpse the rocks beneath. The method is demonstrated by Neville when he falls upon his friend, Bernard, in his posturing Byronic stage, 'like a roll of heavy waters . . . laying bare the pebbles on the shore of my soul'.

13. *The Lifespan*

VIRGINIA WOOLF was sinking the individual life in a more general perspective: life as a span of time granted to all. She began with her own lifespan, marking its stages as she switched from one to another, from youth's search for identity—in her case, the identity of artist—to confront the more daunting challenge of age: to advance on the unknown, what she called 'the fin'. This task she set Bernard, who suffers her depression at youth's end and shares her mature need to leave behind a work of lasting truth. Bernard is Virginia Woolf's spokesman in the long finale to *The Waves*, which is a daring bid to define our lifespan against the infinite time-scale of nature.

Turning away from self-absorption, Virginia Woolf also began to look with new curiosity at the general public. A near-stranger appears in the finale to *The Waves*, whom Bernard, now heavy and elderly, meets in a restaurant along Shaftesbury Avenue and to whom, over dinner, Bernard confides.

He is a specimen reader and, since this is a 'phantom' dinner party, a reader of the future. It is like the eerie encounter between Whitman and future reader in 'Crossing Brooklyn Ferry' where the poet refuses to be shut off behind death's barrier, advancing closer and ever closer to the living reader until he takes him by the hand, whispers in his ear. Whitman's 'you' is a disciple, intoxicated by prophetic promise; Woolf's 'you' is a sensible reader, sceptical of the reach of Bernard's conclusions, and Bernard anxiously watches the half-known face for its varying response: 'You look, eat, smile, are bored, pleased, annoyed—that is all I know', he says.

But the reader's presence is essential. His waiting gaze, his very potency as a possible enemy, calls out Bernard's conclusions to questions posed and tested in the course of one generation: what is the shape of the lifespan? What is the maximum that we can claim for existence?

Bernard (like Lily Briscoe) is unwilling to force conclusions, willing to linger in doubts and uncertainties—to the point of giving up. Where the scientist, recounting his steps, makes up a purposeful story, Bernard registers *all* the steps towards conclusion: the failed notions, the dead-ends: 'It had been too vast an undertaking. . . .'

For Bernard in middle age the tide has ebbed. At life's end, Bernard's creative tide rises to flood the caves of memory. He turns over scenes, stage after stage, figure after figure. He retells memories until they take their final set. Under Bernard's expert touch, the six friends harden as statues who will outlive time's change. He freezes their lives, at their very moment of pulsation, into art, like Yeats's marbles of the dancing floor. The statues embody the achievements of our species: memory, imagination, language, fraternity, effort, and the peculiar gifts reserved for age.

Bernard trusts that the lines of six lives will be coherent if he cuts out what Virginia Woolf called, in her private shorthand, 'non-being':* official honours and doings, the school-leaving ceremony, the job interview, weddings and possibly marriages, buying a house. Bernard, as biographer, assumes that the classic shape of a life lies buried in this clutter of event.

However unconventional this method of composing lives, the compositional principle itself remains intact. Bernard confirms the traditional purpose of biography, to restore meaning to the often humdrum and tragic process of living. His method ensures that the weight of his multiple biography should fall on the constructive moments on which effective lives turn. It also ensures attention to the destructive moments when effort, and maybe life itself, seems pointless. For Virginia Woolf to rise from her own trough, she had to ask—through her six samples—what resources do we have against the biological and psychological minimums of existence? In middle age the curve of Bernard's being swings to its lowest point: 'here it coils useless on the mud where no tide comes'. The up-swing begins when he covers his weak being with the warmth of people on trains: old women clambering with their baskets into third-class carriages. His sympathetic curiosity comes back. In her notes for Bernard's final resurgence, in January 1931, Virginia Woolf wrote: 'I sometimes doubt . . . whether the whole duty of man is to reproduce his kind.' She put science and philosophy

---

* Four years later, Eliot was to write the same biographic theory into 'Burnt Norton'. He used the word 'waste' for the great stretches of the lifespan that are not worth recording in the light of a sublime moment:

> Ridiculous the waste sad time
> That stretches before and after.

before children, then the wave of renewed energy, curiosity, laughter, and, finally, home life. These are our creative resources.

To be creative, the adult must recover, through memory, a child's sense of being. The well-known lines from the 'Immortality Ode', the very lines that Leslie Stephen had quoted at St Ives, were the obvious *donnée* for *The Waves*:

> Though inland far we be,
> Our Souls have sight of that immortal sea
>   Which brought us hither,
>   Can in a moment travel thither,
> And see the Children sport upon the shore,
> And hear the mighty waters rolling evermore.

As one gets older one becomes 'somebody', 'a shell grows over one', Virginia Woolf jotted in her *Waves* notebook. This is the insidious temptation. It takes Percival's death to knock a transparency in Bernard's crust and an almost annihilating depression to knock another. As an old man (in the notes for his final soliloquy) he remembers how, among a party of elder statesmen, 'I then solidified—was somebody: my vanity was gratified.' At such times, he will pass easy opinions and swell with importance and then, he confesses, 'a shell forms upon the soft soul, nacreous, shiny, upon which sensations tap their beaks in vain.'

Bernard finds himself only at the end of his life when he cracks the shell with a new kind of biography. He says in the second draft: 'I perceive that the art of biography is still in its infancy or more properly speaking has yet to be born.'

His biography has two principles. First, that lives are shaped by 'moments of being'—the moment of waking in the nursery, the sponge of sensation, the ring of boys round Percival, the blue madonna, the concert, the intuition of 'one life' at Hampton Court. Six lives rise on the crest of moments with an imaginative residue. The art of living lies in the recognition of these moments that are not the preserve of the powerful, the glamorous, or the gifted, but common to all lives. The six fasten on crucial moments as they happen and seal them in memory. Bernard, reviewing these lives, isolates this skill of creative memory, at its peak in childhood and not measurable by any of the usual criteria of education. The six have cultivated this skill outside the school or college room, in garden or field.

As Bernard turns the pages of his multiple biography, he decides that stories of childhood, school, love, marriage, and death simply are not true, that lives turn on moments of humiliation and triumph that occur now and then, but rarely at times of official crisis or celebration: 'How I distrust neat designs of life', he mutters.

The six have been distinctive in that they have not forced their internal rhythms to coincide with set biographic schemes of marriage and career. Nature's masterplan has rolled out with ease. The second biographic principle is that the life is wave-like. Virginia Woolf expected the nine stages to prove 'that there are waves . . . by wh. life is marked; a rounding off, wh. has nothing to do with events. A natural finishing.'

The Waves demands an unaccustomed submission to this wave-rhythm. We have to pace our reading to the rhythm of a mind that flows back to retell phrases and scenes. It is undoubtedly hard for the trained reader, accustomed to the linear logic of conclusive sentences, to lend his ear to this verbal repetition as the six hoard their memories and turn them over, making a lifelong pursuit of biographic truth.

Even more difficult for the reader is to fill out what is only half-said. Bernard rejects sentences that come down with all their feet on the ground because, he believes, conclusiveness falsifies the truth. The reader has to learn to live with 'the fin', as Virginia Woolf did, with what is half-seen or barely glimpsed.

Rhoda as a young girl in a London drawing-room cannot compose one sentence. Her unvoiced thoughts cannot surface against the consensus of voiced opinion, the flickering tongues of society women and the smooth-worn phrases of gentlemen. There is a low, repeated suggestion that language, as an expression of power, registers too little. 'We only dominate when we make phrases', Bernard says in the notes. Though a professional phrase-maker, he can say, as he approaches his masterpiece: 'I have done with phrases.'

Bernard describes how the six have developed a private 'little language' as an alternative to public discourse. As a group they explore the effect of intimacy on language: they seem to hear one another's unvoiced intent with confident accuracy. From childhood they have known what to make of small gestures and casual words. They posit something better than a standard idiom, for they have trained themselves to 'hear' as well as to speak, until they are skilled in this voiceless language of sympathy.

'Thus I visited each of my friends in turn, trying, with fumbling fingers, to prise open their locked caskets', says Bernard. 'I went from one to the other holding . . . the incomprehensible nature of this our life—for their inspection. Some people go to priests; others to poetry; I to my friends.'

Each of the six mentally 'visits' the five others and, in turn, each is given what he or she most craves: the shifting Bernard is given identity; the ugly Neville, love; the insecure Louis, respect. In other words, they compel one another to release their life-dispensing strength. At the time of writing this, Virginia Woolf wrote in her diary that she used her friends as lamps: 'There's another field I see: by your light. Over there's a hill, I widen my landscape.'

The six friends suggest attributes which civilization may ignore but on which it depends for survival: a capacity to share feeling as well as phrases, an imaginative generosity. Shelley called it 'a going out of our own nature'. He said, what Christ preached, that if a man is to effect 'that sublimest victory' over force, he must imagine, which is to learn to love.

The voices of Bernard, Neville, Jinny, Susan, Louis, and Rhoda are not merely self-reflective. Each voice finds fullness as the biographer of five other people. Neville, unimpressed by Bernard's Byronic pose, helps him back 'into a single being'. Neville, in turn, submits his secret self to Bernard in the shape of a poem. 'Let me then create you', Bernard proposes, silently. '(You have done as much for me.)' This moment of biographic reciprocity is decisive for both lives. 'How curiously one is changed by the addition, even at a distance, of a friend', Neville reflects. 'How useful an office one's friends perform when they recall us.'

In an unpublished essay, Virginia Woolf wrote that Charles Lamb created his friends as he created his essays: 'He made them up, one feels; he endowed them with qualities which were congenial to him; he forced them to play their parts in character, and by his genius has stamped them as he made them for ever.' In the same way, Virginia Woolf created her friends in her imagination; if such people did not exist she would have had to invent them. A fraternity bound by the memory of Percival was her idealization of Bloomsbury bound by the memory of Thoby. On the basis of Thoby, she invented Percival as the hero of fraternity, a secular saviour.

Virginia Woolf came to believe that Thoby, who was reading law at the time of his death, would have eventually become 'Mr. Justice

Stephen'. Thoby appeared in life to be a man of conservative views, preparing to join the dominant order, but the hypothetical middle-aged Thoby of Virginia Woolf's invention turns out to have been all the time on the side of his sisters who had characterized themselves as reformers, revolutionists.

The discrepancy is resolved when Bernard suggests that Percival was a type of late developer. His 'magnificent equanimity (Latin words come naturally)' would have preserved him from meanness until such time as the deep well-spring of right feeling surfaced in action. Had he lived, his sure moral sense would have shown itself in unexpected attacks on injustice. This image of Percival remained intact from the first draft. 'He was to be a man of action. He died young. But if he had lived, undoubtedly his name would have been blessed by a great many obscure Indians, half castes, downtrodden races; & the rumour would have survived of the great Englishman; who rode in a sun helmet; of the just & fearless lawgiver.' The second draft imagines how he 'wd. have taken some unpopular view' and 'stood firm'. The final draft sees him denounce 'some monstrous tyranny'. Through Bernard, Virginia Woolf poured out her elegy to her brother: he would have done justice to people dying of famine and disease, to children, to cheated women. 'He would have protected. About the age of forty he would have shocked the authorities. No lullaby has ever occurred to me capable of singing him to rest.'

The moral ideal summed up by the fictional blend of Thoby with Percival may be traced to the Clapham Sect. It was the image of model reformer that Virginia Woolf wished to preserve, the integrity, energy, and resource of a public servant with the character not to seek power for its own sake. Percival did not go to India to expand the empire but to right a bullock-cart stuck in mud. He exhibits the Clapham traits summed up by Sir James Stephen in an essay which Leslie Stephen gave his daughter when she was fifteen. He had their 'master passion', the desire to relieve distress. He had also 'the judicial nature' and a 'self-possession unassailable by any strong excitement'. Percival's portrait takes its place in a long tradition of family portraiture, including James Stephen's *Memoirs: Written by Himself for the Use of His Children* and Leslie Stephen's life of his brother, all part of what Quentin Bell once called 'the cult of the family'. He went on: 'The Stephen devotion to truth and clarity might take an arid legal form, but it had also a certain austere beauty; the proconsular character of the family had also its admirable and its romantic side.'

Percival's name suggests also the redeemer-knight. The name may have, too, some association with Spencer Perceval, the Tory Prime Minister who was shot in the lobby of the House and died in the arms of the first James Stephen (who had entered Parliament in 1808 under Perceval's auspices). Another Clapham association may be Samuel Wilberforce who was thrown from his horse in 1873 on the Surrey downs at Abinger and killed on the spot. Samuel, like the hypothetical Percival, took up the prevention of cruelty to women and children as well as the treatment of prisoners and, as chaplain to the House of Lords, was able to present eloquent pleas for justice.

Bernard realized that Percival, as an exemplary arbiter of public values, could endure only for a limited time in the minds of his contemporaries. The public standard of their generation will be lost. Perhaps, for Virginia Woolf, Percival was an emblem of a vanishing standard at the beginning of the 1930s.

The extraordinary reach of Bernard's old age starts when, without quite knowing why, he buys himself a portait of Beethoven. He sees, in retrospect, how the loud sing-song of a chorus had obliterated certain periods of his life, for the brakeful of boasting boys going off to cricket in caps and badges became an army marching across Europe. A stolid film of schoolboy dogma had sealed off any hint of strangeness: 'nothing, nothing, nothing broke with its fin that leaden waste of waters.' Then, after his last reunion with his childhood friends, he discovers the real function of a writer: to be the inheritor and continuer of a species that has produced Beethoven and Hampton Court.

He imagines inherited culture as his inhabited house. He is ready to possess 'all its . . . objects, its accumulations of rubbish, and treasures displayed upon tables'. He is tempted, of course, to let tradition prop him, to be more the inheritor than the continuer, but, like Virginia Woolf herself, he never surrenders that glimpse of a submerged form on the empty horizon of his middle age, and so, in old age, can admit the unformed to complement the monuments of the past as his mentor, Beethoven, had balanced his compositions between the classical rhythms inherited from his teacher, Haydn, and odd sounds lurking on the edge of his auditory imagination.

In the eerie late quartets which inspired first Virginia Woolf and
then T. S. Eliot to their greatest works, Beethoven seems to follow
the fin through the waters.*

Throughout the finale to *The Waves*, different kinds of music
rehearse life's phases: the male chorus, the bells of the university
town, the bird-songs of women. Then, as Bernard swells with the
collective energy of his generation, he thinks in terms of the
symphony 'with its concord and its discord, and its tunes on top and
its complicated bass beneath. . . . Each played his own tune, fiddle,
flute, trumpet, drum or whatever the instrument might be.'

Bernard's life has fitted him to recapitulate both the minimal and
maximal possibilities of existence. His swing from the minimum of
abject depression to the maximal possibilities of age starts with
a flicker of the old rhythm in his head, like the dots and dashes
of a pulse. Then, when he meets his friends at Hampton Court, he
is kindled in their light and so, overcomes his separateness.

As chronicler, Bernard lives on beyond his generation. In the last
stage, where he courts immortality, he uses his senses not to glut
identity but to overcome it. By sharing the identity of others he
rides the wave's crest as though he were riding the rhythm of the
universe, transcending time as he rides it.

Bernard disarms future generations of listeners by acknowledg-
ing the 'old brute' still squatting in him. He points to his hairy paw,
holding a glass of fine old brandy. He buttons trousers over the
same organs as a savage.

Hume, who had no religious hopes, is said to have died with
splendid—to Dr Johnson, baffling—equanimity. So Bernard faces
death as he holds his entire experience in view, tier upon tier, his
mind poised above it, immeasurably receptive, replete. He looks at
his hand with its fan of bones laced by blue veins and confirms the
secret of our species' success: 'its astonishing look of aptness,
suppleness and ability to curl softly or suddenly crush—its infinite
sensibility.'

At night, without stirring from his chair, Bernard can range at
will. Age, for him, means the imaginative stretch to rehearse the

* VW's diary makes three references to Beethoven, which show her to have been listening
to late sonatas as she planned the book (18 June 1927) and to a quartet as she worked out
Bernard's final speech (22 Dec. 1930). *Diary*, iii, pp. 139, 246, 339. VW told Gerald Brenan
that she had been reading a life of Beethoven while working on *The Waves* and envied his
power of drawing up into his score, by constant revision, themes which resisted being
brought to the surface (*BG*, p. 290).

daybreak he will not see again. So Virginia Woolf takes us circling back to the dawn of a new generation as the aged Bernard sees the rising sun level its beam at the sleeping house and the bars deepen between the waves as children emerge into the garden.

At its maximal stretch, Bernard's mind can admit its limitation. 'What does the central shadow hold?' he wonders. 'Something? Nothing? I do not know.'

For all that shadow, because of it, the finale is resounding. In admitting the limitation of our species—its inexactitude of vision that makes its dogmas absurd—Bernard's stature grows as, simultaneously, he demonstrates the gifts of our species: its powers of sympathy and imagination, its capacity to communicate by the finest shades of implication and to reflect with inexorable honesty.

The Waves takes this stand against the middle-aged depression in which it was conceived: it is written to justify the existence of human beings as a continuous species. It answers the query of the scientist in *To the Lighthouse* whether we are attractive as a species, whether we should go on.

Bernard finally celebrates six obscure people for their action against 'enemies'. For Rhoda the enemy is the mean-souled expressionlessness of a London shopgirl who sells her stockings after Percival's death. Hers is the mass apathy that can gaze, unmoved, at grief and requires the spice of violent sensationalism to stir dulled senses. For Louis, the enemy are the boasting boys, round-faced chubby little boys, dressed alike, who leave butterflies with their wings pinched off and a smaller boy sobbing in the corner.

'Enemy' is the group's shorthand for whatever spurs in them a wave of resistance. Louis is spurred to economic mastery, Rhoda to the idea of creative order. Jinny melts indifference with the exhilarating touch of a stranger's body. So each of the six sets up the actions that govern their lives.

Then the leaves fell and '*settled with perfect composure on the precise spot where they would await dissolution*'. The finality of the last interlude is the backdrop to the gallantry of Bernard as he rises to the last and loftiest wave of his speech where he sums up six lives and gives them enduring form. He imitates Percival as he rides against death bearing the insignia of the species.

Death is the greatest enemy: one might say that all of life is an action against death. At first Virginia Woolf wanted to show that effort, effort dominates the contest with death—she had marvelled, watching the death of a moth, at its valiant effort to go on moving. In her diary, on 23 November 1926, she noted that life seemed quicker, keener at forty-four than twenty-four—'more desperate I suppose, as the river shoots to Niagara—my new vision of death; active, positive, like all the rest, exciting; & of great importance—as an experience.' But in the end she added a line that gave the last word to the waves: '*The waves broke on the shore.*' Bernard's surging verbal effort is undercut by their curt monotony, yet endures as a writer's supreme fling against death:

And in me too the wave rises. It swells; it arches its back. I am aware once more of a new desire, something rising beneath me like the proud horse whose rider first spurs and then pulls back. What enemy do we now perceive advancing against us, you whom I ride now, as we stand pawing this stretch of pavement? It is death. Death is the enemy. It is death against whom I ride with my spear couched and my hair flying back like a young man's, like Percival's, when he galloped in India. I strike spurs into my horse. Against you I will fling myself, unvanquished and unyielding, O Death!

The waves, which introduce the first stage of the life and round off the last and sound all through, carry and dash human effort. All the while that the six lives unfold, first from the perspective of the actors and then from the perspective of an aging chronicler, they are also seen from the impersonal perspective of what Virginia Woolf called 'insensitive nature'.

Her first memory of the erratic pulse of the waves at St Ives was to unfold as the commanding intuition of maturity: that rhythms of human processes—if attended to without the interference of time-tables—will appear to have something in common with the wave-like rhythms of the physical universe, with the waves of sound and light and the tides of the sea.

She planned the book 'to a rhythm not a plot'. There is the quick waltz rhythm of the city eating-house where Louis feeds as a young shipping clerk. There is the quickening thud of Percival at a gallop. Neville's rhythm is the ebb and flow of conversation under lamp-light in a college room. Rhoda's rhythm is literally the waves, the boats of her imagination rising and sinking on their voyage out. Through these rhythms the six partake of timeless nature.

Writing, the pulse of the sentence or the beat of poetry is, like music, a way of catching the rhythm of nature. Susan's lullaby sounds like an old shell murmuring on the beach. Bernard writing a love letter wants 'speed, the hot, molten effect, the laval flow of sentence into sentence'. He echoes Virginia Woolf's idea that rhythm is the main element in writing: 'Now I am getting [Byron's] beat into my brain.' Neville, inspired by fountains of willows at Cambridge, begins to spout: 'words that have lain dormant now lift, now toss their crests, and fall and rise, and fall and rise again. I am a poet, yes.'

In her late notes for *The Waves* (January 1931) Virginia Woolf says that 'the novel changed when the perspective changed'. *To the Lighthouse* looks at lives from the perspective of historical time; *The Waves* looks at lives from the perspective of eternal time. Historical time sharpens individuality; eternal time blunts it. Looked at *sub specie aeternitatis*, the six, unlike any living characters, have unchangeable forms, graven from nature. Bernard sees Louis carved from stone; Susan's eyes like lumps of crystal; Jinny a flame; Rhoda like clouds that voyage over the dark side of the earth as the other five move through phases of daily life under different angles of the sun.

'I shall pass like a cloud on the waves', Virginia Woolf told herself a few months before she began the book. She saw lives, like her own, pass across their allotted span 'so quick, so quick' yet, she went on, we human beings are successive and continuous. How do we show up in the light of nature's time, represented by the sun's rays at different hours of the day?

As the sun, the traditional measure of time and mortality, rises and sets, so six lives rise, move to their zenith, and set. Each stage of life is measured by a stage of daylight which, all the time, disregards human effort and gets on with its mechanical business. Virginia Woolf deliberately set off the italicized nature interludes from the human voices, so as to set off control from experiment. The result is that, all the while the parallel between physical and human nature is maintained, it is also undermined.

After Percival's death Bernard is shocked by the impervious machine throb of a universe that goes on without him. At his own death the waves continue to break with monotonous regularity. His brave fight against death becomes spectacular in the face of his apprehension of nature's vast and indifferent energy: 'And the light

of the stars falling, as it falls now, on my hand after travelling for
millions upon millions of years—I could get a cold shock from that
for a moment—not more, my imagination is too feeble.'

Virginia Woolf called it a 'violent measure' to strike at human life
from the angle of insensitive nature but the 'sudden directness' of
the results persuaded her that she was on the scent. It seemed like
breaking through gorse. She shouldered her way 'ruthlessly', as
though she were tramping like her father in Cornwall: 'I sacrifice
nothing to seemliness. I press to my centre.'

She first struck from the angle of insensitive nature in the middle
section of *To the Lighthouse*. 'Time Passes' looks impersonally at the
cycle of seasons which wipes out beloved characters, Mrs Ramsay,
Prue, and Andrew, in the shocking casualness of brackets. It is the
perspective of creation itself. *The Waves* begins, like creation, with
an unpeopled universe which is then peopled. It is a narrative
haunted by the eternal mind. Early in the first draft Virginia Woolf
said: 'I am the thing in which all this exists. Certainly without me
it would perish. I can give it order. I perceive what is bound to
happen.' But to take this perspective was to endanger sanity. The
price of that creative power, when it flagged, was to see herself as
a mote on the tides of time. This is perhaps what happened, in-
advertently, on the night of 15 September 1926 when she wrote:

A State of Mind

Woke up perhaps at 3. Oh its beginning its coming—the horror—
physically like a painful wave swelling about the heart—tossing me up.
. . . Down—God, I wish I were dead. Pause. But why am I feeling this? Let
me watch the wave rise. I watch.

She disregarded the trivia to which melancholy attaches itself—
personal failure, ridicule—and pursued this elusive state of mind
for the next four years, deliberately risking herself, so as to stretch
the impersonal perspective of 'Time Passes' to the containing frame
of *The Waves*. On 23 June 1929, just before she embarked on a first
draft, she plunged in utmost melancholy into the deep water of
insensitive nature. 'Lord how deep it is!', she marvelled. 'And as
usual, I feel that if I sink further I shall reach the truth. That is the
only mitigation; a kind of nobility. Solemnity. I shall make myself
face the fact that there is nothing—nothing for any of us. Work,
reading, writing are all disguises; & relations with people. Yes, even

Leonard Woolf

'All that completeness ravished', London, 1941

having children would be useless. . . . I now begin to see . . . [*The Waves*] rather too clearly . . . for my comfort.'

Reading *The Waves*, one swings from the piety compelled by six lives seen close-up to the remote view of these same lives in the impersonal perspective of nature. In *The Waves* human lives represent all that is mutable in nature, all that evolves and wastes in the course of time. The sun and waves provide a fixed measure: there, immutable, from the beginning of earth's time, like Emily Brontë's Yorkshire moor or Hardy's Egdon Heath, against whose expanse of olive-green gorse a man appears as a brown spot. *The Waves* blends familiar biographic detail with a unique diagrammatic detachment so that, as Virginia Woolf uncovered the lines of each life, she could distil a theorem applicable to all lives.

Virginia Woolf's main ambitions came together in *The Waves* and never fused so perfectly again: her wish to frame her own life, her wish to mark her memories of others with a surpassing elegy, and the new wish that rose in her late forties: to penetrate a hidden design.

Although the most impersonal of her works, *The Waves* re-enacts the 'wave of the past' whose precise rise cannot be marked. Certainly it went back to her earliest memory of the waves behind the nursery blind and the garden at Talland House. She remembered as a child looking at a flower in the bed by the front door and realizing, suddenly, that there was a hidden design and 'that we—I mean all human beings—are connected with this; that the whole world is a work of art; that we are parts of the work of art'.

The Waves rehearses, too, the shock of death on the mind of the adolescent emerging, moth-like, from its chrysalis. The waves beat the measure of a life moving always to its end. In April 1925, motoring to Rodmell to spend the Easter weekend with Leonard, Clive Bell, and Duncan Grant, she felt 'again this downy billowy wave beneath us: ah, but how quickly I sink'.

Buoyed by love and friendship—that fertile spring of 1925—she advanced to re-encounter Thoby, no longer a young girl engulfed by loss, but ready to shape his elegy: 'over all this the bloom of the past descends as I write—it becomes sad, beautiful, memorable.' Cambridge, which she visited on 2 May, seemed 'full, like all places, now, of this wave of the past'.

In February 1928 and again in May and in the second draft of *The Waves*, she repeated a comment which she had tossed off while writing *To the Lighthouse*, to the effect that whatever she was writing were not novels: 'I shall invent a new name for them.' When she had asked herself to name the genre back in 1925, she had wondered, half-quizzically: 'Elegy?' Perhaps she saw herself inventing a new genre that would take the poetic and biographic elements of the elegy, which is rooted in personal emotion, and cross these with an impersonal and measured enquiry. The outcome had something in common with experimental science, with its hypothesis (the fin), demonstration (the six lifespans), its control (the interludes of insensitive nature), and result (Bernard's summing-up).

The elegiac mood of the spring of 1925 was quickly subsumed in the impersonal observation that in jungles and storms, in birth and death, humans look the same, make the same queer brews of fellowship, crack the same sort of jokes. 'I sometimes think', she said, 'humanity is a vast wave, undulating: the same.'

After she reeled, intoxicated, across the last pages of *The Waves*, her elegiac aim was fulfilled. 'Anyhow, it is done', she recorded immediately in her diary, '& I have been sitting these 15 minutes in a state of glory, & calm, & some tears, thinking of Thoby. . . .'

Her second triumphant thought was that she had netted something unknown: a sample of the natural universe forever on the horizon of human lives. 'I have netted that fin in the waste of waters which appeared to me over the marshes out of my window at Rodmell when I was coming to the end of To the Lighthouse.'

14. *A Public Voice*

ON 2 October 1932 Virginia Woolf had another prophetic moment which, like her vision of the fin, marked what she called the soul's changes: '. . . now, aged 50, I'm just poised to shoot forth quite free straight & undeflected my bolts whatever they are.'

She resolved to frame a public voice. Like her ideal 'Mr. Justice Stephen', she would show herself as reformer and question the abuses of power. From 1932 she began to call herself an Outsider. This was the start of the last lap in Virginia Woolf's life. She marked its onset, as she had marked the stages of the lifespan in *The Waves*:

These are the soul's changes. I don't believe in ageing. I believe in forever altering one's aspect to the sun. Hence my optimism.

She planned to alter 'cleanly & sanely' by shuffling off distractions: fans, reviews, fame, 'all the glittering scales'. The public voice was to be a far cry from a bravura performance in Bloomsbury. She wished to expose a woman's point of view and called the autumn of 1932 'a great season of liberation'. 'You will understand that all impediments suddenly dropped off. . . . I had no restrictions whatever, & was thus free to define my attitude with a vigour & certainty I have never known before.'

The public stand was backed by a marriage that was now all-sufficing. *The Waves* brought Rhoda and Louis together as 'conspirators': this is how the relation to Leonard took final shape. This peculiar tie strengthened their perspectives on power and made it possible for both in different ways to speak out against it.

After *The Waves*, Leonard became more visible in her writing, his face all peaks and hollows, with deepening grooves on either side of his nose. The diary gives glimpses of their times of happiness and, less often, of Leonard's 'habits' which his wife still hoped to cure: his oppressive silence, his tempers, his rigidity. His room at Monks House she called Hedgehog Hall. He was not a gentleman by her standards: he was hard on people, rude to servants, exacting, despotic, yet these very qualities that caused her, when others noticed, some shame, went together 'with great justice, in some ways; & simplicity too; & doing good things: but in private a very difficult characteristic'. Still, she knew how to defuse anger with a joke. She was never really intimidated; at worst, would get up and curse. The diary reports that there was no real skirmish after 1913–15. A rainy French tour in the spring of 1931 alerted her to 'this warmth, curiosity, attachment in being alone with L. If I dared I would investigate my own sensations with regard to him, but out of laziness, humility, pride, I don't know what reticence—refrain. I who am not reticent.'

During the 1930s they began to admit to themselves that, though they had subscribed to personal freedom, they were, in fact, inseparable. In October 1937, when Virginia thought of going alone to Paris, Leonard said he would rather she didn't.

'Then I was overcome with happiness', she wrote in her diary. 'Then we walked round the square love making—after 25 years can't bear to be separate. Then I walked round the Lake in Regents Park. Then . . . you see it is an enormous pleasure, being wanted: a wife. And our marriage so complete.'

The diary's last hint of their continued love was a disagreement over a greenhouse. 'Yet so happy in our reconciliation', she commented.

'Do you ever think me beautiful now?' she asked.

'The most beautiful of women,' said Leonard.

The last decade of Virginia Woolf's diary turns in on domestic content after 'the hurried London years'. She seems often to be looking away from Bloomsbury to 'the old habitual beauty of England: the silver sheep clustering; & the downs soaring, like birds' wings sweeping up & up. . . . It feeds me, rests me, satisfies me, as nothing else does. . . . This has a holiness. This will go on after I'm dead.' Country walks made her mind 'glow like hot iron'. She liked to tramp across the downs to the cliffs and to glimpse 'the gulls on the purple plough'. Once, at Piddinghoe, she startled Mr Gwynne (lean, aristocratic, with wet pebble eyes) when he found her on his property, scrambling under barbed wire in her wool helmet. She liked, too, to work at her rug, to see to bread-making and preserving and to play bowls on the lawn overlooking the Ouse valley which stretched to Mount Caburn in the distance.

'We get snatches of divine loneliness here', she told her sister, 'we'll play bowls; then I shall read Sévigné; then have grilled ham and mushrooms for dinner; then Mozart—and why not stay here for ever and ever, enjoying this immortal rhythm, in which both eye and soul are at rest? So I said, and for once L. said: You're not such a fool as you seem. . . . I went in; put the kettle on; ran up the stairs looked at the room; almost done; fireplace lovely. . . . Made tea; got out a new loaf; and honey. . . .' The dining-room where they had tea was sunk below the level of the garden 'and dimly green like a fish-pond', Angelica Garnett recalled, with an aquarium in one corner and plants on the window-sills which cast a green light into the room, and through their gaps the legs of visitors could be seen arriving.

Virginia was about to call in Leonard from the ladder on the high tree—'where he looked so beautiful my heart stood still with pride that he ever married me'—when their utopia was invaded by idle grumpy guests. The collapse of that moment of bliss turned her mood to fury.

Eventually, when the Blitz of 1940 marooned them at Rodmell she sank, ironically, into 'peace', free 'on our lovely . . . autumn island' from the battery of visitors who beset her in London. As her world contracted to the village radius, as she thought of friends isolated, like themselves, over winter fires, a sense of a more rural, traditional England of isolated village communities infused *Between the Acts*, and a new kind of history of England which she called, tentatively, *Anon*. It also provoked a startling picture of Leonard as he came, one day, across the marsh, 'looking like a Saxon Earl, because his old coat was torn and the lining flapped round his gumboots'.

This village existence was not a further withdrawal into a precious world of her own but the opposite: an attempt to dig into 'the community feeling' that the war brought out. 'Never felt it so strong before.' She would turn from the private to the public record, from the novel to the annal, and take in the panoply of history, not forgetting the acts of the obscure between the acts of the famous. As far back as December 1927, she had realized that to know the obscure, she must give up self-absorption: 'The dream is too often about myself.' She resolved from then on to 'practise anonymity'. By concentrating on domestic acts too common to be noticed she would frame a voice never heard before, a distinct woman's voice which would be an alternative to the power-hungry rant of political demagogues. In 1932 and 1933 she was impatient with the low, sidelong voice of *The Second Common Reader* and

Flush and anxious to be done with them. She would refuse to believe herself simply a lady prattler, 'for one thing it's not true. But they'll all say so. . . . No, I must . . . create, hardly fiercely, as I feel now more able to do than ever before.'

Virginia Woolf once spoke of 'changes which often make the final period of a writer's career the most interesting of all'. If the last lap is approached not from the angle of her selling successes (*Flush*, *The Years*) but from the angle of her unfinished or projected works (*The Pargiters*, *Between the Acts*, *Anon*, 'Octavia's story'), the diary, talks, essays, and, above all, pamphlets (*Three Guineas*, *Reviewing*), it becomes clear that she was about to transform her career. After nearly a lifetime of personal, elegiac works, written for a small circle, she was seeking a public voice to address a national audience. In short, she wished to become, with age, no less than arbiter of the national conscience and preserver of what she judged the national treasure. An extravagant and, it would seem, impossible aim, but it was characteristic of her daring to rise to the challenge of the polemical 1930s. 'Can there be Grand Old Women of literature', she asked Rose Macaulay, 'or only Grand Old Men? I think I shall prepare to be the Grand Old Woman of English letters.'

To become an Outsider was tantamount to a 'spiritual conversion'. It meant freeing herself of the false obligations of manliness and womanliness so as to discover a new social function for women: to resist and, ideally, in some remote future, to ban war.

As German bombers flew nightly over Rodmell, in August 1940, she shook free from war propaganda which attributed insane love of power to an occasional freak. Recasting the great Clapham issue of slavery, she suggested that we are all enslaved, irrespective of nationality, by 'a subconscious Hitlerism in the hearts of men': the desire to dominate. The word 'slavery' reverberates through her 'Thoughts on Peace in an Air Raid': 'If we could free ourselves from slavery we should free men from tyranny. Hitlers are bred by slaves.'* Her imaginative solution seemed absurd to the power-struck readers of the war generation: that we must find a way to engender creative feeling that will compensate the fighter for the pumped-up thrills of sadism and medals, the strutting aspect of honour, and the loss of his gun.

---

* cf. VW's first polemical piece on the position of women in society (Oct. 1920, repr. *Diary*, ii, Appendix III, p. 342): '. . . The degradation of being a slave is only equalled by the degradation of being a master.'

Like the Claphamites, who persisted with anti-slavery agitation
during the Napoleonic wars, Virginia Woolf looked beyond the
immediate causes of the second world war to the permanent ills
of civilization. Her great grandfather had written a vehement
pamphlet against the institution of slavery;* she wrote a pamphlet
against the institution of war. Her righteous backbone would
stiffen. There was the same delight in plain speaking and the
same conviction that he who has attained higher truth must himself
evangelize.

'Mustn't our next task be the emancipation of man?', she asked
her friend, Shena, Lady Simon, a Manchester City Councillor, in
1940. 'How can we alter the crest and spur of the fighting cock? . . .
So many of the young men, could they get prestige and admiration,
would give up glory and develop what's now so stunted—I mean
the life of natural happiness.'

Virginia Woolf had first concerned herself with the economic
enslavement of women. In her two papers read to the Arts Society
at Newnham and the Odtaa at Girton College in October 1928†
she had kept the tone light: the speaker was herself exempt from
unacknowledged or ill-paid jobs. She had an inherited income. Her
books, she admitted, would have been unthinkable without the
luxury, for a woman, of privacy, summed up by her mock-modest
plea for a room of one's own.

Fired by another speech, in January 1931, to the Society for
Women's Service, she thought of a sequel to *A Room of One's Own*,
a series of polemical essays that would take in education, sex,
and politics. In 1932 she began an 'essay-novel': her plan was to
alternate essays with illustrative fictional scenes set within one
middle-class family, the Pargiters, beginning at the time of her own
birth, the 1880s. The essays were eventually discarded (and the
fiction went on to become *The Years*), but they are pioneering
statements like Mary Wollstonecraft's. Where the *Vindication of the
Rights of Women* is concerned with visible handicaps, *The Pargiters*
examines the more invisible ones. She shows how lack of occupation trivialized the minds of middle-class Victorian girls and their
niggling jealousy, locked in their domestic prison, from which the
only escape was marriage. More hidden, less remediable, is the
awakening of sexual fear. She reveals the able girl-child's blend of

---

* James Stephen: *England Enslaved by Her Own Slave Colonies* (London, 1826).
† Revised as *A Room of One's Own*.

rebellion and submission as she takes in the dominant order that she must learn both to distrust and to obey.

Virginia Woolf then analyses the corresponding distortion of a Victorian young man at Oxford: Edward Pargiter has been trained to deflect his natural response to his cousin, Kitty Malone, into vigorous work and exercise and, if it persists, into a sentimental idealization that leaves a woman cold. When Edward writes a Greek poem to Kitty it never occurs to him to imagine a real woman. In fact, his well-schooled feelings are essentially reflexive, self-admiring.

The light of analysis is finally thrown on Kitty, locked in her parents' false image of a lady which has cut her off from her natural tastes. Her inclination is, she knows, for farming, but she can only dream of an escape from unreality. Beneath the impeccable manner of the Warden's daughter, she is bored by Oxford men who must be talked to about themselves. Secretly, she is kindled by the outspoken honesty of a friend's working-class family,* ambitious for its daughter as well as its son, and by her unmarried tutor, both of whom, though negligible in the power structure, reflect an alternative image of what Kitty might be.

The *Pargiter* essays are based on a note for the 1931 talk, to the effect that a woman is always absorbing a set of values half-an-inch to the right or left of her own. Virginia Woolf warns professional women that, even for them, the task of finding themselves still lies ahead. Their own values, dreams, feelings, will meet with derision. She imagines a man, pervaded by a delicious sense of importance, who finds one day in his library the housemaid comfortably reading Plato and, in the kitchen, the cook composing a Mass in B flat. The man then makes cutting remarks about the way servants compose or read Plato. She cautions women against anger, an enemy within 'who is always sapping your strength and poisoning your happiness'. Her advice is: 'Be patient; be amused.'

Virginia shared the platform that day with Dame Ethel Smyth, who had composed a Mass in D. The seventy-one-year-old ex-suffragist and composer befriended Virginia and helped her voice her thoughts by proving that they were shared, by the example of

---

* VW had in mind Dr Joseph Wright (1855–1930) who rose from working-class origins to become compiler of *The English Dialect Dictionary*. His admiration for his hard-working mother led to unusual sympathy for women. In July 1932 VW read *The Life of Joseph Wright* by his wife, published that year. See *Diary*, iv, pp. 115–16.

her own downright boldness and above all, I think, by calling out the side Virginia had reserved for her fictions. In her first letter on 2 May 1930, Ethel said: 'I never felt . . . that what I *see* of you is the real V because . . . it is the essence I see.' This was a different Virginia from the frail, potty, or playful performer whom so many of her intimates tell us about: Ethel saw 'the divination — the fight'. She called out the fighter, the reformer in Virginia which was stirred by allegiance to her mother, symbol of womanly strength. 'The most violent feeling I am conscious of is . . . for my mother', Ethel wrote. 'She died 38 years ago and I never can think of her without a stab of real passion; amusement, tenderness, pity, admiration are in it and pain. . . .' Ethel called out too the reckless spirit in Virginia, excited by a fling against death. On 11 August 1930, Ethel struck this masterly chord:

No experience however vivid can rob me of that—I am, I am in love with death—with turning away—with the idea (as Plotinus said) of disengaging the eternal from the temporal. . . .

Ethel, like Vita earlier, was in love with Virginia, who kept them both on tenterhooks and remained loyal to Leonard. To Vita she gushed and postured; to Ethel, who shared her views, she dashed down letters of uninhibited candour. Ethel's 'uncastrated cat' style of talk, pouncing, noisy, frank, freed Virginia from her characteristic mix of volubility and reserve. I don't think that she spoke in such an unconsidered way to anyone else. Although there is an element of ridicule in her replies and tactful avoidance of disruptive meetings, she clearly enjoyed the unmasking. She liked Ethel's spunk and public spirit, which she made the basis for the figure of the suffragist, Rose, in *The Years*. Ethel's outspoken manner was quite different from her own training in silence. In 1931 she made a revealing comment in a letter to Ethel:

For months on first knowing you, I said to myself here's one of these talkers. They don't know what feeling is, happily for them. Because everyone I most honour is silent—Nessa, Lytton, Leonard, Maynard: all silent; and so I have trained myself to silence; induced to it also by the terror I have of my own unlimited capacity for feeling. . . .

She went on to ask if her habitual silence came from her fear of 'the unknown force that lurks just under the floor? I never cease to feel that I must step very lightly on top of that volcano.'

Ethel replied that she had nothing to learn about that volcano. '. . . I have never for a second not known that the frozen falcon perches on an incandescent mass below'. There is an exuberant 'Pause—to unstiffen buttocks' and she goes on: 'That you must have set woods alight as you walked through them and beaten your way with your bare feet through rocks and stones and walls when you were young I always imagined.' She understood the peril of the volcano—'I have seen the ground you walk on slightly crack'—and the traditional need to disguise its proximity, but she urged her friend to let it out:

You see, Virginia, I feel very passionately . . . that, once [women] throw off their susceptibility to male notions, something new in the way of light and heat will be diffused in the world.

Virginia Woolf's manuscript notes for the 1931 talk do try out a new blunt, emphatic language:

If I were reviewing books now, I would say [war] was a stupid and violent and hateful and idiotic and trifling and ignoble and mean display. I would say I am bored to death by war books. I detest the masculine point of view. I am bored by his heroism, virtue, and honour. I think the best these men can do is not to talk about themselves anymore.

By 1938, when *Three Guineas* came out, she framed a policy of indifference. The Outsider (who, she insists, is latent in all women) must become indifferent to manly rhetoric, self-importance, and above all warring:

'"Our country",' she will say, 'throughout the greater part of its history has treated me as a slave; it has denied me education or any share in its possessions. . . . Therefore if you insist upon fighting to protect me, or "our" country, let it be understood, soberly and rationally between us, that you are fighting to gratify a sex instinct which I cannot share, to procure benefits which I have not shared and probably will not share. . .'.

Three Guineas is addressed to 'Sir'. Virginia Woolf's imagined public broadens, here, from the professional woman to the educable man. In the 1931 talk she had spoken to women with certain quickness and affectionate ease. She speaks to 'Sir' with cool and patient courtesy. The book's implacable logic is calculated to convince and not, like *A Room*, to disarm. *Three Guineas* is a rational investigation of the dodgy emotions, the unstated assumptions, and evasive terminology that prop patriarchal law. She applies its own methods of laborious argument supported by fact. This argument is unnecessarily prolonged for women readers, but the facts in the footnotes are absorbing, also her subtle analysis of the more covert struggles of nineteenth-century women, of Sophia Jex-Blake who was determined to study medicine and of Charlotte Brontë who, in middle age, wished against her father's will to marry his curate. The most daunting struggles, Virginia Woolf perceives, are not with external obstacles but with oneself, with those notions of self-defeating womanliness which have been so firmly ingrained.

The man, too, she suggests, is enslaved by his fictions. He has made himself a work-slave to protect his fiction of the helpless woman. He has used the same fiction to inflate war fever. The vicious circle goes on: to exact compensation for forcing himself, he becomes 'the sympathy addict . . . calling for replenishment; or as Herr Hitler puts it, the hero requiring recreation, or, as Signor Mussolini puts it, the wounded warrior requiring female dependents to bandage his wounds'. A footnote caps this with a similar claim from an English source:

Never yet have I committed the error of looking on women writers as serious fellow artists. I enjoy them rather as spiritual helpers who, endowed with a sensitive capacity for appreciation, may help the few of us afflicted with genius to bear our cross with good grace. Their true role, therefore, is rather to hold out the sponge to us, cool our brow, while we bleed. If their sympathetic understanding may indeed be put to more romantic use, how we cherish them for it! (William Gerhardi, *Memoirs of a Polyglot*, pp. 320, 321.)

In the late 1930s Virginia Woolf recorded that, as yet, the question of admitting women to the Church or Stock Exchange or Diplomatic Service met some strong emotion that set off 'an alarm bell within us; a confused but tumultuous clamour: You shall not, shall not, shall not . . . '.

She began *Three Guineas* with a calm conviction that, at last, at the age of fifty-five, she had 'stepped out, throwing aside a cloak'. She wrote it in the summer of 1937 with a delirious sense of freedom which whirled her 'like a top miles upon miles over the downs'. She had conceived a right to vote not for one party or another but against the whole edifice of power, and said: 'I feel myself enfranchised till death, & quit of all humbug.'

Three Guineas provoked extreme reactions. Virginia Woolf was called the most brilliant pamphleteer in England. The book was said to mark an epoch. But Leonard was lukewarm and most of her intimates, like Maynard Keynes and Vita, dismissive. None the less she shrugged off opposition. It was a positive relief, she said, to be attacked in *Scrutiny* and sent to Coventry by her friends: 'I do my best work & feel most braced with my back to the wall. It's an odd feeling though, writing against the current: difficult entirely to disregard the current. Yet of course I shall.'

The Outsiders Society, Virginia Woolf claimed, was already in existence. Evidence of it was the mostly unpaid, altruistic work of millions of obscure women. This vast unrecognized work-force practises, unknown to itself, the Outsider principles: to work for the love of the work itself, to retain an experimental attitude, and to cease competition when there is enough to live on.

The true Outsider is not to be found in the limelight. Virginia Woolf herself steadily refused all public honours: the Clark lectures at Cambridge for 1933, the Companion of Honour in 1935, and honorary degrees from Manchester and Liverpool in 1933 and 1939. Privately, she was pleased by the Cambridge offer for the sake of her father who gave the first Clark lectures (on eighteenth-century literature) in 1883. She thought back of 'the uneducated child' reading books in her room and that 'father would have blushed with pleasure could I have told him 30 years ago, that his daughter—my poor little Ginny—was to be asked to succeed him'. But honorary degrees provoked scathing comment:

9th April 1935

The veil of the temple—which, whether university or cathedral, was academic or ecclesiastical, I forget—was to be raised, & as an exception she was to be allowed to enter in. But what about my civilisation? For 2,000 years we have done things without being paid for doing them. You can't bribe me now.

Pail of offal? No; I said while very deeply appreciating the hon . . . . In short one must tell lies, & apply every emollient in our power to the swollen skin of our brothers' so terribly inflamed vanity.

She would not allow herself to be used as an exception. 'It is an utterly corrupt society . . . & I will take nothing that it can give me.' Honorary degrees were mere baubles distributed by the pimps of the brain-selling trade. 'Nothing would induce me to connive at all that humbug. Nor would it give me, even illicitly, any pleasure. I really believe that Nessa & I . . . are without the publicity sense. Now for the polite letters. Dear Vice Chancellor—.'

Tufts of fur on one's head, medals, badges, hoods, she argued, hypnotize the minds of onlookers so that they become rigid. Consider, she said, the glazed eyes of a rabbit caught in the glare of a headlamp. The necessary flexibility of society 'can only be preserved by obscurity'. It was this vast audience of the obscure that she aimed to reach and ultimately to free from the desensitizing glare of advertisement. She believed she could do so only by adopting anonymity. These two words, 'obscurity' and 'anonymity', reverberate as watchwords through the diary and projected works of the latter half of her career.

'. . . I have, at last laid hands upon my philosophy of anonymity', she wrote on 29 October 1933. Her search for a public voice started her thinking of an audience. How might she extend her audience yet further, beyond professional women and men to include worker and villager, the grass roots of England? She found her model in Anon, the unknown poet of the late Middle Ages. 'Clearly I have here in the egg a new method of writing criticism.' She hoped to re-create the fertile, long-forgotten conspiracy between unselfconscious oral poet and the obscure rural audience. The unfinished manuscript, begun on 18 September 1940, was called 'Anon' or 'Reading at Random' or 'Turning the Page'. It consists of two rudimentary chapters, 'Anon' and 'The Reader', which unfold ideas going back seventeen years. The idea for 'Anon' went back to a question in May 1923 as to what happened to the English mind between Chaucer and Shakespeare; 'The Reader' back to an unpublished piece of 1922 on the lost skills of 'Reading'. Though the manuscript is minimal, the fragments suggest a design too bold to be dismissed lightly.

On 28 December 1938 she began reading, deliberately at random, for a 'Common History book', and started writing it between September and November 1940. This history was to turn attention away from England's educated voices, modelled on Greece and Rome, to rediscover the rude native voice of the country. The voice gossips at the farmyard door; it is alternately devout and lusty. It breaks into song like a bird which sings*

* *Anon* opens with a passage from Trevelyan's *History of England* which describes prehistoric Britain as a forest filled with innumerable singing birds. VW's diary notes that she began Trevelyan on 26 Oct. 1940.

because 'Summer is y-comen in' or because it is hungry or merry or
swells with longing for renewed fertility:

> Western wind, when wilt thou blow,
> That the small rain down can rain?
> Christ, that my love were in my arms
> And I in my bed again!*

She proposed this voice that 'is not attached to a person' as a
counter to 'the great modern sins of vanity, egotism, and megalo-
mania'. As women must learn indifference, so audiences must learn
to close their ears to bellowing, iron-willed oratory and listen,
instead, to the merry, loose-lipped voice of nobodies or to women's
little language of intimacy and affection with its nuance of unspoken
intent.

Anon may have been a woman who crooned over her spinning or
to children on a winter's night. In *Mrs. Dalloway* there is a similar
battered woman singing outside Regent's Park Station. Her song
comes from a mouth like a hole in the ground, muddy 'with root
fibres and tangled grasses' and the song is age-old: how once in
May she had walked with—it did not matter—her audience each
supplied a name.

In pre-Renaissance England, Anon's unpretentious voice blended
so easily with those of her listeners that there was no need to
distinguish her by name. This is different from the anonymity
which nineteenth-century women drew round them as a cloak.
Works of Virginia Woolf's last decade tried to re-create this earlier
and more wholesome anonymity, in effect, a verbal bond with a vast
potential audience of working women,† of half-obliterated house-
wives like Isa Oliver, of half-despised widows like Mrs Swithin
(that epitome of the imaginative common reader), and of growing
girls shut off from opportunity, all of whom had no public voice to
lift their thoughts from obscurity and give them due lustre.

In *Between the Acts*, Virginia Woolf posed the problem of an

---

* These lines also hum repeatedly in Louis's head when he misses Rhoda. *W*, p. 145.
They reappear also in 'Reading', the unpublished introduction to *The Common Reader*
(MHP B. 11 d), p. 19.

† VW first met working women at Morley College in 1905–7. After her marriage she was
frequently in touch with the Women's Co-operative Guild. At Hogarth House, 1916–20, she
asked a group of elderly members to tea once a week or fortnight. 'They were sort of mothers'
meetings', Barbara Bagenal recalled. 'She loved talking to these women and, of course, asking
them innumerable questions so that she could learn as much as possible about their lives.'
Recollections of Virginia Woolf, pp. 150–1.

intractably passive, cliché-ridden audience of villagers who watch a pageant of English history. She suspected that the problem was rooted in the history of the popular audience and proposed to explore this history in *Anon*. The book would tackle the inertia of the common reader from both ends: she had to isolate the historical cause and to remedy the present-day result.

The cause she traces to the invention of printing. 'It was Caxton who killed Anon by giving him a name.' The legend of Arthur was fixed in 1485; the audience could no longer share in the making of a communal dream. It became passive, a mere receptacle for the book trade. From the point of view of Anon the printed book was an outrage, for print has a look of finality—a deceptive authority—which daunts the reader's reciprocal effort.

The many drafts of the first chapter, 'Anon', suggest how difficult it was to unwind history from an odd perspective. She argued that the authentic line of English culture stemmed from uncouth people who may have been called Crot, Nin, and Pulley. The Elizabethans, on the other hand, craved the alien ancestry of Greece and Rome. They burdened their pages with proofs of correct intellectual breeding: Pliny, Cicero. They affected eloquence: their language became as ceremonial as their faces fixed on the platter of the ruff. They built themselves round with the ancient classics and studded clothes. So began a cult of self-importance that resulted in a crucial loss: the daily lives and feelings of common folk drop out of sight.

The piece on the Reader picks up this thread at the modern end, with prescriptions for the revival of the common reader. In her paper, 'The Leaning Tower', read to the Workers' Educational Association in Brighton in May 1940, Virginia Woolf had exhorted workers and women, 'the commoners' and 'the outsiders', to join forces as critics. It is inevitable, she conceded, that we commoners, after being excluded from the universities for centuries, will bruise some ancient grass, but she fell back on her father's advice to dare, nevertheless: 'But let us bear in mind a piece of advice that an eminent Victorian who was also an eminent pedestrian once gave to walkers: "Whenever you see a board up with 'Trespassers will be prosecuted', trespass at once".' In future, she assured the workers, 'we are not going to leave writing to be done for us by a small class of well-to-do young men who have only a pinch, a thimbleful of experience to give us'.

The substance of 'The Reader', like 'Reading', is an exposé of a massive confidence trick perpetrated by the middlemen of the book trade. Editors, reviewers, librarians, critics, and academics have persuaded common readers to surrender judgement and swallow 'authoritative' or 'definitive' treatments. As a result, common readers have come to crave a diet of prestigious opinions, not true words. The present-day reader was, she thought, a lost cause, so she would skip the present and try a chapter on the future.

Virginia Woolf was optimistic that, with proper encouragement, common readers could come into their own. She stood shoulder to shoulder with Dr Johnson, who rejoiced 'to concur with the common reader; for by the common sense of readers uncorrupted with literary prejudices . . . must be finally decided all claim to poetical honours.' As a fall-back there might be a service on the lines of the medical profession: private advice for a fee.

Middlemen, she explains, are so corrupting to the reader because they impose modish theories as a reductive grid. Behind their pose of expertise, they are lazy. There is a large class of literate people who can run their eyes down miles of print without 'reading' a word. Her 1939 pamphlet, *Reviewing*, and even more its acid draft, buttonholes the common reader with plain talk. Listen, she says, critiques are written from unsound motives: to pay bills, to settle scores, to flatter, to relieve egotism.* Modern books are written with an uneasy consciousness of a circle of invisible censors. They lack the lone intentness of, say, a Wordsworth poem. Truth cannot be found on show in the literary marketplace; it lives 'in darkness; in silence; where the face is hidden; and only the voice is heard'.

The proper readers become this author's fellow-workers. They must surrender to the author's unique world and bare their minds to the author's signals. By surrender she does not imply passivity; on the contrary, a perpetual exercise of vigilance. To read as the writer's accomplice is to recover the mind's natural functions: the surge of emotion, the play of curiosity, the urge to remember, the need for balance, the wish to compose a whole.

The reader's recovery turns on learning to feel. The author prescribes the 'direct shock' of genuine emotion as a remedy for the inertia of the modern audience, a sickness promoted by the routine

---

* *Diary*, v, 9 Nov. 1939: 'Rev[iewin]g. came out last week. . . . Lit Sup had a tart & peevish leader: the old tone of voice I know so well—rasped & injured. Then YY polite but aghast in the N[ew] S[tatesman].'

brutality, snobbery, and romance of the market-place. We must learn to recognize authentic feeling and let it guide our choice of books:

One principle guides us in making our course and that is [that] the emotion roused in us by each play, poem or story must be so strong that it has the power first to absorb us and then to send us, by a natural reaction, in search of . . . a sensation which appears to complete the one originally felt.

In this way the reader commands responses and so becomes whole. But literature is not an emotional orgy, she is quick to add. It is an effort, often a disappointment. Emotion comes only after exercise of the mind because great writing awakens universal sympathies. It is a greater effort to feel for all lovers and all partings than one's own, to visualize country in general, and wind in general. 'Yet it is these general emotions and these nameless winds that prevail in Homer Virgil Dante and Shakespeare.' The reader, waking from private to universal feelings, recapitulates the mental process of the greatest artists. The continuity of *Anon* was to turn on 'certain emotions always in being; felt by people always'.

Another way of renewing ties between author and reader is through biography. Readers should 'go hunting' for the hidden face of the writer, peer in at basement windows, listen to gossip. 'Somewhere, everywhere, now hidden, now apparent in whatever is written down is the form of a human being.'

Virginia Woolf was living at Monks House after her London home in Mecklenburgh Square was bombed in September 1940. She had never lived permanently in a village and, at times, wondered uneasily if a London sophisticate could possibly commune with the popular voice. She immersed herself now in those works of English literature that do so: the poetry of Anon, Chaucer, Shakespeare, Dickens. She imagined, in *Anon*, the Elizabethans' intoxication with the theatre: men and women, who spent their days loving and cheating in the festering streets around St Paul's, went across the river to the Globe, and there 'heard themselves saying out loud what they had never said yet. They heard their aspirations, their profanities, their ribaldries spoken for them in poetry.' The terrific popular attraction of the play was to see 'their own lives composed'. This phrase suggests the line that Virginia Woolf hoped to trace from Elizabethan drama to the twentieth-century appetite for 'Lives'.

Anon was a critical prop to her own attempt to activate an audience in *Between the Acts*. The dramatist, Miss La Trobe, wills members of the audience to recognize themselves on stage as far back as Chaucer's pilgrims who weave their perpetual backdrop among the trees. As the pageant of English history moves to the modern age, the actors pounce on the villagers with mirrors, forcing them, as it were, on stage. They must recognize themselves as actors. In her primitive way Mrs Manresa (who is after Isa's husband, Giles), flaunts her man-hunting role when she calmly paints her lips in the actors' mirrors. More subtly responsive, Mrs Swithin feels the stir of her unacted part.

'What a small part I've had to play!' she confides during the interval to Miss La Trobe. 'But you've made me feel I could have played . . . Cleopatra!'

After the pageant, Giles and Isa Oliver enact the midnight drama that La Trobe conceives, simultaneously, as her next work. As primeval man and woman they must fight and after they fight they will embrace. Pointz Hall, the shell of civilization, falls away and the two grow enormous as they face each other, as the dog and vixen, their enmity bared 'in the heart of darkness, in the fields of night'. In the final line the age-old drama begins: 'Then the curtain rose. They spoke.'

The last-minute change of title recognized that the novel was not so much about the country house and the pageant as about private dramas going on between the acts. It is a novel about an English audience. It records twenty-four hours in the life of a village 'in the very heart of England' in June 1939. The village is remote, three hours from anywhere, its rural stability still almost untouched by the oncoming menace of the second world war, but already there appears a divide between the man of action, played by Giles Oliver, and the onlookers, old Mrs Swithin, who is reading an Outline of History, and Miss La Trobe, whose unorthodox pageant draws an outline of her own, in effect, another counter-history.

In *The Waves*, Virginia Woolf split herself between Bernard and Rhoda, writer and dreamer. Again, here, she lends herself to the writer, Miss La Trobe, and also to the imaginative reader, Mrs Swithin. Although they have little dialogue, their very existence is reciprocal. Privately, Isa Oliver is of the onlooker party—she conceals her poetry in an account book (as young Virginia Stephen had concealed a diary in 1899 under the covers of a treatise on

logic)—but, in her public role as wife, Isa must act with her
husband. Isa holds to her intact, dreaming self but has to admit that
it is abortive: always unspoken or only a murmur, it can never
surface into drama. Her primary role is to be the typical
Englishwoman: she is thirty-nine, the age of the century; she reads
newspaper reports of rape; she has a solid body like a bolster; her
husband, the typical English gentleman, looks like a cricketer, virile
and immaculate. Their drama is yet to come, when the lights of
civilization go down: they are to fight in barbaric darkness. Though
they will never know the meaning of the play, they must perform
their parts.

Between the Acts was written during the Battle of Britain and
there is never any doubt that, though German guns may, as Giles
predicts, rake the land, the land can absorb the scars (as it had
absorbed the marks of the Romans and the scar on the hill where
they had ploughed to grow wheat during the Napoleonic wars).
Neither is there any doubt that the race will go on: people will
continue to be born. What is in danger is England's treasure,
epitomized by Pointz Hall: its way of life, its books. In the earlier
typescript, when Mrs Swithin tours the house with a visitor,
William Dodge, she confides that she does not care about flesh-
and-blood ancestors, only about 'spirit' ancestors, 'people one's
descended from by way of the mind'. Then she runs her hand over
the books sunk in the wall on the landing 'as if they were pan pipes'.

Giles, in his furious concern for the protection of his country,
scorns this aunt who is, in fact, as alert reader, a prime preserver of
its civilization. Covert signals of recognition pass between the more
literate members of the audience at Pointz Hall, between Dodge
and Mrs Swithin, Isa and Dodge, Isa and the farmer, Haines, but
none will ever surface on the platform of action. All are sadly
ineffective. Dodge, a homosexual, is thought unmanly; Mrs
Swithin, who is whimsical, is called 'Old Flimsy'. So, turning back
to the solitary consciousness, Mrs Swithin and Isa seem to wind up
at the lily pool, staring into its depths.

These people are watchers for hidden faces. Their private
dramas are given in silent soliloquies which are potentially more
dramatic than visible action. Isa's speculation about Haines is one
climax of the book: the unknown man to match the unknown
woman. He is a curious, potent figure, his silence guarding his
'hidden underground bubbling spring', as Virginia Woolf called it

in a draft. His sexual energy never surfaces except covertly, with the char's strumpet daughter. Haines is a man of mysterious but stunted possibilities. In the shelter of his mind ideas grow as blades of grass beneath a stone 'but all white; denied the green that the fresh air of certainty gives'. So Haines remains evasive, a 'perhaps' person; physically solid, but emotionally obscured, tied by marriage to a goose, yet somehow virgin, seductive, untouchable.

These hidden faces in the audience are capable of imaginative response but, for most, Miss La Trobe's pageant is not what they expect. Instead of a sequence of events, she looks for the common denominators of character. As Joan Martyn's fifteenth-century mother had prefigured the Victorian, Mrs Ramsay, so, in this pageant, the fourteenth-century pilgrims reflect 'ourselves'. The Wife of Bath, the Restoration figure of Lady Harpy Harridan, the Victorian figure of Mrs Hardcastle, and, no less prominent in the audience, Mrs Manresa, are continuous and they project into the future. In the earliest dated draft, visitors to Pointz Hall pick up Chaucer in the library and 'some felt, "This is my England. This is visible to me; I am padding along the road; I am the Clerk; I am the Nun; I am the Knight."'

Time chuffs its blank course between the acts of the pageant. In this history the omissions are as striking as the scenes, and leave the audience bewildered. There is no treatment of the army, governments and empire, to the dismay of Colonel and Mrs Mayhew who are looking forward to a Grand Ensemble around the Union Jack. As Joan Martyn had read Lydgate to keep thoughts of war at bay, so this pageant, based on English literature, is a last bid to shore up the variety of character and sense of humour, against the nation's need to fight which must distort national character. Giles, already riveted by the abortive drama of power, stamps on a snake which is choking on a toad and, though this action 'relieved him', it leaves blood on his white shoes. Silently, Isa rebuffs the emotions of the warrior '"Silly little boy, with blood on his boots."' Character will be reduced, as La Trobe foresees in her coming drama, to the rudimentary emotions of cave-dwellers. But despite darkness falling, the day does not end without some inkling of renewal. After the Olivers fight, they will embrace and from this new life will be born. There is this promise of continuity. There is hope too that the changeless pattern of nature—the cows, the shepherd coughing by the farmyard wall, the swallows darting against the trees, and love-making—will outlive war, as Hardy prophesied in 1915 'In Time of "The Breaking of Nations"':

> War's annals will cloud into night
> Ere their story die.

This ambitious attempt to make sense of history in terms of pattern and parallel points again and again to the audience. For English literature, the pageant implies, created this audience which, in turn, in past ages, supplied the material of literature. Old Bart Oliver is a product of the Age of Reason, and Isa's dreams of finding a long-lost Haines are continuous with recognition scenes in Elizabethan romance.

The village audience includes women, yet women are absent from public records. To Trevelyan, Virginia Woolf found, history meant The Crusaders, The University, The House of Commons, The Hundred Years War, The Wars of the Roses, The Dissolution of the Monasteries, The Origin of English Sea-power, and so on. Dare you rewrite history, she had asked students at Newnham and Girton in 1928. Here she does it herself, drawing women forward. The pageant gives prominence to the ages of Elizabeth, Anne, and Victoria and, between these acts, she looks minutely at daily facts in the lives of Mrs Swithin, Isa, and La Trobe. It must be recorded, for instance, that Isa interrupted a rhyme to order the fish and that she 'continued' her father-in-law, though she called him privately 'the old brute'.

Written with a village audience in mind, *Between the Acts* is intentionally simpler and more communicative than the other novels but when Virginia Woolf came to revise the second draft, she found it slight, though Leonard and John Lehmann (then a partner in the Hogarth Press) reassured her that it was a triumph. Her trouble was that she could not, unlike her model Anon, quite trust her audience. Could it be made to see that it, too, plays a part? 'People are gifted' says Mrs Swithin, '—very. The question is— how to bring it out?' At times, Virginia Woolf knows, La Trobe will succeed: Isa fills in the words of the pilgrims and, after the Restoration comedy, an anonymous voice in the audience remarks sceptically, 'all that fuss about nothing'. La Trobe glows. But she loses confidence too easily, for she herself cannot blend into village life: the women in pretty cottages ignore her as a freak and the rustics in pubs, 'dull, gross, hideously bored', pass obscene jokes.

So, in the end, Virginia Woolf made the audience excessively resistant to the pageant and the dramatist frustrated. Taking the entire onus on herself, La Trobe resorts to sermon. 'Consider Ourselves', comes at the audience through the anonymous bray of a megaphone. Consider bomb-droppers and gun-slayers, it says, who do openly what we do slyly when we compete for power: the amiable condescension of the lady of the manor and the writer scraping in the dunghill for sixpenny fame. The sermon, like the mirror scene, is an assault. It is also a desperate effort to close a gap.

Virginia Woolf found that she could not so easily overturn the Modernist premiss of the writer's detachment. Yeats, wishing too to speak from the centre of a common culture, could, as a natural actor, more easily assume the mask of folk poet: 'Talk to me of originality and I will turn on you with rage', he declared in 1937. 'I am a crowd, I am a lonely man, I am nothing.' But Virginia Woolf, with the empirical mind of a novelist, could not assume a position without testing it. Her problem, in a sense, coming from her father, was this relentless honesty. All through *Between the Acts* she is testing her premiss that the gap between creative writer and modern audience could be closed and, as the pageant reaches 'ourselves', La Trobe is forced to admit that it is not possible as yet. In fact, as Leonard Woolf saw, this conclusion was distorted by his wife's extreme diffidence. *Between the Acts* has proved not only more readable, funny, and transparent than the other novels but it also rouses, in sensitive readers, a peculiar affinity with the author: for some, at least, the gap does close.

Miss La Trobe (sometimes called Miss Whatshername) is directing it all from behind the bushes, masterful and faceless, riveted to every pulse of the audience. But the audience is distractable; it so often misses the point. Grating her nails suddenly in the tree's bark, damning the audience, while war planes advance shark-like overhead, La Trobe's desperation signals Virginia Woolf's own. Her drop into 'a trough of despair' in late January 1941 was oddly sudden, Leonard said, there were none of the warning symptoms. La Trobe recovers, her creative tide rises again as she conceives a new play but, except for a few days in February, Virginia Woolf found no release from her conviction of failure.

In the past—in 1904 and 1915—illness had struck, primarily, through her private life. This time it was the rhythm of her creative

ride that took the direct blow. She complained of having lost, as
never before, the urge to write.

In the course of their marriage, Leonard had often feared that she
would break down, especially in 1936 when she was revising *The
Years* and sure of its failure. But there had been no actual bout of
madness since the first world war. Leonard's vigilant eye and quick
action whenever symptoms, like headaches, appeared, kept her sane
from 1915 to 1941, but this time, he said, the blow came without
warning. He was distraught but cut off from the undermining
thoughts which she did not express. Whatever happened in the
three months between late January and her suicide in late March is
buried in sickness and silence, but her writings do suggest the
disturbing thoughts to which sickness attached itself.

Leonard Woolf and John Lehmann, observing her calm during
air raids and general good spirits during the first months of the
Blitz, concluded that it was not the war that disturbed her mind. I
find this hard to believe in view of *Three Guineas* and 'Thoughts on
Peace in an Air Raid'. And it cannot be a coincidence that the two
most dangerous bouts of her sickness exploded, without warning, in
the two wars.

Some time during the autumn of 1940 her solitude, which had for
years been a source of mental courage, now bred mental isolation.
Her Bloomsbury friends, who had been pacifists in the first war,
were now bellicose. She disliked even Leonard's Home Guard
uniform for she saw in military uniform, with its absurd display of
rank, ribbons, medals, a licence given to the most stupid,
vainglorious, and brutish of human instincts. While Leonard was
consumed by the coming horror—when Hitler marched into the
Rhineland he told Virginia that Europe was on the verge of the
greatest smash for six hundred years—Virginia saw not only horror
but the ridiculousness of preparations for war. From the radio on 12
September 1938 came Hitler's savage howl in Nuremberg 'like a
person excruciated; then howls from the audience. . . . Frightening
to think of the faces . . .' and then a composed, cultured BBC voice
to say that evacuees must not take pets. 'A child's game.'

The fourth volume of Leonard Woolf's autobiography, *Downhill
All the Way*, and his books between the wars, *After the Deluge* and
Barbarians at the Gate, all record his growing despair. He saw
nations—Germany, Russia, Spain—become cannibals, attacking
sections of their own populace on a scale never known before. In his

professional capacity as political commentator in the *International Review*, the *Nation* and the *Political Quarterly*, he became a Jeremiah-like witness to the encroaching chaos of a degraded Europe. 'Life became like one of those terrible nightmares in which one tries to flee from some malignant, nameless and formless horror, and one's legs refuse to work, so that one waits helpless and frozen with fear for inevitable annihilation.' The depth of his pessimism was the obverse of his youthful nineteenth-century faith in the partial spread of civilization. And though Leonard's faith was destroyed, to his everlasting bitterness, he retained, with equal tenacity, his old discipleship of G. E. Moore. He had only to close his eyes to see himself back in 1903 in Moore's room in the cloisters of Trinity, worshipping the purity of a character in whom there was no trace of aggression. All his life he strove to fulfil Moore's example of rational judgement — if only as a moral gesture. It was in this independent spirit that he wrote his prophetic books, contemptuous of party lines. He recognized that a few years of horrible slaughter lay ahead but he prophesied, rightly, that barbarous dictators and their political systems carried within them the seeds of their own disintegration. The long-term danger, he saw, was from barbarians within the citadel, the economic barbarism of the democracies and the ideological barbarism of Russia. 'For both these barbarisms destroy freedom and make the idea of a community in which the freedom of each is the condition of the freedom of all an illusion and a sham.'

Leonard could write without hope that his books would have an effect. I think that this explains why, for all his apocalyptic words — 'barbarians', 'deluge', 'annihilation' — he was unshakeable. His intimates saw him as eminently sane, sensible, cool. His wife echoed him — 'This is the prelude to barbarism', she wrote of warstruck London — but she was in one respect his opposite: she was more optimistic about human nature. I have wondered if Leonard's dire rhetoric undermined her hold on life, but I think that, though she recognized the profundity of cosmic grief — she admired it in the Russian novelists — her instinctive and, she felt, English response was protest, not despair. 'The voice of protest . . . seems to have bred in us the instinct to enjoy and fight rather than to suffer and understand.' She saw in English fiction 'our natural delight in humour and comedy, in the beauty of earth, in the activities of the intellect, and in the splendour of the body'. Where Leonard was a prophet of doom, Virginia Woolf was in this sense a fighter. 'Thinking is my fighting', she said in 1940. Her last two books were efforts to stir national morale by locating the native spirit of England in its hidden rural hollows and common historical memories. On Christmas Eve, 1940, she stood at the window, thinking of Alciston farmhouse: 'How England consoles & warms one, in these deep hollows, where the past stands almost stagnant. And the lithe spire across the fields . . . .' Walking that day from Lewes to Rodmell, she had seen a country now scratched but with old colours showing.

Between the Acts and *Anon* were bids to sift England's treasure from the accumulations of the past and to carry it across the present. She needed, then, to look to the future. This was difficult when invasion seemed imminent. Rodmell was only three miles from Newhaven where the German 9th army would have landed if 'Operation Sea Lion' had been carried out. While writing with enjoyment during 1940, Virginia had to concede Leonard's dread of German occupation. 'The least that I could look forward to as a Jew would be to be "beaten up"', he told her. She knew that a Jew's wife would go to a concentration camp, but she could not work up more than mild assent to Leonard's desperate plans.

'There would be no point in waiting', he said. 'We would shut the garage door and commit suicide.' His first idea was that they asphyxiate themselves and he laid by a supply of petrol for that purpose. In June he acquired a supply of 'protective poison' (a lethal dose of morphia) from Adrian Stephen.

'No', Virginia wrote of the first suicide pact, 'I don't want the garage to see the end of me. I've a wish for 10 years more, & to write my book [*Between the Acts*] which as usual darts into my brain.' To her Leonard's plan was 'a common sense dull end—not comparable to a day's walk, & then an evening reading over the fire'. It does seem bizarre that in 1940 it was Leonard who proposed suicide to a rather lukewarm Virginia. He confided that, from about 1938, death had become an obsession.

Virginia replied that she would not wish to live if he died. 'But until then found life what? exciting? Yes I think so.' She encouraged Leonard to agree. Even death itself might be changed 'into an exciting experience—as one did marriage in youth'. Her delight in their natural happiness continued to stimulate her appetite for life.

'What do you think is probably the happiest moment in one's whole life?' she asked a friend, Bobo Mayor, as though talking to herself, and went on: 'I think it's the moment when one is walking in one's garden, perhaps picking off a few dead flowers, and suddenly one thinks: My husband lives in that house — And he loves me.'

Though her collapse itself is inexplicable, it is possible to piece together the thoughts that foiled a resurgence of her public voice. She lost hope of calling up a village audience; she began to fear a certain lifelessness in the 'lower village world', that it would possess and drain her of vitality, like leeches. Evacuated schoolchildren provoked 'infernal boredom'. In her working notebook she set down the king of Brobdingnag's words to Gulliver: 'I cannot but conclude the bulk of your natives to be the most pernicious race of little odious vermin, that nature ever suffered to crawl upon the surface of the earth.' Leslie Stephen, who had quoted the same sentence in his *Swift*, adds that 'indulgence in revolting images is to some extent an indication of a diseased condition of mind'. His daughter saw women like white slugs having tea at Fullers in Brighton. There was a fat smart woman in a red hunting cap and pearls with a large white muffin face and her shabby dependant, 'slightly grilled', also stuffing. 'Brighton a lovecorner for slugs. The powdered, the pampered, the mildly improper.'

She began to think that there might be no cure for the womanliness bred by manliness '—both so hateful'. Towards the end of February she overheard, behind the thin door of the lavatory at the Sussex Grill in Brighton, two girls' soulless yap about 'the boys': Bert 'never did care for big women'. The girls reappear in 'The Watering Place' where the surge of the waves is outdone by the gush of the lavatory which washes their words away. The lavatory epitomizes the larger watering place of Brighton. On the marine parade, women in trousers and high heels with their raffia bags and pearls look like the shells of women, 'as if the real animal had been extracted'. The sea-town, too, is unreal, its skeleton picked out in fairy lights. At night the whole place seems to have sunk down into the water.

In 1904 she had been maddened by imagined obscenities spoken by the ruler. In 1941 she was overcome in a similar way by the unreal 'bombast' of warriors. In a suicidal fragment laid into a draft of *Between the Acts* she pictured herself as the last donkey of a great caravan, burdened with treasures which must be sorted from the dust-pile of the past and borne across a desert. The donkey, she foretells, will collapse on the way.

But there's no lying down; or laying aside; nor forgetting. Such was the command laid on me in the cradle; breathed over me by the restless elm trees; & the thud of the waves. . . . The thongs are burst, that the dead tied round the burden of memories . . . What of me is left when they spill on the ground?

Virginia Woolf's suicide note spoke of voices dinning in her ear which suggested to her that she was going mad. In an earlier version of the donkey fragment she is plagued by the echoes of voices 'always with corrupt murmurs, always with some clink of the baser sort'. None is unspotted with the damp of the old caverns of power. 'These voices merely stir the long hairs that grow in the conch of the ear & make strange music, mad music, jangled & broken sounds; & we must shake our ears, as goats shake away a cloud of bees or cows, fly goaded, lash their sides with their tails, & then we must . . . single out our possessions', refusing guides, for all political leaders are themselves mental prisoners.

She had always hunted London for unnoticed treasures of the past. In 1939 she had climbed down the steps to the Thames near Lower Thames Street, rooting in 'the rathaunted riverine place'. The people on London Bridge had stared. Then she had found Pepys's church and wandered through the Billingsgate and Leadenhall markets and into Fenchurch alleys. About ten days before her depression began she went to inspect the ruins of London. Her feeling for certain alleys and little courts between Chancery Lane and the City amounted to a passion, the closest she came to patriotism: the England of Chaucer, Shakespeare, Pepys, Johnson, and Dickens. 'I went to London Bridge', she related. 'I looked at the river; very misty; some tufts of smoke, perhaps from burning houses. . . . So by Tube to the Temple; & there wandered in the desolate ruins of my old squares: gashed; dismantled; the old red bricks all white powder, something like a builder's yard. Grey dirt & broken windows . . . all that completeness ravished.'

She turned away from the cataclysmic present to the past. She had always intended to devote the final stage of her life to autobiography. To this end she had kept her diary as a future source-book, an unbroken commitment to one volume a year from

1917, when she had been thirty-five. On 24 December 1940, it occurred to her that there was no such thing as a woman's autobiography written with the candour of Rousseau. What would have emerged, we can only guess from the fragmentary 'Sketch' and from the different practice runs: 'Reminiscences', *To the Lighthouse*, *The Waves*. 'I was thinking to myself how would I tell the story of my life. . . . I'm so many things', she had mused over her last stretch of *The Waves*.

In April 1939 she began to sift her memories and, working sporadically, as respite from *Roger Fry* and *Between the Acts*, sketched out the scenes and Victorian characters of her youth. There, again, was the sound of the waves at St Ives; the garden idyll at Talland House; the enigmatic, presiding figure of Julia Stephen, her character obscured by her madonna looks and emphatic gestures. There was Stella, white-faced after her mother's death, slipping away in the summer of 1897. There was Thoby, the future Judge, amused to find a sister mopping up Greek in her back room and enraptured by stories of his friends.

'A Sketch of the Past' is marvellous for its minutely remembered detail of family customs, Victorian manners, and old St Ives before the hotels and crowds. It is the most accurate reproduction of the external case that housed her awakening imagination. The child Virginia looks up over her lesson book in the dining-room and sees the lights changing on the waves. She has an uninterrupted view across the bay to Godrevy Lighthouse. She called these presences 'the third voice', not the private or public voice but something outside herself: 'I see myself perpetually taking the breath of these voices in my sails, and tacking this way and that, in daily life as I yield to them.' At the beginning of 'A Sketch' the third voice irradiates early childhood but, as the memoir goes on, it loses out to the voice of power as it shut off channels of existence: the raging voice of her father 'sinister, blind, animal, savage', a voice reserved for his womenfolk, and then, coming into play, the determined voice of George, blurred with irrational needs.

As the external case lost its radiance, Virginia Woolf was overwhelmed by depression. She had not yet seen her life whole when she abandoned the memoir in November 1940. The ear for the third voice, which would make of autobiography an art as yet unknown, seemed blocked by noisy interference, and external facts simply pile up in the last pages as no more than external facts. The women are hidden, the men caricatures. If anything, the brief 'Reminiscences' of 1907-8 had been better, the portraiture sharper, the view of her father better balanced. Leslie Stephen is not, here, the most lovable of men, the intrepid mountaineer, the vigilant reader, the subtle husband; he is the warped scholar who takes his inadequacy out on women, the prototypical Victorian tyrant, the Mr Barrett of Hyde Park Gate from whom his daughters escaped to Bloomsbury and freedom.

In the 'Reminiscences' she had set herself a limited task: to recall the family dead. In 'A Sketch of the Past' the challenge was to take command of all the rest of her life. But she could not leave the dead and go on. It was as though they signalled with an authority that made the present day unreal. The dead were always there. 'It is strange how the dead leap out on us at street corners, or in dreams.' They backed George when he forced his sisters to go to the balls they loathed: 'And the ghosts of Stella and Mother presided over these scenes.' One day in 1929, when Virginia was speaking to Clive Bell, Thoby's form loomed behind '—that queer ghost'. It still seemed that her own continued life was no more than an excursion without him, and that death would be no more than a return to his company.

She wondered whether some day there would be a device to tap memory. 'Instead of remembering here a scene and there a sound, I shall fit a plug into the wall; and listen in to the past. I shall turn up August 1890. I feel that strong emotion must leave its trace; and it is only a question of discovering how we can get ourselves again attached to it, so that we shall be able to live our lives through from the start.'

The autobiographies of 1907-8 and 1939-40 break off at almost the same point. The 1908 fragment takes the Stephen history close to the present. But the 1940 fragment stuck there, as she immersed her mind ever deeper in those scenes of the past. 'Let me then', she said, 'like a child advancing with bare feet into a cold river, descend again into that stream.'

After she put it down, she opened the black tin boxes which contained her parents' letters and 'got a terrific whiff of the past'. From the violent present, she recalled the hum and song of the Victorian nursery.

'How beautiful they were,' she wrote on 22 December 1940, 'those old people—I mean father & mother—how simple, how clear, how untroubled. . . . How serene & gay even their life reads to me: no mud; no whirlpools.'

The 'Sketch' introduces each stage of childhood and youth from a present-day perspective. The effect is odd: the wartime detail gives a sense not of historical perspective but of time's barrier. Each entry takes a great leap across an almost impassable divide. All through the night before she wrote she raced her mind against the passage of time, forcing a way back past the maturer stages recorded in *The Waves*, back to those haunting figures of early childhood. In her notes for the 'Sketch', Virginia Woolf jotted: '*Our caste*: Upper middle. now destroyed.' In the course of her life she had never seen anyone like her mother and Stella. 'They do not blend in the world of the living at all.' At the end of her life the elegiac impulse, which had once been a source of creativity, became an emotional trap, as when Lily cries 'O Mrs. Ramsay' and, in her grief, her brush drops. 'Death was an attempt to communicate', Mrs Dalloway thinks. 'There was an embrace in death.' Perhaps Virginia Woolf's suicide was in some way an embrace of the past across time's barrier.

The editor of her letters has pointed out that, at the time when she drowned herself in the river near Rodmell, she was not mad. She was afraid of incurable madness. Deliberately and recklessly, she had wooed the dead who could, so easily, claim her. She had spent the afternoon of 21 March arranging her father's old books. Leonard had begged her to put her father away. She did try, at the very end, to replace undermining memories with a more constructive portrait of 'Cousin Octavia', but could not transfer the glow that suffused her immediate family to that sturdy, vigorous, but rather unimaginative co-descendant of the Clapham Sect.*

Octavia Wilberforce, surrounded by family portraits, practised as a doctor in Montpelier Crescent, Brighton. Virginia first visited her on 10 January 1937. She appeared 'a very fresh coloured healthy minded doctor, in black, with loops of silver chain, good teeth, & a candid kind smile which I liked'. Opposite Virginia's plate she had put a china statue of Wilberforce; opposite Leonard's one of Hannah More. This led to a discussion of their family histories and Virginia felt 'flushed & exuberant' as they 'broached many scraps of memories'. Another sign of Virginia's fascination for the Clapham

---

* Octavia's letters show that she was interviewed on 22 Mar. and VW's diary that she was still thinking of the portrait four days before her death. They were not blood relations, but LS's step-grandmother was a Wilberforce.

heritage was a visit, late that year, to Stoke Newington where she pounced on a white stone tomb in the shape of a study table on which 'James Stephen' was carved, 'large & plain, as I suspect he was large & plain'. There was also a long inscription how, with Wilberforce, he took a leading part in the abolition of slavery. She 'was much refreshed by all this'.

Octavia ran a farm with Jersey cows in Henfield. During wartime rationing, she began to bring gifts of milk, cream, and cheese about once a week to Monks House partly to build up Virginia, but there was an understanding with Leonard that these were medical visits. As Octavia rose to go on 28 February Virginia looked at her squarely and said: 'I think I'd like to do a sketch of you. Would you mind?' Octavia, puzzled, protested that there was nothing much to do.

'Yes,' said Virginia eagerly, 'I've already a picture of you as a child at Lavington,* beautiful name, and you could talk to me. You see, I think it would be rather fun to do portraits of living people—anonymously of course.'

Virginia Woolf hoped to find a living counterpart, perhaps, of Florence Nightingale, another granddaughter of Clapham.† Octavia's family had not encouraged her to become a doctor. Nor did her young-lady education help her to qualify. But she had persisted. It was this atypical phase in a contemporary's life that drew Virginia. 'Octavia's story' was to take in 'English youth in 1900'. Virginia often compared herself to Octavia and caricatured her own life as shadowy, disembodied, inactive, blighted by the Victorian patriarchy, in contrast to Octavia's usefulness. This artificial contrast was compounded by shyness on Octavia's part and aloofness on Virginia's, and it is not surprising that their interviews were stilted. It may be that 'Octavia's story' was no more than Virginia's counter to the case-history she had to offer. She distrusted doctors who, in the crises of 1904, 1913, and 1915, had proved ignorant and overbearing.

At first Octavia vowed to treat her gently, but the doctor was soon irritated. Virginia was her own 'worst enemy'. On 22 March

---

* Lavington House, East Lavington, near Chichester, Sussex, the Wilberforce family seat where Octavia was born.

† Octavia was the daughter of Reginald Garton Wilberforce, eldest son of Samuel Wilberforce, son of William Wilberforce. Florence Nightingale was the granddaughter of Sir William Smith, art connoisseur and, as MP for forty-six years, a leading Abolitionist, champion of factory workers, and opponent of religious disabilities.

Octavia tried to jolt her: 'I said I thought this family business was all nonsense, blood thicker than water balderdash. Surprised her anyway.'

Apart from old deaths, Virginia Woolf grieved over the recent deaths of Janet Case and her nephew, Julian Bell, in the Spanish civil war. 'I wake in the night', she wrote after Strachey's death in 1932, 'with a sense of being in an empty hall.' Fry's death in 1934 was 'worse than Lytton's. . . . Such a blank wall. Such a silence: such a poverty. How he reverberated!' Continually she made new friends like Elizabeth Bowen but her first loyalty to the old ties remained. She developed what she called a posthumous friendship with Fry which was 'in some ways more intimate than any I had in life'. As she read his letters she found that 'things I guessed are now revealed; and the actual voice gone'.

Virginia criticized the mausoleum emotions of her father, but the last years of her own diary might, with even more appropriateness, be called a 'mausoleum book'. On 5 May 1937, she went over the morning of her mother's death forty-two years before. The diary races over her own doings and lingers over the dead, even people who were rather peripheral: her cousin, H. A. L. Fisher, and an extended elegy for her mother-in-law for whom, in life, she had had little time. Only Julian Bell resisted the imaginative appropriation: 'My dear Aunt—' she could hear his burst of laughter, as he gripped the sides of his chair.

'The soul deserves to be immortal', Leonard remarked as they walked back from a hotel room in Russell Square where another old friend, Francis Birrell, was dying. Virginia Woolf was tempted, several times, to try a poetic piece that would strain off the soul on a mountain. 'I would like to write a dream story about the top of a mountain', she noted on 22 June 1937. 'About lying in the snow; about rings of colour; silence & the solitude.' This led to her last tragic story, 'The Symbol'.

The symbol of the title is a Swiss mountain which represents, she says in a crossed-out clause, human effort. An elderly English-woman, writing home on a balcony, is following the progress of a climbing-party of young men, including her correspondent's son. Before her eyes, he is casually swallowed by a crevasse. Her placid, reminiscing letter suddenly trails into a line. How is she to go on writing?

This is the scene of Leslie Stephen's Alpine exploits.* He had worshipped the mountains. When he wrote of them his feeling came close to religious awe. Her father had scaled peak after peak but in the story the contemporary young are destroyed. Perhaps she was brooding over the deaths of young men, including her nephew, in the war. Instead of transmuting grief into art, art in this final story—literally the act of writing—is arrested by the prospect of mortality. She told Octavia on 14 March 1941 that it had left her 'desperate—depressed to the lowest depths'.

In her last decade Virginia Woolf tried to overcome the obsession with the dead. She tried to speak for the living and for living traditions. In *The Years* she was the voice of the women of her generation, from the 1880s to the 1930s. In *Between the Acts* she was the performing voice of English society, moving through time, to be sampled in the remote country house, Pointz Hall. In *Anon* she dredged up the native voice of Merry England. Yet private memory continued to tug. In her last months she pursued 'Anon' and autobiography separately, unsure which would push her, like Bernard, to the furthest stretch of age.

Though she could not ride the public wave to its crest, to have seen its possibilities was itself a triumph, though of a different order to that of the artist in *To the Lighthouse*. It was a triumph against mental atrophy, the enemy which Bernard had fought with mounting strength. 'I detest the hardness of old age—I feel it. I rasp. I'm tart', she wrote on 29 December 1940. 'What I need is the old spurt', she groaned on 26 January. In fact, this dryness followed months of great fertility: in November she had been writing three works at once.

It may have been this very fertility that destroyed her. In 1939 she was waiting to take a new imaginative risk: 'I should, if it weren't for the war—glide my way up & up into that exciting layer so rarely lived in: where my mind works so quick it seems asleep; like the aeroplane propellers.' This soaring freedom would either quicken her imaginative work or wreck the balance of her mind. The two effects were extraordinarily close, as when she wrote the finale to *The Waves*. Her imagination would race and her reason would try to hold on. It was a reckless ride, like Bernard's death-defying gallop. She used the same image for *Three Guineas*: 'Oh

* VW uses the name of his famous guide, Melchior Anderegg, for a Swiss proprietor, Herr Melchior, who warns of avalanches.

how violently I have been galloping through these mornings! It has pressed & spurted out of me. If that's any proof of virtue, like a physical volcano.' The bravado of Bernard and the underground spurt of Rhoda seem here to blend.

The gallop could be fatal, as she realized one summer evening in 1932. As she sat with Leonard on the terrace of Monks House and watched the emerald downs draw back into darkness, 'the galloping hooves got wild' in her head, her heart leapt, stopped, leapt again, and, in acute pain, she fainted.

It was therefore necessary to rein the dark dreamer, balancing the wilder novels, *The Voyage Out*, *To the Lighthouse*, *The Waves*, with rather long, documentary novels. Too much exposure to mundaneness, on the other hand, could also break her. After a visit from Elinor Nef, a note-taking faculty wife from Chicago, she shivered and shook and took to bed for two days 'visiting the silent realms again'. She regained them when she slept, walked, or slipped into 'perfectly spontaneous childish life with L.' In *Night and Day*, Katharine Hilbery speaks of a precipice that divides the mind 'on the one side of which the soul was active and in broad daylight, on the other side of which it was contemplative and dark as night'.

This biography has followed the 'dark' side of Virginia Woolf, her exploratory plunges into strange pools. In her speech to professional women she spoke of this plunge as the essential event in the life of a writer. The novelist, she explained, is like a fisherwoman, on the bank of a lake, who lets her rod of reason down into the pool of consciousness. Sometimes she felt a jerk, and the line raced through her fingers as her imagination took to the depths. Then reason had to haul the imagination, panting with rage and disappointment, to the surface because it had gone too far.

Submergence was her image for the hidden act of imaginative daring. Her image of the waves carried her work to completion. Poised on the crest of *The Waves*, Virginia Woolf hailed a new wave to override her settled achievement. This was the pattern of her creative life: a wave ridden to its crest, then sometimes a trough, but always another wave rising far out. She allowed each successive wave to break the previous mould: a poem–novel was followed by an essay–novel which was followed by a drama–novel. Yet, though the form changed, she went on exploring memory: the private memory that shaped an individual artist, the shared memory that shaped a generation, the public memory that shaped a nation. She was always breaking a set shape—it might be the lifespan or the image of women—to explore a shape in the making: so, in her greatest works, she recovered the lost moments on which the life turns or the lost agency of women and their long, silent service to civilization which history has forgotten to record.

The peculiar challenge of a new wave was never immediately clear, only that it compelled a turn in her career. This biography has marked the turning-points that do not coincide with external events: 1892 when a ten-year old child spied the monumental characters of her parents; 1897 when the sisters learnt to walk alone; 1905 when the young woman tramped out the unorthodox form of her novels; 1907-8 when she discovered the uses of memory; 1912-15 when she set up her private life against all marital and mental odds; the fertile spring of 1925; the 'fin' of 1926; and the 'soul's change' of 1932. She conceived each stage of her life as a voyage of discovery, looking forward even to age as an adventure, as she put it on 6 May 1940: 'So the land recedes from my ship which draws out into the sea of old age.'

What happened in January 1941 was an unprecedented failure of an imaginary voyage. She was dismayed to find herself drowning in self-absorption and tried in vain to be at least objective. She wrote on 8 March 1941: 'I mark Henry James's sentence: Observe perpetually. Observe the oncome of age. Observe greed. Observe my own despondency. By that means it becomes serviceable.'

She told Octavia: 'Leonard says I shouldn't think about myself so much, I should think about outside things.' She considered biking in to the Museum daily to read history. The Great Fire of 1666 might supply a perspective on London ruins and fear of invasion might recall 'Armada weather'. A historian's perspective was her last resort, a last effort to uphold an impersonal view of events.

I have wondered why she was beyond Leonard's help, given the strength of their attachment. Her reason was that she feared madness and could not bear to burden him, but—and this can be no more than a guess—there may have been other, less explicable reasons. One possible clue is what Rhoda says of Louis before she commits suicide: 'If we could mount together, if we could perceive from a sufficient height', a unique shared perspective might have

survived, but Louis was drawn to a worldly view—as Leonard came
to sanction war—'and I, resenting compromise and right and wrong
on human lips, trust only in solitude and the violence of death and
thus [we] are divided'.

Even less explicable to Leonard would be the fact that the dead
had always claimed Virginia more completely than anyone living
and that, in a sense, she was always preparing to join them. It was
for her, as for Septimus Warren Smith, an exciting challenge. To
drown was not a horror to Septimus but a passage to the dead,
another voyage of discovery. Neither Septimus nor Mrs Dalloway
believes in mortality: 'since our apparitions, the part of us which
appears, are so momentary compared with the other, the unseen
part of us, which spreads wide, the unseen might survive, be
recovered somehow attached to this person or that, or even
haunting certain places, after death. Perhaps—perhaps.'

On Friday 28 March, Virginia Woolf drowned herself. Both the
note she left for Leonard* and another found on her writing-block
urged him to believe that she owed him all the happiness of her life.
These words were long rehearsed. They can be traced back to
Rachel's death in *The Voyage Out:* 'No two people have ever been
so happy as we have been.' Her last wish was to console Leonard
and to put his goodness on record. She died in this civil manner,
with graceful words on her lips.

Leonard buried her ashes at the edge of Monks House garden at
the foot of a great elm whose boughs were interlaced with another
great elm. They had called the two trees 'Leonard' and 'Virginia'.

On 19 February 1937, Virginia Woolf saw that 'the difficulty
wh[ich] now faces me is how to find a public'.

Her search for this public, set in motion in her last years, seemed
to founder in the whirlpools of her own diffidence and in the cross-
currents of the second world war. Yet her pacifism, unaccept-
able at the time, survived its immediate context. It began to
read convincingly twenty-five years later when self-respecting
Americans of the 1960s refused the phoney emotions of war-
mongers, a mark of civilization as Virginia Woolf conceived it. It is
not surprising that her wide popularity began then and there.

---

* Nigel Nicolson makes a plausible case that this note was written ten days earlier, on
18 Mar. when VW may have attempted to drown herself. *Letters*, vi, Appendix A, pp. 489-91.

The other aim of her final decade was to become, like Bernard, preserver of national achievement. In 'Reading' she identified the national treasure; in *Anon*, the native voice. But in 1941 she abandoned Bernard's enterprise for the alternative scenario which she had framed in the course of *The Waves*: Rhoda's passive end. There is, for Rhoda, no further striving, no renewal after middle age, simply a rounding-off of her life, like a drop falling.

Rhoda has flown ahead of the others, neck outstretched, straight for the statues hewn from nature. Yet she herself is left, like Rachel Vinrace, submerged: bathed in an unfathomed well of unknown modes of being. In this well Rachel sinks silent to the death. Only the writer could bring the silent side to public notice. In Virginia Woolf's first novel, the would-be novelist, Terence Hewet, wishes to fathom silence but remains locked in platitude. But in *The Waves*, she imagined, in Bernard, a novelist or biographer who would be her true spokesman.

Bernard and Rhoda are the public and private voices of Virginia Woolf. Like Bernard, she retold her memories as a professional writer until they took their final set: Percival lounging magnificently on the edge of the playing-field; Louis with his hand on the door knocking for admittance; Helen Ambrose bent, full-blooded but silent, over her sewing; Mr Ramsay vigilant like a stake on a promontory; the Victorian mother reading to her child, a triangle shadowed in the lingering light of a summer's day. All hardened as forms who would outlive time's change. Behind them beat the timeless waves which, for Virginia Woolf, took up their measure—one two one two—in the dawn of consciousness, behind the yellow nursery blind. Writing *The Waves* after nearly fifty years, she looked forward to a time when the spume of memory, her private voice, would sink back, leaving the public voice to go on.

Abbreviations

A L L references to Virginia Woolf's books, unless stated otherwise, are to Hogarth Press editions in London and to Harcourt Brace Jovanovich in the US. Page references are to the uniform edition of Virginia Woolf and to the English editions of all other books.

AROO	*A Room of One's Own*
BA	*Between the Acts*
Berg	Henry W. and Albert A. Berg Collection, The New York Public Library, Astor, Lenox, and Tilden Foundations
BG	*The Bloomsbury Group: A Collection of Memoirs, Commentary and Criticism*, ed. S. P. Rosenbaum, University of Toronto; Croom Helm, 1975
CE	*Collected Essays* (i–iv)
Diary	*The Diary of Virginia Woolf* (i–v), ed. Anne Olivier Bell, assisted by Andrew McNeillie, 1977–84
JR	*Jacob's Room*
JS	Julia Stephen
Letters	*The Letters of Virginia Woolf* (i–vi), ed. Nigel Nicolson, assisted by Joanne Trautmann, 1975–80
LH	*To the Lighthouse*
LS	Leslie Stephen
LW	Leonard Woolf
	Five volumes of his *Autobiography*, Harcourt Brace Jovanovich; Hogarth
LW, i	*Sowing . . . 1880–1904*, 1960
LW, ii	*Growing . . . 1904–1911*, 1961
LW, iii	*Beginning Again . . . 1911–1918*, 1964
LW, iv	*Downhill all the Way . . . 1919–1939*, 1967
LW, v	*The Journey not the Arrival Matters . . . 1939–1969*, 1969
MB	*Moments of Being: Unpublished autobiographical writings*, ed. Jeanne Schulkind. University of Sussex, 1976; Harcourt Brace Jovanovich, 1977
MHP	Monks House Papers, University of Sussex. MHP A are biographic manuscripts; MHP B are literary manuscripts
Mrs. D	*Mrs. Dalloway*
MSS.BA	Drafts of *BA*, including holograph poems. Published as *Pointz Hall: The Earlier and Later Typescripts of* Between the Acts, ed. Mitchell A. Leaska, New York University, 1983

MSS.D   Holograph drafts of *Mrs. D*, British Library, Add. 51044-6 (i–iii)

MS.LH   Holograph draft of *To the Lighthouse*, ed. Susan Dick, University of Toronto, 1982; Hogarth, 1983

MS.Par   Draft of a novel–essay, parts of which became a portion of *The Years*. Published as *The Pargiters*, ed. Mitchell A. Leaska, New York Public Library, 1977; Hogarth, 1978

MSS.VO   Five holograph and typescript drafts of *The Voyage Out*. Berg (one early draft has been published as *Melymbrosia*, ed. Louise A. DeSalvo, New York, 1983)

MSS.W   *The Waves: the two holograph drafts*, ed. J. W. Graham, University of Toronto; Hogarth, 1976

QB   Quentin Bell, *Virginia Woolf: A Biography* (i–ii), Hogarth; Harcourt Brace Jovanovich, 1972

TG   *Three Guineas*

TLS   *Times Literary Supplement*

VB   Vanessa Bell

VO   *The Voyage Out*

VW   Virginia Woolf

W   *The Waves*

Notes

CHAPTER I

3 'if life has a base'. MB, p. 64.

'the waves breaking . . .'. Ibid. 64-5.

photograph. Stella Duckworth's album, Berg. See pl. 2a.

'they were happier . . .'. LH, p. 94.

4 'So many horrors . . .'. Unpublished letter to Julian Bell (1936), Charleston Papers, King's College, Cambridge.

'. . . The ghosts . . .'. Diary, iv (17 Mar. 1932), p. 83.

'. . . The past . . .'. Ibid. iii (18 Mar. 1925), p. 5.

5 'I have some restless searcher . . .'. Ibid. iii (27 Feb. 1926), p. 62.

'some one scene . . .'. 'The Philosophy of Shelley's Poetry' (1900), Selected Criticism, ed. A. Norman Jeffares (Macmillan, 1964, repr. 1973), p. 79.

'How queer . . .'. Diary, iv (4 July 1935), p. 329.

'I must be private . . .'. To Ethel Smyth, Letters, vi (17 Sept. 1938), p. 272.

6 'a certain inevitable disparity'. MSS.W, p. 157.

'Every secret . . .'. Orlando, pp. 189-90.

'I wonder . . .'. Diary, ii (14 Jan. 1920), p. 7.

'blind' moments. 'Sympathy', MHP A.24d.

'shocks'. MB, p. 72.

7 'the synthesis . . .'. Diary, iv (31 May 1933), p. 161. See also Jean O. Love, VW: Sources of Madness and Art (Berkeley: Univ. of Calif. Press, 1977), p. 6: 'She tried . . . by means of her writing, to compose the perfect whole of her experience.'

'built on that . . .'. Diary, ii (22 Mar. 1921), p. 103.

'Books . . .'. Introduction to Mrs. D (NY, 1928), repr. in Virginia Woolf: a collection of criticism, ed. Thomas S. W. Lewis (McGraw-Hill, 1975), p. 35.

8 'the birth of a new species . . .'. Autobiographies: 'The Trembling of the Veil', Book III (Macmillan, 1955, repr. 1977), p. 273.

'trained to silence'. To Ethel Smyth, Letters, iv (29 Dec. 1931), p. 422. See John Mepham, 'Trained to Silence', London Review of Books, (20 Nov.- 4 Dec. 1980).

'invisible presences'. MB, p. 80.

9 she was annoyed. Diary, iv (26 Aug. 1934), p. 239.

'. . . *the Angel of the house* . . .'. Allusion to poem by Coventry Patmore, 'The Angel in the House'. Speech to the London/National Society for Women's Service, 21 Jan. 1931, included in MS.Par, pp. xxvii–xliv. A much reduced version is in *CE*, ii, pp. 284-9, as 'Professions for Women'.

22 Hyde Park Gate. '22 Hyde Park Gate', read to the Memoir Club between Mar. 1920 and 25 May 1921. *MB*, pp. 142-55.

old Mrs Redgrave. Autobiographic fragment, pp. 55-69 in holograph volume entitled 'Essays 1940'. Catalogued in Berg as 'Articles, essays, fiction and reviews, vol. 9.' Part of 'A Sketch of the Past': see revised edn. of *MB*.

raving obscenely. Ibid.

when she was about six. *MB*, p. 69. The sexual interference of VW's half-brothers has been discussed briefly by *QB*, i, p. 44 and at length by Roger Poole, *The unknown Virginia Woolf* (Cambridge, 1978), pp. 28-32, and by Love, pp. 200-8.

'*I still shiver* . . .'. To Ethel Smyth, *Letters*, vi (12 Jan. 1941), pp. 459-60.

10 '*sit passive* . . .'. *MB*, p. 133.

Quentin Bell explained. *QB*, i, pp. 20-1.

'*All our male relations* . . .'. *MB*, p. 132.

'*tough as roots* . . .'. 'Two Women' (1927), *CE*, iv, pp. 61-6. The following comments on education are also from this essay.

Fanny Burney. VW, 'Women Novelists' (1918 review) repr. VW, *Contemporary Writers*, ed. Jean Guiguet (Hogarth, 1965), p. 25.

correspondence of Charlotte Brontë and Robert Southey. The Brontë Letters, ed. Muriel Spark (Macmillan, 1966), pp. 65-7.

11 Night and Day. pp. 117-18.

The Years. p. 357.

Lady Strachey reading. To VB, *Letters*, ii (11 Feb. 1917), p. 144.

Lady Strachey reading and 'many-sided'. Obituary, *Nation & Athenaeum* (22 Dec. 1928) repr. VW, *Books & Portraits*, ed. Mary Lyon (Hogarth, 1977), pp. 208-11.

'*indescribable air of expectation*'. The phrase is taken from *LH*, p. 22 and refers to Mrs Ramsay.

a woman nobly planned. LS referred to the poem, 'She Was a Phantom of Delight', in an essay, 'Forgotten Benefactors'. The essay, written soon after JS's death, was his public tribute to her.

'*her wise brow* . . .'. *MB*, p. 38.

12 '*ineffaceable* . . .'. Ibid. 39.

link with Romantics. Eric Warner has done the first full-length treatment of this crucial topic, 'Some Aspects of Romanticism in the Work of VW', (D. Phil. thesis, Oxford, 1980).

'*one of the loveliest walks imaginable*'. LS to JS (Apr. 1882). All LS quotations in this chapter are from the letters to his wife, Berg.

'*see the Children . . .*'. Wordsworth, 'Ode: Intimations of Immortality from Recollections of Early Childhood': IX.

13 *dish of Cornish cream. MB*, p. 110.

  walk to Trencrom. Ibid. 115.

  '*infernal hotel*'. LS to JS.

14 *Cornwall diary, 1905.* Diary No. 4 (11 Aug. 1905–14 Sept. 1905). Berg.

  this little corner of England. Cornwall diary (11 Aug. 1905).

  re-enacted this visitation. LW, iv, p. 154.

15 'ever since . . .'. *Diary*, v (19 Dec. 1938).

  communal serials. MB, pp. 76–7, 79 and VB, *Notes on Virginia's Childhood*, written for the Memoir Club after VW's death, ed. Richard F. Schaubeck, Jr. (NY: Frank Hallman, 1974). Jean O. Love notes the Brontë resemblance, p. 229.

  tribute. 21 Nov. 1892, printed as 'Stephen versus Gladstone' (Cambridge: Rampant Lions Press, 1967).

16 *serial.* 'A Cockney's Farming Experience and The Experiences of a Pater-familias', ed. Suzanne Henig (San Diego State Univ. Press, 1972). The serial was a collaboration with Thoby.

  LS's love of Virginia. See Jean O. Love, p. 153.

  '*She suddenly asked . . .*'. VB, *Notes on Virginia's Childhood*.

CHAPTER 2

17 *James Russell Lowell.* 'On a Certain Condescension in Foreigners', repr. in *My Study Windows* (Boston, 1871), p. 73.

  '*that old wretch . . .*'. To V. Sackville-West, *Letters*, iii (3 May 1927), p. 374.

  '*a fastidious, delicate mind . . .*'. *Diary*, v (22 Dec. 1940), p. 345.

  from two angles. Ibid. v (25 Apr. 1940), p. 281.

18 Mausoleum Book. All quotations are taken directly from the holograph (Add. 57920) in the British Library (begun May 1895) and from the accompanying 'Calendar of Correspondence', a 157-page summary of letters to and from both wives, begun 13 June 1895. For the final text see *Sir Leslie Stephen's Mausoleum Book*, ed. Alan Bell (Oxford, 1977).

19 '*lopsided*' and '*unreal*'. LS to JS. All subsequent quotations are from these letters (1877–95) in the Berg. Jean O. Love, op. cit. 74, suggests that the infantile behaviour was brought on by the death of LS's mother in the same year as Minny died.

  '*pray God that I may die . . .*'. Julia Cameron to Mrs Jackson (JS's mother), Berg.

'*a deeper and keener sympathy . . .*'. 'Forgotten Benefactors', op. cit. repr. *Social Rights and Duties*, ii (London, 1896), p. 255.

20 *JS's book. Notes from Sick Rooms* (see Biographical Sources below).

the Coniston correspondence. Outlined in the *Mausoleum Book.*

22 '*What he said was true . . . .' LH*, p. 13.

23 *imaginary trial.* MS.LH, pp. 321-4.

'*how old he was*'. See Noel Annan, *Leslie Stephen: His Thought and Character in Relation to His Time* (MacGibbon, 1951; Harvard, 1952), p. 101.

'*like a stridulous grasshopper*'. The behaviour of Saxon Sydney-Turner, on a visit to Bayreuth in 1909, brought back this memory. *Letters*, i (10 Aug. 1909), p. 405.

24 '*gale*'. The phrase comes from MS.LH, p. 247.

painfully divided. Analysed by Jean O. Love, p. 268.

'*entire complete misery*'. MS.LH, p. 323.

LS's deterioration. Noel Annan, p. 97 and *QB* have noted this split in LS's character.

'*one of those bearded . . .*'. *LW*, i, p. 180.

Warboys diary. Entitled: 'Warboys. Summer holidays 1899'. Diary No. 1, 4 Aug.-23 Sept. 1899. Berg.

25 *LS's lamentations to Julia, 1893.* Letter, Berg.

LS and Halford Vaughan. Letter to JS (1881), Berg.

LS's 'leanness' and 'terseness'. Terms used by F. W. Maitland in *The Life and Letters of LS* (Duckworth, 1906; Detroit: Gale Research, 1968), p. 372.

26 '*Dryasdust*'. *Dictionary of National Biography*, iii, p. 1029.

'*no forlorn spectator . . .*'. MS.LH, pp. 71-2.

'*(The strain . . .*'. Ibid. 73.

27 '*Oriental*' *grief. MB*, p. 40.

'*much of the stuff of a Hebrew prophet*'. Ibid.

imprinted. See *LH*, p. 200 and *MB*, p. 91.

CHAPTER 3

28 '*But could one tell the truth?*'. *Diary*, iii (27 June 1925), p. 34. The friend was her brother-in-law, Jack Hills.

'*This is not made up . . .*'. Ibid. (18 Apr. 1926), p. 76.

twenty times faster. Ibid. (23 Feb. 1926), p. 59.

29 *Cézanne. MB*, p. 85.

'*I'm in a terrible state of pleasure . . .*'. *Letters*, iii (25 May 1927), p. 383.

30 '*Indeed, she had . . .*'. *LH*, p. 15.

'*red, energetic ants*'. Ibid. 302.

Tansley's thesis. Ibid. 24.

circus tricks. Ibid. 23.

31 '*Stepping through fields . . .*'. Ibid. 27.

'"*There'll be no landing . . .*"'. Ibid. 17.

'*An unmarried woman . . .*'. Ibid. 80–1.

32 '*a lady of the most delicate charm . . .*'. 'Am I a Snob?' (1936), *MB*, p. 185.

'*Surely she could imitate . . .*'. *LH*, p. 233.

33 *first notes for* LH. See holograph notebook: 'Notes for Writing', 1922–5, Berg.

'*Oh the torture . . .*'. *MB*, p. 90.

'*purifying out of existence . . .*'. *LH*, p. 101.

'*Our apparitions . . .*'. Ibid. 100.

'*muted*' *women*. See Introduction (especially 'Muted Groups and Differing Orders of Perception') to *Perceiving Women*, ed. Shirley Ardener (London: Malaby Press, 1975); also Edwin Ardener, 'Belief and the Problem of Women', pp. 1–2.

'*there was nothing to be said*'. *LH*, p. 54.

'"*I have the feelings of a woman . . .*"'. 'Men and Women', *TLS*, 18 Mar. 1920, repr. *Books and Portraits*, op. cit. 30.

34 *to follow her thought . . .*'. *LH*, p. 43.

'graven in the language of the outlaw'. *Ulysses* (Penguin), pp. 143–4 or (NY: Random House, 1961), p. 143.

'*she imagined how in the chambers . . .*'. *LH*, pp. 82–3.

35 '*like a light . . .*'. Ibid. 160.

'*the most positive of disbelievers*'. *MB*, p. 32.

'*as though she heard . . .*'. Ibid. 35.

the stream of time. MS.LH, p. 196.

'*oh yes . . .*'. Ibid.

unquestionable loveliness. *MB*, pp. 37–8.

36 '*yet he knew*'. *LH*, p. 191. Last words in an American edition, not quite last in the uniform Hogarth edition.

'*anything*'. Ibid. 188.

'*involuntarily . . .*'. Ibid. 189.

37 *Beautiful, even to a child's eye*. *MB*, p. 37.

looked at the photograph. *Sir Leslie Stephen's Mausoleum Book*, pp. 58–9.

'*Unquenchable . . .*'. Quoted by Frances Spalding, *Vanessa Bell* (Weidenfeld; Ticknor, 1983), p. 15.

'*They would come back . . .*'. MS.LH, p. 187.

38 *laugh*. Ibid. 312 and *MB*, p. 81.

'*Ghost . . .*'. *LH*, p. 275.

recurring dream. MS.LH, pp. 303-5.

she would look down a railway carriage. *LH*, p. 279.

'"*Mrs. Ramsay! Mrs. Ramsay!*" . . .'. Ibid. 310.

39 *Vanessa's letter*. Appendix, *Letters*, iii, pp. 572-3.

'*Nothing is stronger . . .*'. MSS.VO: early typescript.

'*still she prevailed . . .*'. MS.LH, p. 262.

'*on more occasions . . .*'. *MB*, p. 40.

CHAPTER 4

43 *1897 diary*. This is the first extant diary by VW, 3 Jan. 1897-1 Jan. 1898, Berg.

44 *Eliot's chrysalis*. 'Fragment Bacchus & Ariadne: 2nd Debate between the Body & Soul' (Feb. 1911), Berg.

sticky tremulous legs . . .'. Autobiographical fragment in holograph vol. entitled 'Essays 1940', Berg. See revised edn. of *MB*.

'*Even now . . .*'. *MB*, p. 53.

'*like a lion . . .*'. *LH*, p. 241.

'*showed himself . . .*'. *MB*, p. 55.

'*down came his fist*'. Ibid. 124-5.

45 '*He grips my hand . . .*'. Ibid. 121.

George's embraces. Poole gives a detailed analysis, pp. 107-12. Phyllis Rose compares the effects of Gerald and George in *Woman of Letters: A Life of VW* (New York: Oxford; Routledge, 1978), pp. 8-9.

'*some restraint . . .*'. *MB*, p. 57.

'*a house . . .*'. *LH*, p. 230.

'*a sea of racing emotions*'. *MB*, p. 58.

'*walked alone*'. Ibid. 57.

'*Nessa and I . . .*'. Ibid. 123.

46 '*We had but a dull sense . . .*'. Ibid. 45.

'*I wish I were dead . . .*'. Noel Annan, op. cit. 102 and *QB*, i, p. 74.

children's deadness. Mark Spilka treats this topic in detail in *VW's Quarrel with Grieving* (Nebraska Univ. Press, 1980).

47 '*We depended on her . . .*'. *MB*, p. 49.

obedience. MS.LH, p. 345.

images of whiteness. *MB*, p. 97.

'*tenacious wire-haired terrier*'. Ibid. 47.

'*meet him face to face . . .*'. Ibid.

Vanessa told her son. Spalding, op. cit. 23.

'*Did mother know?*'. *MB*, p. 101.

48 *Virginia's health and Stella's.* *QB*, i, p. 56.

49 '*Prue Ramsay . . .*'. *LH*, pp. 204–5.

'*I shrink . . .*'. *MB*, p. 117.

50 *friendship with Dickinson.* *QB*, i, pp. 82–4.

pattern of female friendship. Rose, p. 116.

autobiographical fragment. Op. cit.

CHAPTER 5

51 '*Those awful headaches . . .*'. (16 June 1942), Charleston Papers.

52 '*not unnaturally*'. 'Old Bloomsbury', *MB*, p. 161.

twitter at Twickenham. To VB, *Letters*, i (28 July 1910), p. 431.

53 *Ka Cox. Diary*, v (25 May 1938), p. 143.

'*Rashness . . .*'. 'On Being Ill', *CE*, iv, p. 200.

'*what ancient . . .*'. Ibid. 193.

'*the cautious respectability . . .*'. Ibid. 196.

'*a naked soul . . .*'. MSS.D, iii, pp. 9–10.

'*the first man . . .*'. Ibid. i, pp. 58, 61–2. A residue of this appears in the Regent's Park scene in *Mrs. D*, p. 105.

54 '*played out*'. Quoted by *QB*, ii, p. 26.

bed-bugs in Greece. Diary of Foreign Travel, 1906–9, Berg. A typescript also in MHP A.7.

'*I think perhaps . . .*'. *Diary*, i (13 Sept. 1919), p. 298. See also Jean O. Love, op. cit. 3: 'It is most important to note that her madness comprised relatively limited intervals of an extraordinarily productive . . . life.'

'*Things seem . . .*'. Ibid.

55 '*one's lowest ebb . . .*'. Ibid.

'*it might be possible . . .*'. *Mrs. D*, p. 134.

'*have neither . . .*'. Ibid. 136.

'*humiliation . . .*'. *Diary*, v (20 Oct. 1938), p. 181.

'*The blight . . .*'. *The Cause* (1928; repr. Virago, 1978), p. 45.

J. S. Mill. The Subjection of Women (1869; repr. MIT, 1970), pp. 22–3.

Dr Maudesley. Quoted in *The Cause*, p. 251.

Savage's views. Summarized by Stephen Trombley, '*All that summer she was mad*' (London: Junction Books, 1981), p. 126. The chapters on VW's doctors describe some appalling attitudes to and treatments of the mentally ill. I am also indebted to Jane Marcus's sensible article 'On Dr. George Savage' in *The VW Miscellany* (1981).

56 '*And now . . .*'. *Letters*, i (29 June 1906), p. 228.

Stephen instability. See LS's *Life of Sir James Fitzjames Stephen* (London: Smith, Elder, 1895), pp. 10, 52.

'*like gorillas . . .*'. *Diary*, i (7 June 1918), p. 153.

the sinister aspect of material things. See *QB*, ii, p. 15.

'*relic . . .*'. *Mrs. D*, p. 141.

57 '*I wrote the words O Death . . .*'. *Diary*, iv (7 Feb. 1931), p. 10.

the under-mind of a writer. 'The Leaning Tower', *CE*, ii, p. 166.

'*all kinds of wild things*'. *Letters*, i (22? Sept. 1904), p. 142.

58 '*some very curious visions . . .*'. *Diary*, ii (9 Jan. 1924), p. 283.

'*all that I now . . .*'. To Ethel Smyth, *Letters*, iv (16 Oct. 1930), p. 231.

59 *an alarm bell.* *TG*, p. 233.

parget. Mitchell A. Leaska, 'Virginia Woolf, the Pargeter. A Reading of *The Years*', *Bulletin of the New York Public Library* (Winter 1977), pp. 172-210.

'*would certainly have gone crazed . . .*'. *AROO*, p. 74.

60 '*That refuge . . .*'. Ibid. 75-6.

'*Is the time coming . . .*'. *Diary*, i (27 March 1919), p. 259.

ghostly confidants. Holograph of 'Time Passes', dated 30 Apr. 1926. MS.LH, pp. 199-200.

'*Suppose . . .*'. *Diary*, iii (16 May 1927), p. 136.

61 *the question of diagnosis.* I disagree here with Roger Poole, who argues that VW was not mad. There is, though, truth in his argument that a good deal of her so-called illness could be explained by her cultural environment and personal circumstances, also by her novels if they could be read with great caution and delicacy.

term for madness. See Poole, p. 4.

'*slipping tranquilly . . .*'. *Diary*, iii (27 June 1925), p. 33.

'*Rustling among my emotions . . .*'. Ibid. (27 Nov. 1925), p. 46.

'*the appalling fear . . .*'. *Mrs. D*, p. 133.

62 '*oozing . . .*'. Ibid. 136.

imbeciles at Kingston. *Diary*, i (9 Jan. 1915), p. 13.

the Queen's Hall. Ibid. (3 Jan. 1915), p. 5 and n.

'*I begin to loathe . . .*'. *Ibid.*, *p. 5.*

'*I do not like . . .*'. Ibid. (4 Jan. 1915), p. 6.

63 '*to have lost . . .*'. Ibid. (13 Feb. 1915), p. 33.

'*like a diver . . .*'. Ibid. iii (20 July 1925), p. 37.

'*The world did not say . . .*'. *AROO*, p. 79.

warning signs. See *LW*, iii and v; *QB*; and George Spater and Ian Parsons, *A Marriage of True Minds* (Cape and Hogarth, 1977). VW gives a summary of her symptoms in *Diary*, v (24 Nov. 1936).

64 *Poole.* pp. 152-6.

'*Disorder* . . .'. *W*, p. 208.

Bradshaw lecture. Poole, p. 124.

65 '*Once, long ago* . . .'. *Mrs. D*, p. 153.

'*the pictures* . . .'. *Roger Fry*, p. 156.

'*Sir William* . . .'. *Mrs. D*, p. 151.

66 '*counselled submission* . . .'. Ibid. 155.

'*I am now* . . .'. *Diary*, ii (15 Oct. 1923), p. 272.

'*give one the* . . .'. VB to Roger Fry (24 Dec. 1912). Charleston Papers.

'*witless*' Mrs McNab. *LH*, p. 202.

67 *view of a James novel.* To VB, *Letters*, i (19 Aug. 1909), p. 409.

photograph of James. Kept on her table at Asheham. David Garnett, *Great Friends* (Macmillan, 1979; NY: Atheneum, 1980), p. 125.

'*the lava of madness*'. To Ethel Smyth, *Letters*, iv (22 June 1930), p. 180.

CHAPTER 6

68 '*She always said* . . .'. *Notes on Virginia's Childhood*, op. cit.

the training of writers. 'The Leaning Tower' (1940), *CE*, ii, p. 169.

Eliot on education. 'The Naked Man', *Athenaeum* (13 Feb. 1920), p. 208.

diatribe. *QB*, i, Appendix C, p. 205.

dancing classes. *QB*, i, p. 27.

69 '*born beneath green shades*'. MSS.VO. Helen's phrase in the earlier typescript.

'*I inherited* . . .'. *MB*, p. 68.

'*against every form of injustice* . . .'. 'The Clapham Sect', *Edinburgh Review* 80 (1844), p. 26, repr. in *Essays in Ecclesiastical Biography*, ii (Longman, 1849), p. 311.

'*by nature* . . .'. *MB*, pp. 126-7.

70 *Wilberforce's sister.* LS, *The Life of Sir James Fitzjames Stephen* (London: Smith, Elder, 1895), pp. 67-8.

handed on. See chapter on Evangelicalism in Noel Annan, op. cit.; also A. O. J. Cockshut, *Truth to Life* (London: Collins, 1974), pp. 71, 74, 78. In 'The Clapham Sect' Sir James Stephen said that as a coterie, Clapham-ites 'drew many of their canons of criticism from books and talk of their own parentage; and for those outside the pale, there might be, now and then, some failure of charity' (p. 307).

'*sordid motive* . . .'. From a paragraph on Burke in *The History of English Thought in the Eighteenth Century*, ii (London, 1876), p. 223.

'*it is not from want . . .*'. Ibid. 222.

Thomas Clarkson's sketch. Quoted by Sir James Stephen, 'The Clapham Sect', *Essays in Ecclesiastical Biography*, ii, pp. 330-2.

' "*without a skin*" . . .'. In *The Life of Sir James Fitzjames Stephen*, quoted by Cockshut, p. 74.

Mill on 'nervous sensibility'. The Subjection of Women, op. cit. 62.

71 '*surprised . . .*'. *Diary*, iii (28 Nov. 1928), p. 210.

'*To read . . .*'. *CE*, iv, p. 80.

no coxcombry. 'The Clapham Sect', p. 308.

'*The true Claphamite . . .*'. Ibid. 383.

lecture on the right use of books. Delivered to the Shrewsbury Church of England Literary and Scientific Institution, repr. *Literary Addresses*, 2nd Series (London, 1855), p. 7.

'*It makes me angry . . .*'. Letter to JS.

72 '*as he lay back . . .*'. Maitland, p. 476. (Maitland asked VW to contribute some personal memories to his official biography of her father: pp. 474-6).

'*getting the rhythm*'. *Diary*, ii (18 Nov. 1924), p. 322.

'*He read . . .*'. *LH*, pp. 292-3.

'*with fire and ardour*'. Obituary, repr. *Books and Portraits*, op. cit. 210.

73 '*I opened it . . .*'. *MB*, p. 93.

father's study. Autobiographical sketch in holograph volume entitled 'Essays 1940', Berg. See revised edn. of *MB*.

'*all the questions . . .*'. MS.LH, p. 320.

74 *privately written essays.* These have not survived. See *QB*, i, p. 51.

LS and Olive Schreiner. Letter to JS.

'*that is a thing for ladies*'. Letter to JS.

'*Ginia is devouring books . . .*'. *Mausoleum Book*, cited by *QB*, i, p. 51.

75 *LS on Hawthorne.* 'Nathaniel Hawthorne', *Hours in a Library*, i (London, 1892), pp. 169-98.

'*we owe the best relish of the past . . .*'. 'The Old Order', *CE*, i, p. 270.

George Eliot's parties. Mausoleum Book.

Mrs Cameron. Ibid.

76 '*orgy of reading*'. 'Hours in a Library' (1916), *CE*, ii, p. 35.

77 '*and consort . . .*'. Ibid. 36.

'*pure convention*'. *MB*, pp. 135-6.

LS on Jane Carlyle. VW to Violet Dickinson, *Letters*, i (4 May? 1903), p. 76.

78 *Hardy's view of LS.* 'The Schreckhorn', *Poems of Thomas Hardy*, selected by T. R. M. Creighton (Macmillan, 1974), p. 107.

'*like fate*'. Maitland, p. 364.

79 *'weird powers . . .'.* Ibid.

'Lucy Gray'. VW probably read this in Palgrave's *Golden Treasury*. (Several of her poetic allusions are to poems in this collection of lyrics.)

'It was his fate . . .'. LH, pp. 71-2.

80 *'is the most abject treachery . . .'. AROO*, p. 160.

'The Modern Essay'. CE, ii, p. 48.

the Cambridge analytical mind. MB, p. 126.

'did not deny . . .'. Essay on Jowett, see also Annan, p. 132.

'relieved of a cumbrous burden'. Some Early Impressions (Hogarth, 1924), p. 70. Written in 1903 and published in the *National Review* that year.

'granitic' mind. LW, iv, p. 80.

'lapidary'. Ibid. i, p. 184.

81 *visited St Sophia.* Diary of Foreign Travel, Berg.

'always logic-chopping'. Quote from LS's letters, Maitland, p. 306.

'crippling'. MB, p. 126. Cited by Rose, p. 19.

'our facts . . .'. MSS.VO: earlier typescript.

82 *Mill's model. On Liberty* (Penguin), pp. 109-10.

'and show us . . .'. MB, pp. 45-6.

83 *'Books are the things I enjoy . . .'.* Diary No. 2, entitled 'Hyde Park Gate' (30 June 1903-1 Oct. 1903?), Berg.

envy. To Thoby, *Letters*, i (May 1903), p. 77. Quoted by *QB*, i, p. 70.

84 *'I felt . . .'. MB*, p. 108.

'Greek is my daily bread . . .'. Letters, i (17? June 1900), p. 35.

'central private life'. Autobiographical fragment (1940), op. cit. See Rose, pp. 28-9.

85 *Greek studies.* Holograph notes, MHP A.21. Dated 1 Dec. 1907-11 Jan. 1909.

'a sadness . . .'. 'On Not Knowing Greek', *CE*, i, p. 13.

'a counsellor . . .'. Obituary by VW for *The Times* (1937), MHP B.26c.

Case's outrage. VW to VB, *Letters*, i (25? July 1911), p. 472.

'please know . . .'. Letters, vi (22 Mar. 1937), p. 114.

86 *report on teaching at Morley College. QB*, i, Appendix B, pp. 202-4.

The Journal of Mistress Joan Martyn. Berg. Ed. Susan M. Squier and Louise A. DeSalvo, *Twentieth Century Literature* (Fall/Winter 1979), pp. 237-69.

'By the way . . .'. Letters, i, p. 190.

'solidly read . . .'. Ibid. (July 1905), p. 202.

'making out . . .'. Ibid. (4 Aug. 1906), p. 234.

88 *'that things . . .'. Middlemarch*, 'Finale'.

89 *long flirtation. QB* has a full account, i, pp. 132-6.

'*We talked* . . .'. I have drawn on VW's account of a rather later encounter, a post-war meal at Verrays in Regent Street. *Diary*, i (15 Feb. 1919), p. 240.

'*My dear Virginia* . . .'. Clive Bell's letters to VW, MHP.

'*Seriously* . . .'. *Letters*, i (6 May 1908), p. 330.

'*I think* . . .'. Ibid. (19 Aug. 1908), p. 356.

'*the gayest human being* . . .'. Clive Bell, *Old Friends* (Chatto, 1956; Harcourt, 1957), p. 99.

'*with soft deep eyes* . . .'. To VW (14 Feb. 1909), MHP.

90 '*You have* . . .'. Letter (19 July 1917), ibid.

to the French. Letter (11 Aug. 1907), ibid.

write about women. Letter (6 Sept.? 1910), ibid.

'*barley*' *image.* Letter (4 Nov. 1908), ibid.

'*I just go on* . . .'. To VW (3 Aug. 1908), ibid.

high expectation. John Russell, 'Clive Bell', *Encounter* 23 (Dec. 1964), 47–9, repr. *BG*, pp. 197–201.

Clive Bell's comments on VO. *QB*, i, Appendix D, pp. 207–10.

91 '*Then you come* . . .'. *Letters*, i (May 1908), pp. 333–4.

CHAPTER 7

92 '*We need not* . . .'. To Clive Bell, ibid. (7? Feb. 1909), p. 382.

'*re-form* . . . *multitudes* . . .'. Ibid. (19 Aug. 1908), p. 356. Quoted by *QB*, i, p. 137.

George Eliot quotation. 'Prelude', *Middlemarch*.

' "*It's awfully difficult* . . ." '. *VO*, pp. 180–1.

George Eliot's heroines. 'George Eliot', *CE*, i, p. 204.

VO *as* Bildungsroman. See John Bayley, 'The Diminishment of Consciousness: A Paradox in the Art of VW' and Gillian Beer, 'Virginia Woolf and Prehistory' in *VW: A Centenary Perspective*, ed. Eric Warner (Macmillan, 1984).

93 '*She must reach* . . .'. 'George Eliot', p. 204.

Hyde Park Gate diary. Diary No. 2, op. cit. Berg.

travel diary. Diary of Foreign Travel, Berg.

first chapter. The chapter is entitled 'The Hero'. MHP A. 26d. Another unpublished story 'Phyllis and Rosamund', dated 20–3 June 1906, expresses the same disgruntlement with good society. MHP A.23f.

Jane Carlyle. 'The Letters of Jane Welsh Carlyle', *Guardian* (2 Aug. 1905), p. 1295. See also *CE*, iv, p. 36: 'Her letters owe their incomparable brilliancy to the hawklike swoop and descent of her mind upon facts. . . . She sees through clear water, down to the rocks at the bottom.'

94 *Charlotte Brontë.* See 'Mrs Gaskell', *TLS* (29 Sept. 1910), repr. VW, *Books and Portraits*, p. 140.

Shelley. Review of the Shelley–Hitchener letters, *TLS* (5 Mar. 1908), repr. *Books and Portraits*, pp. 154–7.

Elizabeth I. 'The Girlhood of Queen Elizabeth', ibid. (30 Dec. 1909), repr. *Books and Portraits*, pp. 173–7.

Lady Hester Stanhope. Ibid. (20 Jan. 1910), repr. *Books and Portraits*, pp. 195–200.

Strachey's Stanhope. Athenaeum (4 Apr. 1919), repr. *Biographical Essays* (Chatto, 1960), pp. 211–18.

95 *'With scanty education . . .'. Books and Portraits*, p. 196.

'Memoirs of a Novelist'. MHP B.9a.

'to write a very subtle work . . .'. To Clive Bell, *Letters*, i (15 Apr. 1908), p. 325.

97 *Bell to VW.* Letter (27 Oct. 1909), MHP.

wrecked ships. VO, pp. 23–4.

'great white monsters . . .'. Ibid. 18.

'like a fish . . .'. Ibid. 198.

evidence of five drafts. For a full description see Louise A. DeSalvo, *Virginia Woolf's First Voyage. A Novel in the Making* (Macmillan, 1980).

burnt several more. QB, i, p. 126 suggests that she burnt seven drafts.

'infinite strange shapes'. To Clive Bell, *Letters*, i (19 Aug. 1908), p. 356.

98 *'as a chiselled block'.* Ibid. (15 Apr. 1908), p. 325.

'My boldness . . .'. Ibid. (7 Feb. 1909), p. 383.

'the feel of running water'. Ibid.

99 *'one great advantage'. VO*, pp. 31–2.

'bare passages of biography'. To Clive Bell, *Letters*, i (7? Feb. 1909), p. 382.

'verbatim'. To VB, ibid. (10 Aug. 1908), p. 349.

'Never was there . . .'. Ibid.

100 *'Since the time . . .'. VO*, p. 323.

Ralegh's description. Hakluyt, ed. E. J. Payne (London, 1880), p. 362.

different people. 'Trafficks and Discoveries': a review of *English Seamen in The Sixteenth Century* by J. A. Froude and *Hakluyt's Voyages, Travels, and Discoveries of the English Nation, TLS* (12 Dec. 1918), p. 618.

'in which people were imprisoned'. VO, p. 29.

'two sinister grey vessels . . .'. Ibid. 75.

101 *'quaint, sprightly . . .'.* Ibid. 67.

fear of her half-brother. Poole, p. 36.

'Still and cold . . .'. VO, p. 86.

'*I shall never . . .*'. MSS.VO. This quote comes from the later typescript.

'*creeping . . .*'. Ibid.

'*When shall we be free? . . .*'. *The Years*, p. 320.

'*a perpetual discovery*'. Ibid. 413.

'*a wonderful power . . .*'. *VO*, p. 273.

102 *Clive Bell's accusation and VW's reply.* *QB*, i, Appendix D, pp. 209, 211.

Oxford and Cambridge dons. *VO*, p. 172.

'*the masculine conception . . .*'. Ibid. 253.

'*"My good creature . . ."*'. Ibid. 43.

'*"Lloyd George . . ."*'. Ibid. 211.

rewrites the Victorian ideal. Gillian Beer, op. cit., suggests that VW 'rewrote' the Victorians.

103 '*"Does she reason . . ."*'. *VO*, p. 244.

'*"There it was . . ."*'. Ibid. 258.

'*who built up . . .*'. Ibid. 259.

'*She reviewed . . .*'. Ibid. 260.

104 '*"I can believe . . ."*'. Ibid.

'*With one foot . . .*'. Ibid. 245–6.

'*She was more lonely . . .*'. Ibid. 29.

105 '*"should live separate . . ."*'. Ibid. 182.

'*because of the extraordinary freedom . . .*'. Ibid. 298.

'*You could say anything . . .*'. Ibid. 297.

'*her mind dwelt . . .*'. Ibid. 206.

'*"What is it to be in love?". . .*'. Ibid. 207.

Louise DeSalvo. In *Virginia Woolf's First Voyage.*

106 '*into the heart of the night*'. *VO*, p. 325.

Heart of Darkness. Avrom Fleishman has linked the two novels in *Virginia Woolf: A Critical Reading* (Baltimore: Johns Hopkins, 1975), p. 1.

'*He was drawn on . . .*'. *VO*, p. 326.

107 '*"We are happy together.". . .*'. Ibid. 332.

Beethoven's Opus 112. Hermione Lee identifies this in *The Novels of VW* (Methuen, 1977), p. 43.

'*the sense of being . . .*'. Emerson, 'Self-Reliance'.

108 '*I attain . . . a symmetry . . .*'. Diary of Foreign Travel, quoted by *QB*, i, p. 138.

'*"What novels . . ."*'. *VO*, p. 262. See John Preston, 'The Silence of the Novel', *Modern Language Review* (Apr. 1979), pp. 257–67, on a 'silent discourse' between novelist and reader in *Mansfield Park*.

'*that roar . . .*'. *Middlemarch*, ch. 20.

'*the secret . . .*'. *Adam Bede*, ch. 17.

109 *notes on womanhood. VO*, pp. 356-7.

'*Rachel said nothing. . . .*'. Ibid. 357.

less talk. Compare the later typescript.

110 '*reality dwelling . . .*'. *VO*, p. 35.

'*would explode . . .*'. Ibid. 18.

'*The sea . . .*'. *Letters*, i (20 Apr. 1908), p. 326. The letter came from St Ives.

111 '*You don't realise . . .*'. Ibid. (15 Apr. 1908), p. 325.

'*arrow-like speed*'. *MB*, p. 39.

112 *the light of a butterfly's wing. LH*, pp. 78, 264.

'*Confronted . . .*'. 'The Decay of Essay-writing', *Academy and Literature* (25 Feb. 1905), pp. 165-6.

'*Very gentle . . .*'. *VO*, p. 220.

CHAPTER 8

115 '*to give you my life*'. *W*, p. 169.

'*a convenience . . .*'. Ibid. 181.

polemical piece. 'The Intellectual Status of Women', a brilliant letter to the *New Statesman* (Oct. 1920), repr. *Diary*, ii, Appendix III, pp. 339-42.

revolt against Hyde Park Gate. 'Old Bloomsbury', *MB*, p. 159: 'From my angle then, one approaches Bloomsbury through Hyde Park Gate.'

116 '*dash*'. 4 Mar. 1905 in Diary no. 3, headed 'New Forest' (Xmas 1904-31 May 1905), Berg.

furnishings, Spalding, p. 46.

Fitzroy Square. Described by Duncan Grant, who lived in this square at the time, *BG*, p. 65.

117 *feminized.* I owe this point to Michelle Totah.

bawdy talk. Diary (1909), MHP Add.13.

Vanessa dancing. Recalled by Adrian Stephen in a letter to VB, *c.*1942, Charleston Papers, King's College, Cambridge.

Sydney Waterlow. Holograph diary (3 Jan. 1911), Berg.

the Foundling Hospital. MB, p. 179.

'*the Chinese shoe . . .*'. Ibid. 88.

'*one passionate . . .*'. Ibid. 148-9.

118 '*the Greek slave years*'. Ibid. 106.

expression of blazing defiance. Reported by David Garnett in review of *MB*, *New Statesman* (11 June 1976), pp. 777-8.

that disastrous evening. MB, pp. 151-3.

'*A Garden Dance*'. Hyde Park Gate diary.

'*a farmyard . . .*'. *VO*, pp. 176-8.

'*Kiss me . . .*'. '22 Hyde Park Gate', *MB*, p. 147.

119 '*evidently adored*' *George*. Dr Octavia Wilberforce in a résumé of VW's problems and last days to an American friend, MHP.

to comfort her. MB, p. 160.

'*Sleep had almost come . . .*'. Ibid. 155.

may have been irresistible. See Love, op. cit. 207.

'*in a position . . .*'. Notes on Hyde Park Gate for 'A Sketch of the Past'. MHP A.13a.

'*Go and tear it up*'. *MB*, p. 130.

stickler. Anne Olivier Bell's note in *Diary*, i, p. 61.

'*the good boy . . .*'. VW to Violet Dickinson (11? Oct. 1903), *Letters*, i, p. 101.

George's hypocrisy. Poole, p. 111.

120 '*a very low down affair*'. *MB*, p. 169.

'*a kind of duck-weed*'. The connection between this phrase and Duckworth was made by Mitchell A. Leaska in *Bulletin of the New York Public Library* Vol. 80 (Winter 1977), p. 181.

'*like two swans . . .*'. The reappearance of duckweed noted by Leaska, ibid.

frozen in her white dress. Poole, p. 112 n. Rose prints this picture, p. 25.

'*Thoughts upon Social Success*'. Hyde Park Gate diary.

121 '*Old mother nature . . .*'. Diary of Foreign Travel.

Margaret Schlegel. Howard's End, ch. 15.

Diary (8 Mar. 1905). Diary no. 3 (Xmas 1904-27 May 1905).

first cigarette. Diary (28 Apr. 1905) and *MB*, p. 164.

Thursday discussions. 'Old Bloomsbury', *MB*, pp. 168-9.

not rarefied. VB, 'Notes on Bloomsbury', a Memoir Club essay (1951), repr. *BG*, p. 79.

122 '*Never have I . . .*'. *MB*, p. 168.

'*You might . . .*'. (23 June 1911?) Charleston Papers.

barricade. See the beautifully written account of VB by her daughter, Angelica Garnett, in *Recollections of VW*, ed. Joan Russell Noble (London: Peter Owen, 1972), pp. 83-8.

pretensions. QB, i, Appendix C, pp. 205-6 and Rose, p. 39.

123 *ridicule of poems.* See p. 100 n. above.

'*To dwell upon Bloomsbury . . .*'. To Harmon H. Goldstone, *Letters*, v (16 Aug. 1932), p. 91.

portrait of Saxon Sydney-Turner. MHP A.13c. Entitled 'One of our Great Men'.

VW's 'Victorianism'. Old Friends, pp. 100-1.

Strachey meets the Visigoths. Quoted by Michael Holroyd, *Lytton Strachey: A Critical Biography*, i (Heinemann, 1967; Holt, Rinehart, & Winston, 1968), p. 397 (cut from the revised edn.).

'slightly stingy appearance'. Diary, i (24 Jan. 1919), p. 236.

124 *'Excessive paleness . . .'.* Quoted by Holroyd, revised edn., 1973, p. 168.

waterspiders. 'My Early Beliefs' (1938), a paper delivered to the Memoir Club, repr. *BG*, p. 64.

the schoolfriend saga. MB, p. 165.

the trembling Woolf. Ibid. 166.

'if 6 people died . . .'. Diary, iii (27 Nov. 1925), p. 48.

125 *Forster as butterfly. MB*, p. 176 and *Diary*, i (24 July 1919), p. 295.

Thoby in the novels. QB, i, p. 112.

'I had him . . .'. Letters, iv (15 Oct. 1931), p. 391.

common grief. QB, i, p. 113.

126 *Strachey on Thoby.* Letters to LW, Berg.

Stevenson. The words are recalled roughly in *Diary*, v (12 Oct. 1937), p. 113, after her nephew, Julian Bell, was killed in Spain. 'In Memoriam' comes from *Underwoods*, which she may have read in *Poems* (Chatto, 1906), p. 38.

'Sympathy'. MHP A. 24d. Typescript, undated. 1907-10 has been suggested, but the structure is so like that of 'The Mark on the Wall' (1917) that the date may be later, i.e. closer to the composition of *JR*.

127 *'the ramshackle . . .'.* MS.LH, p. 241.

affection. Quentin Bell comes to this precise conclusion in his Introduction to *Diary*, i, p. xxvii: 'The strength of their union was not, in the end, based upon a similarity of ideas and outlook. It was based on affection.'

'hold yourself . . .'. MB, p. 84.

'Harry saw . . .'. The Wise Virgins: A Story of Words, Opinions and a Few Emotions (Edward Arnold, 1914), p. 68.

128 *'She had not . . .'. LH*, p. 144.

'spectator'. Letter, Charleston Papers.

Forster's 'saved'. A. O. J. Cockshut links this word in *The Longest Journey* with the Clapham Sect in *Truth to Life*, p. 78.

Annan on LW. Review of *LW*: v, *The Political Quarterly*, 41 (Jan.-Mar. 1970), pp. 35-41, repr. *BG*, pp. 187-94.

the group's portrait. I owe this point to Michelle Totah.

Mary Hutchinson. Richard Shone, *Bloomsbury Portraits* (Phaidon; Dutton, 1976), p. 175.

129 Studland Beach. Ibid. 76.

'*Do you think we have . . .*'. *Letters*, vi (17 Aug. 1937), p. 158.

The Tub. Shone, p. 177.

Portrait of a Lady. Ibid. 139.

Vanessa Bell at Charleston. Shone, colour plate VII (opposite p. 256).

130 *life at Charleston.* Shone, p. 18.

pool of calm. Angelica Garnett, op. cit. 85, described VB as 'calm, like a pool . . .'.

Vanessa Bell, *1942.* Shone, p. 12. Shone describes this as a portrait of 'a late Victorian of consequence'. p. 19.

'*grave & rather sarcastic . . .*'. To JS (16 Apr. 1881).

131 '*like a broad river*'. *Ottoline at Garsington: Memoirs of Lady Ottoline Morrell 1915–1918*, ed. Robert Gathorne-Hardy (Faber, 1974; Knopf, 1975), p. 51.

'*Vanessa icy . . .*'. Holograph diary, op. cit. (2 Dec. 1910).

VB's undemonstrativeness. To JS (14 Apr. 1881).

'*when she is demonstrative . . .*'. *QB*, ii, p. 203.

CHAPTER 9

132 *Leonard's letters, except one.* MHP.

133 '*I hope the Mandril . . .*'. Berg. I am indebted to Leon Berger for his transcript.

'*I have always . . .*'. *LW*, ii, pp. 151–2.

'*—then I say . . .*'. *Letters*, i (1 May 1912), pp. 496–7.

'*proper passion*'. See ch. 2 above.

134 '*There is nothing sweeter . . .*'. *MB*, p. 105.

men '*had*' women. Ibid. 104.

135 '*the stupidest . . .*'. *LH*, p. 158.

'*Women . . .*'. Ibid. 159–60.

a Valkyrie. Review of *MB*, *New Statesman* (11 June 1976), pp. 777–8.

'*Shall you kiss me . . .*'. *Letters*, i (14 Aug. 1908), p. 355.

'*There are bullocks . . .*'. Ibid. (10 Aug. 1909), p. 406.

'*How pleasant . . .*'. Ibid. ii, p. 124.

136 *letters of Mérimée.* Read during visit to Greece. Diary of Foreign Travel.

love of Wordsworth for sister. Review of Wordsworth's letters, *TLS* (2 Apr. 1908).

'*There are such beings . . .*'. To Fanny Knight (18 Nov. 1814), *Jane Austen's Letters*, ed. R. W. Chapman (Oxford, 1952), p. 409.

'*I confess . . .*'. *Night and Day*, p. 156.

Strachey's appearance. Frances Partridge's lovely description in *Memories*, (Gollancz; Little, Brown, 1981), pp. 77-8.

137 *'Oh I was right . . .'. Diary*, ii (17 Oct. 1924), p. 317.

'softest to impressions . . .'. Ibid. i (12 Dec. 1917), p. 89.

'from the sight of the tail . . .'. Ibid. ii (5 Apr. 1918), p. 131.

'repined . . .'. Ibid. i (15 Nov. 1919), p. 311.

'So I think of you . . .'. Letters, i, p. 374.

'Your destiny . . .'. Quoted in *A Marriage of True Minds*, p. 56.

a young hawk. See VW's description of Louis in MSS.W, p. 52. For other good descriptions of LW see Gerald Brenan, *South from Granada* (Hamish Hamilton, 1957), pp. 139-40, and also Richard Kennedy, *A Boy at the Hogarth Press* (1972; repr. Penguin, 1978), p. 20.

138 *coupling. A Marriage of True Minds*, p. 53: '. . . seeking his satisfaction from the readily available prostitutes of Jaffna.' See also Strachey's replies, Berg.

unidentified paper. 'The wise man . . .'. n.d., Leonard Woolf Papers. I P, University of Sussex.

LW's diary. In 63 vols., Leonard Woolf Papers, II R.

'Has Cascara acted?'. (11 Mar. 1914).

'not only in his face'. To Violet Dickinson (24 June 1912) *Letters*, i, p. 505.

139 *quote from Micah. LW*, i, p. 26.

Annan on Woolf. BG, pp. 187-94.

'Every man . . .'. Letter from LS to his mother-in-law, quoted by Maitland, p. 314.

'the most Victorian . . .'. LW, i, pp. 183-4.

140 *temple of Segesta.* Ibid. 183.

Syrian wanderer. 'Aspasia' paper, Leonard Woolf Papers, II D. 7a, University of Sussex.

'but from the first . . .'. Letters, i (June 1912), p. 503.

'the spring. . .'. 'Aspasia' paper, op. cit.

'We've seen nothing . . .'. Letters, ii (17 Aug. 1912), pp. 3-4.

141 *'the proper business'.* To Lytton Strachey, ibid. (1 Sept. 1912), p. 5.

'Why do you think . . .'. Ibid. (4 Sept. 1912), pp. 6-7.

'We've talked incessantly . . .'. To Molly MacCarthy, ibid. 9.

'I like continuing . . .'. Diary, ii (11 May 1920), p. 36.

'Lappin and Lapinova'. A Haunted House (1944, repr. 1973), pp. 69-78.

143 *'Immundus Mongoosius Felicissimus . . .'. Letters*, ii, p. 35.

'Come along marmots . . .'. Ibid. 95.

'a cypher language'. Orlando, p. 254.

145 *'my rapid bold Mong'. Letters*, ii (31 Oct. 1917), p. 193.

'*I daresay . . .*'. *Diary*, i (28 Dec. 1919), p. 318.

'*It will be a joy . . .*'. *Letters*, ii (11 Sept. 1919), p. 388.

contract. MHP, described by *QB*, ii, p. 19.

146 '*It's so frightfully tame . . .*'. *Letters*, ii (29 and 30 Oct. 1917), pp. 191, 193.

147 *Carlyles' letters*. 'More Carlyle Letters', *TLS* (1 Apr. 1909), p. 126.

148 '*Some winy smell . . .*'. *LH*, pp. 270–1.

'*I remember . . .*'. MSS.VO: early typescript.

'*into the tropics*'. *MB*, p. 166.

LW's sense of his Jewishness. Roger Poole, op. cit. 78.

149 '*I'm half afraid . . .*'. *Letters*, i, p. 496.

'*like hills . . .*'. *The Wise Virgins*, p. 118.

'*Her life was an adventure . . .*'. Ibid. 222.

'*to the extreme of wildness . . .*'. *Letters*, i (1 May 1912), p. 496.

'*a certain fierceness*'. *The Wise Virgins*, p. 62.

'*extraordinarily gentle*'. LW's diary (27 Apr. 1912). In code, transliterated by Anne Olivier Bell.

'*no more than a rock*'. *Letters*, i (1 May 1912), p. 496.

150 *to rise up against him*. To VW (29 Apr. 1912).

'*so dear . . .*'. To VW (24 May 1912).

Mill. The Subjection of Women, pp. 24–5.

'*Aspasia*'. An extract quoted in *A Marriage of True Minds*, pp. 61–2.

151 *to Ka Cox*. *Letters*, ii, pp. 6–7.

The Wise Virgins. Poole, pp. 78–102, was the first to use this novel as a source of LW's attitudes.

'*I admire your women . . .*'. *The Wise Virgins*, p. 77.

'*very affectionate*'. Ibid. 118.

152 '*Katharine's Opinion . . .*'. Ibid. 149.

Bella Woolf to LW. Letters, Leonard Woolf Papers.

'*his curious pessimistic temper . . .*'. *Diary*, iv (23 Oct? 1931), p. 51.

153 '*We wait hunched up . . .*'. *The Wise Virgins*, p. 156.

'*To feel people . . .*'. Ibid. 158.

'*She liked his sensibility . . .*'. Ibid. 122.

Lytton Strachey's criticism. Letter (14 Dec. 1913), Berg.

154 *bitter skirmish*. *Diary*, iv (11 Mar. 1935), p. 286.

in the middle of The Wise Virgins. *Letters*, ii, p. 23.

VW read The Wise Virgins. *Diary*, i (31 Jan. 1915), p. 32. Cited by Poole, p. 101.

155 *killed it dead*. Cited by Poole, p. 99.

medical ignorance. For details see Stephen Trombley, op. cit.

156 *woollen combinations.* Barbara Bagenal, *Recollections of Virginia Woolf*, p. 150.

'*but on the 5th . . .*'. *Diary*, iii (2 Aug. 1926), p. 105.

'*How lovely is the privacy . . .*'. MSS.W, pp. 367–8.

'*purpled with the shadows . . .*'. Ibid. 291. I have corrected 'tortured' with 'tortures'.

157 '*shivering and unhappy soul*'. Ibid. 292.

'*formidable, bony . . .*'. Ibid. Cancelled line.

recovered illusions. Diary, i, p. 73.

'*idiot games*'. *LH*, Time Passes, VII.

'*So, unhesitatingly . . .*'. MS.LH, p. 280.

158 *prefer to have £3. Diary*, iii (20 Apr. 1925), p. 11.

' "*And your husband . . .*" '. VW to Ka Cox, *Letters*, ii (Nov.? 1912), p. 11.

'*We were kept awake . . .*'. Ibid. (11 Apr. 1920), pp. 428–9.

'*divine contentment*'. *Diary*, i (3, 4, 5 Nov. 1917), p. 70.

'*one's personality . . .*'. Ibid. (2 Nov. 1917), p. 70.

159 '*No-one except a very modest person . . .*'. Ibid. (6 Jan. 1915), p. 9.

'*Stop*'. Ibid. (19 Jan. 1915), p. 23.

'*stony*'. *Diary*, iv (15 Apr. 1935), p. 300.

'*I think the worse . . .*'. Ibid. iii (9 Mar. 1926), p. 66.

'*L. may be severe . . .*'. Ibid. (14 Dec. 1929), p. 273.

'*I snuggled in . . .*'. Ibid. (14 June 1925).

160 '*L. and I . . .*'. Ibid. (8 Apr. 1925), pp. 8–9.

'*If it were now to die . . .*'. *Othello*, II. i.

CHAPTER 10

161 '*how this preposterous masculine fiction . . .*'. To Margaret Llewelyn Davies, *Letters*, ii (23 Jan. 1916), p. 76.

'*One by one . . .*'. *LH*, p. 195.

Northanger Abbey. Ch. 14.

'*If you object . . .*'. MS.Par, first essay, p. 9. See also 'Modes and Manners of the Nineteenth Century', *TLS* (24 Feb. 1910), repr. *Books & Portraits*, p. 23: '. . . we are left out, and history, in our opinion, lacks an eye.' Similarly, Henry James, in *The Sense of the Past*, speaks of 'the little notes of truth for which the common lens of history . . . was not sufficiently fine'.

162 *Steiner. After Babel: Aspects of Language and Translation* (Oxford, 1975), pp. 29–30.

'*The Roman Road*'. *Selected Poems of Thomas Hardy*, pp. 92–3.

she subdues barbarity. LH, p. 77.

'*to die gloriously . . .*'. Ibid. 32.

163 '*in his mud-coloured uniform . . .*'. *The Years*, p. 308.

Miss Parry. Mrs. D, pp. 268–9.

'*stayed the corruption . . .*'. *LH*, pp. 215–16.

164 '*vulgar brag*'. Letter to JS (Aug. 1877), Berg.

165 '*imprint a respect . . .*'. *Diary*, i (30 Oct. 1918), p. 211.

'*whether any . . .*'. To VB, *Letters*, ii (13 Nov. 1918), p. 293.

'*sleepy & torpid . . .*'. *Diary*, i (19, 20, 24 July 1919), pp. 292–4.

'*treasure*'. See 'A Haunted House', 'Reading', and poems laid into MSS.BA.

treasures in Jacob's Room. p. 133. Quoted by Hermione Lee, op. cit. 89.

'*Unconsciously . . .*'. *LW*, iv, p. 16.

conceived at Wissett. Letter to VB, quoted by *QB*, ii, p. 32.

166 '*modest mouse-coloured . . .*'. *A Haunted House*, p. 43.

'*The romantic figure*'. See Eric Warner, 'Some Aspects of Romanticism in the Work of Virginia Woolf', op. cit.

167 '*elephant-bodied . . .*'. *BA*, pp. 13–14.

'*opening . . .*'. To VB, *Letters*, ii (2 Apr. 1920), p. 426.

Emma Vaughan. To VB, ibid. (22 May 1917), p. 156.

'*a cool waiting wit . . .*'. MSS.D, i, p. 18.

'*the spectator . . .*'. *Diary*, i (30 Nov. 1918), p. 222.

168 '*but a procession . . .*'. *JR*, p. 115.

statues. VW refers specifically to *Greek* statues but this is inaccurate. The Greeks did finish the backs. Information supplied by Peta Fowler.

'*In Flanders Fields*'. By John McRae, who died in Base Hospital, 1918.

169 '*Clean, white . . .*'. *JR*, p. 13.

'*Had he been put on . . .*'. *MB*, pp. 119–20. Allusion identified by Jeanne Schulkind.

Catullus' elegy. Poem No. 101. John Griffiths supplied this source and parallel circumstance.

'*at the mouth . . .*'. *JR*, pp. 117–18.

171 '*a wall*'. *Diary*, ii (26 Jan. 1920), p. 14.

'*sterile acrobatics*'. Ibid. (14 Feb. 1922), p. 161.

'*& the draggled girl . . .*'. Ibid. i (12 Apr. 1919), p. 263.

172 '*much in the spirit . . .*'. Ibid. ii (8 June 1920), p. 47.

posthumous volume. The Middle Years.

'*The Old Order*' (*1917*). *CE*, i, pp. 270–6.

'*At 60 . . .*'. *Diary*, iii, p. 58.

'*the shadow . . .*'. Ibid. i, p. 266.

'*go down to Treveal . . .*'. Ibid. ii, p. 103. She was planning a spring visit to Cornwall.

'*& find . . .*'. Ibid. i (20 Apr. 1919), p. 266.

173 '*It's enough . . .*'. Ibid. (15 Mar. 1919), p. 253.

A Writer's Diary. 1953. These extracts contain nothing from her notebooks which she kept separately.

German prisoners. *Diary*, i (10 Sept. 1917), p. 49.

Kitty and Mrs Dalloway. Ibid. ii (8 Oct. 1922), p. 206.

'*strangely unaccented*'. Ibid. (15 Feb. 1923), pp. 234–5.

'*like an over ripe grape . . .*'. Ibid. (15 Sept. 1924), p. 313.

174 '*the shadow . . .*'. 'The Old Order', *CE*, i, p. 270.

'*How he suffers! . . .*'. *Diary*, iv (5 Feb. 1935), p. 277.

'*bronze mask*'. Ibid. v (16 Feb. 1940), p. 268.

visit to Mary Sheepshanks. Ibid. ii (13 June 1923), p. 246.

'*lapse*'. Ibid. i (15 Feb. 1919), p. 239.

'*La Figlia che Piange*'. T. S. Eliot, *Prufrock and Other Observations* (1917).

'*the finished . . . the raw*'. *Diary*, iv (23 Nov. 1933), p. 189.

'*to be as subtle . . .*'. 'The Letters of Henry James' (1920), *CE*, i, p. 285. She seems to be writing more of herself here than of James.

175 *incredible felicities.* I am using her words to describe James's letters.

'*something incommunicable . . .*'. Ibid.

'*aloofness . . .*'. 'The Old Order', p. 276.

'*the soul*'. *Diary*, ii (19 Feb. 1923), p. 234. See also iii (27 Feb. 1926), p. 62.

'*I'm amused . . .*'. Ibid. i (28 Dec. 1919), p. 317.

CHAPTER 11

176 '*new departure*'. Ibid. 236.

Forster. 'Anonymity: An Enquiry', *Two Cheers for Democracy* (Penguin), p. 97.

voice and manner. South from Granada, pp. 139–40, repr. *BG*, pp. 283–95.

'*I see through . . .*'. *Diary*, iii (27 Feb. 1926), p. 63.

177 *impetuosity of address.* The phrase comes from *QB*, i, p. 67.

Stephen Spender. Review, *Observer* (30 Oct. 1977).

'*And I don't like . . .*'. *Letters*, iii (4 Sept. 1924), p. 131.

'*Let us consider letters . . .*'. *JR*, pp. 91–2.

178 '*Reading*'. MHP B.11d. Undated 41-page typescript, but the evidence of the diary suggests Mar. 1922. This must be distinguished from 'Reading', *CE*, ii, pp. 12–33.

'*Flee fro the prees . . .*'. 'Truth: Balade de Bon Conseyl', one of Chaucer's short poems, quoted on p. 22 of 'Reading'.

'*I feel as if . . .*'. *Diary*, ii (19 June 1923), p. 248.

without mincing. Ibid. (28 July 1923), p. 259.

'*& this I must prize . . .*'. Ibid.

'*I feel time racing . . .*'. Ibid. ii (22 Jan. 1922), p. 158.

'*close to the fact*'. Ibid. (14 Oct. 1922), pp. 207–8.

'*Often now . . .*'. Ibid. 246.

179 *VW in basement*. Richard Kennedy, *A Boy at the Hogarth Press* (1972; repr. Penguin, 1978), p. 36. These reminiscences are accompanied by amusing drawings.

a protective skin. *LW*, iv, pp. 52–3.

'*It is a mistake . . .*'. *Diary*, ii (22 Aug. 1922), p. 193.

180 '*My only interest . . .*'. Ibid. (18 Feb. 1922), p. 168.

'*an image . . .*'. Ibid. 221.

'*London itself . . .*'. Hyde Park Gate diary (1903), Berg.

'*people would have seen . . .*'. *Diary*, ii (17 Oct. 1924), p. 317.

Tomlin's bust. 1931, the National Portrait Gallery, London.

the cracked Englishwoman. *Memories*, p. 236.

181 '*nothing shakes . . .*'. *Diary*, ii (23 June 1920), p. 49.

the public. 'Mr. Bennett and Mrs. Brown', *CE*, i, p. 332.

second-rate works. 'Jane Austen', ibid. 147.

'*Middlemarch . . .*'. 'George Eliot', ibid. 201.

'*the stable . . .*'. 'On Not Knowing Greek', ibid. 4.

182 '*In your modesty . . .*'. 'Mr. Bennett and Mrs. Brown', p. 336.

183 '*Am I a fanatical enthusiast . . .*'. *Diary*, iii (23 Feb. 1926), p. 60.

LW's view of work. *LW*, v, p. 128.

'*Why?*'. Kennedy, op. cit. 23.

'*Spartan*'. *Diary*, iii (28 June 1923), pp. 250–1.

184 '*But my God—*'. Ibid. (7 Dec. 1925), p. 49.

'*We could both wish . . .*'. Ibid. i (11 Oct. 1917), p. 58.

'*to an oddly complete understanding*'. Ibid. (7 May 1918), p. 150.

185 '*And then we talked . . .*'. Ibid. ii (31 May 1920), pp. 44–5, with useful editorial note. Quoted by *QB*, ii, pp. 70–1.

'*a woman caring . . .*'. *Diary*, ii (25 Aug. 1920), pp. 61-2.

'*I hear his voice . . .*'. *The Letters and Journals of Katherine Mansfield: A Selection*, ed. C. K. Stead (Penguin, 1977), pp. 62, 65.

186 '*with the special voice . . .*'. *Prelude*: XI, *Collected Stories* (Constable, 1945; repr. 1973), p. 53.

'*Ah, I have found . . .*'. *Diary*, ii (12 Mar. 1922), p. 171.

'*not the shadow . . .*'. *LW*, iii, p. 204.

Mansfield to VW. 27 Dec. 1920, MHP.

'*Everything . . .*'. *Diary*, ii (16 Jan. 1923), p. 226.

187 '*ravenous . . .*'. Letter to VW (1928). All her letters to VW are in Berg.

'*Sapphist tendencies*'. Letters from VB to VW (16 May 1909; 5 and 17 July 1910), Berg. Cited by Jean O. Love, p. 279.

188 '*scandalous*'. See Vita's letters.

androgyny short-lived. I owe this point to Marni Stanley.

'*every woman . . .*'. *Mrs. D*, p. 109.

'*caves*'. *Diary*, ii (30 Aug. 1923), p. 263.

189 '*I alternately laugh . . .*'. Ibid. iii (18 June 1925), p. 32.

lovable character. Forster gave this advice after *Night and Day:* ibid. i (6 Nov. 1919), p. 310.

'*hidden satire . . .*'. Ibid. ii (17 July 1922), p. 180.

'*slippery mud*'. Ibid. (4 June 1923), pp. 243-4.

'*have neither kindness . . .*'. *Mrs. D*, p. 136.

first plan. The manuscript of *JR*, iii, pp. 131, 153, Berg.

revised idea. *Diary*, iii, p. 207.

190 *QB observes. QB*, i, p. 80 n.

'*the paragon . . .*'. *MB*, p. 143.

'*It would be intolerable . . .*'. *Mrs. Dalloway's Party*, ed. Stella McNichol (Hogarth, 1973), p. 26.

'*She had a perpetual sense . . .*'. *Mrs. D*, p. 15.

'*the power . . .*'. Peter Walsh thinks this, p. 120.

'*To be conscious . . .*'. 'The Clapham Sect', *Essays in Ecclesiastical Biography*, p. 309.

191 '*unknown*' *face*. MSS.D, iii, p. 92.

'*to breast her enemy*'. Ibid. 98-9.

192 '*some distaste . . .*'. *Diary*, iii (18 June 1925), p. 32. See Jane Novak, *The Razor Edge of Balance: A Study of VW* (Univ. of Miami, 1975), p. 125.

like LW. The connection is suggested by David Garnett, *Great Friends*, pp. 125-6.

'*the death . . .*'. *Mrs. D*, p. 91.

complete the character. To Harmon H. Goldstone, *Letters*, v (19 Mar. 1932), p. 36.

193 *RF on modern art.* Quoted by VW in a chapter on the 1st and 2nd Post-Impressionist Exhibitions of 1910 and 1912, *Roger Fry*, pp. 177–8. See Avrom Fleishman, *The Novels of VW*, pp. 16–17.

the mind in its natural state. Colin Blakemore, *The Mechanics of the Mind* (Cambridge, 1977), p. 51.

'*Quiet descended . . .*'. *Mrs. D*, p. 61.

194 '*slip easily . . .*'. 'The Mark on the Wall', *A Haunted House*, p. 42.

'*not entirely real*'. Ibid. 44, 47.

'*crack*'. 'Lady Fanshawe's Memoirs', *TLS* (26 July 1907), p. 234.

reading Proust. *Diary*, ii (10 Feb. 1923), p. 234.

'*He searches out . . .*'. Ibid. iii (8 Apr. 1925), p. 7.

'*so perfectly receptive*'. 'Phases of Fiction', *CE*, ii, p. 83.

'*a sentence . . .*'. Review (19 May 1923), repr. *Contemporary Writers*, ed. Jean Guiguet (Hogarth, 1965), p. 124; and repr. *VW: Women and Writing*, ed. Michele Barrett (Women's Press, 1979), p. 191.

'*a vibration . . .*'. MSS.D, i, p. 5.

195 '*inaudible way*'. *Diary*, iii (15 June 1929), p. 232.

'*Aren't things spoilt . . .*'. MS.LH, p. 214.

'*I am a woman . . .*'. *Diary*, iii (31 May 1929), p. 231.

Joyce. For the influence of Joyce on VW see Guiguet, *VW and Her Works* (Hogarth, 1965), especially pp. 240–5.

inner world of nightmare. T. S. Eliot, 'Cyril Tourneur', *Selected Essays* (Harcourt, 1950), p. 166.

'*the moderns . . .*'. 'Mrs. Dalloway in Bond Street', p. 23.

'*From the contagion . . .*'. Shelley, 'Adonais': XL.

'*Fear no more . . .*'. *Cymbeline*, IV. ii.

196 '*of life beyond . . .*'. *Mrs. D*, p. 39.

'*universal love*'. Ibid. 103.

'*The merit . . .*'. 18 June 1923, in one of four diary-like notebooks, Berg.

initial diagram. 'Notes for Writing', a holograph notebook dated Mar. 1922–Mar. 1925, Berg.

ten years. MS.LH, Appendix A, p.11 and Appendix B: outline of 'Time Passes'.

197 '*I enclosed . . .*'. *MB*, p. 84.

'*can think back . . .*'. *AROO*, p. 146.

tried on mother's dress. In John Lehmann, *VW and Her World* (Thames and Hudson, 1975), p. 22. See opposite pl. 6.

198 *'It was for the old ghosts . . .'. The Sense of the Past.* I am indebted to Julia Briggs for attention to this in *Night Visitors: The Rise and Fall of the English Ghost Story* (Faber, 1977), pp. 114-16.

'Mother and child . . .'. LH, pp. 85, 271-2.

199 *the mass of the hedge.* Ibid. 243. See also pp. 246, 279, 297.

'had over and over . . .'. Ibid. 70.

'alone spoke the truth'. Ibid. 288.

'never tampered . . .'. Ibid. 13.

'"We perished, each alone"'. Ibid. 256. He quotes Cowper, 'The Castaway'.

'I think I might . . .'. Diary, iii, p. 38.

'The blessed thing . . .'. Ibid. 109.

200 *'I meant* nothing *by The Lighthouse'. Letters*, iii (27 May 1927), p. 385. Cf. comment in *Diary*, iii (13 Sept. 1926), pp. 109-10: 'I am making some use of symbolism.'

'misty-looking tower . . .'. LH, p. 286.

'stark and straight'. Ibid.

'I will find some theory about fiction . . .'. Diary, iii (7 Dec. 1925), p. 50. The immediate context is a plan for a book on fiction which emerged eventually as 'Phases of Fiction', 1929.

201 *'One must keep on looking . . .'. LH*, p. 309.

'It became a miracle . . .'. MS.*LH*, p. 348.

202 *'I could hear her voice . . .'. MB*, p. 80.

CHAPTER 12

203 *'No biographer . . .'. Diary*, iii (4 Sept. 1927), p. 153.

depression. Ibid. (15, 28, 30 Sept. 1926), pp. 110-13.

'I am glad . . .'. Ibid. (28 Sept. 1926), p. 112.

'of my own strangeness . . .'. Ibid. (27 Feb. 1926), p. 62.

204 The Prelude. 1850 text, Book VII, ll. 461-5, noted in *Diary*, iii, pp. 247-8. *The Prelude*, she said in 1911, was one of the greatest books ever written (*Letters*, i, p. 460).

205 *'But observe how dots and dashes . . .'. W*, p. 134.

'At 46 . . .'. Diary, iii (21 Apr. 1928), p. 180.

206 *'Draw a little apart . . .'.* 'Impassioned Prose' (on De Quincey) *TLS* (16 Sept. 1926), repr. *CE*, i, p. 172. See also *LH*, p. 289: One way of knowing people was 'to know the outline, not the detail'.

Wordsworth's immortal sea. 'Ode: Intimations of Immortality from Recollections of Early Childhood': IX.

207 '*sense sublime*'. For suggestive connections with 'Tintern Abbey' see Eric Warner, op. cit. 222.

'*Prelude*'. MSS.W, p. 192, 'verso'.

sailing boats. Recalled for Maitland's biography and again in *MB*, p. 77.

208 '. . . *those first affections*'. 'Immortality Ode': IX.

'*into England*'. MSS.W, p. 431.

cricket match. More prominent in the first draft.

notes on Thoby. MHP A.13a.

209 '*a figure*'. *MB*, p. 120.

QB on Thoby Stephen. QB, i, p. 22.

Strachey on Sir James Fitzjames Stephen. 'The First Earl of Lytton', *Independent Review* (Mar. 1907). Quoted by Holroyd, i (1967), pp. 359–60.

Percival reading. MSS.W, p. 565.

'*monolithic*'. Letter of 1905, quoted by Holroyd, p. 140.

'*Beautiful statues* . . .'. Diary of Foreign Travel, 1906.

210 'bared her brows . . .'. *W*, pp. 52–4.

211 '*Then she lay* . . .'. MSS.W, p. 188.

'*Our differences* . . .'. *W*, p. 101.

Louis stone-carved. Ibid. 84.

'*Now let us say* . . .'. Ibid. 89.

'*Like minnows* . . .'. Ibid. 98.

'*the outermost parts* . . .'. Ibid.

212 '*Here, incredible* . . .'. Ibid. 85.

'*The yellow canopy* . . .'. Ibid. 105.

213 '*complete maturity* . . .'. Exercise book headed 'Additions to Waves etc.' (30 June 1931), MHP B.2e. In MSS.W: Appendix A, p. 64.

'*I remember* . . .'. *W*, p. 109.

notes, autumn 1930. Notebook, MSS.W, p. 755.

'*Nothing that has been said* . . .'. *W*, p. 112.

'*a perfect dwelling-place*'. Ibid. 116.

214 '*Very little* . . .'. Ibid.

'*that flings* . . .'. Ibid. 117.

'*runs on a snag*'. Entry dated 3 Nov. 1930, MSS.W, p. 761.

'*Percival was flowering* . . .'. *W*, p. 144.

first part of VW's plan. She elaborated on the first part in Sept.–Oct. 1930.

215 '*His eyes will see* . . .'. *W*, p. 122.

sixty-five. Bernard's age, in the ninth episode, is given in the drafts.

'One has pierced me . . .'. *W*, p. 126.

216 'I am no longer January'. Ibid. 122.

'glutted . . .'. Ibid. 123.

'we grow old'. Ibid. 126.

'scene by scene . . .'. Ibid. 127.

'But now I am compact . . .'. Ibid. 119.

217 London Bridge 'falling down . . .'. The Waste Land (1922).

Bernard sees the fin. *W*, pp. 134–5.

Whitman. 'Out of the Cradle Endlessly Rocking'.

218 'What dissolution . . .'. *W*, p. 145.

'the summit . . .'. Ibid. 135.

'I admit . . .'. Ibid. 138.

'Blindness returns . . .'. Ibid. 204.

'Your voices . . .'. Ibid. 158.

219 'as a man . . .'. Ibid. 154.

visit to Hampton Court. Diary, iii, p. 324.

the mood of Macbeth. Macbeth, v. iii.

220 'What has permanence?'. *W*, p. 161.

clouds of cold mortality. Shelley, 'Adonais': LIV.

'Let us . . .'. *W*, p. 162.

'My ruined life . . .'. Ibid. 163.

'to press out . . .'. Ibid. 165.

221 'silence falling . . .'. Ibid. 159.

'down the river'. Ibid. 166–7.

222 'so to look'. MSS.W, p. 167.

'I have been . . .'. Ibid. 377.

'The six characters . . .'. Letters, iv (27 Oct. 1931), p. 397. I am indebted to Eric Warner for pointing this out.

223 'He is gone!'. *W*, p. 96.

'safety'. Ibid. 176.

'hung like clothes . . .'. Ibid. 154.

'bestial'. Ibid. 94.

225 'suspects me of rapture . . .'. Ibid. 46.

slow flood. Ibid. 74.

'she rode at the day . . .'. Ibid. 195.

'the squeak of trams . . .'. Ibid. 196.

226 'like a piece . . .'. Ibid. 173.

tongue of an ant-eater. Ibid. 174.

'*to follow the curve . . .*'. Ibid. 63.

'*My life has a rapidity . . .*'. Ibid. 92.

'*rebuke . . .*'. Ibid. 128.

227 '*withdrawn together . . .*'. Ibid. 101.

'*O western wind . . .*'. Quoted ibid. 145.

228 '*the most constantly passionate . . .*'. MSS.W, p. 359.

'*Lappin and Lapinova*'. See p. 142 above.

'*Every day . . .*'. W, p. 91.

photo of storm-troopers. LW, v, p. 14.

229 '*protective façade . . .*'. Ibid. i, p. 98.

'*It is a stigma . . .*'. W, p. 69.

Steiner. In Bluebeard's Castle (Faber, 1971), p. 38. The whole argument is more complex and subtle.

'*Lord! . . .*'. Letters, v (8 Aug. 1934), p. 321.

'*malevolent . . .*'. W, p. 66.

'*the silent people . . .*'. MSS.W, p. 707.

urban squalor. Allen McLaurin comments on the similarity of the city landscape in the poems of T. S. Eliot. *Virginia Woolf: The Echoes Enslaved* (Cambridge, 1973), p. 134.

'*He fascinated me . . .*'. W, p. 179.

'*I do not see . . .*'. Ibid. 156.

230 '*pale*', '*marmoreal*'. Ibid. 66, 156; *Diary*, ii (16 Feb. 1921), p. 90.

prophetic. MSS.W, p. 315.

'*All tremors . . .*'. W, p. 8.

'*dungeons . . .*'. The phrase is there already in first draft, MSS.W, p. 291. W, p. 155.

231 *Wordsworth quotation. The Prelude*, Book I, ll. 393–9.

'*pure spirit shall flow . . .*'. Shelley, 'Adonais': XXXVIII.

reading Shelley. MSS.W, pp. 127–9.

'*fiery' purity.* Ibid. first draft, p. 325.

'*gone now like the desert heat*'. W, p. 144.

'*Life is . . .*'. *Diary*, iii (30 Sept. 1926), p. 113. Puddle recalled also in *MB*, p. 78. Rhoda, too, sees 'the puddle' and 'cannot cross it.' W, p. 113.

232 '*ride rough waters . . .*'. Ibid. 114.

'*my spirit's bark . . .*'. 'Adonais': LV.

drifts of ice. MSS.W, p. 510.

VW's dream. Recalled by John Lehmann, talk at Manchester College, Oxford (July 1975).

pulse for pulse. From Emerson's sermon 'The Genuine Man', preached in 1832: 'His heart beats pulse for pulse with the heart of the Universe.' I am indebted to Faith Williams for the reference.

storm. W, p. 76.

'*The livid foam . . .*'. MSS.W, p. 512. See first draft, p. 202, for an earlier version.

identity dissolves. Another account in MSS.W, p. 134.

knock against a tree. Louie Mayer, cook-general at Monks House, *Recollections of Virginia Woolf*, p. 159.

233 '*Now I will relinquish . . .*'. *W*, p. 117.

epitome. See 'The Narrow Bridge of Art', *New York Herald Tribune* (14 Aug. 1927) repr. *CE*, ii, pp. 224–5.

'*a kind of poetic algebra*'. Eric Warner, op. cit. 326.

234 *VW on the Brontës. CE*, i, pp. 188–9.

'*like a roll of heavy waters . . .*'. *W*, p. 64.

CHAPTER 13

235 '*phantom' dinner.* So described in an outline on 3 Nov. 1930 in notebook, MSS.W, p. 757.

'*You look . . .*'. *W*, p. 208.

236 '*It had been too vast . . .*'. Ibid. 201.

'*non-being*'. *MB*, p. 70.

'*here it coils . . .*'. *W*, p. 191.

'*I sometimes doubt . . .*'. MSS.W, p. 764.

237 *LS and the 'Immortality Ode'.* Letter to JS, Berg.

'*somebody*'. MSS.W, p. 762.

knock a transparency. W, p. 187.

'*I then solidified . . .*'. MSS.W, p. 762.

'*a shell . . .*'. *W*, p. 181.

'*I perceive that the art of biography . . .*'. MSS.W, p. 684.

238 *stories of childhood, etc. W*, p. 169.

Nature's masterplan. Appropriated from Eric Warner.

'*that there are waves . . .*'. Notebook (3 Nov. 1930), MSS.W, p. 758.

'*We only dominate . . .*'. (3 Jan. 1931), MSS.W, p. 764.

'*I have done with phrases*'. *W*, p. 209.

239 '*Thus I visited . . .*'. Ibid. 189.

'*There's another field* . . .'. *Diary*, iii (2 Sept. 1930), p. 316.

'*a going out* . . .'. *A Defence of Poetry*.

'*into a single being*'. *W*, p. 64.

'*Let me* . . .'. Ibid. 61.

'*How curiously* . . .'. Ibid. 60.

'*He made them up* . . .'. MHP B.11a. A review of *The Letters of Thomas Manning to Charles Lamb*, ed. G. A. Anderson.

'*Mr. Justice Stephen*'. *MB*, p. 120.

240 *reformers, revolutionists.* See p. 69 above.

'*magnificent equanimity* . . .'. *W*, p. 172.

'*He was to be a man of action* . . .'. MSS.W, p. 347.

'*wd. have taken some unpopular view*'. Ibid. 561.

'*some monstrous tyranny*'. *W*, p. 108.

'*He would have protected* . . .'. Ibid. 172.

Clapham traits. 'The Clapham Sect', op. cit. 290. (Sir James dwells here on Henry Thornton).

'*cult of the family*'. See Introduction to *Diary*, i, p. xxiii.

241 '*nothing* . . .'. *W*, p. 174.

the inheritor. Ibid. 180.

242 *Beethoven's late quartets.* The influence of these quartets on *The Waves* is noted by QB, ii, p. 130.

'*with its concord* . . .'. *W*, p. 182.

'*its astonishing look of aptness* . . .'. Ibid. 206.

243 '*What does the central shadow* . . .'. Ibid. 207.

'settled . . .'. Ibid. 167.

244 *effort, effort. Diary*, iii (22 Dec. 1930), p. 339.

the death of a moth. 'The Death of the Moth', *CE*, i, pp. 359–61.

life keener at forty-four. Diary, iii, p. 117.

'The waves broke . . .'. *W*, p. 211.

'*And in me too the wave rises* . . .'. Ibid.

'*to a rhythm* . . .'. *Diary*, iii (2 Sept. 1930), p. 316.

245 *rhythm the basis of writing.* See p. 72 above.

'*speed* . . .'. *W*, p. 57.

'*words* . . .'. Ibid. 59.

'*the novel changed* . . .'. Notebook, MSS.W, p. 765.

'*I shall pass* . . .'. *Diary*, iii (4 Jan. 1929), p. 218.

'*And the light of the stars* . . .'. *W*, p. 190.

246 *'ruthlessly'*. *Diary*, iii (26 Dec. 1929), p. 275.

the perspective of creation. See J. W. Graham, 'Point of View in *The Waves*: Some Services of the Style', *Univ. of Toronto Quarterly*, xxxix (Apr. 1970), pp. 193–211.

the eternal mind. Wordsworth, 'Immortality Ode': VIII.

'I am the thing . . .'. MSS.W, p. 39, quoted by Graham.

'A State of Mind'. *Diary*, iii, p. 110.

containing frame. Eric Warner's phrase.

'Lord how deep . . .'. *Diary*, iii, p. 235.

247 *'that we . . .'*. MB, pp. 72–3.

'again this downy billowy wave . . .'. *Diary*, iii (19 Apr. 1925), p. 10.

'over all this the bloom of the past . . .'. Ibid.

'full, like all places . . .'. Ibid. (4 May 1925), p. 16.

248 not novels. Ibid. (18 Feb. 1928), p. 176 and ibid. (31 May 1928), p. 185. J. W. Graham has noted her comment in the second draft of *The Waves*: 'The author would be glad if the following pages were not read as a novel.' MSS.W, p. 582.

CHAPTER 14

249 *'. . . now, aged 50 . . .'*. *Diary*, iv, p. 125.

an Outsider. First essay (dated 11 Oct. 1932), MS.Par, p. 7.

'These are the soul's changes . . .'. *Diary*, iv (2 Oct. 1932), p. 125.

'cleanly & sanely'. Ibid.

'a great season . . .'. Ibid. (31 Dec. 1932), pp. 134–5.

'habits'. Ibid. (11 Mar. 1935), p. 287.

oppressive silence. Like Renny in *The Years*, p. 307.

Hedgehog Hall. *Diary*, iii (5 Aug. 1929), p. 238: 'Leonard's new room, Hedgehog Hall a-building.'

not a gentleman. Ibid. iv (25 June 1935), p. 326.

250 French tour. Ibid. (Apr. 1935), p. 18.

thought of Paris. Ibid. v, p. 115.

'Yet so happy . . .'. Ibid. (28 July 1939), p. 228.

'the hurried London years'. Ibid. (9 Dec. 1939), p. 250.

'old habitual beauty . . .'. Ibid. iv (16 Sept. 1932), p. 124.

'the gulls . . .'. Ibid. (2 Oct. 1932), p. 126.

Mr Gwynne. Ibid. v (6 Jan. 1940), p. 257.

'We get snatches . . .'. *Letters*, vi (8 Oct. 1938), p. 286.

251 *'and dimly green . . .'*. Recollections of *VW*, p. 87.

'*on our lovely . . . autumn island*'. *Diary*, v (12 Oct. 1940), quoted in *LW*, pp. 71–2.

Anon. *Diary*, v (23 Nov. 1940), p. 340.

Leonard as Earl. To Ethel Smyth, *Letters*, vi (1 Feb. 1941), p. 466.

'*the community feeling*'. *Diary*, v (15 Apr. 1939), p. 215.

from novel to annal. Ibid. (29 Apr. 1939), p. 217.

'*The dream . . .*'. Ibid. iii (22 Dec. 1927), pp. 168–9.

252 '*for one thing . . .*'. Ibid. iv (2 Oct. 1933), p. 181, when *Flush* was published.

'*changes . . .*'. 'Jane Austen', *CE*, i, p. 151. She is noting, here, that Austen died at the height of her powers when still subject to these 'changes'.

'*Octavia's story*'. Not a title, simply the descriptive term used in her diary, (24 Mar. 1941), quoted by *LW*, v, p. 90.

'*Can there be Grand Old Women . . .*'. *Recollections of VW*, p. 165.

'*spiritual conversion*'. *Diary*, v (20 May 1938), p. 141.

'*Thoughts on Peace . . .*'. *CE*, iv, pp. 173–7.

253 *delight in plain speaking, etc.* These traits defined as the Clapham heritage by Noel Annan, p. 110.

'*Mustn't our . . .*'. *Letters*, vi (22 Jan. 1940), pp. 379–80.

speech, 1931. MS.Par, pp. xxvii–xliv.

like Mary Wollstonecraft's. Mitchell Leaska's suggestion in an excellent Introduction to MS.Par, p. vii.

254 *enemy within*. MS.Par, pp. xli, xliv.

255 *Ethel Smyth's letters to VW*. Berg.

Ethel and Rose. See Grace Radin, *Virginia Woolf's The Years* (Knoxville: Univ. of Tennessee, 1981), pp. 5–6.

'*For months . . .*'. *Letters*, iv (29 Dec. 1931), p. 422.

256 '*. . . I have never . . .*'. 31 Dec. 1931. Adrienne Rich notes in the Berg folder that this is the reply to VW's letter of 29 Dec.

'*You see, Virginia . . .*'. Undated.

'*If I were reviewing . . .*'. 21 Jan. 1931, MS.Par, Appendix, p. 164.

'"*Our country*" . . .'. *TG*, p. 197.

257 '*the sympathy addict . . .*'. Ibid. 203.

'*Never yet . . .*'. Ibid. 314–15.

'*an alarm bell . . .*'. Ibid. 233.

'*stepped out . . .*'. *Diary*, v (9 Apr. 1937), p. 78.

'*like a top . . .*'. Ibid. (12 Mar. 1938), p. 130.

'*I feel myself enfranchised . . .*'. Ibid. (28 Apr. 1938), p. 137.

258 *'brilliant pamphleteer'*. In *TLS* (4 June 1938), reported in *Diary*, v (3 June 1938). Review repr. in *VW: The Critical Heritage*, ed. Robin Majumdar and Allen McLaurin (Routledge, 1975), pp. 400–1.

dislike of TG. *QB*, ii, pp. 204–5.

'I do my best work . . .'. *Diary*, v (22 Nov. 1938), p. 189.

Outsider principles. TG, pp. 203–4.

'The veil . . .'. *Diary*, iv, p. 298.

'It is an utterly corrupt society . . .'. Ibid. (25 Mar. 1933), p. 147.

baubles. TG, p. 171.

259 *'Nothing would induce . . .'*. *Diary*, iv (25 Mar. 1933), p. 148.

hypnotize. TG, pp. 207–8.

'can only be preserved by obscurity'. Ibid. 208.

'. . . I have . . .'. *Diary*, iv, p. 186.

'Clearly I have . . .'. Ibid. v (19 Feb. 1937), p. 57.

'Anon' and 'The Reader'. Berg. Ed. Brenda R. Silver, *Twentieth Century Literature*, 3/4 (Fall/Winter, 1979), pp. 356–441. 'Anon' exists in three versions in the Berg and, since there was no final text, I draw freely on all versions.

'Reading'. MHP B.11d, op. cit. See ch. 11, p. 178.

began reading. Reading Notes: MHP B.2c, from G. B. Harrison's *Elizabethan Journal*, Trevelyan's *History*, *Coriolanus*, Eileen Power's *Medieval English Nunneries*, Aubrey on Spenser, and Henslowe's diary. The initial idea came to her on 14 Oct. 1938 (*Diary*): 'some kind of critical book . . . ranging all through English lit: as I've read it & noted it during the past 20 years.'

'Common History book'. *Diary*, v (12 Sept. 1940), p. 318.

260 *'the great modern sins . . .'*. *TG*, p. 149.

Anon may have crooned ballads. AROO, p. 74.

battered woman. *Mrs. D*, pp. 123–5 with additional detail from MSS.D, i, pp. 95–8.

261 *'The Leaning Tower'*. *CE*, ii, p. 181.

262 *Dr Johnson*. Last paragraph of *Lives of the English Poets* (Thomas Gray).

without 'reading'. 'The Reader', *Twentieth Century Literature*, p. 428.

Reviewing. MHP B.11c. Hogarth sixpenny pamphlet series No. 4, repr. *CE*, ii, pp. 204–15.

'Wordsworth . . .'. *Diary*, v (7 Aug. 1939), p. 229.

'in darkness; in silence . . .'. 'Reading', MHP B.11d, p. 3.

fellow-workers. 'How Should One Read a Book', *CE*, ii, p. 2.

263 *'One principle guides . . .'*. 'Reading', MHP B.11d, pp. 22–4.

'*certain emotions* . . .'. Notes for Reading at Random (18 Sept. 1940), *Twentieth Century Literature*, p. 374.

'*Somewhere, everywhere* . . .'. 'Reading', *CE*, ii, p. 29.

'*heard themselves* . . .'. 'Anon', *Twentieth Century Literature*, p. 396.

264 '*What a small part* . . .'. *BA*, p. 179.

'*in the heart of darkness* . . .'. Ibid. 256.

last-minute title. Title was changed from *Pointz Hall* to *Between the Acts* on 26 Feb. 1941 (*Diary*).

265 '*spirit*' *ancestors*. MSS.BA, p. 86.

runs her hand. *BA*, p. 85.

'*hidden underground* . . .'. MSS.BA, p. 38.

266 '*perhaps*'. Ibid. 37.

Chaucer. Ibid. 49. Dated 2 Apr. 1938.

'*relieved him*'. *BA*, p. 119.

'"*Silly little boy* . . ."'. Ibid. 133.

267 *Trevelyan's history*. *AROO*, pp. 67–8.

'*continued*'. *BA*, p. 24.

'*People are gifted* . . .'. Ibid. 73.

'*dull, gross* . . .'. MSS.BA, p. 176.

268 *sermon*. *BA*, pp. 218–19.

Yeats. 'A General Introduction for My Work', *Selected Criticism*, ed. A. Norman Jeffares (Macmillan, repr. 1973), p. 266.

grating. *BA*, p. 210.

'*a trough of despair*'. Quoted by *LW*, v, p. 78.

269 *hard to believe*. Roger Poole first expressed this doubt, p. 222.

the greatest smash. *Diary*, v (13 Mar. 1936), p. 17.

'*like a person excruciated* . . .'. Ibid. (13 Sept. 1938), p. 169.

'*A child's game*'. Ibid. (2 Oct. 1938), p. 178.

270 '*Life became* . . .'. *LW*, v, p. 11.

to close his eyes. Ibid. 47–9.

'*For both these barbarisms* . . .'. Last sentence of *Barbarians at the Gate* (Gollancz, 1939), pp. 218–19.

'*This is the prelude to barbarism*'. 'London in War', three pages laid into MSS.BA. MHP A.20.

'*The voice of protest* . . .'. 'Modern Fiction', *CE*, ii, pp. 109–10.

271 '*Thinking* . . .'. *Diary*, v (15 May 1940), p. 285.

'*How England consoles* . . .'. Ibid. (24 Dec. 1940), p. 346.

invasion. Nigel Nicolson's footnote, *Letters*, vi, p. 432.

'*The least* . . .'. *LW*, v, p. 46.

'*We would shut* . . .'. Ibid.

'*protective poison*'. Ibid. 15 and *QB*, ii, pp. 216–17.

'*I don't want the garage* . . .'. Quoted by *LW*, v, p. 46.

'*But until then* . . .'. *Diary*, v (11 Dec. 1938), p. 190.

death exciting. Ibid. (18 Jan. 1939), p. 200.

272 '*What do you think* . . .'. Letter from Bobo Mayor (26 May 1964), Univ. of Sussex, quoted in *A Marriage of True Minds*, p. 62.

'*lower village world*'. To Shena, Lady Simon, *Letters*, vi (25 Jan. 1941), p. 464.

'*infernal boredom*'. *Diary*, v (26 Feb. 1941), quoted in *LW*, v, p. 89.

working notebook. MHP B.2d., p. 38.

Leslie Stephen. Swift (1882; repr. London 1902), p. 179.

white slugs. Diary, v (26 Feb. 1941), quoted in *LW*, v, p. 88.

'*—both so hateful*'. To Shena, loc. cit.

Bert 'never did . . .'. *Diary*, v (26 Feb. 1941), quoted in *LW*, v, p. 87.

'*The Watering Place*'. MHP A.28. Earlier draft, 'The Ladies' Lavatory' is in 'Flush and Other Essays', Berg.

'*bombast*'. Quoted in *LW*, v, p. 46.

273 *donkey fragment.* Holograph entitled 'Possible Poems', MSS.BA, p. 504. Undated, but Mitchell A. Leaska suggests it was written between the summer and Oct. 1940. (Another version of this fragment to be found in the Berg's later typescript: part II, p. 131. See MSS.BA, pp. 557–8.) Extracts appear in *BA*, pp. 182–3.

feeling for certain alleys. To Ethel Smyth, *Letters*, vi (12 Sept. 1940 and 12 Jan. 1941) pp. 431, 460.

'*I went to London Bridge* . . .'. *Diary*, v (15 Jan. 1941), p. 353.

274 *a woman's autobiography.* To Ethel Smyth, *Letters*, vi, p. 453.

'*I was thinking* . . .'. Notebook (30 Jan. 1931), MSS.W, p. 767.

over her lesson book. MB, p. 110.

view across the Bay. Ibid. 111.

'*the third voice*'. Ibid. 115.

'*sinister, blind* . . .'. Ibid. 126.

275 '*It is strange* . . .'. *W*, p. 194.

'*And the ghosts* . . .'. *MB*, p. 135.

'*—that queer ghost*'. *Diary*, iii (26 Dec. 1929), p. 275.

no more than an excursion. Cited by *QB*, i, p. 112.

'*Instead of remembering* . . .'. *MB*, p. 67.

'*Let me then* . . .'. 19 July 1939, *MB*, p. 98.

'*How beautiful . . .*'. *Diary*, v, p. 345.

276 '*Our caste . . .*'. MHP A.13a.

'*They do not blend . . .*'. *MB*, p. 97.

'*Death was . . .*'. *Mrs. D*, pp. 277–8.

editor of her letters. Nigel Nicolson, Introduction to *Letters*, vi, p. xvii.

her father's old books. To Lady Tweedsmuir, *Letters*, vi, p. 483.

277 *visit to Stoke Newington. Diary*, v (12 July 1937), p. 102. The family of VW's paternal great-grandmother, Anne Stent, came from Stoke Newington. Her great-grandfather's second wife, Wilberforce's sister, was also buried there.

'*I think . . .*'. Octavia's conversations with VW were reported in six letters to Elizabeth Robins in NY, MHP.

'*worst enemy*'. To Elizabeth Robins.

278 '*I said . . .*'. Ibid.

'*I wake . . .*'. *Diary*, iv (8 Feb. 1932), p. 74.

'*worse than Lytton's . . .*'. Ibid. (17 Oct. 1934), p. 253.

'*in some ways . . .*'. Ibid. (30 Dec. 1935), p. 361.

'*My dear Aunt—*'. Ibid. v (28 Aug. 1938), p. 164.

'*The soul . . .*'. Ibid. iv (18 Dec. 1934), p. 266.

'*I would . . .*'. Ibid. v, p. 95.

'*The Symbol*'. Dated and presumably begun 1 Mar. 1941. MHP A.24e.

279 *worshipped the mountains.* e.g. LS, 'The Alps in Winter', *Men, Books and Mountains*, ed. S. O. A. Ullman (London 1956).

'*I detest . . .*'. *Diary*, v, p. 347.

'*What I need is the old spurt*'. Ibid., p. 355.

'*I should . . .*'. Ibid. (11 Apr. 1939), p. 214.

'*Oh how violently . . .*'. Ibid. (12 Oct. 1937), p. 112.

280 '*the galloping hooves . . .*'. Ibid. iv (17 Aug. 1932), p. 121.

'*visiting the silent realms . . .*'. Ibid. (12 Aug. 1933), p. 171.

'*perfectly spontaneous . . .*'. Ibid. 172.

'*on the one side . . .*'. *Night and Day*, p. 358.

speech. MS.Par, pp. xxvii–xliv.

281 '*So the land recedes . . .*'. *Diary*, v, p. 283.

'*I mark . . .*'. Ibid., pp. 357–8.

biking in to the Museum. Ibid. (8 Mar. 1941), p. 358.

the Great Fire. Ibid. (1 Jan. 1941), p. 351.

'*Armada weather*'. Ibid. (12 Sept. 1940), p. 318.

'*If we could mount . . .*'. *W*, p. 164.

282 *a passage to the dead.* Detail from the manuscript. See p. 53 above.

'*since our apparitions* . . .'. *Mrs. D*, p. 230.

suicide note. Letters, vi, p. 481.

'*No two people* . . .'. *VO*, p. 431. This is repeated almost verbatim in the first suicide note (dated by Nicolson 18? Mar.) and repeated in other words on 28 Mar. Noted by Leaska, *The Novels of VW*, p. 25; also by Poole, p. 34. A facsimile of the first letter to LW is published on p. 185 of *A Marriage of True Minds*.

two trees. LW, v, p. 96. There is a photograph of the two elms on p. 179 of *A Marriage of True Minds*.

'*the difficulty* . . .'. *Diary*, v (19 Feb. 1937), p. 57.

Biographical Sources

THIS bibliography is limited to works that link Virginia Woolf's life and work. For a comprehensive list of her writings see B. J. Kirkpatrick, *A Bibliography of Virginia Woolf*, 3rd edn. (Oxford, 1980). Virginia Woolf's works are published by the Hogarth Press and Harcourt Brace Jovanovich unless stated otherwise. For details see Abbreviations. For criticism see Robin Majumdar, *Virginia Woolf: An Annotated Bibliography of Criticism 1915-1974* (NY and London: Garland, 1976).

PRIMARY SOURCES

The three main repositories of VW's papers are the Berg Collection, The New York Public Library; the Monks House Papers at the University of Sussex; and the Charleston Papers at King's College, Cambridge.

The most useful unpublished sources are the six early diaries, in the Berg Collection, which give some entrée to the dark but formative years between the death of Stella in 1897 and the beginning of the first novel in 1908. In these years Virginia Stephen tended to keep diaries while on vacation and, of these, the Cornwall diary, dated 11 Aug.-14 Sept. 1905, is extraordinarily suggestive of her future development as modern novelist.

Another early portent of future experiment is the fictional 'Memoirs of a Novelist' (1909) at Sussex. There, too, are VW's notes on her brother, Thoby Stephen, a central figure in two of her novels, and a story called 'Sympathy' which contains the seeds of these novels. Also at Sussex are VW's last sketches, 'The Watering Place' and 'The Symbol'. Neither sketch is especially good but they help explain her state of mind early in 1941 as she sank into depression. Some thoughts of the mad Septimus Warren Smith in the three-volume holograph of *Mrs. Dalloway* (in the Department of Manuscripts, British Library Reference Division) are also revealing of VW's state of mind when she appeared deranged.

The reading lists that VW devised for herself, her twenty-six volumes of reading notes (in the Berg) with additional notes (at Sussex) together with the ten working notebooks of articles, essays, fiction, and reviews, 1925-40 (in the Berg) are packed with telling detail of what VW had in her mind at a given time.

The most useful scholarship began thirty years after VW's death with the editing of the great mass of her papers, above all Anne Olivier Bell's five-volume edition of *The Diary of Virginia Woolf*. Anyone who has examined the holograph volumes will agree that this may well prove the editing feat of the century, with its accurate attention to minute detail and its preservation of family memories that would otherwise have been lost. Other essential editions are the *Letters* in six volumes which Nigel Nicolson, too, has clarified with extensive notes; *Moments of Being: Unpublished Autobiographic Writings of Virginia Woolf*, edited by Jeanne Schulkind, which is VW's own guide to the defining moments of her youth; and the fascinating drafts of two of her novels: *The Pargiters: The Novel-Essay Portion of* The Years, edited by Mitchell A. Leaska, and the two holograph drafts of *The Waves*, edited by J. W. Graham. Dedicated scholars will want to sift through other drafts that have been published: *Melymbrosia*, an early version of *The Voyage Out*, edited by Louise A. De-Salvo (New York Public Library); *Mrs. Dalloway's Party: A Short Story Sequence*, edited by Stella McNichol; the holograph draft of *To the Lighthouse*, edited by Susan Dick; and *Pointz Hall*, two typescript drafts of *Between the Acts*, edited by Mitchell A. Leaska. He appends the two holograph versions of a prose-poem, 'What do I ask?', which give some idea of what led VW to commit suicide, pp. 503–5, 557–8. But more important are two short pieces: a brilliant story of 1906, 'The Journal of Mistress Joan Martyn', edited by Susan M. Squier and Louise A. De-Salvo and published in the Virginia Woolf issue of *Twentieth Century Literature* (Fall/Winter 1979) together with her last unfinished book, *Anon*. Here the editor, Brenda Silver, had the difficult task of choosing one of several versions, all in a rudimentary state. Her chosen version is carefully edited with excellent notes, but the unedited versions of the first chapter are worth a visit to the Berg.

SECONDARY SOURCES

To understand Leslie Stephen's relation to VW it is necessary to sense his immense attraction. This is revealed most clearly in unpublished letters to Julia Stephen, 1877–95 (Berg) and in his holograph 'Calendar of Correspondence' (British Library). The other crucial batch of unpublished letters is from Leonard Woolf to VW (at Sussex) which shows unexpected passion in their relationship. The Berg Collection has also large batches of letters from Vanessa Bell, Victoria Sackville-West, and Ethel Smyth to VW. For further detail on these relationships see Frances Spalding, *Vanessa Bell* (Weidenfeld and Nicolson; Ticknor and Field, 1983); Nigel Nicolson, *Portrait of a Marriage* (Weidenfeld and Nicolson, 1973; NY: Atheneum); and Christopher St John, *Ethel Smyth: A Biography* (Longmans, 1959). In the case of Katherine Mansfield's relation to VW, less is to be gained from those biographies which dwell on spite rather than discern points of contact in their writing.

For the Clapham heritage in VW's background see 'The Clapham Sect' in *Essays in Ecclesiastical Biography*, ii, by Sir James Stephen (Longmans, 1849). For other family influences see James Stephen, *The Memoirs of James Stephen written by Himself for the Use of His Children*, edited by Merle M. Bevington (Hogarth, 1954); Leslie Stephen's writings, in particular *Sir Leslie Stephen's Mausoleum Book*, edited by Alan Bell (Oxford, 1977) and his *Life of Sir James Fitzjames Stephen* (Smith, Elder, 1895); F. W. Maitland, *The Life and Letters of Leslie Stephen* (Duckworth 1906; Detroit: Gale Research, 1968), in particular the pages which his daughter herself contributed, pp. 474–6; and Noel Gilroy Annan, *Leslie Stephen: his thought and character in relation to his time* (MacGibbon and Kee, 1951; Cambridge, Mass.: Harvard University Press, 1952). The character of Julia Stephen may be discerned in her only publication, *Notes from Sick Rooms* (Smith, Elder, 1883; Orono, 1980).

Family portraits of VW will always provide a main route through her life: Leonard Woolf's five-volume *Autobiography* (Hogarth and Harcourt, 1960–9) and Quentin Bell's two-volume *Virginia Woolf: A Biography* (Hogarth and Harcourt, 1972). Both works are articulate, humorous, and convincing, with an unsurpassable sense of what it was like to know VW day by day. Although neither ventures on literary criticism, their occasional comments on the major novels are well judged, e.g. Leonard Woolf's estimate of *The Waves* as her masterpiece.

An opposing camp was set up by Roger Poole in *The unknown Virginia Woolf* (Cambridge, 1978) which puts Leonard Woolf in a critical light and argues that VW's madness may be, at least to some extent, explicable. This line was followed in Stephen Trombley's attack on the treatment of VW: '*All that summer she was mad*': *Virginia Woolf and Her Doctors* (London: Junction Books, 1981). He exposes frightful medical practices and attitudes of ignorant arrogance that vindicate VW's resistance to doctors and nurses. These two studies provoked polarized responses and have to be sifted with care to extract the grains of truth from extreme positions. While Poole and Trombley follow a psychological line, Phyllis Rose has a feminist bias. *Woman of Letters: A Life of Virginia Woolf* (NY: Oxford; Routledge, 1978) stresses VW's 'affair' with Vita Sackville-West and boosts the works of the 1920s, particularly *Orlando* and *A Room of One's Own*, over what she sees as a decline in the 1930s, starting with *The Waves*. Though this line, in the end, distorts VW's achievement, Rose's initial aim is refreshing: to dispel the image of the Invalid Lady of Bloomsbury with a portrait of an energetic and resourceful VW: 'I would prefer to see less emphasis on despair, more on resilience in the literary history of women.' The feminist interest in VW is far from exhausted but, so far, it has been predictable rather than subtle. In the main, critics have followed the paradigms laid down by the family biographers, as Jean O. Love in VW: *Sources of Madness and Art* (Berkeley: University of California Press, 1977), a detailed psychological study of Virginia Stephen's childhood and youth which contains useful summaries of Leslie Stephen's letters. The established view of Leonard Woolf's nurture of VW is fleshed out by George Spater and Ian Parsons in *A Marriage of True Minds* (Cape and Hogarth, 1977). Despite its tempting subtitle, *An Intimate Portrait of Leonard and Virginia Woolf*, it is fact-filled (in the manner of Leonard Woolf) rather than intimate.

More revealing, often, are the glimpses of VW in brief reminiscences. The two most perceptive are by William Plomer in *The Autobiography of William Plomer* (Cape, 1975) and by her niece, Angelica Garnett, in *Recollections of Virginia Woolf*, edited by Joan Russell Noble (London: Peter Owen, 1972). All the contributions to this collection are direct and believable. One of the best is by VW's cook, Louie Mayer. Other living glimpses may be found in Vanessa Bell, *Notes on Virginia's Childhood*, edited by Richard F. Schaubeck, Jr. (NY: Frank Hallman, 1974); Clive Bell, *Old Friends: Personal Recollections* (Chatto, 1956; Harcourt, 1957); David Garnett, *Great Friends* (Macmillan, 1979; NY: Atheneum, 1980); Richard Kennedy, *A Boy at the Hogarth Press* (Penguin, 1978); Ottoline Morrell, *Ottoline at Garsington: Memoirs of Lady Ottoline Morrell 1915-1918*, edited by Robert Gathorne-Hardy (Faber, 1974; Knopf, 1975); and Frances Partridge, *Memories*, published in US as *Love in Bloomsbury* (Gollancz; Little, Brown, 1981). See also S. P. Rosenbaum (ed.), *The Bloomsbury Group: A Collection of Memoirs, Commentary and Criticism* (Croom Helm; University of Toronto, 1975). This is a thorough compendium, but for a detached and keen judgement of VW's milieu see Richard Shone's Introduction to *Bloomsbury Portraits: Vanessa Bell, Duncan Grant, and their circle* (Oxford: Phaidon; Dutton, 1976).

The most sensitive critical assessments of the essentials of VW's career come so far not from specialists but, as she would have liked, from the common reader. They appear in two reviews, one by Rosemary Dinnage in *TLS* (18 Apr. 1980) and the other, a longer review-essay by John Mepham, 'Trained to Silence', *London Review of Books* (20 Nov.-4 Dec. 1980). A new perspective on VW's ties with the Romantic poets is opened up by Eric Warner, 'Some Aspects of Romanticism in the Work of Virginia Woolf' (Oxford thesis, 1980). These modest assessments are truer to VW than many critical studies which are too laborious or too partisan, in either case following some set route. A reader who has liked VW's writings might approach her again either through her life, the immediate material of her art, or through her great predecessors, Jane Austen, George Eliot, and Henry James, with their insight into domestic enclosures and the hidden lives of women.

Photographs, portraits, and places are sources at least as suggestive as books. Julia Margaret Cameron's many photographs of VW's mother (National Portrait Gallery, London; see also *A Victorian Album*, edited by Graham Ovenden, NY: Da Capo Press, 1975) try to elicit this woman's rare soul as VW was to do in *To the Lighthouse*. As Frances Spalding says, Mrs Cameron 'did not "take" photographs, she immortalized her sitters.' Vanessa Bell's faceless portraits of her sister provide an inspired comment on her hidden nature in contrast to, say, the sharp, insistent image-making of Man Ray who, in the 1920s, photographed VW as an advanced Modern.

For occasional snaps, see Stella Duckworth's album (Berg) with its records of the Stephen family at play in the late 1880s and 1890s, and also Leonard Woolf's five albums (owned by the Harvard Theatre Collection, Harvard College Library). Pictures of Leslie Stephen illustrate his mutability: the pathos of the Watts portrait (reproduced by Maitland); the lanky climber in the Alps (reproduced by Annan); and the aged, eminent Victorian knighted in 1902 and photographed by Beresford (reproduced by Quentin Bell). Looming in the wings, here, is his twenty-year-old daughter, her pointed face much like her father's but rather shadowy behind him.

Certain places, apart from the home bases of Bloomsbury squares and Sussex downs, had for VW a peculiar imaginative resonance: the different faces of London (see VW, *The London Scene*, Hogarth; Random House, 1982), especially the old parts of the City; Hampton Court; and, above all, the Cornwall shore. VW is one of those writers who must be heard as well as read: the strong, irregular rhythm of her prose corresponds to the beat of the waves.

Index

The following contractions have been used:

VB for Vanessa Bell
VW for Virginia Woolf
LS for Leslie Stephen
JS for Julia Stephen